Power and Dysfunction

The New South Wales Board for the
Protection of Aborigines 1883–1940

Aboriginal History Incorporated

Aboriginal History Inc. is a part of the Australian Centre for Indigenous History, Research School of Social Sciences, The Australian National University, and gratefully acknowledges the support of the School of History and the National Centre for Indigenous Studies, The Australian National University. Aboriginal History Inc. is administered by an Editorial Board which is responsible for all unsigned material. Views and opinions expressed by the author are not necessarily shared by Board members.

Contacting Aboriginal History

All correspondence should be addressed to the Editors, Aboriginal History Inc., ACIH, School of History, RSSS, 9 Fellows Road (Coombs Building), The Australian National University, Acton, ACT, 2601, or aboriginalhistoryinc@gmail.com.

WARNING: Readers are notified that this publication may contain names or images of deceased persons.

Power and Dysfunction

The New South Wales Board for the
Protection of Aborigines 1883–1940

RICHARD EGAN

PRESS

Published by ANU Press and Aboriginal History Inc.
The Australian National University
Acton ACT 2601, Australia
Email: anupress@anu.edu.au

Available to download for free at press.anu.edu.au

ISBN (print): 9781760464721
ISBN (online): 9781760464738

WorldCat (print): 1273734272
WorldCat (online): 1273742980

DOI: 10.22459/PD.2021

This title is published under a Creative Commons Attribution-NonCommercial-NoDerivatives 4.0 International (CC BY-NC-ND 4.0).

The full licence terms are available at
creativecommons.org/licenses/by-nc-nd/4.0/legalcode

Cover design and layout by ANU Press

This book is published under the aegis of the Aboriginal History Editorial Committee of the ANU Press.

This edition © 2021 ANU Press and Aboriginal History Inc.

Contents

List of figures	vii
Foreword	xiii
Acknowledgements	xv
Terminology	xix
Introduction	1
1. A faltering start to 'protection', 1883	19
2. Policy drift, 1883–1897	49
3. The zealot from Parramatta	93
4. The 'almost white' children, 1904–1910	125
5. Enter the bureaucrats, 1916	151
6. The girls return	189
7. If the 'white parents object'	229
8. Winds of change	257
Conclusion	291
Appendix 1: Board members in order of appearance	297
Appendix 2: Member attendance for all Board members from 1883 until 1916	325
Appendix 3: Member attendance for all Board members from 1916 until 1939	327
Appendix 4: Statistics of removals (see Chapter 6)	329
Bibliography	337

List of figures

Figure 1.1: George Thornton. 38
Figure 1.2: Richard Hill. 43
Figure 2.1: Edmund Walcott Fosbery. 52
Figure 2.2: Philip Gidley King. 54
Figure 2.3: Attendance of the first 16 members of the Board up to 1897. 57
Figure 2.4: Number of years members spent on the Board. 57
Figure 2.5: William H. Suttor. 58
Figure 2.6: Robert Hoddle Driberg White. 59
Figure 2.7: Map of Dharawal Country and Environs. 67
Figure 2.8: Map of the Shoalhaven showing Aboriginal population centres. 72
Figure 2.9: 'The Courthouse' (Nowra 1910). 76
Figure 3.1: George Edward Ardill. 94
Figure 3.2: Our Boys Farm Home, Camden. Two Aboriginal boys can be seen, second from the far right and one in front of the matron. 96
Figure 3.3: Naval Training Ship *Vernon*. 99
Figure 3.4: The Christian Endeavour Mission Church. 109
Figure 3.5: Aboriginal population at La Perouse, 1885–1900. 111
Figure 3.6: John Stuart Hawthorn. 115
Figure 3.7: Lady Timbery, Queen of La Perouse. 117

Figure 3.8: John See. 121

Figure 4.1: Robert T. Donaldson. 128

Figure 4.2: Edward Dowling. 138

Figure 4.3: Thomas Garvin. 140

Figure 4.4: Board member attendance by percentage during the lead-up to the *Aborigines Protection Act 1909*. 141

Figure 4.5: Robert Scobie. 146

Figure 5.1: Edward Burns Harkness. 173

Figure 5.2: Number of Board meetings held each year by the 'new' Board from 1916 to 1939. 181

Figure 6.1: Map of New South Wales Aboriginal Land Council boundaries. 205

Figure 6.2: Numbers and regions from where Aboriginal girls were removed and subsequently placed in apprenticeships (1916–28). Total: 456. 206

Figure 6.3: Numbers of Aboriginal girls removed from locations within the North Western region (1916–28). Total: 133. 207

Figure 6.4: Numbers and regions from where Aboriginal boys were removed and subsequently placed into apprenticeships (1916–28). Total: 159. 208

Figure 6.5: Numbers of Aboriginal boys removed from locations within the North Western region (1916–28). Total: 84. 208

Figure 6.6: Mean total Aboriginal populations at major Aboriginal concentration centres from 1911 to 1915. Numbers of children are included in the total population columns and are also represented separately. 209

Figure 6.7: Numbers of 'full-blood' and 'half-caste' children at location points between 1911 and 1912 from where 10 or more girls were subsequently removed. 210

Figure 6.8: Location points in Sydney for the placement of Aboriginal girls who had been removed from their communities. 212

Figure 6.9: Location points in rural New South Wales for the placement Aboriginal girls who had been removed from their communities. 213

Figure 6.10: The top 30 location points across New South Wales for the placement of Aboriginal girls removed from their communities. 214

Figure 6.11: Location points across New South Wales for the placement of Aboriginal boys. 215

Figure 6.12: The top 30 location points across New South Wales for the placement of Aboriginal boys removed from their communities. 215

Figure 6.13: Numbers of children removed from Dharawal population centres (1916–28). 217

Figure 6.14: Domestic placement history of one Dharawal apprentice. 218

Figure 7.1: The manager's house at Roseby Park Aboriginal Station. 229

Figure 7.2: View from Greenwell Point across to Orient Point (Roseby Park); this was the punt journey for young Barbara Timbery to attend school. 230

Figure 7.3: Internal note from Minister for Education, John Perry, 6 March 1902. 237

Figure 7.4: Aboriginal schools established between 1883 and 1915. 238

Figure 7.5: Map of the Shoalhaven. 239

Figure 7.6: Peter Board. 244

Figure 8.1: B.C. Harkness. 258

Figure 8.2: William John MacKay. 268

Figure 8.3: Mark Davidson. 272

Figure 8.4: George Edward Ardill. 275

Figure 8.5: The Day of Mourning. 281

Figure 8.6: Day of Mourning. 281

Figure A1.1: George Thornton. 297

Figure A1.2: Richard Hill. 297
Figure A1.3: Philip Gidley King. 298
Figure A1.4: William J. Foster. 299
Figure A1.5: Edmund Walcott Fosbery. 300
Figure A1.6: Harman John Tarrant. 300
Figure A1.7: William H. Suttor. 302
Figure A1.8: Robert Hoddle Driberg White. 303
Figure A1.9: John See. 304
Figure A1.10: George Edward Ardill. 305
Figure A1.11: Edward Dowling. 307
Figure A1.12: Robert Scobie. 308
Figure A1.13: Thomas Garvin. 308
Figure A1.14: Robert Thomas Donaldson. 309
Figure A1.15: Peter Board. 310
Figure A1.16: Robert T. Paton. 311
Figure A1.17: George Stuart Briner. 315
Figure A1.18: Edward Burns Harkness. 316
Figure A1.19: Brian James Doe. 317
Figure A1.20: Roy S. Vincent. 319
Figure A1.21: George R. Thomas. 321
Figure A1.22: Bertie Clarence Harkness. 321
Figure A1.23: William John MacKay. 323
Figure A1.24: George Edward Ardill. 323
Figure A2.1: Board member attendance from 1883 to 1916. 325
Figure A3.1: Board member attendance from 1916 to 1939. 327
Figure A4.1: Numbers of Aboriginal girls removed from institutions and interstate who were placed in apprenticeships (1916–28). Total: 45. 329

Figure A4.2: Numbers of Aboriginal girls removed from locations within the Wiradjuri region (1916–28). Total: 69.   330

Figure A4.3: Numbers of Aboriginal girls removed from locations within the Northern region (1916–28). Total: 66.   330

Figure A4.4: Numbers of Aboriginal girls removed from locations within the Mid-North Coast region (1916–28). Total: 57.   331

Figure A4.5: Numbers of Aboriginal girls removed from locations within the North Coast region (1916–28). Total: 49.   331

Figure A4.6: Numbers of Aboriginal girls removed from locations within the South Coast region (1916–28). Total: 39.   332

Figure A4.7: Number of Aboriginal girls removed from locations within the Central region (1916–28). Total: 22.   332

Figure A4.8: Numbers of Aboriginal girls removed from locations within the Sydney/Newcastle region (1916–28). Total: 11.   333

Figure A4.9: Numbers of Aboriginal girls removed from two locations in the Western region (1916–28). Total: 3.   333

Figure A4.10: Numbers of Aboriginal boys removed from institutions who were placed in apprenticeships (1916–28). Total: 15.   334

Figure A4.11: Numbers of Aboriginal boys removed from locations within the Wiradjuri region (1916–28). Total: 13.   334

Figure A4.12: Numbers of Aboriginal boys removed from locations within the Northern region (1916–28). Total: 9.   335

Figure A4.13: Numbers of Aboriginal boys removed from locations within the Mid-North Coast region (1916–28). Total: 11.   335

Figure A4.14: Numbers of Aboriginal boys removed from locations within the North Coast region (1916–28). Total: 13.   335

Figure A4.15: Numbers of Aboriginal boys removed from locations within the South Coast region (1916–28). Total: 5.   336

Figure A4.16: Numbers of Aboriginal boys removed from locations within the Central region (1916–28). Total: 9.   336

Figure A4.17: Numbers of Aboriginal boys removed from locations within the Sydney/Newcastle region (1916–28). Total: 8.   336

Foreword

For several decades from the late nineteenth century, the New South Wales Aborigines Protection Board (APB) had extraordinary powers over the lives of Aboriginal people. Indeed, it obtained progressively greater control, with often devastating consequences for the very people it was charged with protecting. In their 1938 pamphlet, *Aborigines Claim Citizens Rights!*, the Aboriginal activists William Ferguson and Jack Patten condemned the Board for its hypocrisy and for its 'cruelty and callousness towards the Aborigines'.[1]

The impact of the New South Wales APB's policies on Aboriginal people has been the focus of much scholarly energy in recent decades, especially in relation to its child removal policies and practices. Richard Egan is therefore to be commended for the valuable and original contribution he has made to this scholarship. Despite the APB being an influential body, with oversight of a department that implemented a range of discriminatory policies, its internal dynamics and ways of operating have not been a major focus of previous scholarship. Egan fills this gap by concentrating specifically on the role of the Board: on how (or indeed if) its members interacted with Aboriginal people; and on which members drove the agenda. It is an important scholarly contribution because, in contrast to other Australian states where significant individuals exerted influence as 'chief protectors' or 'native commissioners', Aboriginal policy in New South Wales was driven by a somewhat amorphous 'board'.

The centrepiece of this book is its analysis of the 64 men who served on the APB from 1883 to 1940. The book functions in part as a group biography of the APB, using both quantitative and qualitative methods. It includes carefully researched profiles of the often woefully ill-equipped men appointed to the Board, as well as a statistical analysis of members'

---

1   Patten and Ferguson, *Aborigines Claim Citizens Rights!*, 3.

length of tenure and rates of meeting attendance. Egan is able to show that Aboriginal policy was shaped for the most part by a much smaller group of Board members, perhaps fewer than a dozen, who are subject to more detailed biographical analysis. He also demonstrates that, following a reconstruction of the Board in 1916, it was far less active in its oversight of policy, leaving Aboriginal affairs in the hands of a largely unaccountable 'cabal' of departmental officers.

In writing a history of the APB, Egan is very conscious that the lived experiences of Aboriginal people who were subject to its policies are a crucial part of this history. He gives numerous examples of how the Board's policies and practices affected Aboriginal people across the state, with a particular focus on the Dharawal people of the coastal regions south of Sydney. He has also undertaken an extensive study of APB data on child removals and placements, which is supported by graphs and maps, and complemented by useful interpretations and conclusions regarding the meanings and limitations of that data. He shows that there was no clear logic to patterns of Aboriginal child removal, which might have been influenced, for example, by local station managers.

While Egan does not ignore the subjects of protective policy in New South Wales, his focus is nonetheless on the agents of this policy. He identifies three key periods in the history of the Board: a foundational period from 1883 characterised by a more laissez faire approach to Aboriginal policy; a second more activist period from 1897, which included passage of the *Aborigines Protection Act 1909* (NSW) and an increase in rates of child removal; and a final period from 1916, which saw real power pass to a small group of officials working for the Board. It is a deeply researched and nuanced book, which reveals how the administrative activity of the Board and its officers had a dehumanising effect, with the Aboriginal presence in New South Wales constructed in abstract terms and perceived as a social problem. The book exposes what is at times a startling indifference to Aboriginal people's rights and interests.

I had the privilege of examining the doctoral thesis upon which this book is based, and it is wonderful to see it published. It provides a nuanced account of the APB – including its power and influence, but also its dysfunction and failures – and is a unique and valuable contribution to the history of Aboriginal policy in New South Wales.

Samuel Furphy, The Australian National University, March 2021

Acknowledgements

I wish to acknowledge the support of the Australian Academy of the Humanities through the provision of a grant to assist in the publication of this work. This organisation has a fellowship of over 600 humanitarians leaders in Australia and a commitment to the pursuit of excellence within the field. I am most grateful to the Academy for their financial contribution to this publication.

This book had its genesis in a PhD thesis I completed in 2019, so much of my debt is owed to those who assisted me then. I would like to thank my two thesis supervisors for all their expertise and support throughout that four-year process. Lisa Ford provided advice and encouragement from the outset of my research and her regular and close editing of my work was invaluable. Lisa kept me on task, tightened my prose and provided honest appraisal. Grace Karskens' reassurance, support, chapter editing and reflective comments were essential to a successful outcome. I would also like to thank Anne O'Brien for her early advice on a protection board member, for reading my material and for her professional advice. Her empathy and positive input were comforting.

I would also like to thank Peter Read for always being on hand to answer my questions and provide advice. Russell McGregor's early encouragement of my thesis proposal was very much appreciated. Also, my sincere thanks to the following for meeting with me and sharing their professional support for my project: Samuel Furphy, Tim Rowse, Naomi Parry (phone conversation), Heather Goodall (email correspondence), Mike Donaldson and Paul Irish. I would like to thank Victoria Haskins who was instrumental in allowing me to access the restricted files from some of Joan Kingsley-Strack's archive held at the National Library of Australia. A further thanks to Samuel Furphy for providing editorial advice on my manuscript and for providing the Foreword to this book.

I would like to thank Anne Wright as the head of the Indigenous Family History Unit in the Department of Education and Aboriginal Affairs. Anne welcomed me to the Aboriginal Protection Board archive and enabled me to access the material at a very convenient location in her Sydney offices on a regular basis throughout the first two years of my research. Anne's friendly, supportive and cooperative demeanour helped me through some long days with the protection board minutes and ward registers.

To all the library staff at the Mitchell Library and State Library of New South Wales (SLNSW), the National Library of Australia (NLA) and the Australian Institute of Aboriginal and Torres Strait Islander Studies, sincere thanks for your courteous and efficient service. A special thanks to Linda Glenda Veitch and Southnary Tan, from SLNSW, who helped me track down the 1916 New South Wales protection board report, which has been an elusive document for many scholars. Also, to the staff at State Records New South Wales, a sincere thanks for your regular support with my research and at times going beyond the normal retrieval process; a special thanks to John Cann who tracked down some reference numbers for me when I was unable to visit the Records office in Kingswood. I have greatly appreciated the correspondence from the SLNSW and the NLA for their prompt and helpful service regarding all copyright issues. A special thanks to Rosemary Sempell from the NSW Parliamentary Library for all her efforts to provide me with images and copyright approvals.

I would like to thank Ruth Simms for her friendly chats concerning Dharawal in the Shoalhaven in the early stages of my research. A sincere thanks to Sonny Simms, Les Bursill and Bryan Smith for allowing me an interview and being so candid and generous with their stories from Dharawal Country relating to the Aboriginal Protection/Welfare Boards of NSW.

My sincere thanks go to Gillian Souter who, towards the end of my research, made crucial edits and provided constructive advice to all my chapters.

I would like to thank Peter Johnson for the preparation of several maps and for his pleasant and friendly manner.

I owe a broader debt to the many scholars whose works I have drawn upon extensively. They have toiled for years in libraries and other institutions thumbing through many files of primary source material so that we can be better informed from their interpretations of the past. Without such works this work would not have been possible.

I would like to thank Rani Kerin of the ANU Press Aboriginal History editorial board for her extensive correspondence and assistance regarding the technical aspects of the preparation of my manuscript and her overall supportive interest in my project.

Finally, I am indebted to my wife. Lyn has 'carried' me over the last five years and protected me from many domestic chores and other obligations. Just as importantly, she has assisted in major editing and proofing of my chapters and helped me significantly with statistical analysis in several chapters. Without her support and practical assistance this venture would not have been possible.

Terminology

Two distinct groups of Indigenous Australians are officially recognised in Australia: the people of the Torres Strait Islands and those Aboriginal people of the mainland and Tasmania. The term Indigenous Australians is used to embrace both Aboriginal people and Torres Strait Islander people. As this discussion centres mainly on the geographical area of New South Wales I have used the term 'Aboriginal people'. I have only used the term 'Indigenous' when referring to the whole of Australia. I have occasionally used the term 'Aborigine' if appropriate to the context. Where appropriate I have used a language name such as Wiradjuri, or a clan name such as Cadigal. When quoting directly from primary source material, the more offensive terms such as 'full-bloods', 'half-castes', 'octoroons', 'quadroons', 'blacks' and 'natives' have been retained.

An Aboriginal 'station' was run by a station manager who was usually the teacher at the station school. His wife acted as the matron, whose duties were to 'exercise oversight of all women, with special charge of girls and young children' and oversee all domestic duties. Some large stations, like Cumeroogunga, had extra help through an assistant manager or a nurse, and, on occasion, 'general employees are also engaged'.[1]

An Aboriginal 'reserve' was dedicated land for the use of Aboriginal people. Some reserves had an Aboriginal school, staffed by a teacher-matron who was 'almost entirely' under the control of the Department of Education.[2] There were no permanent managers on the reserves and

---

1   *Aborigines Protection, Report and Recommendations of the Public Service Board of New South Wales*, 4 April 1940, Government Printer NSW, 6/4501.1, 11.
2   *Aborigines Protection, Report and Recommendations of the Public Service Board of New South Wales*, 4 April 1940, 11.

the Aboriginal Protection Board provided the residents with rations and supplies if required. All general oversight responsibilities were undertaken by the local police.

The term 'mission' was used, predominately by Aboriginal people, when referring to their time spent on either a station or a reserve and does not necessarily refer to a place that was begun by missionaries such as Warangesda or Cumeroogunga. Aboriginal camps were found in many places across New South Wales but primarily on the outskirts of country towns close to amenities. Most residents of these camps refused to reside on supervised stations or the reserves.

Introduction

Wiradjuri Labor man William Ferguson and Yorta Yorta activist Jack Patten, both from southern central New South Wales, had become seasoned campaigners for Aboriginal rights by the end of the 1930s. They were in no doubt about the intentions of Aboriginal 'protection' in Australia when they published their 1938 pamphlet, *Aborigines Claim Citizens Rights!*

> By your cruelty and callousness towards the Aborigines you stand condemned in the eyes of the civilised world ... If you openly admit that the purpose of your Aborigines Legislation has been, and now is, to exterminate the Aborigines completely so that not a trace of them or their descendants remains, we could describe you as brutal, but honest ... You hypocritically claim that you are trying to 'protect' us; but your modern policy of 'protection' (so called) is killing us off just as surely as the pioneer policy of giving us poisoned damper and shooting us down like dingoes.[1]

After 55 years of the New South Wales Board for the Protection of Aborigines (hereafter referred to as the Board or the APB) 'protecting' the lives of Aboriginal people in that state, this was the harsh reality. How could the Board, established ostensibly to provide and care for Aboriginal survivors of colonialism, be attacked so vehemently by Aboriginal activists? What had taken place between the Board's creation in 1883 and the Australia Day celebrations of 1938 to illicit such a response? Were Patten and Ferguson accurate in their characterisation of the Board? History has proved them right.

In 1883 the Board was issued with brief instructions from the New South Wales Government through the colonial secretary. It was to provide land 'where the blacks might resort' and be employed, ensure that the children

---

1   Patten and Ferguson, *Aborigines Claim Citizens Rights!*, 3–4.

were educated and that the aged and sick were cared for and that the 'strong, active and healthy' be engaged in useful work.[2] There was little guidance from the government as to how the Board was to proceed and what agencies it could employ to carry out its directive. It soon found one. After only four weeks of operation the shock resignation of the Board's first chair, George Thornton, who had been made Chief Protector of Aborigines in late 1881, made way for the Inspector-General of Police, Edmund Fosbery, to be appointed to the Board. Fosbery's arrival to the Board set the tone of operation for the next 57 years. The Board relied almost entirely on the New South Wales Police Force to carry out its operations on the ground. This outcome inextricably tied the police to Aboriginal affairs in New South Wales. By the beginning of the twentieth century, the Board's early emphasis on assistance, education and employment had switched to crafting policies that sought to control, segregate and remove. For the next 40 years the Aboriginal people of New South Wales were subject to, in one form or another, the coercive and restrictive policies of the Board.

The men who sat on the Board for its first 57 years came from different backgrounds but had commonalities. They were white, privileged, educated professionals, and generally well-connected in public life. They included humanitarians, philanthropists, businessmen, politicians and public servants. Why they joined the Board is often unclear. Some genuinely felt that they could make a difference to the deplorable plight of many Aboriginal people; others nurtured agendas akin to religious zealotry and sought to mould the underprivileged or destitute according to their own visions of reform. For some, it was simply part of their job as public servants in the New South Wales Government.[3]

Thus far, historians have focused primarily on the policies of the Board and their impact upon Aboriginal people in New South Wales rather than on the internal workings of the Board itself. This emphasis is understandable: the segregated reserves and stations, the separate and inferior education system, the removal of children, the attempt to 'merge' Aboriginal people into white society and the dispersal of communities that disrupted Aboriginal life are the important narratives. However, less

---

2   *Protection of the Aborigines (Minute of the Colonial Secretary, Together with Reports)*, Legislative Assembly, New South Wales, 2 March 1883, 2.
3   In 1916 the APB members were drawn from the following New South Wales parliamentary ministries: the colonial secretary's department, agriculture, public health, education and the police.

attention has been paid to the Board itself, and to the political and social trends, and key individuals, that shaped the Board's policy direction; this book endeavours to fill this gap.

New South Wales post-contact historiography

Research on the early contact period between the British and Aboriginal people of the Sydney region has been the subject of several histories with interests in both sides of the frontier.[4] Although my study begins 100 years after this period, recent scholarship by Grace Karskens in *The Colony* and Paul Irish in *Hidden in Plain View* both highlight an important feature of this research. Karskens brought to her readers the voices of Aboriginal people heard and recorded by the settlers of Sydney. She points out that Aboriginal people were an integral part of Sydney life, and that after the spearing of Arthur Phillip at Manly Cove in September 1790, the 'Aboriginal people were *always* [my emphasis] among the city's population'.[5] Building on Karskens's work, Paul Irish has completely dispelled the myth that the Sydney Aboriginal people were all gone by the time Mahroot of the 'Botany tribe' gave his testimony to the 1845 select committee into the 'Condition of the Aborigines'.[6] Irish shows how Aboriginal people in the Sydney region not only survived the early contact period, they never left. They maintained their culture, kin and land connections traversing back and forth along well-known 'beats' (tracks, trails and paths) in what he terms the 'affiliated coastal zone'. The Aboriginal people of Sydney, Woolloomooloo, Manly, Rose Bay, Vaucluse, Botany and La Perouse have always been there.[7]

Both Karskens and Irish dispel myths that 'crippled' the Board after 1883. The common belief in the late nineteenth and early twentieth centuries that Aboriginal people would 'die out' never eventuated, and the Board never came to terms with this reality. Its blinkered view was reflected in policy hiatus and failure.

---

4   Willey, *When the Sky Fell Down*; Smith, *Bennelong: King Bungaree;* Clendinnen, *Dancing with Strangers*.
5   Karskens, *The Colony*, 385.
6   *Aborigines: Minutes of Evidence taken before the Select Committee on the Aborigines*, Mahroot alias the Boatswain, 8 September 1845, 1–5.
7   Irish, *Hidden in Plain View*, 25.

Of particular interest to this study is Peter Read's research and subsequent work on Wiradjuri history.[8] Read's study of the Wiradjuri's battle to survive in the wake of invasion, dispossession and the frontier wars, and their subsequent struggle under the oppressive polices of the APB, provides a foundation upon which to explore further the dynamics of the Board, particularly after the government's restructure of the Board after 1916. This government intervention and restructure of the Board had severe ramifications for the Aboriginal people of New South Wales. Read's later work on the Stolen Generations is well known and, using the same archive he examined, my research has a focus on the locations from which Aboriginal apprentices were removed and traces their multiple placements across the state.

Heather Goodall's research on Aboriginal communities in New South Wales from 1909 and 1939 and her subsequent book *Invasion to Embassy* are indispensable resources for this study.[9] My research confirms her assessment of the Board's early period as 'a small administrative body [with] no legislative base'.[10] However, I attempt to explain why this was so. I argue that the nature and circumstances surrounding the establishment of the Board influenced its early operation and, moreover, the Board chair, Edmund Fosbery, was disinclined to act decisively on policy. This reluctance worked in favour of Aboriginal people as it forestalled the introduction of restrictive measures that followed after Fosbery's retirement. Victoria Haskins has provided invaluable insights into the operations of the Board in the latter stages of its life, revealing the Board's methods and its all-controlling influence over Aboriginal girls removed from their communities.[11] I have explored this further by exposing the gross dysfunction and lack of accountability of the Board during this period. I also highlight an obvious disconnect between Board members and outside influences, its collective paranoia, and sense of being under siege in the late 1930s.

---

8   Read, 'The History of the Wiradjuri people of NSW 1909–1969'; *A Hundred Years War*. See also Read, *A Rape of the Soul so Profound*; '"Breaking up These Camps Entirely"'.
9   Goodall, 'A History of Aboriginal Communities in New South Wales 1909–1939'; *Invasion to Embassy*.
10 Goodall, *Invasion to Embassy*, 2008, 108. Goodall, 'A History of Aboriginal Communities in New South Wales 1909–1939'.
11 Haskins, *One Bright Spot*.

Naomi Parry's research on the treatment of black and white children in welfare in New South Wales and Tasmania underscores the importance of one Board member, George Ardill.[12] I build on this discussion by describing his influence in the removal of Aboriginal children in New South Wales and his evangelical obsession. His judgement and character were questioned by his contemporaries, and I speculate as to the reason for his needless appointment to the Board: his lone wolf operational style dominated, and he accumulated significant power.

Jim Fletcher's forensic exploration of the New South Wales School Files and other Department of Education archival material has exposed the substandard education provided to Aboriginal children and the extent to which Aboriginal children were excluded from public schools.[13] I have focused on the Board's limited power in this area. The Board was unable to prevent such exclusions and failed in its stated policy of allowing small numbers of Aboriginal children to be admitted to local schools. It was powerless in the face of the white parental prejudice against Aboriginal children and was marginalised when the Department of Education acquiesced to this pressure group.

My research also extends the work undertaken by Anna Doukakis in her exhaustive study of parliamentarians' contributions to the debate on Aboriginal issues up to 1916.[14] I emphasise and canvass the debates – which exposed the internal dynamics of the Board – that took place in 1918 and 1936 on two important legislative amendments to the *Aborigines Protection Act 1909*.

My other debts to scholars of the Board are more specific and are acknowledged in the chapters that follow.

Protectionism

The Board was established, ostensibly, to 'protect' the Aboriginals of New South Wales, but as will been seen, over time, the word 'protect' almost became a misnomer. Protectionism became an instrument of government to achieve other ends. The history of 'protection' can be traced back to the

---

12 Parry, 'Such a Longing'.
13 Fletcher, *Clean, Clad and Courteous*.
14 Doukakis, *The Aboriginal People*.

empires of Rome and China, and conquests across Central Asia and the Middle East, where promises to protect the lives of subjects were made upon their submission. In the medieval period, royal protection 'helped to structure' the monarchies; protection 'was a global phenomenon'.[15]

Recent scholarship centred on protectionism, humanitarianism and colonial governance has provided a new lens through which to view the history of empires. Lauren Benton and Adam Clulow conclude that protectionism was significant in the 'politics of empires' and indeed was a 'framework for interpolity relations' and a strategy for rule.[16] They likened such protective regimes to passports that 'facilitated movement, framed commercial interactions and generated translatable political terms'.[17] This resurgence of interest in nineteenth-century British colonialism has seen 'significant attention paid to humanitarians and their conflicts, compromises, and collusions with projects of settler encroachment on indigenous peoples' lands'.[18] With a focus on the British Empire between 1815 and 1860, Alan Lester and Fae Dussart pose the question: how can the 'violent settler colonization' of Australia, New Zealand, southern Africa and North America be reconciled with 'Humanitarian' government positions? From a number of examples that focus on particular individuals throughout the empire, they argue the broader point that 'violent colonial conquest was foundational to and intrinsic to the shared history of British humanitarianism and governmentality'.[19] They develop this argument by

> seeing the individuals who sought to effect humanitarianism within colonial contexts in which they lived, and to which they contributed, as dynamic assemblages within which they had some, albeit limited, capacity to effect change.[20]

By examining the relationship between the Dja Dja Wurrung people, to the north of Melbourne, and the assistant protector, Edward Stone Parker, in the Port Phillip Protectorate in New South Wales 1839–49, Lester and Dussart demonstrate some enduring features of protectionism and governmentality function in this humanitarian space.[21] Protector Parker's orders from the chief protector, George Augustus Robinson, were to travel

---

15 Benton, Clulow and Attwood, eds, *Protection and Empire*, 3.
16 Benton, Clulow and Attwood, eds, *Protection and Empire*, 2–3.
17 Benton, Clulow and Attwood, eds, *Protection and Empire*, 8.
18 Lester and Dussart, *Colonization and the Origins of Humanitarian Governance*, 4.
19 Lester and Dussart, *Colonization and the Origins of Humanitarian Governance*, 1.
20 Lester and Dussart, *Colonization and the Origins of Humanitarian Governance*, 6.
21 Lester and Dussart, *Colonization and the Origins of Humanitarian Governance*, 114–15.

with the Dja Dja Wurrung, to 'proselytise and both dissuade and shield from the worst frontier violence and, at some point, encourage them to settle on reserves'.[22] Parker soon realised that he would not be able to move around with the Dja Dja Wurrung people as the larger language group broke up into smaller clans and travelled independently for long periods of time. He also had to establish a station (which was not his remit) to protect the declining numbers in the face of European expansion and settler violence. He was then forced to relocate at the demands of his clientele.[23] Parker soon realised that Aboriginal people were not passive players in this 'protection space'. As a result, Parker's ability to effect change himself was limited. It was the 'Aborigines themselves [who] set the terms of engagement with Parker's project, according to their own political geographies'.[24] Joanna Cruikshank and Mark McMillian, in their research on mid-nineteenth-century Victoria, describe how Aboriginal people 'asserted their own expectations and laws in ways that helped to shape how protection plans emerged'.[25] Samuel Furphy and Amanda Nettelbeck make the point that 'protection was a particularly unstable concept' that could be administered in a variety of ways by a range of players.[26]

Christina Twomey and Katherine Ellinghaus argue that scholars often see protectionism and humanitarianism as one and the same, but in fact they should not be conflated, as protectionism 'deserves more singular attention'. Protectionism should not just be seen through the prism of British settler colonialism but as a broad, world-shaping process, with its origins in European colonialism. They argue that this world-shaping process includes three streams of scholarship. First, how indentured labour and slaves were treated. Second, how some of the subjects of protective policies were able to utilise the 'discourse [of protectionism] to their advantage' as the records reveal the perspectives of Indigenous populations. And third, how the ideas of protection led to the formulation of other laws and policies that did not include the word 'protect'.[27] To illustrate an example of this last stream, Amanda Nettelbeck reasons that during the 1840s the protectorates of Port Phillip, South Australia and Western Australia sought to control the mobility of Aboriginal people as each was

---

22   Ford, 'Protecting the Peace on the Edges of Empire', 175.
23   Lester and Dussart, *Colonization and the Origins of Humanitarian Governance*, 146–53.
24   Lester and Dussart, *Colonization and the Origins of Humanitarian Governance*, 153.
25   Furphy and Nettelbeck, *Imagining Protection in the Antipodean Colonies*, 6.
26   Furphy and Nettelbeck, *Imagining Protection in the Antipodean Colonies*, 6–7.
27   Twomey and Ellinghaus, eds, 'Protection: Global Genealogies, Local Practices', 3–4.

part of a wider government agenda to 'make them amenable to settler society's cultural and legal codes'.[28] Although the protectorates were fundamentally about protecting, they sat within a 'broader framework' of government control and regulation. However, the demand by a settler petition in 1853 that Aboriginal people should come under the *Vagrancy Act 1835* (NSW) was met with wide derision in the New South Wales Legislative Council, as it would be an anathema to declare almost the entire Aboriginal population as vagrants when it was their natural 'disposition' to move across country.[29] Nevertheless, in the latter decades of the nineteenth century, with increasing dispossession forcing more Aboriginal people towards the towns and cities with no prospect of work, the vagrancy laws of incarceration became more appealing to government bodies and indeed the protectorates. The vagrancy laws became the instrument for separating the races to prevent sexual mixing, maintaining an Aboriginal labour force for white businesses and for punishments relating to begging and loitering. Nettelbeck contends that by the 'end of nineteenth century, the term "vagrant" had become routinely employed to describe Indigenous people as irreversibly destitute … and that in the cause of their own protection they should be confined to government reserves'.[30] This example parallels the story of the New South Wales Board for the Protection of Aborigines. As will be seen in subsequent chapters, the original policies of protection and assistance to Aboriginal people in the early 1880s in New South Wales became, over time, far less about protecting but more about controlling, segregating and punishing.

Lisa Ford notes that the 'project of Aboriginal protection has a rich historiography [and is] deeply entwined with the study of webs of empire'.[31] The implementation of protectionism on the frontiers of a far-flung outpost of the British Empire led to a vast array of outcomes, some foreseen and many unforeseen.

---

28 Nettelbeck, 'Creating the Aboriginal Vagrant', 80.
29 Nettelbeck, 'Creating the Aboriginal Vagrant', 83.
30 Nettelbeck, 'Creating the Aboriginal Vagrant', 99.
31 Ford, 'Protecting the Peace on the Edges of Empire' 175.

Biography

This is a work invested in the life stories of Board members. Only the briefest biographical sketches have been possible, but they help to identify the Board members, their backgrounds and their 'contribution' to the Board in order to assess their relative impact. As Ann Laura Stoler argues, it was 'not only empires that reshaped the "interior frontiers" of the nation; [it was also] the people who moved within, between and outside of imperial boundaries'.[32] David Lambert, Alan Lester and Tony Ballantyne have all demonstrated the importance of life stories to a greater understanding of the British Empire.[33] Samuel Furphy's book *Edward M. Curr and the Tide of History*, which details the impact of Curr's writings on colonial Victoria and describes Curr's role on the Victorian Board for the Protection of Aborigines, confirms the importance of biography in shaping Aboriginal history. His discussion of the Victorian Board also highlights the differences of opinion between Board members that have direct parallels with the New South Wales experience.[34] Curr's interests, proclivities and personality influenced his impact on the Victorian Protection Board just as those of key members, G.E. Ardill and parliamentarian Robert T. Donaldson affected their roles on the New South Wales Board.

Biography has, at times, been considered the 'poor relation' to 'serious' history; yet, many historians are 'rediscovering an interest in individuals and subjective experiences'.[35] This is because it sheds light on a 'range of differing historical periods and problems', bringing 'individuals and groups' into the 'framework of historical analysis'.[36] Biographical compilations, or collective biographies, have classical roots, but evolved over centuries into compilations that reflected the growth of nation states

---

32 Quoted in Lambert and Lester, *Colonial Lives*, 13.
33 Lambert and Lester, *Colonial Lives*. Tony Ballantyne notes it was not just the connection between the metropole and the colony that was important, it was also the web of 'cultural traffic ... that developed into a cultural mesh of networks' across the empire that facilitated an exchange of ideas and imperial institutions that circulated between colonies. Ballantyne, *Orientalism and Race*, 13–17.
34 Furphy notes that Curr did not agree with his colleagues on the issue of 'assimilation or absorption'. He saw no distinction between 'half-caste' and 'full-blood' and wished all the Coranderrk Aboriginal people removed to a remote station on the Murray River. Furphy, *Edward M. Curr and the Tide of History*, 141. See also Furphy, '"They Formed a Little Family as it Were"', 95–116. Furphy highlights the power of a small group of Board members which has parallels with the New South Wales Protection Board post 1916. He also writes of their 'falling out' over the removal of the manager John Green from Corranderrk as the Kulin fight for the survival of their reserve took centre stage.
35 Cowman, 'Collective Biography', 83.
36 Caine, *Biography and History*, 1.

or political movements such as feminism.[37] Krista Cowman argues that, in the later part of twentieth century, two further types of collective biography developed, each described as 'group biography'. The first of these concerned the 'origins, activities and philosophies of groups themselves', augmented by information (from original dictionary entries) on individual members. A second type is the study of the biographical subjects and their connection in some way through 'family, metier or politics'.[38]

A biographical approach is key to understanding how the New South Wales Protection Board functioned. Indeed, this study is in part a project in group biography, though this approach has its limitations. First, it is most relevant for the first two phases of the Board between 1883 and 1916 when most Board members (apart from the chair, who was a government appointee) offered their services. What motivated these men, pre-1916, to join the Board had a good deal to do with shared elements in their backgrounds, religious persuasions, humanitarian interests and professions. After 1916 the bulk of membership was appointed by the government – what linked this group was a salaried government appointment, and an apparent disinterest in Aboriginal welfare. Individual biography is even more important to this story as Board members did not all come to the Board with a common purpose; moreover, the Board's loose and ambiguous intentions did not lend itself to a common interest and goals. The 'protection' of Aboriginal people encompassed a vast array of issues to deal with and, as will be seen, the impetus and carriage of these were driven by individuals. Here the sketchy individual biographies gathered in the Appendices are key to explaining the motivations and actions of the Board.

Many biographical works by or about Aboriginal people have shed light on the nature of the Board. Stan Grant's insightful recollections of his early life, his family and its roots, and on matters of race, go to the deep-seated problem with which the Board never came to terms – how to deal with those Aboriginal people who were not considered to be 'full-bloods'.[39] Ella Simon's autobiographical portrayal of Purfleet (Taree) in its early years as a station graphically describes how Board personnel arrived unannounced, evicted some families from their homes

---

37   See Caine, *Biography and History*, 48–56; and Cowman, 'Collective Biography', 86–89.
38   Cowman, 'Collective Biography', 88.
39   Grant, *Tears of Strangers*.

and proceeded to impose a managerial authority. Her work exposes the Board's uncaring and perfunctory approach to its clientele.[40] The stories of Jimmie Barker at Brewarrina, as related by Janet Matthews, and Thorp Clarke's biography of Doug Nicholls shed much light on the role of the station managers and their use of wide powers over the residents.[41]

What shaped the Board

By the late 1930s, the Board had acquired extraordinary powers over Aboriginal people. It could direct any Aboriginal person on or off a reserve or station; remove any Aboriginal child from their family into an institution or into service; collect the wages of 'any Aborigine' and hold them in trust; authorise the medical inspection of any 'Aborigine'; order any 'Aborigines to move from their camp to another camp-site, or from towns and townships'; and prevent any Aboriginal person from leaving New South Wales.[42] No other member of the Australian community was dealt with in this fashion – Aboriginal people had been singled out as special subjects of intensive state control.

Despite exercising these extraordinary powers, throughout its entire life, the Board remained a small administrative entity with no obvious operational rules or procedures, and no requirements for member attendance. Its only requirement was to submit an annual report to the New South Wales Government. Some public and parliamentary voices raised alarm at the treatment of Indigenous Australians, but their voices were few. There was a public indifference to the plight of Aboriginal people. Russell McGregor writes that at the turn of the century the 'Federation Fathers gave no thought to how Aboriginal people might be included in the nation to be'.[43] This overall indifference to Aboriginal people was consolidated by popular belief and 'scientific' perspectives. Anthropologists Baldwin Spencer and Frank Gillen noted in 1899 'that the "Australian aborigines are the most primitive or backward race" on earth ... [and] ... they were doomed, and little more could be done other

---

40 Simon, *Through My Eyes*, 88–91.
41 Matthews (as told to), *The Two Worlds of Jimmy Barker*; Clark, *The Boy form Cumeroogunga*.
42 Patten and Ferguson, *Aborigines Claim Citizen Rights!* 7–8. See also the *Aborigines Protection Act 1909* (NSW); *Aborigines Protection Amending Act 1915* (NSW); *Aborigines Protection (Amendment) Act 1918* (NSW); *Aborigines Protection (Amendment) Act 1936* (NSW).
43 McGregor, *Indifferent Inclusion*, xvii.

than to make their "path to final extinction … as pleasant as possible"'.⁴⁴ Not only was there a general indifference to the first Australians, the 1901 Australian Constitution shut out Aboriginal people from Australian society. Section 51(xxvi) precluded the Commonwealth from making laws with respect to Aboriginal people and Section 127 excluded them from the national census. Nothing could be clearer. McGregor contends that, at the time of 'Federation, it seemed to settler Australians that the Aboriginal race literally had no future. A forward-looking nation foresaw an Australia devoid of Aboriginal people'.⁴⁵ Collectively, the Board held the same view.

To demonstrate how the Board operated on the ground, I have drawn upon some of the Board's interactions with Dharawal people, whose Country lies to the south and south-west of Sydney. To 'ground' this approach, I have consulted several authors that have documented Dharawal history since 1788, including Grace Karskens, J.L. Kohen, Keith Willey, Inga Clendinnen and Keith Vincent Smith, whose works focus on the Sydney region but connect with Dharawal history.⁴⁶ Research from Michael Organ and C. Speechley, Anne Marie Whitaker and Carol Liston provide the early picture of the Dharawal and European interaction south of Sydney.⁴⁷ Michael Bennett's research details the employment and agency of Aboriginal workers in the Shoalhaven and Illawarra.⁴⁸

The Dharawal have a peculiar role in the Board's formation, as their 'beats', or well-worn tracks, trails and paths, up and down the coast and inland, linked communities from the Shoalhaven right through to the north shore of Sydney.⁴⁹ It was this regular interaction between the Dharawal and Sydney clans and groups on the north coast that was partly responsible for the government's appointment of a Protector of Aborigines, and later the establishment of the Board. Dharawal people also participated in some exemplary moments of resistance, particularly in opposing the removal of their children from public schools.⁵⁰ For this reason, the Dharawal provide

---

44   McGregor, *Indifferent Inclusion*, xvii.
45   McGregor, *Indifferent Inclusion*, xx.
46   Karskens, *The Colony*; Kohen, *The Darug and Their Neighbours*; Willey, *When the Sky Fell Down*; Clendinnen, *Dancing with Strangers*; Smith, *Eora: Mapping Aboriginal History 1770–1850*.
47   Organ and Speechley, *Illawarra Aborigines*; Whitaker, *Appin: The Story of Macquarie Town*; Liston, 'The Dharawal and Gandangara in colonial Campbelltown', 49–59.
48   Bennett, 'For a Labourer Worthy of His Hire'.
49   Irish, *Hidden in Plain View*, 17.
50   Chapter 7 describes how some Aboriginal individuals challenged the Education Department and the Board over the exclusion of their children from public schools.

an excellent focus through which to explore the Board's operational methods, to demonstrate the limits of Board power and policy as well as the Board's incursions into communities. I have endeavoured to provide an Aboriginal perspective where possible and have been grateful to the contributions from some Dharawal people who allowed me to interview them. Some individuals and organisations were reluctant to discuss the lives of their grandparents and great-grandparents for obvious reasons.

Chapter outlines

I have employed a chronological approach to facilitate what I have determined to be three distinct phases or periods of the Board spanning its 57 years. The following chapters largely represent these phases.

Chapter 1, which examines factors leading up to the Board's establishment, shows the halting and chaotic origins of the Board. I provide a brief background sketch of the dramatic decline in the Aboriginal population after the British invasion from 1788, and the first formal attempt at protection, initiated from London in the Port Phillip District in 1838. The chapter's focus is, however, on the direct antecedents to the establishment of the New South Wales Board and the circumstances surrounding its formation. Broadly, three factors forced the New South Wales Government to intervene in Aboriginal affairs. First was the strong advocacy of missionaries Daniel Matthews and John Gribble to fund their two missions in central southern New South Wales. Second was the subtle and persistent push from Aboriginal people for reserve land. The third factor was a very public controversy over the Aboriginal people residing at the government boatshed at Circular Quay in 1881. The subsequent appointment of George Thornton, in late 1881, as an 'Aborigines Protector' by the Parkes Government was not enough to quell the disquiet over Aboriginal issues. The position of 'Aborigines Protector' was removed by the incoming Stuart Government and, in an acrimonious atmosphere, a Protection Board was established.

Chapter 2 examines the first period of the Board, from 1883 to 1897. The Board established key infrastructure to assist primarily the aged and infirm, and to instruct the children. Nevertheless, it failed to meet the material needs of Aboriginal people, remained aloof from its clientele and did not reflect on its policy positions. I offer a brief sketch of Board members, outline initial policy platforms and, using Dharawal examples, explore how the early Board 'interacted' with Aboriginal people. The chapter highlights the Board's inability to develop coherent policy. It had outlined a legislative wish list in its first annual report, including the full 'custody and control of aborigines of all ages and sexes in a like manner as a parent'.[51] Yet it did not actively pursue a legislative mandate until the early twentieth century. Indeed, it took 27 years to achieve enabling legislation in 1909. Also, as a result of its interaction with Aboriginal people, the Board recognised certain unexpected challenges such as the increasing number of Aboriginal people entering the reserves and stations, continued lack of funding, the regular exclusion of Aboriginal children from public schools, and the increase in the 'half-caste' population. But it failed to respond to any of these with coherent policy. Furthermore, a tense and acrimonious relationship with a parallel organisation – the Aborigines Protection Association (APA), which maintained control over the three largest Aboriginal stations – caused ongoing financial and policy frustration for the Board.[52] In 1897, after 14 years, the APA finally relinquished power to the Board.

The arrival of two forceful leaders on the Board from 1897 to 1916 ushered in a second phase of the Board's history, in which it gained legislative power and wielded it to the detriment of Aboriginal communities. In 1897, George Edward Ardill joined the Board and remained until 1916. His lengthy stay resulted in a more proactive Board approach to the removal of Aboriginal children and to a renewed effort to gain a legislative mandate. Chapter 3 demonstrates how Ardill became a dominant force on an otherwise apathetic Board. Ardill's evangelical zeal and dogged approach set the Board on a policy course that would continue until its reconstitution in 1916. The arrival of another powerful, crusading individual, Robert T. Donaldson, further augmented the impact of the Board. Chapter 4 explains his influence. He came to the Board highly recommended and was a forceful politician with a combative style. A man who saw the 'big picture' and professed to 'know' Aboriginal people, Donaldson spoke regularly in parliament and in public, advocating the removal of Aboriginal children, particularly the 'almost white' girls,

---

51 *Protection of Aborigines: Report of the Board* (the APB Report: hereafter *APBR)* 1884, 2. Accessed via 'NSW', To Remove and Protect, AIATSIS: aiatsis.gov.au/sites/default/files/docs/digitised_collections/remove/22818.pdf, accessed 1 November 2018.
52 Maloga and Warangesda had been established by missionaries Daniel Matthews and John Gribble, respectively, in the mid-1870s, and they were taken over by the high-powered Sydney organisation the APA. Brewarrina was added in 1886. See Chapter 1 for details.

from the camps, reserves and stations and their placement into domestic apprenticeships. This became his crusade. He did much to secure the passage of the *Aborigines Protection Act 1909* (NSW) and was even more influential in the passage of the 1915 amendment that allowed the Board to bypass the courts to remove children. Chapter 5 explains why the Board was reconstituted in 1916. Ardill was, in part, responsible for the change. He created a controversy over payments to members, the Board went on strike and a furore erupted over the appointment of a new inspector. With rumours of an imminent reconstitution, three members – including the previous Inspector-General of Police, Thomas Garvin – resigned in protest.

This upheaval ushered in the last phase of the Board's history. Gone were any remaining humanitarians, those with an interest in Aboriginal policy, businessmen and high-profile individuals. From 1916, the Board was predominately staffed by public servants, all compliant with government, and with no special interest in Aboriginal affairs. Significant change occurred: the frequency of Board meetings was drastically reduced, the agendas filtered and the annual reports curtailed. This allowed, either by design or evolution, for a small clique or cabal within the structure of the Board to dominate policy and act with little oversight. Board agents (including Donaldson) immediately embarked on the systematic removal of Aboriginal children from their communities. They wielded considerable authority over Aboriginal people and their hand was further strengthened with an additional amendment (although mitigated by the parliament) to the Act in 1918 that enabled the Board to expel more Aboriginal people from the reserves and stations.

In Chapters 6 and 7, I demonstrate two of the Board's most destructive influences upon the Aboriginal communities of New South Wales: its removal of children into apprenticeships and its failure to provide or demand access for Aboriginal children to a full and equal education. Paradoxically, both issues also revealed the Board's limitations as well as its power and arrogance. Chapter 6 explores the Board's inability to prevent Aboriginal girls from returning home after their apprenticeships and Chapter 7 shows its impotence and indifference in preventing Aboriginal children from being excluded from local public schools. Chapter 8 describes how the Board crumbled in the face of powerful Aboriginal critiques in the 1930s. The Board could not accept the increasing influence of Aboriginal voices such as Fred Maynard, William Cooper, William Ferguson, Pearl Gibbs and Jack Patten, who demanded an end to 'protection' and the Board. In return, the Board saw them as impertinent and as agitators. It had built up a 'wall of secrecy and paranoia' since 1918 that made it the object of humanitarian critique. The APB's dysfunctional structure and blinkered personnel could not feel the 'winds of change' from any direction, and it reaped the consequences.

I explore how this poorly designed APB worked in practice under an ever-expanding legislative mandate. Paradoxically, the Board's loose structure, flawed processes and lack of overall accountability combined to make it both a powerful and dangerous entity and, at times, an ineffectual and dysfunctional one, unable to implement policies. This book demonstrates that the Board was profoundly influenced by a few individuals whose enthusiasms shaped Aboriginal life in the face of the indifference of other Board members. By understanding its structural dysfunctions and personnel, we can better understand why it pursued particular policies, what other key institutions (such as the Education Department) influenced Aboriginal lives, and how Aboriginal people themselves sometimes managed to challenge policy and change outcomes by exploring gaps in the Board's power.

Far more than a blemish

The story of the Board and its impact upon Aboriginal people is a sorry chapter in Australia's history; far more than a mere blemish as prime minister John Howard once described.[53] Below is an attempt to analyse one government bureaucracy and provide some meaningful analysis of what shaped its direction – a path that gave rise to such a fervent protest by 100 Aboriginal people at the Day of Mourning in Sydney on 26 January 1938.

Pervading much of the life of the Board was the common belief in the late nineteenth and early twentieth centuries that Aboriginal people would 'die out'. It worked on the premise that the 'full-blood' Aboriginal people would soon be gone, and those of 'lighter skin' would be absorbed in the mainstream community – the Board could then close the reserves and stations and cease the issue of rations. This did not eventuate, and the

---

53 John Howard made it clear that his government would not go further than express 'regrets' concerning what happened to Aboriginal people but conceded that it was the most 'blemished' chapter of Australia's history. See Manne, ed., *Whitewash*, 2003, 4.

Board never came to terms with this reality. Consequently, it railed against the presence of Aboriginal people, their mobility and their determination to be part of Australian society.

When Aboriginal people meet for the first time, so much is already understood. Aboriginal people of New South Wales, who came under the direct attention of the Board, and indeed those who did not, have all suffered in one form or another from the same stigma, racism and exclusion from white Australia. What began as assistance and support changed to coercion, removal, control and segregation. Racist attitudes and Board incompetence, indolence, zealotry, misplaced care and indifference combined to do great harm to the Aboriginal people of New South Wales for over five decades.

1

A faltering start to 'protection', 1883

Although the 'mother colony' of New South Wales was the birthplace of European occupation and Aboriginal dispossession, it was slow to address the parlous situation of many of its Aboriginal people throughout the nineteenth century. When the first attempt at ameliorating the condition of the surviving Aboriginal population came via the Port Phillip Protectorate in 1838, it was undertaken only on the southernmost frontier of the colony in what would become Victoria. After the failure of the protectorate in 1849, and the establishment of the Colony of Victoria in 1851, the New South Wales Government did not undertake any formal measures to address the appalling consequences of the dispossession of its Aboriginal people for the next 30 years. It required pressure from other quarters, in the late 1870s, to force the government to begin its stumbling attempts to establish a formal protective body to ameliorate the condition of those Aboriginal people in need.

Amity and kindness in tatters

When the Cadigal and Cameragal watched John Hunter and Arthur Phillip enter Port Jackson in two cutters on 21 January 1788, they had little reason to suspect that their way of life was under threat. The pale strangers would probably stay for a while and leave as they had done 18 years beforehand when James Cook and Joseph Banks arrived in Botany Bay, 16 kilometres to the south. However, the raising of the Union Jack on 26 January at Sydney Cove would change everything.

Under instructions from King George III, Arthur Phillip was to open a dialogue with the 'native' inhabitants and encourage all to live in 'amity and kindness' – it did not last long. Phillip, frustrated by the lack of contact with local Aboriginal clans, captured two Aboriginal men to enforce dialogue. Within two years relations had deteriorated and Phillip launched a punitive expedition against the local Aboriginal people for the spearing of a convict. There was now a new norm: one of retribution for any Aboriginal transgressions against the interests of the fledgling colony.

No one knows how many Indigenous people lived in Australia in 1788.[1] Bain Attwood and Stephen G. Foster estimate an Aboriginal population across the continent of 750,000 at the time of occupation.[2] Political historian Colin Tatz suggests somewhere between 250,000 and 750,000.[3] Archaeologist John Mulvaney estimated somewhere between 500,000 and 1 million.[4] Jan Kociumbas offers that 'writers now argue that 750,000 or even a million is a more likely figure'.[5] Recently, Raymond Evans and Robert Orsted-Jensen, in their research on the Queensland frontier, have concluded that the pre-contact population in Queensland alone was between 250,000 and 300,000.[6]

Table 1.1: Decline in the Aboriginal population, 1788 to 1861.

State/Territory	Estimated levels in 1788	Estimated levels in 1861	Decline
New South Wales	48,000	15,000	68.75%
Victoria	15,000	2,384	84.10%
Tasmania	4,500	18	99.60%
South Australia	15,000	9,000	40.00%
Queensland	120,000	60,000	50.00%
Western Australia	62,000	44,500	28.22%
Northern Territory	50,000	48,500	3.00%

Source: Smith, *The Aboriginal Population of Australia*, Table 8.2.1, 208.

---

1   There is still much speculation about population levels of Indigenous Australians at the time of the British occupation and it never can be definitively determined. See: Reynolds, *The Forgotten War*, 122; Jones, *The Structure and Growth of Australia's Aboriginal Population*, 2–3; Attwood and Foster, *Frontier Conflict*, 5; Broome, *Aboriginal Australians*, 1994, 11; Day, *Claiming a Continent*, 88; Mulvaney, *Encounters in Place*, xv. There is less dispute, however, about the fact that the Aboriginal population declined dramatically after the British occupation from 1788.
2   Attwood and Foster, *Frontier Conflict*, 5.
3   Tatz, *With Intent to Destroy*, 74.
4   Mulvaney, *Encounters in Place*, xv.
5   Kociumbas, 'Genocide and Modernity in Colonial Australia', 84.
6   Evans and Orsted-Jensen, '"I Cannot Say the Numbers that were Killed": Assessing Violent Mortality on the Queensland Frontier'. Paper presented at 'Conflict in History', 6.

Nearly four decades since first published, L.R. Smith's exhaustive Aboriginal population study, covering the entire country, is still useful (see Table 1.1). Although his starting base of 314,000 across the whole continent in 1788 is very conservative, to the point of being misleading, his record of decline is alarming.[7] If one uses an estimate of the Aboriginal population of 750,000 across the continent in 1788, then using Smith's 1861 levels, the decline in the population is more appalling.

The rapid decline in the Aboriginal population was due, in the first instance, to the introduction of diseases. The outbreak of smallpox, known as *Gal-gal-la* by the Sydney clans in April 1789, was the first major catastrophic event for the Aboriginal population of the Sydney region. Marine officer Watkin Tench, in April/May 1879, wrote that:

> [an] extraordinary calamity was now observed among the natives … in all the coves and inlets of the harbour … Pustules, similar to those occasioned by smallpox, were thickly spread on the bodies.[8]

Grace Karskens writes that we 'don't know how many people died', but 'some scholars estimate that 80 per cent of people died in the 1789 epidemic'.[9]

Other diseases reduced the population as well. Economic historian Noel Butlin considered venereal disease as a major impediment to the recovery of the Aboriginal population after the smallpox epidemics.[10] Richard Broome asserts that disease 'proved the greatest killer' and the 'gradual loss of life' due to dysentery, scarlet fever, influenza, typhus, measles and whooping cough were just as devastating as a major epidemic like smallpox.[11] The sudden story of smallpox was cataclysmic but the slow catastrophe for Aboriginal people that unfolded afterwards is the important narrative.

The dispossession of Aboriginal land was total. By 1821, only 33 years after Phillip's arrival, all the land within a 70-kilometre radius of Sydney was occupied by nearly 94 per cent of the colony's white population.[12]

---

7   Smith, *The Aboriginal Population of Australia*, 208.
8   Flannery, ed., *Watkin Tench 1788*, 102–3.
9   Karskens, *The Colony*, 377.
10 Bennett, 'For a Labourer Worthy of His Hire', 128.
11 Broome, *Aboriginal Australians*, 2010, 63–65.
12 Ford and Roberts, 'Expansion, 1820–1850', 122.

Under Governor Brisbane (1821–25), further expansion out from Sydney took place. The land grant system of 'Tickets of Occupation' allowed for 'land-hungry pastoralists to use unsurveyed land in remote corners of the colony'.[13] In the Hunter region, settlement spread along the Paterson and Williams rivers and up to the Liverpool plains. The Bathurst area was occupied by pastoralists who pushed even further along the Cudgegong and Talbragar rivers. The reduction of the wool tariff in 1823 unleashed what became known as the 'squatting age' where squatters occupied the land without the 'imprimatur of the state'.[14] From Bathurst, heading north-west towards Wellington Valley, the number of sheep runs increased dramatically. In 1821 there were over 27,000 sheep and by 1826 sheep numbers had risen to 92,000.[15] It was this frenetic pastoralist activity that resulted in the swift dispossession of Aboriginal people and a significant depletion of their resources.

Aboriginal groups defended their Country by spearing sheep, cattle and settlers; the settlers and the mounted police responded with brutal efficiency. To justify violent reprisals, the colonists adopted 'an emerging legal fiction' that Aboriginal people 'trespassed on the property of the British Monarch'.[16] Henry Reynolds, in his seminal work *The Other Side of the Frontier*, reckoned that 20,000 Aboriginal people had died on the frontier across the whole of Australia.[17] In a more recent book, *The Forgotten War*, Reynolds states that his earlier figure of 20,000 should be heavily revised 'upwards to 30,000 and beyond, perhaps well beyond'.[18]

The numbers will never be precise, but the destruction and dispossession were apparent to all. As Tom Griffiths observes, 'many colonists accepted murder in their midst' but they also realised it could not be 'openly discussed'; there were 'good reasons to remain silent'.[19] Many reasoned that this was all the inevitable product of the march of civilisation – a natural outcome and indeed God's will. Ann Curthoys notes that pro-slavery arguments based on the notion that 'Africans had been created separately by God as a lower and different order of being' were a powerful

---

13 Ford and Roberts, 'Expansion, 1820–1850, 126. The 'Ticket of Occupation' could be obtained for a small fee, and the owner could graze 'flocks or herds within two miles of a named locality'. See Perry, 'The Spread of Rural Settlement in New South Wales, 1788–1826', 383.
14 Ford and Roberts, 'Expansion, 1820–1850', 128–29.
15 Perry, 'The Spread of Rural Settlement in New South Wales, 1788–1826', 383.
16 Ford and Roberts, 'Expansion 1820–1850', 128–29.
17 Reynolds, *The Other Side of the Frontier*, 121–22.
18 Reynolds, *The Forgotten War*, 134.
19 Griffiths, *Hunters and Collectors*, 106.

idea during the frontier wars; the 'denial of Aboriginal humanity' was frequently expressed when frontier violence was at its height and was used as a justification for dispossession by force.[20] In the first trial following the Myall Creek Massacre of 1838, where 11 white men were acquitted for the slaughter of 28 Aboriginal people, one juror opined:

> I look upon the blacks as a set of monkies … I knew well they [the white men] were guilty of the murder, but I, for one, would never see a white suffer for shooting a black.[21]

But the anti-slavery view that Aboriginal people were 'at least, human beings, created of one blood by the Creator with Europeans', did hold sway in the mid-1830s.[22] In Britain, after the emancipation of slaves throughout the British Empire, there emerged a strong movement to protect the indigenous people of the empire.

Protection in New South Wales

In the Australian context during the nineteenth and early twentieth centuries, Aboriginal protection came in many forms – a variation that was amplified from the period of colonial self-government when restrictive legislation created different protective regimes in every state. Early attempts in New South Wales to protect Aboriginal Australians from settler depredations were localised. In 1825 the London Mission Society offered Lancelot Threlkeld 10,000 acres on the shores of Lake Macquarie to set up a mission. He was instructed to learn the language of the Awabakal people, open a school and teach the Aboriginal people carpentry and agriculture.[23] However, due to internal society wrangling, the mission folded in April 1828.[24] Another mission deep in Wiradjuri Country at Wellington Valley was established by Samuel Marsden in 1830. Wiradjuri were cautious, fearing the missionaries may mistreat them as white settlers had done.[25] Internal ructions, a suspicious clientele, no missionary appreciation of Aboriginal culture and values and an

---

20 Curthoys, 'Race and Ethnicity', 67.
21 *The Australian*, 8 December 1838, 2.
22 Curthoys, 'Race and Ethnicity', 67.
23 Harris, *One Blood*, 52. Threlkeld often represented Aboriginal people in court as they were unable to swear an oath on the bible; he undertook a translation of the bible into Awabakal, and openly spoke against massacres that had occurred in the region. Harris, *One Blood*, 54.
24 Harris, *One Blood*, 52.
25 Harris, *One Blood*, 65–66.

increasingly obsessive and aggressive Reverend Watson saw the mission go the same way as Threlkeld's in the early 1840s.[26] The next impetus for some protective measures did not come from Sydney but from London. The 'Exeter Hall' humanitarians had cast an eye across the British colonies and found dreadful excesses against the indigenous populations.

It took reports home to Britain of the impact of the new wave of pastoralism on Aboriginal people to transform sporadic early efforts into a protection policy. The pressure to redress the depredations upon indigenous people across the British colonies came from 'British philanthropists including those of evangelical, protestant, non-conformist and humanitarian persuasion'.[27] Michael Christie notes that the 'Exeter Hall' movement had successfully brought about the abolition of slavery in 1833 and now focused on the 'plight of all indigenous people in the British colonies'.[28] The genesis of the increased interest in the indigenous peoples had been the continuing hostilities in the Cape Colony in Africa between the British and the Xhosa, but broadened to all colonies.

Efforts to protect indigenous people throughout the empire were spearheaded by leading humanitarian Thomas Fowell Buxton.[29] A House of Commons Select Committee on the 'Native Inhabitants of British Settlements' was formed and heard witnesses from 31 July 1835 until 19 May 1837. It detailed such injustices as loss of land, the deliberate killing of indigenous people and the introduction of alcohol and

---

26   Read, *A Hundred Years War*, 17–18. Read writes of an incident, in December 1839, where Watson had come to take a two-year-old child from his Aboriginal mother (he claimed she had sold the child to him for £11), but she refused. Watson went into a rage, gathered the local constables and returned to take the child. An attempt to restrain him by another missionary failed and he stormed into the house and took the child. Within two weeks all the Wiradjuri had left the mission. Watson was removed by his employer in 1840 and the Reverend James William Gunther, who had replaced Handt, abandoned the mission shortly after. Read, *A Hundred Years War*, 21.
27   Christie, *Aborigines in Colonial Victoria*, 81.
28   Christie, *Aborigines in Colonial Victoria*, 81. It was named 'Exeter Hall' as the group used to hold their meetings at that place in the Strand.
29   Although Thomas Fowell Buxton has been largely recognised as the driver of the committee, Zoe Laidlaw argues that the evidence and argument presented was certainly not his alone. Her article, 'Aunt Anna's Report: The Buxton Women and the Aborigines Select Committee, 1835–37', 1–28, reveals the role played by the women in the Buxton extended family in the crucial preparation of material and argument to present to the select committee. Priscilla, a daughter, and Anna, a cousin, were both Quaker women steeped in practical philanthropy who pursued intellectual interests, and both played significant roles in the presentations to the Select Committee.

prostitution.³⁰ In the Australian context, the violence against Aboriginal women, the 'seduction of women by white men' and the impact of venereal disease were the most prevalent themes.³¹ Little had been done to protect these women from the violence or the 'contamination of the dregs of our countrymen'.³² It is worth noting that the report blames the 'poorer class' of settler and not the rich pastoralists.

In January 1838, Lord Glenelg, Secretary of State for the Colonies, informed the Governor of New South Wales, George Gipps, that it had been decided to appoint a Chief Protector of Aborigines, with its principal station in Port Phillip; he would be aided by four assistant protectors each responsible for the Aboriginal people within a district.³³ When George Robinson – the newly appointed chief protector – and his assistants arrived in Sydney in September 1838 to take up their appointments, they were immersed in the maelstrom of the trial over the Myall Creek Massacre. They soon became the object of antagonism from settler society.³⁴ The protectorate only lasted 10 years: it failed from incompetence, impracticability and resistance from settler society.³⁵ The collapse of the Port Phillip Protectorate in 1848 resulted in a hiatus of government activity from Sydney for nearly four decades.

London's attempt at protection in New South Wales was limited. The site of the experiment, in the southern frontier of the New South Wales colony, was geographically small. Had the attempt been made in the vast expanses of New South Wales proper there is nothing to suggest it would have fared

---

30   Christie, *Aborigines in Colonial Victoria*, 85. There is a wide body of literature concerning the report of the select committee, protectionism and the humanitarian movement of the period. For example, see Laidlaw's work, mentioned above, as well as her work in 'Heathens, Slaves and Aborigines: Thomas Hodgkin's Critique of Missions and Anti-Slavery', 133–61, and *Integrating Metropolitan, Colonial and Imperial Histories – The Aborigines Select Committee of 1835–37*. See also Mitchell, '"The Galling Yoke of Slavery": Race and Separation in Colonial Port Phillip',125–37; and Lester and Dussart, *Colonization and the Origins of Humanitarian Governance*.
31   Elbourne, 'The Sin of the Settler', 7.
32   *Report from the Select Committee on Aborigines (British Settlements); with the Minutes of Evidence, Appendix and Index*, House of Commons, 26 June 1837, VQ. 354.9400814/10, 10. House of Commons Parliamentary Papers Online, State Library of New South Wales (hereafter SLNSW).
33   For literature concerning the 'protectors' see Christie, *Aborigines in Colonial Victoria*, 87–137. Rae-Ellis, *Black Robinson: Protector of Aborigines*; Reed, 'Rethinking William Thomas: "Friend" of the Aborigines', 87–99; Arkley, *The Hated Protector: The Story of Charles Wightman Sievewright, Protector of Aborigines, 1839–42*.
34   Harris, *One Blood*, 156.
35   For settler society resistance, see Curthoys and Mitchell, 'The Advent of Self-Government 1840s–90', 157; and Mitchell, 'Are We in Danger of a Hostile Visit from the Aborigines? Dispossession and the Rise of Self-Government in NSW', 298.

any better. Susan Johnston suggests that 'failure of the Protectorate led to a pessimism which consigned native policy to "the abyss of neglect"'.[36] As a result, attempts at protection after the failure of the protectorate were largely private.

Nevertheless, despite the failure of the Port Phillip Protectorate, another official protective structure had been put in place. The House of Commons Select Committee of 1837 had also instructed the protectors to bring the Aborigines within 'the pale of the law'. Outside of Port Philip, protection was therefore 'imagined through the prism of the magistracy, the courts, and criminal law'.[37] When George Gipps replaced Bourke as Governor of New South Wales in 1838, Lord Glenelg had already proclaimed that all Aborigines were to be considered subjects of the Crown – hence they were to be treated equally under law. Governor Gipps's proclamation in May 1839 enshrined this into law, giving the Commissioners of Lands extensive powers beyond the 'boundaries of location'. As Lisa Ford notes, the commissioners were now to be 'magistrates of the territory' and 'Coroners would investigate Aboriginal deaths as they would white ones'.[38]

Police and magistrates were and remained the most important purveyors of government protection throughout the continent. Increasingly, they acquitted this duty by over-policing.[39] Throughout Australia, protection was conflated with legal punishment of Aborigines, while the violent business of dispossession continued as many magistrates 'were pastoralist themselves'. Government protection was reduced to blanket distribution (described below) and population reports.[40]

Peculiar antecedents to the Board

The first antecedent to the establishment of the Board occurred in the mid-1840s, when a group of prominent men with an interest in the welfare of Aboriginal people, particularly those around coastal Sydney, established the Sydney Aborigines Committee. Paul Irish has written about this little-known committee, and places it at the forefront of

---

36 Quoted in Smithson, 'A Misunderstood Gift', 105.
37 Ford, 'Protecting the Peace on the Edges of Empire', 180.
38 Ford, 'Protecting the Peace on the Edges of Empire', 186.
39 Nettelbeck and Smandych, 'Policing Indigenous Peoples on Two Colonial Frontiers', 356–75.
40 Ford, 'Protecting the Peace on the Edges of Empire', 186.

assistance to local Aboriginal people at the time.[41] Although this group cannot be credited with the formation of the Protection Board in 1883, one member of the committee, George Thornton, would become the 'Protector of Aborigines' in 1881, and an inaugural member of the Board in 1883. It was Thornton's opinion of how to assist Aboriginal people that was a point of contention within the committee.

Bob Nichols, former editor of the liberal newspaper *The Australian*, and supporter of both self-government and an end to convict transportation, formed the Sydney Aborigines Committee in 1844.[42] Other key members were George Hill and Daniel Egan. All three 'shared a common background of local birth, convict roots and a long association with Sydney'.[43] George Thornton joined the committee in 1854 and would establish himself as a significant figure in Sydney society as Lord Mayor on two occasions (1853 and 1857), as a member of the Legislative Assembly in 1858, as a Freemason and founding provincial grand master, and, in 1860, by becoming the first chair of the Woollahra Borough Council.[44]

The Sydney Aborigines Committee primarily organised the distribution of blankets to the Sydney Aboriginal groups. Irish has comprehensively examined the different viewpoints of members, notably Bob Nichols and George Thornton, about the yearly issue of blankets to Aboriginal people. Nichols was comfortable with Aboriginal people coming from other districts to receive their supply in Sydney. In contrast, Thornton believed they should remain in their own districts and not come to Sydney.[45] This difference of opinion would prove crucial in the openly divisive public debate in the early 1880s concerning assistance to Aboriginal people in the Sydney environs.

It is curious that Thornton held so strongly to the belief that Aboriginal people should receive aid *only* in their districts. He, of all people, would have been aware of how widely Aboriginal people travelled around the coast as he spent a good deal of time with Sydney Aboriginal people in his early years on fishing trips in the Coogee area and on camping trips with them around Wollongong, Kiama and Jervis Bay. He would have had 'considerable opportunity to understand the long-distance connections

---

41 Irish, 'Hidden in Plain View', 174–83.
42 Irish, 'Hidden in Plain View', 175.
43 Irish, 'Hidden in Plain View', 174.
44 Rutledge, 'Thornton, George (1819–1901)'.
45 Irish, 'Hidden in Plain View', 178.

and beats, that were a feature of Aboriginal lives'.[46] Some years later the Reverend T.J. Curtis, a Presbyterian minister from Redfern, exposed a basic flaw in Thornton's position on rationing. Curtis explained that an Aboriginal man would, by necessity (traditional law), come from a different district to that of his wife. Thus, it would be practically impossible to demand that they 'should return to and continue to dwell in their respective districts' when most individual family members were made up from more than one district.[47] Thornton's narrow approach to rationing would have ramifications when he took up the position of 'Protector of Aborigines' in 1881.

A further call in the New South Wales Parliament for the protection of Aboriginal people came in 1861 from a 'retired merchant and ex-Navy man', John Lamb, but nothing was forthcoming.[48] It was not until 1876 when the pastoralist William Henry Suttor (Jr) called for a Select Committee 'to inquire and report on the Aboriginal inhabitants of the Colony' that the parliament felt 'obliged to care for the Aborigines because their land had been taken, liquor introduced, and … their game had been killed or driven away'.[49] But again, no action was taken; parliamentary discussion 'of Aborigines returned mostly to irregular questions about blankets'.[50]

Conversely, Victoria, after it achieved responsible government and a bicameral parliament in 1856, moved quickly to establish a 'protective' body. A group of 'churchgoers, philanthropists, ethnologists and a small number of concerned ex-squatters' lobbied the government after they had been galvanised by a piece in the Melbourne *Argus* written by editor and owner Edward Wilson.[51] In 1856 Wilson launched a stinging rebuke of the paltry amount of money spent on the Aboriginal population in Victoria. He pointed out that since Victoria had become a separate colony, it had gained millions of pounds from the sale of gold, beef, mutton and wool – all sourced from expropriated Aboriginal land.[52] He implored the colony to fully compensate the remaining Aboriginal people regardless of the cost. Within two years Victoria had launched a Select Committee into

---

46 Irish, 'Hidden in Plain View', 178.
47 *Sydney Morning Herald* (hereafter *SMH*), 6 January 1883, 7.
48 Doukakis, *The Aboriginal People*, 28–29.
49 Doukakis, *The Aboriginal People*, 32.
50 Doukakis, *The Aboriginal People*, 32.
51 Christie, *Aborigines in Colonial Victoria*, 153.
52 Christie, *Aborigines in Colonial Victoria*, 152.

the 'present condition of the Aborigines', and in 1860 the Central Board for the Protection of Aborigines was established. Despite the ostensibly good intentions of the move towards formal protection, Victoria would produce, before Federation, the most restrictive legislation of all subsequent Aboriginal jurisdictions.[53]

The second antecedent to the formation of the Board was sparked by two missionaries. The first was Daniel Matthews, whom Ann Curthoys asserts was the most influential figure in the establishment of the Board.[54]

The missionary lobbyist

Daniel Matthews, the son of a strict Wesleyan ship's captain, came to Australia as a teenager in 1853 and encountered Aboriginal people on the gold fields in Bendigo.[55] Theologian John Harris suggests that Matthews was 'saddened to see drunken Aboriginal people begging around grog shanties and appalled to see white men plying them'.[56] He began a campaign of writing to almost every paper in Victoria and New South Wales, and connected with the Aboriginal people in central northern Victoria. In 1856, along with his brother William, he purchased three blocks of land with some river frontage on the New South Wales side of the Murray River some 20 kilometres east of Echuca.[57] The land was a regular gathering place for Aboriginal people and he retained its traditional name of Maloga. His decision to establish a mission may have been due to his contact with the Aboriginal reserve at Coranderrk in Victoria and his friendship with the manager John Green. At Coranderrk, life 'was orderly, Christian and productive'; Matthews came to believe that 'Aborigines could, if assisted, become good members of society'.[58] He voiced his concerns for the plight of Aboriginal people regularly in the press. On 29 May 1866 he wrote to the editor of the Melbourne *Age*:

---

53   Broome, *Aboriginal Victorians*, 192.
54   Curthoys, 'Race and Ethnicity', 177.
55   Harris, *One Blood*, 220. For other accounts of Daniel Matthews and the Maloga Mission, see Cato, *Mister Maloga*; Curthoys, 'Race and Ethnicity', Chapter 3; Barwick, 'A Little More than Kin', 143–79.
56   Harris, *One Blood*, 220.
57   Harris, *One Blood*, 221.
58   Curthoys, 'Race and Ethnicity', 181.

> As a community have not the people of this colony and the Government largely benefited by the land taken from this uncivilized Race. And are we not morally bound in return at least to ameliorate the conditions of the 1900 aborigines who hitherto [have] been taught the most degrading vices.[59]

In April 1870, Matthews convened a meeting in Echuca with the intention of establishing a mission. Twelve men attended and Matthews estimated that the expenses during the first year would be £400. A committee was formed but funds were slow to come, and only £39.15.6 had been raised over two and half years.[60] The Maloga Mission was officially opened in 1874. Matthews 'scoured the country for destitute Aboriginal people to bring them to Maloga' and, along with his zealous wife Janet, believed Aboriginal people could live dignified and worthwhile Christian lives, if given a chance.[61] Over the next five years the mission struggled for money and there were periods of acute food shortages.[62] In September 1878 Matthews travelled to Sydney to publicise his mission and raise some support; he spoke to members of parliament and 'men of high standing and philanthropic principle'.[63] At Temperance Hall in Sydney on 14 October 1878, Daniel Matthews shared stories with the 20 assembled to refute the commonly held beliefs in the inability of the Aboriginal people to succeed. The chair, Mr J. Roseby, addressed the meeting:

> The interests of the aborigines have been neglected by us as a people for many years; the impression apparently having been that it was useless to try and civilize these poor benighted blacks. In Victoria however, schools and stations had been opened that had proved successful [and we hope] to see the Government of this colony do more than had yet been done for the benefit of the poor blacks.[64]

---

59 Daniel Matthews Papers, 1861–1917, A3384, Vol. 1, Part 2.
60 Curthoys, 'Race and Ethnicity', 183.
61 Broome, *Aboriginal Australians,* 1994, 76.
62 Curthoys, 'Race and Ethnicity', 195.
63 Quoted in Curthoys, 'Race and Ethnicity', 202.
64 *SMH,* 15 October 1878, 3.

From the Temperance Hall meeting, the 'Committee to Aid the Maloga Mission' was formed. Mr Edward G.W. Palmer was appointed secretary and a petition that 'steps should be at once taken to afford them [the Aborigines] requisite protection' was adopted and presented to the governor.[65]

Requests for financial assistance from the government failed.[66] Not deterred, a deputation from the Temperance Hall meeting called upon the colonial secretary on 2 June 1879. It informed the colonial secretary, Henry Parkes, that although little could be done for the adult population it was thought that the 'training of the children came within the province of the Government'.[67] Governor Lord Augustus Loftus, in his opening speech of parliament, remarked:

> It has been long felt that the aborigines of the colony have not been sufficiently cared for and you will be invited to deliberate upon the best means of affording more certain and effectual aid to such as remain of these unfortunate people.[68]

The address was described in the press as the 'first time in the history of Australia that these unfortunate people have had the honour of being referred to in a Vice-Regal speech'.[69]

The Maloga Committee moved to expand its reach, broaden its concerns and 'press for substantial changes in policy towards Aborigines'.[70] On 16 February 1880, the Aborigines Protection Association (APA) was established at Temperance Hall in Pitt Street, Sydney. Its primary focus was 'for the purpose of ameliorating the condition of the aboriginal tribes of this colony'.[71] The APA boasted many very powerful men from parliament and the clergy, and individuals with philanthropic interests. The first meeting of the committee comprised the Reverend Canon H.S. King, R. Hill Esq. JP, R. Barbour Esq. MLA, the Reverend T.J. Curtis, G.C. Tutting Esq. JP, John Lupton, E.G.W. Palmer and Daniel Matthews. The patron of the APA was Lord Augustus Loftus, the governor of New South Wales, and Sir John Robertson (joint leader of the government

---

65 *SMH*, 15 October 1878, 3.
66 Curthoys, 'Race and Ethnicity', 203.
67 Daniel Matthews Papers 1861–1917, A3384, Vol. 1, Part 2.
68 Daniel Matthews Papers 1861–1917, A3384, Vol. 1, Part 2.
69 Daniel Matthews Papers 1861–1917, A3384, Vol. 1, Part 2.
70 Curthoys, 'Race and Ethnicity', 209.
71 *Evening News*, 11 June 1880, 3.

with Sir Henry Parkes) became the president of the association. Overall, the council of the association consisted of one bishop, seven reverends, nine members of parliament and 13 men who were either philanthropists or had an interest in Aboriginal issues.[72] In the preface to its first report, the APA highlighted the two problems that would continue to shape Aboriginal policy for the next 60 years:

> a state of things the most repugnant to pure Christian feelings has sprung up. Hundreds of young half-castes – the unmistakable tokens of the white man's sin – are now running wild in the interior, being destitute of all physical comfort, and sunk in the lowest moral degradation.

> The condition of the old blacks is one of absolute wretchedness. Drink, and other vicious habits contracted from the whites, have reduced them to the lowest possible level, and are fast driving them, as a race, from the face of the earth. Something, therefore, must be done to alter this terrible state of things, and ... speedily.[73]

In 1880 the APA put the blame at the feet of the colonists. The Reverend M. Wilkinson moved that Aboriginal people had a 'strong and urgent claim for consideration and protection at the hands of colonists who have displaced them from their hunting grounds'.[74] Six months later, in the Legislative Assembly, APA member (and future Protection Board member) John Foster stated that colonists had neglected the remnants of the Aboriginal race and the best method of protection was to 'give financial support to APA projects'.[75] For the next 17 years the APA would continue its high profile in Aboriginal affairs, have a direct influence on the establishment of the Protection Board and exist as a parallel organisation, albeit in an uneasy relationship with the Board, until 1897.

The camp of mercy

At the time of the formation of the APA, another missionary, the Reverend J.B. Gribble, played a similar role to that of Daniel Matthews. Gribble, a lay preacher and registered minister of the Congregational Church, was

---

72 Daniel Matthews Papers, 1861–1917, A3384, Vol. 1, Part 2.
73 *Report of the New South Wales Aborigines Protection Society*, Sydney, 30 June 1881, Daniel Matthews Papers 1861–1917, A3384, Vol. 2, Parts 1 & 2.
74 Quoted in Curthoys, 'Good Christians and Useful Workers', 47.
75 Curthoys, 'Good Christians and Useful Workers', 48.

a resident of Jerilderie in Victoria with a 'comfortable and profitable' parish in the registry of Deniliquin.[76] Jane Lydon writes that his 'associates were activists' and often 'critical of official Aboriginal policy'.[77] Gribble, who was acquainted with Matthews, had been travelling widely up and down the pastoral stations along the Murray, passing on the Lord's message, and had taken an interest in the mission at Maloga.[78] In May 1878 these men joined forces and embarked on a journey to select a site in the Riverina. They found a suitable one: 600 acres on the Waddi Rural Reserve near Darlington Point on the banks of the Murrumbidgee River.[79] In March 1880 Gribble resigned his ministry and accompanied by his wife, children and some 'aboriginal girls ... and several black males' set off with two wagons loaded with rations and belongings to establish his mission that he called Warangesda.[80]

Within a month, and with two huts nearing completion, Gribble received a letter from the Lands Department in Sydney informing him to cease work immediately; he was obliged to travel to Sydney and speak with the government.[81] Gribble had never been to Sydney. He rode to the nearest railway station at Wagga Wagga, over 100 miles away, and reached Sydney as a total stranger. The Reverend Joshua Hargraves, the Rector of St David's, Surrey Hills, who was visiting the association, noted Gribble and his obvious distressed condition and introduced himself. Thus began a friendship that lasted until Gribble's death 1893.[82] Hargraves accompanied Gribble to see Premier Henry Parkes and a favourable outcome ensued; the land upon which the mission had been placed was granted to Gribble and he was appointed teacher of the 'provisional school for aborigines at a salary of £60'.[83] With the support of Hargraves, the APA and now the premier, Gribble returned to Warangesda somewhat buoyed.

---

76 Gulambali and Elphick, *The Camp of Mercy*, 1.
77 Lydon, 'Christian Heroes? John Gribble, Exeter Hall and Antislavery on Western Australia's Frontier', 61.
78 Gribble's diary entry on 19 January 1878 describes a visit to the 'blacks camps' at Moira Lakes with both Daniel and Janet Matthews. Gribble Papers, MS 1514/1, Item 2 (Australian Institute of Aboriginal and Torres Strait Islander Studies, hereafter AIATSIS).
79 Curthoys, 'Race and Ethnicity', 210.
80 Gulambali and Elphick, *The Camp of Mercy*, 2. The word 'Warangesda' came from 'Camp of Mercy', from 'warang' the word for camp in Wiradjuri, and 'esda', meaning 'mercy' in Hebrew. See Harris, *One Blood*, 414.
81 Gulambali and Elphick, *The Camp of Mercy*, 3.
82 *Narrandera Argus*, 18 April 1950, 3.
83 *Narrandera Argus*, 18 April 1950, 3. There is a discrepancy here, as Gulambali and Elphick suggest it was £90.

The high level of activity by Matthews, Gribble and the APA in lobbying for funds pressured the government to respond. Matthews pushed hard to secure funding. His diary of May 1881 records a hectic schedule: meeting with a Wesleyan congregation at Redfern on the 1st, meeting with Mr Palmer on the 2nd, and, on the 4th, to

> Circular Quay, Govt. Boat Shed, saw the blacks. Kate a half-caste girl confined a month ago – baby died – about 18, [unclear where she had been confined but she resided at the boatshed] very delicate – sad case.[84]

Matthews's deep commitment to the welfare of Aboriginal people cannot be disputed, but he and Gribble were also driven by financial necessity and they were not averse to arousing alarm for gain. They suggested that the 'superior races' had a moral obligation to the 'lesser races'. They advised politicians that the 'blacks were capable of hard work', if they were properly taught by the missionaries, but hinted that failure to support the missions might have dangerous consequences. Gribble warned of 'an up-rising of wild half-castes in the very midst of a Christian community'.[85] The government was caught between allowing the missionaries to continue their charitable and religious work while recognising that it had an obligation to do more.

There is little doubt that persistent pressure of these two individuals upon the New South Wales Government to participate in Aboriginal affairs had pricked the conscience of the politicians to at least open a dialogue on what needed to be done to assist its Aboriginal population.

Aboriginal people campaign for reserve land

The third antecedent to the formation of the Board was the Aboriginal push for reserve land. In contrast to Curthoys, Heather Goodall argues that too much emphasis has been placed on the work of the missionary Daniel Matthews to stir the government and not enough given to the pressure applied by Aboriginal people themselves in their demands for land. Goodall records that over the period 1861 to 1884, of the

---

84 Daniel Matthews Papers 1861–1917, A3384, Vol. 1, Part 2.
85 Read, *A Hundred Years War*, 30–31.

31 reserves allocated to Aboriginal people across the colony, 26 had been initiated and demanded by Aboriginal people.[86] Between 1874 and 1883, at least 12 reserves, ranging in size from 6 to 400 acres, were granted to 'individual aborigines'.[87] By the early 1880s Aboriginal people were already well-versed in lobbying the government for reserve land. Aboriginal people made direct approaches to the government and the press; recruited white figures such as police or missionaries to progress their claims; or took direct action through leasing, buying or reoccupying/squatting on land to build houses and develop agriculture.[88]

A powerful example of Aboriginal people employing white figures to assist in their demands for land occurred in the Shoalhaven in Dharawal Country.[89] Jack Bawn and his people from the Shoalhaven River had come to a large ceremonial gathering of south coast and highlands Aboriginal people on the Braidwood goldfields in 1872. The local police officer, Martin Brennan, was present at the gathering and recorded the meeting in his *Reminiscences of the Gold Fields*:

> A large corroboree was held … at which representatives from Broulee, Shoalhaven and coastal districts attended. When the festival was over, sixty-two blacks called upon me. Jack Bawn and Alick were the leaders … I asked Jack what they wanted. [He replied] We have come to you to intercede for us in getting the Government to do something for us. Araluen Billy, our king, is old and cannot live long; my wife Kitty and self are old too. I have assisted the police for many years and we want to get some land that we can call our own in reality, where we can settle down, and which the old people can call their home … we think the blacks are entitled to live in their own country.[90]

Brennan said he would do what he could. He wrote to a Judge McFarlane regarding the request and was asked to furnish the judge with all the 'particulars you know concerning this interesting race'.[91] Brennan supplied him with 'eight sheets of foolscap' and the judge made representations to Governor Robinson and informed Brennan that the matter would be placed before Premier Henry Parkes. Shortly afterwards, Brennan was

---

86 Goodall, 'Land in Our Own Country', 9.
87 Curthoys, 'Good Christians and Useful Workers', 36.
88 Goodall, 'Land in Our Own Country', 3–8.
89 Goodall, 'Land in Our Own Country', 5.
90 Brennan, *Reminiscences of the Gold Fields*, 213.
91 Brennan, *Reminiscences of the Gold Fields*, 213.

instructed to survey 40 acres of Crown lands along the Shoalhaven River for Jack and his people. Brennan accompanied Jack and others to inspect the site.[92] Unfortunately the reserve was never gazetted. Brennan said there were bushrangers in the area and there would be reprisals against Jack as he had previously assisted the police.[93] Heather Goodall suggests that Jack and his people were 'unable to occupy the land because of hostility from surrounding white farmers'.[94] Probably both reasons were in play.

This example (although unsuccessful) demonstrated the quiet but insistent way that Aboriginal people lobbied the government for land to which they were entitled. The government would not have been able to ignore this subtle and persistent pressure, considering that no less than 26 reserves had been successfully acquired by Aboriginal people by the early 1880s. However, it was not Aboriginal demands for land that was the most immediate pressure point for the government. Rather, Aboriginal people taking up residence at the government boatshed at Circular Quay became the catalyst for government action.

The Circular Quay boatshed

The final antecedent to the establishment of the Board and an immediate impetus for the government position of an 'Aboriginal protector' was a single, very public controversy about Aboriginal occupation of a boatshed on the east side of Circular Quay in 1881. Anna Doukakis suggested that the occupiers of the boatshed were 'displaced South Coast Aborigines'.[95] In contrast, Paul Irish argues that there was certainly not a migration of Aboriginal people into Sydney in the 1870s. Blanket distribution records, between 1861 and 1880, both in coastal Sydney and all south coast centres, remained very stable suggesting that there was no large movement of Aboriginal people to Sydney. Locations at Rushcutters Bay, Rose Bay, Circular Quay, North Sydney, Manly, Botany and La Perouse had all been centres of longstanding occupancy by Aboriginal communities. Irish contends that the 'only truly new settlement' to be established, in the late 1870s, was at the government boatshed on the eastern side

---

92   Brennan, *Reminiscences of the Gold Fields*, 213–14.
93   Brennan, *Reminiscences of the Gold Fields*, 214.
94   Goodall, 'Land in Our Own Country', 5.
95   Doukakis, *The Aboriginal People*, 41.

of Circular Quay (where the Opera House forecourt now stands).⁹⁶ The boatshed was used as a 'repair and storage shed' for government boats, but when it fell into disuse 'Aboriginal people moved in'.⁹⁷ While it is unclear why Aboriginal people began to occupy the boatshed it may have 'functioned … as a staging post for visits to the city, and a gathering place for Aboriginal people entering Sydney by steamer'.⁹⁸ Irish also adds that Aboriginal people had occupied the outer Domain since the early 1850s, but by the late 1870s the forest was 'dying of natural decay' and they may have sought another location. Irish notes that the population at the boatshed fluctuated between 10 and 30 residents, that people stayed for several weeks at a time, and that it was both a workplace to make decorative shell baskets and a 'domestic and social space'.⁹⁹

By early 1881 the Aboriginal boatshed residents were attracting significant criticism from authorities. The police reported on the behaviour of the Aboriginal people and their 'unruly presence during the day around the busier quay wharves and city streets to the south'.¹⁰⁰ Police Sub-Inspector S.D. Johnston noted that the Aboriginal people who sheltered at the boatshed 'have been a perfect nuisance' and he recommended that 'those remaining be supplied with a free passage by steamer to Kiama and Shoalhaven, and the police see them on board'.¹⁰¹ Edmund Fosbery, Inspector-General of Police, stated that it is 'extremely desirable that the aboriginals should as far as practicable' be discouraged from coming to Sydney and that rations should be issued to them in the districts to which they belong.¹⁰² The negative reports were all from the police. Irish submits that public opinion was not necessarily against the occupation of the boatshed by Aboriginal people and that the press was 'more likely to lampoon the urban Aboriginal presence as harmless, if unsightly'.¹⁰³ The APA had garnered a good deal of community and parliamentary support to help Aboriginal people in general and, despite the urging of the police, the Parkes–Robertson Government seemed reluctant to act without a clear solution.¹⁰⁴

---

96   Irish, *Hidden in Plain View*, 108.
97   Irish, *Hidden in Plain View*, 109–10.
98   Irish, 'Hidden in Plain View', 197.
99   Irish, *Hidden in Plain View*, 110.
100 Irish, 'Hidden in Plain View', 203.
101 Thornton, *Aborigines: Report of the Protector, to 31 December 1882*, 894.
102 Thornton, *Aborigines: Report of the Protector, to 31 December 1882*, 894–95.
103 Irish, 'Hidden in Plain View', 209.
104 Irish, 'Hidden in Plain View', 210.

The issue over the boatshed was an opportunity for George Thornton (Figure 1.1). Since the controversy over the blanket issue in 1857 (i.e. where he believed that Aboriginal people should only receive rations in their own district), Thornton had maintained an interest in Aboriginal issues. He was a founding councillor of the APA in 1880 and had been involved in the administration of the mission at Warangesda.[105] As president of the Sydney Rowing Club, he would have been very familiar with the Aboriginal residents at the boatshed 'as he rowed or walked past' to his monthly meetings.[106] Irish argues that Thornton chose to act in early 1881 because he recognised that government intervention in Aboriginal affairs was imminent and he wanted his agenda of 'localised rationing' to prevail; so he created a 'moral panic' to force the removal of the Aboriginal people from the boatshed.[107]

Figure 1.1: George Thornton.
Source: Parliamentary Archives, NSW Parliament Collection (ThorntonG-936).

Thornton wrote to the principal under-secretary concerning the Aboriginal camp at the boatshed, pointing out that they were 'supplied with food and rations by the Government, but are constantly drunk, fighting, swearing [and are] a public nuisance'. He claimed that the Aboriginal people had come from elsewhere to Sydney and that there was not 'one person left of the Sydney or Botany tribes' and urged that no rations should be given to these people unless 'within the limits of their own districts'. This of course was untrue.[108] He suggested that his letter be forwarded to the water police magistrate who would confirm his views; he concluded his letter with the claim that I 'have a good knowledge of the people,

---

105 Jackson-Nakano, *The Kamberri*, 101.
106 Irish, 'Hidden in Plain View', 208.
107 Irish, 'Hidden in Plain View', 207–10.
108 Irish, *Hidden in Plain View*, 2017, 108–9.

and to be second to no-one in the Colony as their friend, and one desirous of having kindness – useful kindness – done to them'.[109] He also spruiked his own credentials and availability for service by submitting to Parkes 'your government should appoint a gentleman (only one) who should be sort of a *Protector* to the aborigines of this Colony'.[110]

In February 1881 Parkes appeared to side with Thornton's views and offered him a role in distributing rations to Aboriginal people in their districts, but he never made the appointment.[111] However, the death by drowning of a young Aboriginal boy, Joe Bundle, in July 1881 forced the government's hand on the boatshed issue. The day after the tragedy there were claims that European men were living at the boatshed in contravention of the *Vagrants Act 1835* and Inspector-General Edmund Fosbery ordered the removal of the Aboriginal residents. Irish asserts that this was surely a pretext to break up the camp as visitations by Europeans to the boatshed had been well known for months.[112] A letter from Sub-Inspector Donohoe to Fosbery on 15 July 1881 stated:

> went to the 'blacks camp' and told them that they would not be allowed to stay and about ten in number went at once to the North Shore, and equal number went to Manly, and one wished to go by train to Cootamundra ... the boat-shed is now clear of aborigines.[113]

Appointment of 'Protector of the Aborigines'

With 'progress' at the boatshed, Thornton wrote to Parkes at the end of 1881 and reminded him of his offer to assist the government. As Parkes was about to leave the country he 'hastily appointed' Thornton as the 'Protector of the Aborigines of New South Wales'.[114] Thornton had got his wish. Doukakis argues that he was chosen because he was a good friend of Parkes and had the potential to save the government money and

---

109 Thornton, *Aborigines: Report of the Protector, to 31 December 1882*, 6–7. This letter (dated 18 January 1881) is one of a number included in his report to the parliament.
110 Quoted in Doukakis, *The Aboriginal People*, 40.
111 Irish, 'Hidden in Plain View', 210.
112 Irish, 'Hidden in Plain View', 214.
113 Thornton, *Aborigines: Report of the Protector, to 31 December 1882*, 896.
114 Irish, 'Hidden in Plain View', 220.

embarrassment.[115] Whatever the case, Thornton was thrust into a job that neither he nor the government had thought through. His official letter of appointment is unrevealing as to his exact duties. He was instructed to give 'articles of food and clothing', to 'expend monies set apart for ... sustenance' and to 'give advice and instruction to those who may be variously concerned in the care' of the Aboriginal people.[116] Other than that he would proceed as he saw fit.

This was indicative of how the New South Wales Government would now approach Aboriginal affairs. Its approach was reactive, hasty and provided little direction to those given responsibility for Aboriginal affairs. Without any other resource base, George Thornton deferred immediately to the New South Wales police to furnish him with all the details with which to produce two reports: one in August 1882 (a progress report) and the final one in the December of the same year. Other than his reports, there are no records of what Thornton did during his brief period as protector. He did not formally record any trips that he undertook, who he employed to carry out the work of the protectorate, or any procedures he utilised. Nevertheless, his final report remains an important record of the state of Aboriginal affairs at the time.

Not averse to self-praise, Thornton characterised his final report as 'most comprehensive and interesting ... showing in detail every obtainable particular in respect of the aborigines all over the Colony'.[117] He divided the colony into nine regions and noted every police station that dealt with Aboriginal people. Each station recorded the number of Aboriginal people under its supervision; whether they were employed or received aid, blankets, clothing or fishing materials; whether they had any addictive habits or received medical aid; whether the children received educational instruction; and any special information of likely interest. Thornton ascertained that the Aboriginal population comprised 'pure-bred' adults 4,994, 'pure-bred' children (under 14 years of age) 1,546, adult 'half-castes' 1,108, children 'half-castes' (under 14 years of age) 1,271: total

---

115 Doukakis, *The Aboriginal People*, 40.
116 Official appointment of Thornton as Protector, 29 December 1881, Thornton Papers, MS 3290, National Library of Australia (hereafter NLA).
117 Thornton, *Aborigines: Report of the Protector, to 31 December 1882*, 1.

population, 8,919.[118] Many politicians were surprised at the figure, as it was thought that there may have only been 1,000 Aboriginal people left in the colony.[119]

He listed 41 districts where 'aid has been afforded' (flour, tea, sugar, etc.) and mentioned that other districts had also been supplied with fishing gear and boats. Thornton was of the strong opinion that 'reserves of land should be made ... for the purposes of the aborigines, to enable them to form homesteads, to cultivate grain, vegetables, fruit ... for their own support and comfort', and was of the firm belief that the 'half-castes' should be 'compelled to work in aid of their own requirements'. He stressed that the missions at Maloga and Warangesda, funded and controlled by the APA, 'were the creation of private enterprise and benevolence ... and quite outside the power and interference of the protectorate'.[120] He also expressed his firm belief that Aboriginal people could not be truly converted to Christianity.[121]

The first indication of government disquiet over Aboriginal affairs after Thornton's appointment as protector came with the establishment of a government inquiry into the two missions at Maloga and Warangesda. Also, Thornton's insistence that Aboriginal people could not be Christianised now put him at odds with powerful figures in the APA – an organisation deeply committed to the benefits of Christianity.[122] Over the next year, from mid-1882, relations between the APA and Thornton deteriorated and descended in to open warfare over general policy and over Thornton's alleged neglect of Aboriginal groups in the Sydney area.

Inquiry into Maloga and Warangesda

Joint leader of the government John Robertson was also president of the APA. He informed his APA members that the government was considering more financial support to both missions, but wanted to conduct its own inquiry into their viability. In late March 1882 the APA approached the government to seek leave for John Marks – MLC and treasurer of the APA – and the protector George Thornton to undertake the inspection

---

118 Thornton, *Aborigines: Report of the Protector, to 31 December 1882*, 1.
119 Doukakis, *The Aboriginal People*, 46.
120 Thornton, *Aborigines: Report of the Protector, to 31 December 1882*, 2–3.
121 Curthoys, 'Good Christians and Useful Workers', 51.
122 Curthoys, 'Good Christians and Useful Workers', 51.

of the stations at Maloga and Warangesda.[123] The government announced that Marks, Thornton and E.W. Palmer, the secretary of the APA, would undertake such duties.[124]

Curiously, and for reasons unknown, Thornton did not commit to the inquiry, causing a delay in the start date. Embarrassingly for the APA, their regular subscribers were reluctant to fund the organisation until the outcome of the inquiry and Daniel Matthews, with limited funds, had to send many of 'the blacks' away from the Maloga Mission to 'find subsistence elsewhere'. Despite a formal letter from the APA to Thornton seeking his involvement, he was 'unable to leave Sydney'.[125] Consequently, Edmund Fosbery, Inspector-General of Police, acting on behalf of the government, and Phillip Gidley King (MLC and the newly chosen vice-chair of the APA), acting on behalf of George Thornton, were appointed to the lead the inquiry.[126]

There seems little doubt the Parkes–Robertson Government had no control over these powerful personalities with long-vested interest in Aboriginal affairs. Thornton's refusal to head the inquiry, the interruption to funding of the APA and Matthews' turning Aboriginal people away from Maloga due to lack of funds resulted in escalating tensions between Thornton and the APA. This strained relationship erupted into a full-scale public row in January 1883.

The report authored by Fosbery and King acknowledged the devotion of Matthews and Gribble but suggested that if future stations were formed under government control the 'services of persons should be obtained with such qualifications as will in all respects ensure the goodwill and co-operation of the neighbouring population and the confidence of the public'.[127] They did acknowledge, however, that the missions served a purpose and recommended improvement to both sites, and also that aid – in the form of blankets, food and clothing – be continued, and that medical assistance be made available. King and Fosbery were concerned about the children and urged that they should not be kept on the missions, especially the 'half-castes or quadroons, some of who are so

---

123 *SMH*, 5 April 1882, 5.
124 *SMH*, 9 June 1882, 7.
125 *SMH*, 9 June 1882, 7.
126 *Evening News*, 23 June 1882, 3.
127 *Aboriginal Mission Stations at Warangesda and Maloga (Report On Working Of.)*, NSW Legislative Assembly, 18 January 1883, 3.

fair [skinned] as to be indistinguishable from Europeans'. They suggested that their 'half-caste mothers would 'willingly part with them' if assured that it would be 'for their benefit'. The removed children should be:

> trained as to fit them to take their places as domestic servants, or amongst the industrial classes; and this ... would be best attained by 'boarding out' the young of both sexes.[128]

The report concluded by stating that the present system of allowing 'blacks free passages in the railways' should cease in order to prevent them 'wandering about from place to place'. It further advised that the government should take over the responsibilities and duties of the APA as the 'society may not always be able ... to meet and provide for' the needs of Aboriginal people.[129]

Figure 1.2: Richard Hill.
Source: Parliamentary Archives, NSW Parliament Collection (HillR).

Although it was clear that Fosbery and King were advocating government control of Aboriginal protection, still the government resisted intervention. This indecision prompted a question from MLC and APA member Richard Hill as to when the government proposed to bring in a bill concerning Aboriginal people. Hill was informed that the government was 'not at present in a position to make any definite promise'.[130] Richard Hill (Figure 1.2), born 1810, was a carpenter, butcher with his own slaughterhouse, orchard owner, pastoralist and politician.[131] He had had a longstanding involvement with Aboriginal people that began

---

128 *Aboriginal Mission Stations at Warangesda and Maloga (Report On Working Of)*, NSW Legislative Assembly, 18 January 1883, 3.
129 *Aboriginal Mission Stations at Warangesda and Maloga (Report On Working Of)*, NSW Legislative Assembly, 18 January 1883, 3.
130 NSW, *Parliamentary Debates*, Legislative Council, 20 September 1882, 472 (A. Campbell).
131 Rutledge, 'Hill, Richard (1810–1895)'.

in the 1830s when he was a young man in Sydney and had witnessed Aboriginal people gather in large numbers; 'I may say fairly that I have seen hundreds assemble on "Hyde Park" on more than one occasion, either to corroboree … or for a man to "stand punishment"'.[132] His earliest formal involvement in Aboriginal issues came as a member of the Select Committee of Parliament, called for by pastoralist William Henry Suttor (Jr) in 1876.[133] He became a councillor of the APA in 1881 and had close contact with the Aboriginal people at La Perouse and Botany. He knew many Aboriginal people in the Sydney area, accompanied Daniel Matthews on visits to Botany and Circular Quay, helped provide rations for them and had a keen interest generally in Aboriginal issues. Hill's longstanding involvement with Aboriginal people may well have placed him in contention for the 'Protector' role, but Thornton was a powerful figure.

The Parkes–Robertson Government fell on 4 January 1883 without any definitive action on Aboriginal affairs. Alexander Stuart, the new premier, was a devout Anglican, member of the Church of England General Synod and good friend of John Gribble. The APA had found a friend. Stuart had not been impressed with the previous administration's 'inactivity on Aboriginal matters'.[134] The incoming government was a trigger for the APA to attack Thornton. Member for Upper Hunter and APA member John McElphone, responding to reports that rations had not been provided to the Aboriginal people at La Perouse over Christmas, got to his feet in the Assembly on 4 January 1883 and launched an assault on Thornton. McElphone claimed Thornton had completely 'neglected his duties' and called for his resignation.[135] In a letter to the *Sydney Morning Herald*, the Reverend T.J. Curtis, a Presbyterian minister from Redfern and inaugural member of the APA, praised the great work that Richard Hill had done in providing rations to the 'La Perouse blacks' over the years and he lamented the fact that Hill had been passed over in favour of Thornton as protector as being 'a grave mistake and a gross wrong'.[136] On 18 January, the King/Fosbery report was tabled and that applied further pressure on Thornton; although with no direct mention of Thornton, one recommendation

---

132 Hill and Thornton, *Notes on the Aborigines of New South Wales*, 1.
133 Doukakis, *The Aboriginal People*, 31.
134 Goodall, *Invasion to Embassy*, 2008, 106.
135 Quoted in Irish, 'Hidden in Plain View', 222.
136 *SMH*, 6 January 1883, 7.

was the immediate 'assistance in the shape of food and clothing' to both missions – a clear signal of Thornton's neglect as protector.[137] In early 1883 Thornton was under siege.

It was from this furore that the Board emerged. The previous government had allowed these tensions to simmer either through indifference or indecisiveness. It would be the Stuart Government that would take determined action. Yet, it still put in place a body that was severely hamstrung.

The Board for the Protection of Aborigines

A minute from the colonial secretary, 26 February 1883, outlined the government's position. After careful consideration of the reports by Thornton, letters and newspaper articles on the 'La Perouse blacks' and the King/Fosbery report on the missions at Maloga and Warangesda, Alexander Stuart concluded: 'much more must be done … before there can be any national feeling of satisfaction that the Colony has done its duty by the remnant of the aboriginal race'.[138]

Stuart praised the efforts of Thornton, particularly his progress report that detailed the number of Aboriginal people in the colony and their circumstances, but he was, however, 'constrained to think … that the Protectorate should not be in the hands of one person only … but should reside in a Board … of officials [and] gentlemen'. Stuart acknowledged the work of the APA, stated that it should continue and encouraged the establishment of other stations across the colony, but – contrary to the advice of King and Fosbery – Stuart argued that they should *not* (my emphasis) be under government control. He cited Victorian and South Australian examples of where marked progress had been made and reasoned that New South Wales should not hide behind any such notion that 'it is impossible to reclaim them from their nomadic habits, or from their ignorant superstition and degraded condition'.[139] Stuart had

---

137 *Aboriginal Mission Stations at Warangesda and Maloga (Report On Working Of.)*, New South Wales Legislative Assembly, 18 January 1883, 4.
138 *Protection of the Aborigines (Minute of the Colonial Secretary, Together with Reports)*, Legislative Assembly, New South Wales, 2 March 1883, 3.
139 *Protection of the Aborigines (Minute of the Colonial Secretary, Together with Reports)*, Legislative Assembly, New South Wales, 2 March 1883, 1–3.

walked a fine line: he praised Thornton for his efforts and survey work and also allowed for the APA to have a continuing and commanding role in Aboriginal affairs.

Stuart proposed that a Board be formed of between five to seven members to be funded on an annual basis as a supplement to private benevolence, that it be subject to the control of the colonial secretary, that it provide an annual report; that a secretary be appointed to assist the Board, and that police magistrates or 'gentlemen' be invited to act as district agents to support the Board.[140] There was, however, no Bill: the new Board would have no legislative powers. A notification in the *Government Gazette*, dated 5 June 1883, formally established the Board for the Protection of Aborigines.[141] The Board's mandate was limited and sketchy and it was placed in a support role to the APA. Premier Stuart offered only broad direction, advising that every effort should be made 'for the elevation of the race' by providing 'rudimentary instruction … by aiding in the cost of maintenance or clothing … grants of land, gift of boats or implements for industrial work'.[142] The inaugural members were George Thornton, Richard Hill (MLC), Philip Gidley King (MLC), W.J. Foster (barrister-at-law) (MLA), Hugh Robison (Inspector of Public Charities) and Alexander Gordon, barrister and Queen's Counsel (MLC).

The appointment of George Thornton was intriguing. Perhaps the government felt that his overall knowledge, long association with Aboriginal people and his recent report as protector would be valuable assets to the new body. That fact that he was elected chair was even more remarkable, considering that three other Board members (King, Hill and Foster) were all APA members. However, for reasons unclear, Thornton resigned his position after a month. He was replaced (but not as chair) by Edmund Fosbery, Inspector-General of Police.

One can only speculate on Thornton's departure. There was obvious historical tension between Hill and Thornton over the issue of rations. Thornton may have also struggled with a consultative approach after operating as sole protector and decision-maker, or he may have regarded

---

140 *Protection of the Aborigines (Minute of the Colonial Secretary, Together with Reports)*, Legislative Assembly, New South Wales, 2 March 1883, 3.
141 The correct name for the Board between the years 1883–1940 was The Board for the Protection of Aborigines, but common usage has been the Aborigines Protection Board – hence I have used the acronym APB or interchanged it with the 'Board'.
142 *Protection of the Aborigines (Minute of the Colonial Secretary, Together with Reports)*, Legislative Assembly, New South Wales, 26 February 1883, 2.

the establishment of the Board as a slight on his efforts. Jim Fletcher surmised that Thornton likely felt it pointless to remain on a Board that was so heavily weighted against his viewpoint.[143] Unfortunately, there are no APB minutes for the first six years to shed any light on his departure. An entry in the first Board report of March 1884 states: 'Mr Thornton was elected to the Chairmanship, but we regret to say he resigned his connection with the Board after the fourth meeting'.[144] After his exit he played no further formal role in Aboriginal affairs. He died in 1901.

Armed with Thornton's report of 1882, which provided the most up-to-date census of Aboriginal people and the general areas in which they were located, the Board began its work. The six Board members functioned as a committee until Edmund Fosbery emerged, over the course of the year, as chair.[145]

An unsure path

The path to Aboriginal 'Protection' in New South Wales was far from smooth and the immediate steps leading to the creation of the Board had been a tortuous affair, yet the creation of a six-member Board seemed a workable outcome. However, Stuart's firm belief that the Board should only supplement the work of community benevolence towards the Aboriginal population placed the Board in a secondary position to the influential APA. It confirmed, in fact, that the government did not want to take full control of Aboriginal affairs; it preferred a strong religious and benevolent presence over secular rule. The absence of any legislative authority for the Board cemented that position.

The men of the Board met weekly at 114 Phillip Street, Sydney, in the afternoon and made decisions and determined policy as the need arose. They were powerful men, comfortable in their own abilities, authority and decision-making. It is speculation as to whether they realised the enormity of their task: overseeing the protection and welfare of nearly 9,000 Aboriginal people stretched wide across the colony. The Board's cautious beginnings are the focus of the next chapter.

---

143 Fletcher, *Clean, Clad and Courteous*, 57.
144 *Protection of the Aborigines: Report of the Board* (the APB report: hereafter *APBR*) 1883–84, 1. Accessed via: aiatsis.gov.au/sites/default/files/docs/digitised_collections/remove/22818.pdf, accessed 1 November 2018.
145 Fosbery was seconded into the position, against his wishes, sometime before the first Board report was issued in 1884. Further explanation is provided in Chapter 2.

2
Policy drift, 1883–1897

In June 1883, the newly established Board for the Protection of Aborigines (the APB) had been given responsibility for the Aboriginal population within the colony of New South Wales. The inaugural six Board members, all in full-time professional employment, attended to the matters of the APB one afternoon each week. In its first full year of operation, the Board expended £3,425.13.6 on an Aboriginal population calculated to be 8,091, which equated to just under eight and a half shillings per person.[1] What was to be done with the Aboriginal people of the colony of New South Wales was theirs to determine; a largely laissez faire approach from Premier Alex Stuart allowed the Board free rein. Unlike the colony of Victoria, which undertook a comprehensive survey in 1858–59 before it established its own Aborigines Protection Board in 1860, the New South Wales Board had no such broad review to access. As mentioned in Chapter 1, George Thornton's report of 1882 and a two-page King and Fosbery assessment of the two existing missions at Maloga and Warangesda were the only two recent New South Wales documents the Board could draw upon to build a policy framework.[2]

---

1   *Protection of the Aborigines: Report of the Board* (the APB Report: hereafter *APBR*) 1885–86, 1–4. Accessed via 'NSW', To Remove and Protect, AIATSIS: aiatsis.gov.au/sites/default/files/docs/digitised_collections/remove/22813.pdf. The Board never had to support the total Aboriginal population. Many Aboriginal people worked and lived away from the reserves and stations or did not request assistance. Nevertheless, it was a paltry amount of money considering that Daniel Matthews had sought, in 1879, £500 to run just one mission of some 153 individuals. See Curthoys, 'Race and Ethnicity', 203.
2   The Victorian survey (*1858–9, Victoria, Report of the Select Committee of the Legislative Council, The Aborigines*) canvassed a much wider group of people across Victoria, did not rely upon the police to compile the report and was a significant document of some 88 pages. Thornton's report (*Aborigines: Report of the Protector, to 31 December 1882*) was a result of police reports and reflected the views of one man. The report *Aboriginal Mission Stations at Warangesda and Maloga* (New South Wales Legislative Assembly, 18 January 1883) was limited to an evaluation of the two missions, although it did articulate some policy directions.

The New South Wales Board could have adopted the Victorian model. The Victorian Protection Board gained legislative power in 1869 and established six reserves and forced almost half the Aboriginal people in the state onto those reserves.[3] By the time the New South Wales Board was established in 1883, the Victorian Protection Board was already planning intrusive and brutal legislation (passed in 1886) that would enable it to drive its 'half-caste' Aboriginal population off the reserves and into the mainstream community.[4] Others would follow Victoria's lead. Bain Attwood states that throughout the late nineteenth and twentieth centuries, 'indigenes faced a second onslaught, from agents of European "civilisation" who sought to change and reshape their minds and hearts, making them anew'.[5] This attempt to reshape came relatively quickly in Victoria; in New South Wales it took much longer to arrive.[6]

Under the leadership of Edmund Fosbery, Inspector-General of Police, the New South Wales Board began cautiously. Created in an atmosphere of rancour, with no legislative power, goals or benchmarks and with limited funds, it probably could have done little else. George Thornton's 1882 report had been largely gathered from information provided by every police station across New South Wales; with Fosbery now at the helm, it was unsurprising that the Board would very quickly defer to the network of the New South Wales Police Force to carry out its operations. The police became a permanent crutch for the Board; their presence among Aboriginal communities was pervasive. In a sense, the police 'became' the Board.

Over the first decade and a half up to 1897, the Board was in a period of policy drift – Fosbery's Board avoided the issue of developing new policy positions in the face of changing circumstances. It found comfort in the status quo. Several factors reflected this position. First, having proposed a legislative agenda within its first year of operation, the Board failed to pursue this agenda for the next 15. Second, the Board remained aloof from its Aboriginal constituents and, rather than initiating programs, or policies, it reacted to requests. Also, some trends appeared as a result

---

3   McGrath, ed., *Contested Ground*, 136.
4   The 'Half-Caste' Act of 1886 allowed 'full-bloods', and 'half-castes' over 34 years of age and their offspring to remain on the reserves. All others had to leave. See McGrath, ed., *Contested Ground*, 139–40.
5   Attwood, *The Making of the Aborigines*, 1.
6   Queensland achieved legalisation in 1897, Western Australia in 1905, New South Wales in 1909, and South Australia and Northern Territory in 1911.

of the Board's interaction with Aboriginal people, but the Board did not actively respond to them. More Aboriginal people were presenting at reserves and stations, which strained Board finances. The Board was forced to build more Aboriginal schools because Aboriginal children were excluded by white parents from attending public schools. Furthermore, the composition of the Aboriginal population (according to Board racial classifications) was changing, with a significant decrease in the 'full-blood' population and an increase in the 'half-caste' population. Although the Board recognised and publicly reported all these changes and responded to them in an ad hoc way, it did not craft a considered policy response. Lastly, although not a direct restraint on the Board's overall policy development, the continued and unwelcome involvement of the Aborigines Protection Association (APA) – which ran three of the most populous Aboriginal stations in the colony – was a constant drain on Board finances and a persistent reminder that it was not in complete control of Aboriginal affairs.

The reasons for the overall policy inertia are less obvious, but I argue that they rest, to a large degree, with Fosbery. He showed no desire to go down the 'Victorian path' of restrictive legislation and held to this view throughout his tenure. Further, of the new members to the Board over this period, none had the will, the time or the ability to influence policy change. These 'lesser' members contributed to policy drift through transitory membership or lack of engagement. Moreover, from the Board's perspective, Fosbery's police force was doing a 'sterling job' overseeing the unmanaged reserves and providing statistical data across the colony to fill the Board's annual reports. During this period, the Board found more purpose in its own reporting of its 'achievements' than in addressing fundamental policy issues regarding the living conditions of Aboriginal people or the future relations between Aboriginal people and mainstream Australia. On the policy front, Fosbery's Board was in a 'holding pattern'. It was not on Fosbery's watch that the most severe measures were imposed upon Aboriginal people; this came under different personnel. As Attwood noted, the attempt to 'reshape' and 'make anew' did come to New South Wales but it was driven by harder and more task-orientated men than Fosbery.

Early Board personnel

Assessing the policy impact of individual Board members over the 57-year life of the Board is difficult. In the absence of recorded member contributions in the Board minutes and limited attribution to their impact generally, any definitive appraisal is unachievable. There are, however, some key indicators of performance and commitment: time spent on the Board, attendance patterns, press statements, parliamentary contributions, obituaries and biographies. All these assist in making some assessment about the effectiveness of members. Appendix 1 has details of the 64 serving members of the Board from 1883 until 1940. Brief mention is made in the following chapters of some members in 'each phase' of the Board, with extended reference to those who had impact on Board policy and those who were particularly notable for their *inaction*.

Figure 2.1: Edmund Walcott Fosbery.
Source: Australian Police (australianpolice.com.au). Courtesy: Greg Collander.

Of the inaugural members, Edmund Fosbery (Figure 2.1), Richard Hill and Philip Gidley King served lengthy terms, while Alexander Gordon, Hugh Robison and John Foster were all gone within five years. Apart from Fosbery, who steered the Board through its first 20 years, and Hill's likely consistent and valuable input, none of the other original members had any significant influence on policy direction.

After Thornton's resignation, the Board functioned without a chair until Edmund Fosbery (Thornton's replacement) became chair sometime between March 1884 and April 1885.⁷ He was a reluctant appointee to the chair, the second Board report recorded:

> as the Inspector-General has been able to attend our meetings more regularly than other members, and as he is constantly at hand to give instructions to the Secretary regarding the business of the Department, we unanimously decided upon electing Mr Fosbery to the position of the Chairman of the Board, which he accepted in deference to our wishes, whilst earnestly desiring that another selection should be made.⁸

Fosbery was 'well-connected' as he held several influential positions within Sydney institutions and societies, but he was first and foremost a career policeman.⁹ After joining the service in 1861 he rose to the top job of Inspector-General of Police in 1874.¹⁰

Fosbery had obvious authority and as Board chair he wielded substantial power. He remained as chair of the APB until 1903, missing only one year in 1888 when he went on leave. Effectively, he was chair for 18 years and, by extrapolation from extant Board minutes, Fosbery chaired over 850 meetings.¹¹ More is said of Fosbery's influence below, but his election as chair was significant as it set a longstanding precedent for the full life of the Board – the chair would *always* be the Inspector-General of Police. This ensured that the New South Wales Police Force would be inextricably involved with Aboriginal people of New South Wales for the next 60 years.

Philip Gidley King (Figure 2.2) was a much less engaged member and his credentials for a role on the APB are not substantial. His co-authorship with Edmund Fosbery of the report on the Warangesda and Maloga missions was probably pivotal in his appointment as an inaugural member of the APB. He served on the APB for 14 years. However, close analysis of his attendance reflects limited engagement. Also, during his

---

7   There is no reference to a specific date of Fosbery's elevation to the chair, but it occurred between these dates. See *APBR* 1883–84 and 1885–86 (accessed via 'NSW', To Remove and Protect, AIATSIS: aiatsis.gov.au/sites/default/files/docs/digitised_collections/remove/22818.pdf and aiatsis.gov.au/sites/default/files/docs/digitised_collections/remove/22813.pdf, respectively).
8   *APBR* 1885–86, 3.
9   Golder, *Politics, Patronage and Public Works*, 187.
10 Rutledge and Dickey, 'Fosbery, Edmund Walcott (1834–1919)'.
11 There are significant gaps in the Board minutes of meetings: the first six years from 1883 to September 1890, from July 1901 to May 1905 and from December 1906 to March 1910.

24 years in parliament he made only one specific utterance on Aboriginal matters.[12] In response to a report by the Department of Public Instruction in 1887 on the pupils at Warangesda Aboriginal school, he believed that it was the 'natural process' that the 'full-blood' population would disappear and that 'half-castes' would soon be 'lost in the complete dilution of the superior race'.[13] Perhaps therein lies the reason for his lack of commitment to his role on the Board. It is also telling that, after almost a decade and a half of membership, the Board did not recognise or celebrate his service on his departure in late 1897.

Figure 2.2: Philip Gidley King.
Source: Parliamentary Archives, NSW Parliament Collection (King Philip Gidley-752).

Richard Hill's contribution to the Board (Figure 1.2) was considerable and there is little doubt about his support for Aboriginal people. However, as a parliamentarian, he was not vocal on Aboriginal issues. His obituary states that, although he was a member of both Houses of Parliament, he 'did not take a very active part in politics'.[14] He spent just over nine years from 1868 until 1877 in the Assembly and then served in the Legislative Council from 1880 until 1895. To spend 24 years in the state parliament with seemingly little impact is telling. During the entire 12 years he was an APB member his voice was not once raised in the Legislative Council on behalf of Aboriginal people; Anna Doukakis records that Hill made only two speeches related to Aboriginal people, both predated the APB, and both were regarded as negative towards Aboriginal people. However, Paul Irish makes the point that the 'almost unfailing attendance of stalwart members' Hill and Fosbery at the Board's meetings, 'allowed a consistency to develop in Board dealings despite the lack of legal power'.[15] Hill would most certainly have been called upon for his opinions at the weekly Board meetings. His connections with

---

12 Anna Doukakis made no reference to King in all her research on member contributions in parliament.
13 Fletcher, *Documents in the History of Aboriginal Education in New South Wales*, 82.
14 *Sydney Morning Herald* (hereafter *SMH*), 21 August 1895, 8.
15 Irish, 'Hidden in Plain View', 242.

Aboriginal people were rich. The fact that he did not raise Aboriginal issues in parliament did not negate the fact that he had an intimate knowledge of many Sydney Aboriginal people and consistently assisted them over time. Hill and his son George had been 'active in distributing rations to Aboriginal people at Botany' and he had also employed the Aboriginal couple George and Emma Timbery from La Perouse in his Sydney home.[16] When Daniel Matthews was recruiting Aboriginal people for his Maloga mission, he took 25 of them, on the eve of their departure, to Hill's house for blankets and refreshments.[17] Irish records even after George Thornton was appointed protector and sought to restrict rationing to only those residing in their 'districts', Hill did not change his long-term practice of providing meat and rations to whom he pleased. He 'took his obligations seriously' and there was 'no compelling reason for Hill and others to abandon such behaviour simply because of Thornton's appointment'.[18] Hill knew and understood Aboriginal people and had empathy for them.

While on the Board, in the early 1890s, Hill at age 83 took responsibility for organising and supervising the supply of boats, equipment and rations at La Perouse.[19] He made his contribution by continuing to work closely with Aboriginal people, a practice he had begun well before the Board. The nature of his relationships with Aboriginal people may well have compelled him to be a restraining influence against any suggestion of a legislative agenda. Hill came to the Board when he was 73 years old and he died, still a member, aged 85; he most probably engaged more with Aboriginal people than any other Board member during this period.

There is no evidence to suggest that the other three members played any significant role in policy determination. According to Doukakis, Board member Attorney General William J. Foster made one 'neutral' contribution on Aboriginal matters in the parliament.[20] His time on the Board was relatively short (four years), but the 1887 annual Board report acknowledged:

---

16   Irish, *Hidden in Plain View*, 116.
17   Irish, *Hidden in Plain View*, 116.
18   Irish, *Hidden in Plain View*, 118–19.
19   Hill offered to undertake the purchase of a sail and to have two boats painted. *APB Minutes* (hereafter *APBM*), 10 November 1892, Item 10; organised an additional third boat. *APBM*, 7 December 1893, Item 10; and he organised for two Aboriginal people to be supplied with rations and for the sale of a boat. *APBM*, 28 December 1893, Item 6. All *APBM* accessed via: Minute Books (Aborigines Welfare Board), NRS 2, NSW Department of Aboriginal Affairs, Sydney.
20   Neutral in the sense that it was neither positive or negative towards Aboriginal people. Doukakis, *The Aboriginal People*, 162.

> During the past year we have been deprived of the valuable services of the Honourable W.J. Foster, M.P., who found it necessary to retire, the pressure of his other public duties preventing him from devoting the attention he desired to the work of the Board, though taking a deep interest in it.[21]

Parliamentarian, barrister and Queens's Counsel Alexander Gordon spent under two years on the Board. The Board recognised his efforts:

> We regret to record ... the retirement of the Hon. A. Gordon ... having taken a deep interest in the welfare of the Aborigines, and cordially rendering us valuable assistance in the work we had undertaken to discharge.[22]

Hugh Robison, as Inspector of Charities, was perhaps an obvious choice for the Board as its main function was, in the beginning, very like that of a charitable organisation; his expertise in the area may have been thought useful. He served for a period of five years, but his departure drew a less complimentary Board response: 'Mr Hugh Robison, who served as a member of the Board from 5 June 1883, resigned on the 15 October last'.[23] For attendance patterns of all members up to 1897 see Figure 2.3.

It is impossible to gauge the level of involvement from Foster, Gordon, and Robison, as attendance records do not exist for these three, and Thornton had left after the first month. However, as the overall attendance patterns reveal, Fosbery and Hill most likely would have contributed much to the decisions made in this early period, and King would have contributed little.

---

21 *APBR* 1887, 1. Accessed via 'NSW', To Remove and Protect, AIATSIS: aiatsis.gov.au/sites/default/files/docs/digitised_collections/remove/22812.pdf.
22 *APBR* 1886, 2. Accessed via 'NSW', To Remove and Protect, AIATSIS: aiatsis.gov.au/sites/default/files/docs/digitised_collections/remove/22808.pdf.
23 *APBR* 1888, 1. Accessed via 'NSW', To Remove and Protect, AIATSIS: aiatsis.gov.au/sites/default/files/docs/digitised_collections/remove/22809.pdf.

2. POLICY DRIFT, 1883–1897

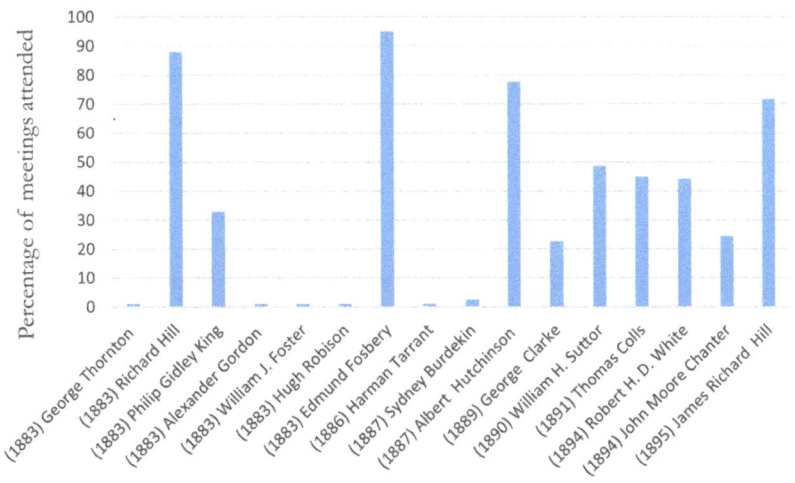

Figure 2.3: Attendance of the first 16 members of the Board up to 1897.
Source: Author's analysis of Board minutes for appropriate years. Please note attendance details do not exist for Thornton, Gordon, Foster, Robison and Tarrant.

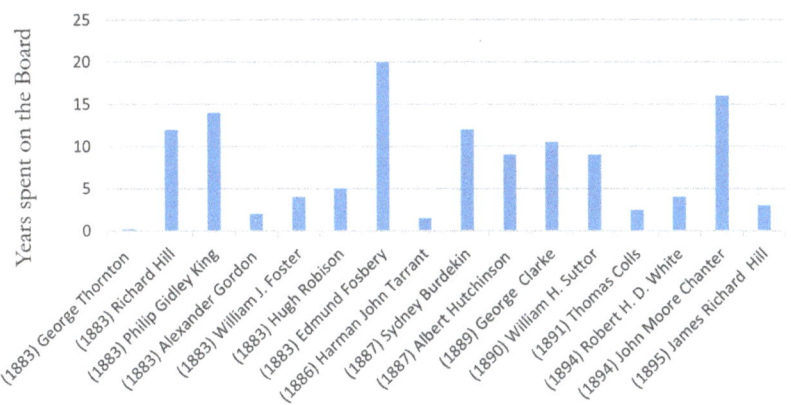

Figure 2.4: Number of years members spent on the Board.
Source: Author's analysis of Board minutes for appropriate years.

The Board's membership did not remain stable from 1883 until 1897, and of the nine new members who joined the Board from 1886 none appeared to influence Board policy or direction. Little is known of the contributions made by Thomas Colls and George O'Malley Clarke. However, the views of three other members are identifiable. Justice of the Peace Albert Maxwell Hutchinson joined the Board on 26 August 1887 and served for nine years. The Board report of 1897 noted:

> We regret to have to record the death … of Mr Albert Maxwell Hutchinson, who, during the nine years he held a seat on the Board, took a deep interest in furthering every object which had in view the improvement of the condition of the aborigines.[24]

He was a consistent attender over a long time (see Figures 2.3 and 2.4) and, it would appear, a solid contributor.

Figure 2.5: William H. Suttor.
Source: Parliamentary Archives, NSW Parliament Collection (SuttorWH-(jr)).

William Henry Suttor (Figure 2.5) joined the Board on 25 July 1890 and remained for nine years. Suttor published an essay on early Christian missions in 1899 and his views on Aboriginal people were disparaging. While he accepted that Aboriginal people had been exposed to white brutality and un-Christian behaviour, they 'were entirely governed by fear and self-interest, passion and indolence, and they had no innate conception of any moral responsibility whatever'. He considered that the end had already come for the Aboriginal people of the colony: 'although we may feel that … we somewhat neglected our obvious duty, I am not prepared to say that

---

24   *APBR* 1897, 1. Accessed via *Journal of the Legislative Council*, Q328.9106/7, *NSW Parliamentary Papers, Consolidated Index* (hereafter *Journal of LC*), State Library of New South Wales (hereafter SLNSW), Vol. 56, Part 1, 607.

their fate has not been the best thing for them'.²⁵ His obituary in the *Australian Town and Country Journal* sheds no further light on his contribution to Aboriginal affairs.²⁶

It is important to note that views like this did not discount anyone from joining the Board. In fact, they are perfectly consistent with views on 'protection' as noted. If a gentleman was a respected member of the community, there appeared no apparent barrier to joining the Board if one offered one's services.

Figure 2.6: Robert Hoddle Driberg White.
Source: Parliamentary Archives, NSW Parliament Collection (White Robert).

In 1884, Robert Hoddle Driberg White (Figure 2.6), member for Gloucester, rose in parliament and spoke of the 'deplorable condition of the aborigines'. He stated that many were unable to obtain enough food to survive and some were in a 'state of almost starvation' and that many had died. He concluded by saying that he would 'bring under the notice of the board' as to the current 'state of want' for Aboriginal people, many of whom were in his electorate.²⁷ Ten years later he was appointed to the APB on 16 February 1894 and left in May 1898. While on the Board in 1895 he provided a report on the 'inferior quality' of the flour supplied to the 'Aborigines' at Lake Illawarra and produced a sample of flour at a Board meeting explaining how it would not be able to make bread.²⁸ He seemed to understand and sympathise with the hardships Aboriginal people suffered in New South Wales.

Legislative member for the seat of Murray and later Deniliquin, John Moore Chanter was appointed to the Board on 31 August 1894 and resigned sometime during 1910. W.H. Suttor and Board member Thomas Colls had put his name forward as 'he has always taken an interest in the

---

25   Suttor, *Early Christian Missions Among our Aborigines*, 1889, DSM/572.9901/S, Mitchell Library (hereafter ML) (no page numbers provided).
26   *Australian Town and Country Journal*, 4 October 1905, 53.
27   NSW, *Parliamentary Debates*, Legislative Council, 17 April 1884, 2845 (Robert White).
28   *APBM*, 14 March 1895, Item 8.

Aborigines'.[29] Before joining the Board, he had been a regular critic of it. In 1890 he was scathing of the Board for not doing enough for the 'protection of the aborigines'. Chanter spoke highly of the Aboriginal station at Cumeroogunga where the 'natives' were industrious, had 'excellent houses constructed of sawn timber and iron roofs', and lived by themselves in a 'very respectable manner'. He believed that the Aboriginal people 'will gradually merge into the rest of our population, and will become good citizens'.[30] When Aboriginal children were excluded from the public school at Gulargambone in 1899 he was quick to challenge the relevant minister in parliament:

> Is he aware that eleven aboriginal children, fully and properly clothed, were sent [by the Board] to the public school at Gulargambone [and 10 days later] were told by the teacher not to attend the school again?[31]

Chanter appeared to be the most likely to raise issues or provide opinion on a policy level, but Anna Doukakis submits that once a Board member, his criticism of the APB and general outspokenness ceased.[32] Two obituaries, one from the *Riverina Recorder* and other in the *Jerilderie Herald and Urana Advertiser*, shed little extra light on Chanter in the field of Aboriginal affairs.[33]

Although these men were at times outspoken on Aboriginal issues, and some of them sympathetic for the Aboriginal cause, they did not actively seek more power for the Board or provide policy direction or positions.

The 'doomed race' theory

The Board began operations holding limiting assumptions about its clientele, assumptions that were shared by broader society. The 'doomed race' theory underpinned much discussion about Aboriginal policy in the late nineteenth century. It was characterised by two misplaced beliefs: that the Aboriginal population could not withstand the 'march' of British

---

29 *APBM*, 9 August 1894, Item 9.
30 NSW, *Parliamentary Debates*, Legislative Assembly, 18 February 1892, 5455 (John Chanter).
31 NSW, *Parliamentary Debates*, Legislative Assembly, 8 March 1899, 505 (John Chanter).
32 Doukakis, *The Aboriginal People*, 70.
33 *Riverina Recorder*, 14 March 1931, 2; and *Jerilderie Herald and Urana Advertiser*, 12 March 1931, 2.

'civilisation', and that Aboriginal people were incapable of taking an equal place with whites at the table of citizenship as the colonies approached nationhood.[34]

The racial scientists of the late eighteenth and early nineteenth centuries had placed the Australian Aboriginal person at the 'bottom of the racial hierarchy along with the Tierra del Fuegians and the Hottentots of Africa', based on 'Divine Providence'.[35] Russell McGregor asserts that while there were obvious physical reasons why the Aboriginal population in Australia was declining through hostile encounters, disease, lack of medical attention and through the act of dispossession, even scientists believed that there was some 'mysterious agency' at work that was the 'hand of God'.[36]

Charles Darwin's evolutionary theories did not alter the view that population collapse among indigenous peoples was considered 'God's work'; instead, they simply provided another explanation for 'their lowly status' and confirmed their disappearance under the 'Natural Law of Survival of the Fittest'.[37] By the late nineteenth century the scientific world had made up its mind on the Aboriginal people of Australia. The vice-president of the Royal Society of Tasmania, James Barnard, made the following assertion in 1890:

> It has become an axiom that, following the law of evolution and survival of the fittest, the inferior races of mankind must give place to the highest type of man, and this law is adequate to account for the gradual decline in numbers of the aboriginal inhabitants of a country before the march of civilisation.[38]

Compounding the notion that Aboriginal people would die out was the desire of settler society to exclude Aboriginal people from any future 'progress' of the colony. Henry Reynolds, argues that 'for every public figure who defended' Aboriginal people there were 'many more who condemned them'.[39] Many of those who denigrated Aboriginal people were influenced by the proponents of phrenology, such as Royal Navy

---

34 Attwood, *Telling the Truth about Aboriginal History*, 22. See also Holland, 'The Impact of "Doomed Race" Assumptions in the Administration of Queensland's Indigenous Population by the Chief protectors of Aboriginals from 1897 to 1942', 14–19.
35 McGregor, 'The Doomed Race', 14.
36 McGregor, *Imagined Destinies*, 15.
37 McGregor, 'The Doomed Race', 14.
38 Quoted in McGregor, 'The Doomed Race', 14.
39 Reynolds, *Nowhere People*, 97.

Captain J.L. Stokes who, although sympathetic to Aboriginal people, accepted in the mid-1840s that 'if the principles of that science are admitted to be true, these savages are woefully deficient in all qualities which contribute to man's moral supremacy'.[40] The editor of *The Age* wrote in 1880 that when two races 'of different stages of development' are brought into contact then the 'inferior race is doomed to wither and disappear'.[41] Bain Attwood suggests that following the decades after 1850 it became a 'matter of common sense' among the colonists that 'Aborigines were either a race doomed to die out or a child race in need of European tutorship'.[42] McGregor asserts that, as the nineteenth-century ended, Aboriginal people were 'shut out' of the national community as they were 'deemed incapable of exercising the rights of citizenship or appreciating its responsibilities'.[43]

The Board's interaction with Aboriginal people during this period was guided by these assumptions. The Board would assist the 'full-blood' population – the old and needy – until there were none left. What was to be done with the 'half-caste', 'quadroon' and 'octoroon' population was less clear. The Board's policies on this issue were vague and non-committal. Herein lay the Board's key blind spot for the next 57 years: it never came to terms with the fact that Aboriginal people, despite any arbitrary racial classifications imposed by white authorities, regarded themselves as Aboriginal. Moreover, Aboriginal people were not dying out. Ann Curthoys observes, in the late 1870s (before the Board was established), that 'if the Aborigines were disappearing, then they were taking longer than anticipated'.[44] Due to a decrease in demand for pastoral labour and a move to a more agricultural base there was an increased Aboriginal presence closer to towns and cities. Through their 'requests for boats, entry into the city of Sydney, response to private missionary efforts, and applications for land, they presented colonists with a new situation'.[45] In its first 15 years the Board struggled to come to terms with this reality.

---

40   Quoted in Reynolds, *Nowhere People*, 99.
41   Quoted in Reynolds, *Nowhere People*, 100.
42   Attwood, *Telling the Truth about Aboriginal History*, 139.
43   McGregor, *Indifferent Inclusion*, xx. See also Attwood, *Telling the Truth about Aboriginal History*, 139.
44   Curthoys, 'Race and Ethnicity', 175.
45   Curthoys, 'Race and Ethnicity', 175.

Policy settings: A 'quiet and comfortable abode'

In 1883, Premier and Colonial Secretary Alex Stuart's early instructions to the Board were brief: provide suitable land where Aboriginal people can be employed, educate the children (especially the 'half-castes'), look after the aged and sick and engage the 'strong, active, and healthy' in useful work.[46] Following his religious bias, Stuart recommended that the primary role should remain with the APA; while not ruling out the place of government stations, he believed that it was 'a sounder principle to encourage benevolent effort in this manner'.[47] Consequently, the Board was sidelined from controlling the only two existing missions in the colony.

The Board's first report provides an outline of its policy positions. It proposed a somewhat idyllic regime whereby willing Aboriginal parents could establish 'a quiet and comfortable abode', preferably by the 'coast or on the banks of main rivers', to live with their children and that persons of 'good character' would supervise these homes and schools for the children.[48] Aboriginal people would be encouraged to live in separate reserves away from towns and cities. Dedicated Aboriginal reserves had already been created before the Board was established. Heather Goodall records that 32 reserves were founded between 1861 and 1884; of the 32 reserves, 27 were a result of Aboriginal demands or occupation – that is, where Aboriginal people 'had already reoccupied the land and had begun farming'.[49] The Board inherited 25 reserves with a total area of 3,500 acres.[50] It subsequently made additional applications for more reserve land to the Minister for Lands.[51] As Stuart had outlined, food and clothing would be supplied only to those in need and to children attending school whose parents were 'unable to provide' for them.[52] There was an expectation that all able-bodied men and boys should maintain

---

46 *Protection of the Aborigines (Minute of the Colonial Secretary, Together with Reports)*, Legislative Assembly, New South Wales, 2 March 1883, 2.
47 *Protection of the Aborigines (Minute of the Colonial Secretary, Together with Reports)*, Legislative Assembly, New South Wales, 2 March 1883, 2. As mentioned previously, Stuart was a devout Anglican, a member of the Church of England Synod and a close friend of missionary John Gribble.
48 *APBR* 1883–84, 3.
49 Goodall, *Invasion to Embassy*, 2008, 103.
50 Goodall, *Invasion to Embassy*, 2008, 102.
51 *APBR* 1883–84, 4.
52 *APBR* 1883–84, 2.

themselves by 'labour on the station or at neighbouring homesteads'.⁵³ Demonstrating some realism, the Board cautioned against a one-size-fits-all approach and advised that 'no inflexible rules ... could be laid down, as the habits and circumstances of the aborigines vary greatly in different districts'.⁵⁴ Fosbery's Board adopted a much more benign approach compared to what would follow.

The Board considered that 'where the aboriginal children are decently clad and sufficiently fed', they should be able to attend local schools. The *Public Instruction Act 1880* (NSW) had declared that all children – regardless of their race, colour or creed – should receive a free education.⁵⁵ The Board encouraged Aboriginal children to go to school and provided 'incentives' to the parents.

> We have striven to induce parents to send their children to school ... chiefly by providing decent clothing for them and granting a half-ration of food to all who regularly attend.⁵⁶

From the Board's third annual report onwards, it regularly recorded the number of children attending school.⁵⁷ Early reports did, however, recognise that there could be objections to the presence of Aboriginal children in predominately white classrooms and flagged the idea of separate Aboriginal schools if numbers warranted.⁵⁸ However, the Board felt more secure in its overall policy when on 3 December 1884, the Department of Public Instruction declared that 'where a sufficient number of aboriginal children can be grouped together for instruction' they could be taught in a separate 'Aboriginal' school but where there are 'only a few such children' they could attend the nearest public school, provided they were 'habitually clean, decently clad, and that they conduct themselves with propriety both in and out of school'.⁵⁹ The Board confidently announced that 'any prejudice which may have existed against the admission of aboriginal and half-caste children into the Public Schools will, it is to be hoped, be now entirely removed'.⁶⁰

---

53 *Aboriginal Mission Stations at Warangesda and Maloga (Report on Working Of.)*, New South Wales Legislative Assembly, 18 January 1883, 4.
54 *APBR* 1883–84, 1.
55 NSW, *Parliamentary Debates*, Legislative Assembly, 20 November 1879, 274 (Henry Parkes).
56 *APBR* 1885–86, 2.
57 'As far as can be ascertained, there are at the present time 520 Aboriginal and half-caste children receiving instruction, chiefly in Public Schools', *APBR* 1885–86, 2.
58 *APBR* 1883–84, 3.
59 *APBR* 1885–86, 2.
60 *APBR* 1885–86, 2.

Fosbery and King's report on the missions at Maloga and Warangesda proposed that children should not remain on the reserves; both the boys and girls 'should be further trained as to fit them to take their places as domestic servants, or amongst the industrial classes' and that they be 'boarded out'.[61] However, the Board's first report was less than optimistic on this direction. The Board stated that it approached the 'subject of boarding-out aboriginal and half-caste children with more hope than confidence' but thought the 'means of making the experiment should be provided'.[62] The Board did not elaborate.

The Board was more detailed in its legislative agenda. Citing the 'favourable results' from the Victorian legislation of 1869, it defined its priorities in 1884. It sought to have 'custody and control of aborigines of all ages and sexes in like manner as a parent'; vest power in the Board or minister to own 'all property provided for the aborigines'; supervise, confirm or annul 'all agreements between aborigines and any other person'; impose penalties on persons 'harbouring any aborigine' without Board consent; and authorise the minister or the Board to grant Aboriginal people exemptions from the Bill.[63] These would be sweeping powers, particularly its first priority to have *full* control and custody of *all* Aboriginal people.[64] Interestingly, despite this list of priority powers, the first Board members never actively advocated for enabling legislation to be passed.

The Board did not pursue other policies outlined in its first report with any more alacrity. As the years went by its annual report gradually increased in size with more statistical data, reports on the reserves, stations and districts, and with expenditure accountability. But, from one year to the next, there was no thorough analysis of policy direction; it was never clear what the Board was trying to achieve. Arguably, the Board's immediate task was enormous, perhaps even impossible. Six men, all with other jobs, sitting one afternoon a week, were tasked with the responsibility for nearly 9,000 Aboriginal people spread across the far-flung expanse of New South Wales.[65] The 1883–84 Board report stated: 'Numerous applications for

---

61   *Aboriginal Mission Stations at Warangesda and Maloga (Report on Working Of.)*, New South Wales Legislative Assembly, 18 January 1883, 3.
62   *APBR* 1883–84, 4.
63   *APBR* 1883–84, 2.
64   *APBR* 1883–84, 2.
65   George Thornton's report of 1883 reckoned on a total Aboriginal population of 8,919.

Government aid have been received from or on behalf of the aborigines scattered throughout the Colony'.[66] Board members, realising the scale of its task, may well have been overwhelmed.

The Stuart Government had not stipulated the mechanisms by which aid would be delivered nor the work of the Board to be undertaken. However, Edmund Fosbery's early appointment, which was unforeseen, conveniently enabled the Board to utilise the full network of the police to undertake its functions.[67] How the Board 'connected' with Aboriginal people is best viewed at the local level. Dharawal experiences illustrate the Board's methods.

APB and interaction with Dharawal

Dharawal (Tharawal/Turawal/Thurwal) is said to be the

> language spoken by the mobs/bands of Aboriginal people who had a relationship with the area south of Botany Bay and Georges River, west to Appin, south as far as Goulburn and to Wreck Bay near Nowra.[68]

Jim Kohen cautions that the 'problems which confront researchers who try to reconstruct the boundaries between Aboriginal groups across Australia are many'. It is important that boundaries be identified but they should truly reflect 'how the land is and was perceived by the traditional owners'.[69] Put simply, if you are Dharawal then this would be 'because it is the country of your father'.[70] Therefore the boundaries designated in Figure 2.7 should be regarded as approximate.

---

66   *APBR* 1883–84, 2.
67   The Victorian Central Board for the Protection of Aborigines did not have the same reliance on the police. It had a network of local committees across the colony and Honorary Correspondents in the more remote regions. *Central Board for Aborigines in the Colony of Victoria, First Report, 1861*, 3.
68   Bursill, Jacobs, Lennis, Timbery-Beller and Ryan, *Dharawal*, 9.
69   Kohen, 'Mapping Aboriginal Linguistic and Clan Boundaries in the Sydney Region', 32.
70   Bursill, Jacobs, Lennis, Timbery-Beller and Ryan, *Dharawal*, 9.

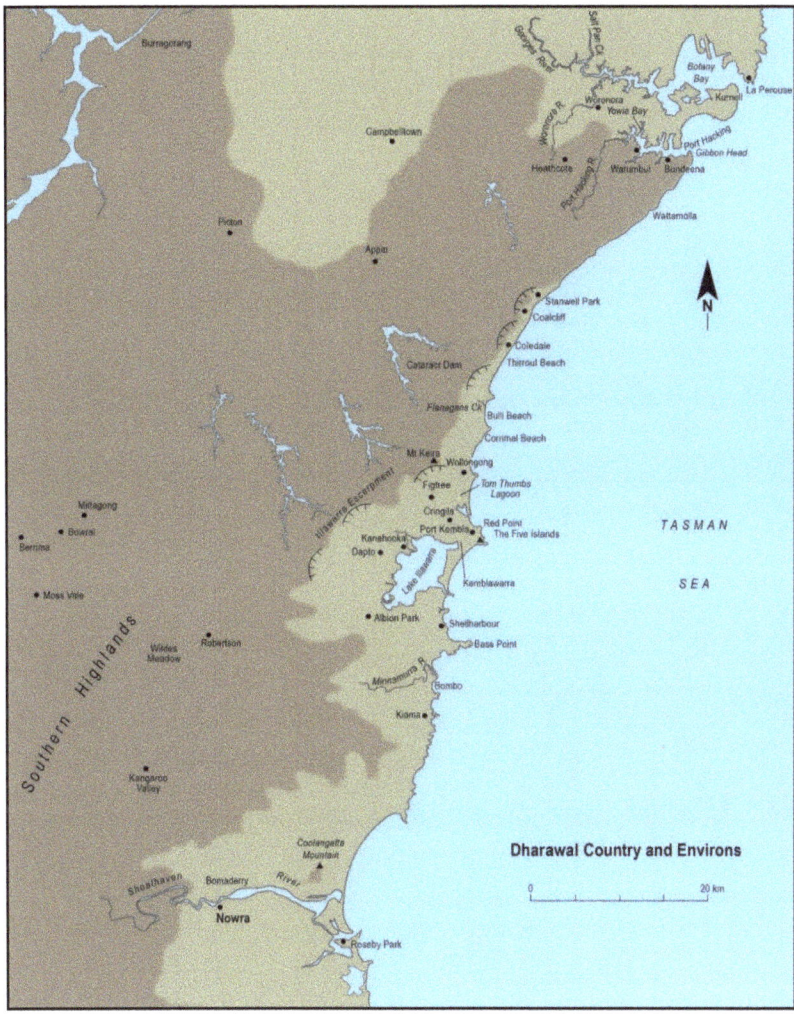

Figure 2.7: Map of Dharawal Country and Environs.
The dark shading represents the high country and not a boundary.
Source: Mike Donaldson, Les Bursill and Mary Jacobs. Cartographer: Peter Johnson, Cordeaux Heights, New South Wales.

Dharawal location points

The APB's early interaction with the Dharawal was not dissimilar to that of any other Aboriginal language group throughout the colony in the early stages of its work – the Board waited until it received requests from local police, Aboriginal people, community members or politicians, and then responded. At the end of its first year, the Board had identified the following location points within Dharawal Country and supplied certain rations and supplies. The Dharawal locations below are directly quoted from a complete alphabetical list of locations across the colony:

> Botany – Supplied with rations, clothes, huts, and medical attendance.
>
> Camden – Rations and medical attention supplied.
>
> Cox's River – Rations supplied to four old and infirm aborigines and seven children.
>
> Illawarra – Had their boat repaired.
>
> Jervis Bay – Clothing, sail, oars, rope, paint, fishing-lines and hooks; also rations supplied to aborigines.
>
> Kangaroo Valley – Rations supplied to two old and infirm aborigines.
>
> Kiama – Rations supplied to three old and infirm aborigines and six children.
>
> Nowra – Oars, rope, fishing-lines, hooks, paint, clothes, and rations supplied.
>
> Picton – Rations supplied.
>
> Shellharbour – Rations supplied.
>
> Shoalhaven – Boat repaired.[71]

George Thornton's report of 1883 would have been invaluable to the Board. It listed all the police stations across the colony from which supplies and rations had previously been distributed. For each location point, Thornton provided a variety of information: population, those employed, those in need of rations and why, conditions of boats supplied, children in school, how medical treatment was delivered, and any special information likely to be of interest.[72] For example, in the Shoalhaven, in the southern part of Dharawal country, Thornton noted that the Aboriginal population was 143, most of the 'half-castes' were employed; that they lived 'by fishing and government rations'; that there were 'three boats in the district, one at Terara, one Broughton Creek, and one at Jervis Bay' and all were in 'good order'. He gauged that about 'thirty half-caste children are at school at Coolangatta and five are at Jervis Bay'.[73]

---

71 *APBR* 1883–84, Appendix B.
72 Thornton, *Aborigines: Report of the Protector, to 31 December 1882*, Appendix, 10–11.
73 Thornton, *Aborigines: Report of the Protector, to 31 December 1882*, Appendix, 12.

2. POLICY DRIFT, 1883–1897

This was only the briefest sketch, but still valuable information for the Board. Likely though, the Board was unaware of specific details. For example, in the Shoalhaven many Aboriginal people were engaged in work. The Alexander Berry estate established in 1822 at the base of Cullunghutti (Coolangatta) Mountain was a significant employer of Aboriginal labour right up until the turn of the century when most of the Aboriginal residents were 'transferred' to Roseby Park.[74] Ninety-two Aboriginal people worked on the estate from 1822 to 1872.[75] Michael Bennett explains that those who worked did so for a variety of reasons. Work provided them with European goods and subsistence items to replace traditional foods, but more importantly 'it enabled Aboriginal people to continue living on their land in proximity to important sites such as Coolangatta Mountain'.[76] At the time the Board was established most Aboriginal people within the Shoalhaven and the Illawarra were able to provide for themselves.[77]

Whether any Board member – perhaps with the exception Richard Hill – grasped the idea that Aboriginal people wanted to remain on Country and sought employment and schooling for their children, is speculative. However, the Board's selection of reserve land would indicate they did not.

Of the 25 Aboriginal reserves that the Board inherited in 1883, three were in Dharawal Country. A closer analysis of these three reserves reveals how the Board was either indifferent to, or had little regard for, the needs of Aboriginal people if the reserves were to be occupied. Two reserves (No. 26 and No. 27) were close to each other (only 1.5 miles apart). They were approximately 30 miles west of Picton on Byrnes Creek, which flows into the present Warragamba Dam. Reserve No. 26 consisted of 300 acres and Reserve No. 27 consisted of 100 acres. The third reserve (No. 101) was on the northeast of Jervis Bay, across the water from Huskisson. However, the three reserves were never occupied by Aboriginal people. Although a Lands Department report stated that Reserve No. 26 had some good grassland and 7 acres were suitable for cultivation, Aboriginal people in the area had chosen instead, to occupy a nearby farm at Burragorang called

---

74   The residents moved to Roseby Park in 1900 and it was notified in 1906 as an official reserve.
75   *Cullunghutti: The Mountain and its People*, 91–93. See also Bennett, 'For a Labourer Worthy of His Hire', particularly Chapters 6, 7 and 8.
76   Bennett, 'For a Labourer Worthy of His Hire', 181.
77   Bennett, 'For a Labourer Worthy of His Hire', 246.

St Joseph's.[78] The same report noted that the farm had been 'purchased by the late father Dillon … and on which they [Aboriginal residents] make a very fair living rearing stock and growing maize'. A police report of 23 October 1882 noted that the farm was in a very good position 35 miles from Picton and consisted of seven acres of good cleared land: 'It was purchased by the Reverend G J Dillion … in 1876 for £200 for the use of the Aborigines'.[79] The farm at Burragorang provided Aboriginal people with what they needed: employment and nearby schooling.[80]

Reserve No. 27 was even less appealing because it had no water – a report stated 'Aborigines object to live on this Reserve there is no water on it and no school near to it'.[81] A decade later, the APB report of 1891 confirmed Aboriginal resistance, stating that reserves in the Wollondilly area had been 'set aside' for Aboriginal people but 'they can not be induced to occupy them'. It also recorded that the Aboriginal people living at the Burragorang farm still make a 'fair living from it rearing stock and growing maize'.[82]

The Lands Department report for the third reserve (No. 101) at Jervis Bay, read:

> Situated about 28 miles from Nowra and 8 miles from Huskisson by water … the Reserve is a level plain. About 300 acres of it is barren ground covered with low scrub, rushes and grass-tree. The whole frontage to Jervis Bay is sandy beach over which in rough weather a very heavy surf breaks, but at the ocean end there is creek … this is sheltered from the Bay by rocks and is a nice harbour for small boats. There is freshwater in this creek all year round [and has a] total area of 700 acres.

Another entry on 6 August 1890 in the same report noted:

---

78   Reserve No. 26, notified 9 December 1878, Parish of Peaks, County of Westmorland, Locality Picton, Register of Aboriginal Reserves, 1875–1904, Reference Numbers 2/8349. Reel 2847, Aborigines Welfare Board Archives, NRS 23, State Records of New South Wales (hereafter SRNSW).
79   Reserve No. 26, notified 9 December 1878, Parish of Peaks, County of Westmorland, Locality Picton, Register of Aboriginal Reserves, 1875–1904, Reference Numbers 2/8349. Reel 2847, Aborigines Welfare Board Archives, NRS 23 (SRNSW).
80   The Board report for the year 1890 stated that 'fifteen children are receiving instruction at the Public School in the Picton District, *APBR* 1890, 7. Accessed via *Journal of LC*, Vol. 47, Part 2 (SLNSW).
81   Reserve No. 27, Parish of Peaks, County of Westmorland, Locality Picton, Register of Aboriginal Reserves, 1875–1904, Reference Numbers 2/8349. Reel 2847, Aborigines Welfare Board Archives, NRS 23 (SRNSW).
82   *APBR* 1891–92, 7.

[the] Aborigines refuse to reside there but if they could be induced to do so no better spot could be found in the district upon which to centralise the whole of the aborigines in the Police Districts of the Shoalhaven and Dowling.[83]

Aboriginal people made clear choices about where they were going to live. If reserve land was barren, had no water, was not close to schools and was distant from employment, they would not move there. Also, in the case of the Jervis Bay reserve, the not-so-subtle advice that it would be a suitable place for all the Aboriginal communities of the Shoalhaven and those further to the south was a blatant attempt to remove all the Aboriginal people from the two districts and isolate them, just as George Augustus Robinson had done to small groups of Tasmanian Aboriginal people when he moved them to Flinders Island.[84]

Two points can be made here. Due to its limited funds, the Board was more than happy for Aboriginal people to be independent of the Board. Also, in what would become the Board's modus operandi, it never recognised that those who needed assistance still wanted employment opportunities, to maintain connections with Country and kin, and their children educated: they did not want to be isolated.

The Shoalhaven and the reliance on the police

The local police were integral to the Board's operations and information gathering throughout its existence. The first detailed account from the Shoalhaven is found in the Board's second annual report. Police Sergeant Brayne from Jervis Bay wrote:

> 22 half-castes and aboriginals attending school: most of them are quick at learning. Some of them come a distance to school, leave home on Monday, and return on Friday evening. They live in a hut with an old aboriginal couple, who cook the food for them and keep them clean; they appear eager to learn. Mr. Beetson, Public School Teacher, also Mrs. Beetson, take a great interest in

---

83   Reserve 101, notified 26 September 1881, Parish of Woolumboola, County of St Vincent, Locality Jervis Bay. The Dowling district was further south, taking in Milton and Ulladulla. Register of Aboriginal Reserves, 1875–1904, Reference Numbers 2/8349. Reel 2847, Aborigines Welfare Board Archives, NRS 23 (SRNSW).
84   Ryan, *Tasmanian Aborigines*, 219–53; Brantlinger, *Dark Vanishings*, 124–28.

them. Mrs. Beetson gave great assistance in making the clothes for them. The aborigines and half-castes in the district are all very comfortable, none in want of necessaries of life. Most of the young men work and have given up wandering. No drunkenness. Messrs. Dwyer and Pitt, Inspectors of Schools, were surprised at the intelligence of the children when they examined the school.[85]

Brayne's report referred to the school at Huskisson at Currambene Creek (Figure 2.8). It was not clear how many of the children lived in the hut with the old Aboriginal couple but officer Brayne was keen to stress that all seemed well at Jervis Bay. Reports such as these from local police officers were the primary means from which the Board gained information about conditions on the ground. In this case, Brayne's report also highlighted the lengths that some Aboriginal families went to for their children to receive an education, including allowing them to spend four nights away from home each week.

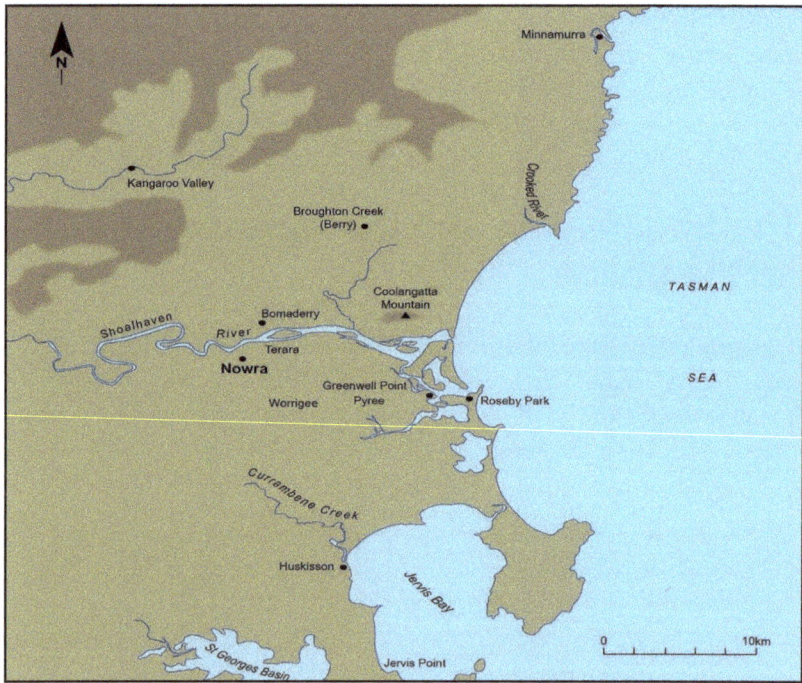

Figure 2.8: Map of the Shoalhaven showing Aboriginal population centres.
Source: Peter Johnson, cartographer, Cordeaux Heights, New South Wales.

85   *APBR* 1885, 2.

2. POLICY DRIFT, 1883–1897

Table 2.1: Board minute entries: first five items (as recorded) relating to Dharawal Country.[86]

Date	Nature of item	Action
25 September 1890	John Riley, Aboriginal, Burragorang, – applying for a grant of land.	Refer to Mr Ryeland for a report as to applicant's circumstances and if land is already reserved is adequate.
30 October 1890	Letter from Mr Thornton, MP, recommending that 'Aborigines' at Jervis Bay be supplied with a boat.	Embody contents of report in a letter to Mr Thornton.
23 December 1890	Police forwarding an extract from the 'Valley Pioneer' with reference to Hugh Anderson's Statements regarding Aborigines at Kangaroo Valley.[87]	(no action recorded)
16 April 1891	Police (Nowra) applying for authority to expend £4.10.0 in the purchase of a flat-bottomed boat, to convey children at Greenwell Point to school.	Approved.
11 June 1891	Police (Nowra) reporting on condition of Aboriginal Camp at Ulladulla recommending rations and erection of three two-roomed huts for 'aged Aborigines'.	Approve rations for children and expend £5.0.0 to best advantage for huts.

Source: Author's analysis of APB Board minutes, 1890–1893.

Apart from the stations at Cumeroogunga, Warangesda and, from 1887, Brewarrina, which were run by the APA and presented annual reports to the Board, all other official information to the Board was provided by the New South Wales police.[88] An analysis of the APB Board minute items that concerned Dharawal Country over a three-year period from 1890 to 1893 reveals 18 entries. They demonstrate how the Board's actions were almost entirely a result of requests from the police. Table 2.1 shows the first five entries and reveals how the Board noted agenda items and responded to them. All entries were limited in detail; there is no record of any discussion on the items raised. The Board responses are cursory, often dismissive, and if requests were refused the Board afforded little or

---

86 *APBM* 1890–1891.
87 Hugh Anderson was an Aboriginal man from Cumeroogunga who attempted to form a mission at Kangaroo Valley in the late 1880s and claimed that his mission had been 'starved out' of the Valley. See: *Cullunghutti: The Mountain and its People*, 214.
88 However, after February 1895, the Board established local boards attached to Aboriginal-managed stations (the first of which was the Grafton Home). These became additional sources of information.

no explanation. Of the 18 entries from the Shoalhaven, 15 (83 per cent) came either directly from, or via, the police at Nowra in the form of requests for rations, reserve land or medical treatment, and as tenders for supplies. Of the other three entries: one was from John Riley, an Aboriginal man requesting land, which was subsequently refused with no explanation;[89] one from the mayor of Nowra who requested that the 'aborigines be supplied with a boat';[90] and the third came from George Thornton (MLA and ex-protector) recommending that the Aboriginal people at Jervis Bay also be supplied with a boat.[91]

From 1889, the Board, through its annual reports, regularly thanked the police for their work: the 'Board has to depend largely upon the officers and members of the constabulary throughout the Colony ... for carrying out its operations';[92] and 'appreciation ... of the assistance so cheerfully rendered by the members of the Police Force throughout the Colony'.[93] Another role for the police was the distribution of blankets, but other people were also participants in what was clearly an annual ritual.

'I seconds the motion'

The Board inherited the entrenched tradition of providing a yearly blanket to Aboriginal people but played a minimal role in distribution. The annual blanket distribution was a complicated institution: it evolved over a number of stages, each determined by 'shifting imperatives of peace-keeping'.[94] The institution of 'gifts' began with Macquarie's annual Parramatta feasts each December with the distribution of 'badges of distinction', food and clothing.[95] Michael Smithson notes that it was Governor Darling who first introduced the annual blanket distribution in 1826. To regain control of events on the frontier after the 1824 declaration of Martial Law in Wiradjuri Country, Darling saw the issue

---

89 John Riley was refused his grant by the Board on 16 October 1890 with no reason given, *APBM*, 16 October 1890 (no item number).
90 *APBM*, 19 May 1892 (no item numbers specified in this period).
91 *APBM*, 30 October 1890.
92 *APBR* 1889, 1. Accessed via 'NSW', To Remove and Protect, AIATSIS: aiatsis.gov.au/sites/default/files/docs/digitised_collections/remove/22828.pdf.
93 *APBR* 1894–95, 3. Accessed via 'NSW', To Remove and Protect, AIATSIS: aiatsis.gov.au/sites/default/files/docs/digitised_collections/remove/22879.pdf.
94 O'Brien, 'Kitchen Fragments and Garden Stuff', 162.
95 Reece, 'Feasts and Blankets, 192.

of blankets as a practical tool to reduce frontier violence and as a reward for individuals who had assisted in capturing bushrangers.[96] The blanket became an instrument of 'protection' *for* settler society.

Governor Richard Bourke decreed that the distribution of clothing would be more effective at the beginning of winter. The 'Macquarie feasts' would now be held on 1 May and 'magistrates and settlers were required to inform Aborigines in their area that blankets would not be issued at the "Parramatta feast" but would be sent instead to stations and police officers for distribution on 10th May'.[97]

In 1838 Governor Gipps qualified the distribution. He declared that only those Aboriginal people who had rendered services would be supplied with blankets and those who were troublesome would be omitted.[98] Over time, Gipps dramatically reduced the number of blankets distributed and, under financial pressures, he discontinued the practice in 1844. Many blanket agents complained of the cessation and some aged and infirm Aboriginal people 'perished for want of warm clothing'.[99] On the advice of the 1845 Select Committee on Aborigines the new governor, Fitzroy, reintroduced the policy in 1848. Anne O'Brien observes that 'Indigenous people had become dependent on blankets in the winter and that they were also a form of official recognition'.[100] Smithson argues that Aboriginal people had always regarded the gift of the blanket as a right, 'an obligation owed by Europeans who made use of the resources on lands traditionally owned by Aborigines'.[101] When Gipps stopped the issue, or only gave to some, this caused power relations to be further disrupted.[102] Europeans never really understood the complex relationship and meaning of the blanket issue from an Aboriginal perspective.[103]

---

96   Smithson, 'A Misunderstood Gift', 75; see also O'Brien, 'Kitchen Fragments and Garden Stuff', 162.
97   Reece, 'Feasts and Blankets', 196.
98   Reece, 'Feasts and Blankets', 200.
99   Reece, 'Feasts and Blankets', 202.
100 O'Brien, 'Kitchen Fragments and Garden Stuff', 162.
101 Smithson, 'A Misunderstood Gift', 86.
102 O'Brien, 'Kitchen Fragments and Garden Stuff', 163.
103 Smithson, 'A Misunderstood Gift', 104.

POWER AND DYSFUNCTION

Figure 2.9: 'The Courthouse' (Nowra 1910).
Source: From the collections of the Wollongong City Libraries and the Illawarra Historical Society (Wollongong City Council Policy number 9.6).

In Dharawal Country, the annual occasion to provide a blanket to all Aboriginal people was a moment of ceremony and of ritual. The distribution involved the police and local magistrates, but also the white community. On 1 April 1858, a group of 25 Aboriginal people travelled to the Wollongong Courthouse to receive their blankets, and some known Aboriginal 'leaders' led the group in three cheers for the Queen. The *Illawarra Mercury* on 25 April 1858 reported that 23 blankets were issued at Kiama, drawing a rousing chorus of cheers to Queen Victoria.[104]

The blanket distribution at the Nowra Courthouse (Figure 2.9) in 1883 provides a closer look at the ritual. Nowra did not have an Aboriginal reserve within proximity to the township but was the contact point between the police and the Shoalhaven Aboriginal people.

To receive a blanket and special ration on the day of distribution, Aboriginal people came from places such as Huskisson (referred to as Jervis Bay), Coolangatta, Greenwell Point, Broughton Creek and Crooked River. The *Shoalhaven Telegraph* of May 1883 reported:

> As stated in our last issue, owing to the severity of the weather it was determined to distribute the blankets to the blacks on the first instant instead of the 24th. Due notice having been given, our sable colonists, male and female, adult and juvenile, mustered in strong force at the Courthouse at Nowra on Tuesday last, when … with

---

104 Bennett, 'For a Labourer Worthy of His Hire', 203.

> the assistance of the police, distributed the blankets to the number of 81. There were not Aboriginals to that number present; as some were unavoidably absent, through sickness or other causes. As on former occasions, several benevolent ladies now provided a substantial meal for our vagrant and disinherited country people. Mrs Scott of Nowra, and Mrs Rev. J Best, provided sandwiches, buns, and tea in abundance, to the great gratification of their swarthy visitors.

Clearly, this was a well-worn event at the Courthouse. The assembled were aware of the people who were unable to attend, and their blankets were distributed to others to pass on. Food was organised. It was also acknowledged that the Aboriginal people had been dispossessed. What followed revealed the ritual involved with the blanket issue.

> The Rev. Joseph Best and the Rev. Luke Parr addressed these black people, alternatively, and their words were listened to with respectful attention, each male darkie uncovering his head while the clergymen were speaking to them. At the conclusion of the proceedings, a pure son of the soil, – without any traces of that colour which bears witness against the invading race – stepped forward, with his head uncovered and called for three cheers for the ladies who had so kindly treated them to a meal. Another darkie said, 'I seconds the motion'; and forthwith three ringing hearty cheers were given. The demeanour of these poor people showed that they are not slow to recognise an act of kindness … Considering all the wrongs to which these aboriginals have been subjected … it is highly gratifying to find that there are those, though they may be few, are not slow in doing a kindness.[105]

The extract is revealing on several levels. First it showed an unequal reciprocity. The Aboriginal people respectfully participated in the ceremony of the occasion, thanked the ladies for the meal and their thanks were demonstrated by 'three cheers'. This goes to the heart of Smithson's argument that acknowledgements of dispossession and of recompense were bound up in this annual blanket issue to Aboriginal people. Second, this was a well-beaten path for both black and white residents. There was no going back; both parties recognised the predicament. The tradition served as 'circuit-breaker' to a very unsatisfactory situation. The Board had no role in this ritual; the blankets came from the government store

---

105 *Shoalhaven Telegraph*, 3 May 1883, 2.

and were provided outside of Board funding.[106] In this early period of the Board it was a reactive body; it remained aloof and allowed those on the ground to carry on with regular traditions. In some instances, it did nothing when it should have taken some responsibility.

The 'classroom is of bark covered with blankets'

The Board had responsibility for the education of Aboriginal children. But it appeared completely indifferent to events surrounding the education of Aboriginal children at Kangaroo Valley in 1890. In early 1890, Hughie Anderson, an Aboriginal missionary, requested educational materials and a tent to facilitate the education of the Aboriginal children at a bush camp in Kangaroo Valley. In March 1890, Sergeant Sykes (of Nowra Police) wrote to the Chief Superintendent of Police outlining Anderson's request.[107] Sykes recorded 'there are a number of children in the camp to whom instruction could be imparted on the spot if the Protectorate [meaning the APB] supplied him with a tent 20 x 15 [feet]' and school supplies.[108]

Police Constable Reynolds (of Nowra police) reported that there was a 'half-caste' named Frank Foster at the 'Aborigines camp' and that he was trained as a school teacher at Maloga Mission Station up on the Murray River. Reynolds advised that the local public school at Kangaroo Valley was a little more than a mile away, but they have a 'great objection to attending the public school as they say the white children are always making fun of them'.[109] It was not uncommon for Aboriginal children to be the brunt of name-calling or worse.[110]

---

106 The first Board report to itemise the financial breakdown of these expenses was in 1892–93: 'Government Stores: Blankets, clothing, oars, and Stationery, £2,504.0.0', Appendix C, 8. This funding was independent of Board funding. *APBR* 1892–93. Accessed via *Journal of LC,* Vol. 50, Part 2, 327 (SLNSW).
107 It is unclear where this camp was located. However, in August 1890 an Aboriginal reserve of 320 acres was notified in Kangaroo Valley fronting the Shoalhaven River. Most likely the 'camp' was within this area before it was notified. Register of Aboriginal Reserves, 1875–1904, Reference Numbers 2/8349. Reel 2847 Aborigines Welfare Board Archives, NRS 23 (SRNSW).
108 Sergeant Sykes, Nowra Police to Superintendent of Police E District, 31 March 1890, Kangaroo Valley School Files, 1876–1913, 5/16418.2, Bundle A, Item 17543.
109 Constable Reynolds to Sergeant Sykes at Nowra, 1 April 1890, Kangaroo Valley School Files, 1876–1913, 5/16418.2, Bundle A, (no item number).
110 Landon and Tonkin, *Jackson's Track: Memoir of a Dreamtime Place*, 202–3.

The district inspector of schools, Richards, confirmed the police reports and stated that the camp was 'not under the control of the Aborigines Protection Board or similar organisation' and that Anderson was in charge. The current makeshift 'classroom' at the camp was of 'bark covered with blankets', which was waterproof 'but not in severe weather'. He reported that the teacher, Frank Foster, was 'an intelligent half-caste, 19 years of age; and has certainly received some training'. Accordingly, he recommended that a tent and teaching materials be supplied, that the 'present arrangement is preferable to having them taught at a Public School', and that the APB be informed.[111]

The regional inspector of schools, Pitt, presented contrary advice. Pitt was aware of the all the circumstances, claimed to know each Aboriginal person at the camp and placed 'no reliance on them whatever'. He alleged the children did attend the local public school and were treated well and that there are no grounds for their withdrawal. He stipulated that there was 'no certainty of their stay at the present camp', and that if the materials recommended were granted them 'no care would be taken of them, but left to ruin and rot'. He declared that he could not support the camp school and that the 'Aborigines Protectorate' (the Board) be informed that the existing school at Kangaroo Valley is

> both available and suitable for the children of the Black's camp, and further, that the protectorate be respectfully invited to cooperate in the matter – to clothe and ration them, in order to facilitate the children's attendance at school.[112]

The chief inspector of schools opposed Pitt's suggestions:

> The children of the blacks as a rule are dirty and verminous and they injure the schools where they attend. If this man Anderson is a fit man for the task he might be allowed a small sum to encourage him in his work.[113]

---

111 Internal Departmental note from District Inspector, 26 April 1890, Kangaroo Valley School Files, 1876–1913, 5/16418.2, Bundle A, Item 21241.
112 Memorandum to the Colonial Secretary from Inspector Pitt, 20 May 1890, Kangaroo Valley School Files, 1876–1913, 5/16418.2, Bundle A, Item 23261.
113 Memorandum to the Colonial Secretary from Inspector Pitt, 20 May 1890, Kangaroo Valley School Files, 1876–1913, 5/16418.2, Bundle A, Item 23261.

Three months later in June 1890 the chief inspector of schools noted that missionary Anderson was about to leave the colony and 'that the camp will cease to exist'. He recommended therefore 'that no further action be taken on this matter at present'.[114]

The role of the Board in these events is unclear but three points can be made. First, the minutes for the APB meetings are not available for this period, so it is not known whether the situation at Kangaroo Valley was brought to the attention of the Board. Second, there is no correspondence from the Board in the school files on this matter and no reference (that I can find) to any Board correspondence elsewhere. Third, if the APB was at all concerned about the schooling of Aboriginal children some response after the initial inquires and reports from two police officers would be expected. Interestingly, Pitt's report only sought to *inform* the Board of the situation and what may be possible. There is no suggestion that anyone needed to *defer* to the Board as a matter of course or that it should take a lead role, but Pitt was obviously frustrated that the Board had taken no interest at all in the matter.

On another level, the situation in Kangaroo Valley revealed the second-class system of education for Aboriginal children. Although acknowledging the more than adequate training and capabilities of teacher Frank Foster, both the police and District Inspector Richards were more than happy for him to continue teaching without any remuneration, in what could be described as appalling conditions. The local constable may have been sympathetic to the fact that the children were treated badly at the local public school and therefore favoured the continuation of the Aboriginal 'camp school'. But the stark reality was that within the township of Kangaroo Valley, it seemed perfectly normal that a bush/camp school for the Aboriginal children, with no funding or properly paid teacher, should exist alongside the fully funded local public school.

Pitt was clearly convinced that the Aboriginal children should go to the local public school. But his reasons for advising so were less humanitarian than racist. He complained that any supplies given to Aboriginal people would be wasted and ruined. He dismissed out of hand the complaints about ill-treatment and he also wanted the APB to do its job. The chief inspector's comments are probably the most damning. He saw the

---

114 Note from Inspector to District Inspector (no date of letter but stamped 10 June 1890), Kangaroo Valley School Files, 1876–1913, 5/16418.2, Bundle A.

Aboriginal children as 'dirty and verminous' and injurious to white pupils – and not just the Kangaroo Valley 'blacks', but all of them. Such views, from one of the highest-ranking men in the Department of Education says much about the policy direction of educating Aboriginal children in the colony.

The situation at Kangaroo Valley in 1890 exposed the remoteness of the APB from everyday issues faced by Indigenous people. Over a period of three months some response from the Board would have been expected. The Aboriginal camp and the children's education were the Board's responsibilities. The Board's inaction could only be attributed to incompetence, a policy vacuum for this situation or an abrogation of responsibility. Likely it was a combination of all three.

Trends emerging over the first 15 years

If the Board remained aloof from the processes of blanket distribution and the education of Aboriginal children, it nevertheless played a growing (if remote) role in the lives of Aboriginal people in other spheres. The first extensive Board report was in 1891. Twenty-three 'dense' pages listed police reports on 72 districts across the colony, census data from 185 location points, expenditure on rations and clothing and, in specified localities, medical expenses and overall expenditure statements. The reports continued in this vein until 1915.[115] Through its reports, the Board satisfied the demand of the colonial secretary to be 'accountable'. It knew, statistically, all about the clientele under its jurisdiction – its annual report had, in fact, become its raison d'être. Susan Greer argues that before the Board could understand its task, it had to turn the Aboriginal population into 'useable information': it had to collect data on the number of residents, locations, age and 'caste', births and deaths, who received medical treatment, who was receiving rations and what works were carried out on stations and reserves, and give a full disclosure of where the money had gone.[116] The written report was thus an important instrument of Board power over the Aboriginal population. Fosbery and his Board took the reporting seriously, far more so than later Board members. Whether or not Fosbery saw the reporting 'as an instrument of power',

---

115 The Board was reconstituted in 1916 and the reporting changed dramatically thereafter: this is discussed in Chapter 5.
116 Greer, 'Governing Indigenous Peoples', 163–66.

his reports were certainly a record of 'achievement' and a demarcation of the Board's domain. Tim Rowse draws attention to that fact that colonial governments, using subjugated Indigenous population statistics, created a sense of 'national community'. [117]

Nevertheless, these Board reports that show the growing engagement between the state and Aboriginal people – chiefly through the distribution of rations and growth in reserves and stations – did not lead Fosbery's Board to affect any policies to accommodate these changed circumstances and trends. It remained paralysed on the policy front.

As can be seen in Table 2.2, the number of geographical location points across the colony for distribution of rations and supplies grew steadily from 51 in the year ending 1884 up to 146 in the year ending 1896. This increase mirrored an increase in the number of Aboriginal reserves from the original 25 in 1883 to 113 in 1897.[118] The Board only engaged with 9.2 per cent of the total estimated Aboriginal community in 1884, but by 1897 that had increased to 35 per cent of the total estimated population. Also, there was a large increase in the numbers of Aboriginal people seeking rations in the year ending 1888. The Board explained this partly because it had become 'generally known that the Government made such provision[s]' and the Aboriginal people had begun to trust the Board to provide.[119] Likely also, it reflected the growing distress of the Aboriginal population.

---

[117] Rowse, 'The Statistical Table as Colonial Knowledge', 51. Rowse cites four examples, one of which was that of protector Edward Stone Parker's precise statistical table of Aboriginal people coming and going from his Loddon protectorate. Parker managed to 'evoke in arithmetical terms an entity that did not necessarily exist: a *resident* [my emphasis] Aboriginal population' (67). It was an important perception for the Government – a permanent Aboriginal population.

[118] *APBR* 1898, 2. Accessed via *Journal of LC,* Vol. 57, Part 1 (SLNSW).

[119] *APBR* 1890, 1. Accessed via *Journal of LC,* Vol. 47, Part 2 (SLNSW). Peter Read also suggests that while numbers were increasing, only about 'half the populations at Warangesda and Brungle, and the other unmanaged reserves, could be considered even semi-permanent'; the stations were becoming 'convenient stopping places'. Read, *A Hundred Years War,* 43.

Table 2.2: **Number of location points for rations and supplies, expenditure and support as a percentage of population across the colony, 1883–1897.**

Year (ending Dec.)	Number of location points	Number of people receiving rations and supplies	Spending on rations and supplies (£ s. d.)	Census*	Percentage of total population receiving rations	Overall Board expenditure (£ s. d.)
1883	67	unknown	unknown	8,471	unknown	–
1884	51	741	£2,417.13.6	8,091	9.2%	£2,417.13.6
1885	62	846	£2,975.6.5	7,984	10.6%	£2,975.6.5
1886	71	976	£3,603.13.10	7,684	12.7%	£3,603.13.10
1887	82	845	£4,021.13.9	7,092	11.9%	£4,021.13.9
1888	96	1,386	£5,192.4.7	7,485	18.5%	£5,192.4.7
1889	113	1,509	£5,275.13.3	7,529	20.0%	£11,300.0.0**
1890	121	1,324	£6,129.18.4	7,700	17.2%	£12,622.2.11
1891	125	1,420	£7,130.9.11	7,473	19.0%	£14,078.19.8
1892	127	1,581	£9,019.7.6	7,349	22.0%	£17,030.3.8
1893	138	1,614	£7,809.3.1	7,255	22.2%	£15,253.14.0
1894	138	1,920	£7,947.0.10	7,021	27.3%	£15,311.8.3
1895	139	2,189	£8,595.18.4	7,046	31.1%	£17,050.0.11
1896	148	2,184	£9,581.3.6	6,984	31.3%	£17,311.17.6
1897***	146	2,452	£9,266.3.7	7,084	35.0%	£16,732.12.0

Notes:

* The Board regularly made the qualification that it was difficult to obtain accurate figures 'owing to the wandering habits of the race'.

** This was *not* a major increase in funding. The Board reports (from 1890) now included extra costs upon the government such as freight charges, Board secretary's salary, aid to the APA (£2 for every £1 raised), medical assistance, Public Instruction Department funds for schools, government stores and other sundry items.

*** All statistics for Cumeroogunga, Warangesda and Brewarrina were included for the first time.

Source: APB reports for relevant years. Census was obtained from Alan T. Duncan, 'A Survey of the Education of Aborigines in New South Wales, Vols. 1 & 2', 281.

The steady increase in numbers receiving rations and supplies shown in Table 2.2 throughout the 1890s does not necessarily reflect proactivity by the Board. Rather, it coincided with the economic downturn of the decade. Pastoralism, the 'backbone of the economy', went into decline throwing many people out of work. Coupled with this was a collapse of the financial institutions, and when the Commercial Bank of Australia 'suspended operations' in 1893, panic set in, 'accounts were frozen, bills not paid' and the country was gripped by depression.[120] A severe drought that began in 1895 (and that persisted for seven years) ensured there would be no recovery until the turn of the century. Many Aboriginal workers lost their jobs and were forced onto the reserves to survive.[121] The point to be made here is that more Aboriginal people were now engaging with the Board, living on managed stations and unmanaged reserves, receiving rations and supplies. This was not what the Board had envisaged; it had assumed from the outset that the Aboriginal population would decline. If Fosbery and his Board had a view on this unexpected pattern, it was not apparent. The annual reports were duly presented with evermore regional reporting and statistical information, but without overview or analysis.

The second trend to emerge was the average expenditure per person per year for rations and supplies fluctuated over the 14-year period (see Table 2.3) with a peak in 1892 of an average of £5.7 per person per annum. This dropped by 33.3 per cent to £3.8 per person per annum in 1897.

One would expect over time, with original funding at a low level and with increasing numbers requiring assistance, a steady rise in the expenditure per person would occur. Yet the overall trend was to retain the status quo. For the year 1886 expenditure was £3.7 per person per annum and 11 years later, for the year 1897, it was virtually the same at £3.8.

Table 2.3: Board expenditure per Aboriginal person per year.

Year (ending Dec.)	Numbers receiving rations and supplies	Expenditure (£)	Expenditure per person per year (£)
1884	741	2,417	3.3
1885	846	2,975	3.5
1886	976	3,603	3.7
1887	845	4,021	4.8
1888	1,386	5,192	3.7
1889	1,509	5,275	3.5
1890	1,342	6,129	4.6
1891	1,420	7,130	5.0
1892	1,581	9,019	5.7
1893	1,614	7,809	4.8

120 Molony, *History of Australia*, 163–65.
121 Goodall, *Invasion to Embassy*, 2008, 132.

Year (ending Dec.)	Numbers receiving rations and supplies	Expenditure (£)	Expenditure per person per year (£)
1894	1,920	7,947	4.1
1895	2,189	8,595	3.9
1896	2,184	9,581	4.4
1897	2,452	9,266	3.8

Source: All Board reports from 1883–84 to 1898.

The Board did raise its concerns regarding a lack of funding.[122] In 1897 the Board identified the need:

> Huts are required on many reserves; farming appliances, boats, fencing, [etc.] are also needed; but action of the Board is greatly restricted by the want of necessary funds. The expenditure is not large, and the Vote is administered with rigid economy. The Board therefore express an earnest hope that this appeal for more liberal provision will receive favourable consideration by the Government.[123]

The Depression of the 1890s stretched the government's capacity to increase funding, so 'belt-tightening' was to be expected. Yet the government had either not been listening to the Board or had been unpersuaded by its entreaties for several years. The Board began its operations from a very low funding base. In the year ending 1884, the Board expended £3.7 per person per annum. George Thornton had suggested in 1882 (no doubt an ambit claim) that an annual figure of £150,000 was required each year to support the Aboriginal population.[124] That would have been £18.14.0 per person per annum. Fifteen years later, in 1897, the government expenditure of £16,732.12.0 for a total population of 7,084 Aboriginal people (£2.7.3 per person per annum) seemed grossly inadequate. Even if one counts only those Aboriginal people receiving rations and supplies from the Board in 1897, the total expenditure of £16,732.12.0 on 2,452 recipients would average only £6.8 per person per annum, less than a third of that estimated by Thornton in 1882. Limited funding for the Board was a perennial problem and it was powerless to secure more.

---

122 See *APBR* 1887–88, 2. Accessed via 'NSW', To Remove and Protect, AIATSIS: aiatsis.gov.au/sites/default/files/docs/digitised_collections/remove/22812.pdf; *APBR* 1889, 2. Subsequent reports up to 1897 make the point regularly but in an oblique way by exposing the enormous subsidisation of the APA.
123 *APBR* 1898, 1.
124 Thornton, *Aborigines: Report of the Protector, to 31 December 1882*, 2.

A third trend during this period was the increase in the number of Aboriginal schools. In 1885 there were 146 Aboriginal children in school. Twelve years later, in 1897, there were 690 in both Aboriginal schools and local public schools: an increase of 544 students, or an average of only 42 *extra* Aboriginal children going to school each year across the whole colony.[125] This was not a big increase at all. However, the number of separate Aboriginal schools had increased dramatically. There were two Aboriginal schools (Maloga and Warangesda) operating in 1883. By 1897, 11 more separate Aboriginal schools had been established: Brewarrina, Wallaga Lake on the south coast, Brungle near Tumut; Barrington inland from Taree, Pelican Island in the Macleay River district, Cabbage Tree Island at the mouth of Port Stephens, Wauchope and Rollands Plans near Port Macquarie, Forster on the mid-north coast, Cowra, and Grafton.[126] The Board had not sought this expansion. The increase was due to 'white pressure' that had excluded Aboriginal children from the public schools (discussed in Chapter 7).[127]

Fourth, while the overall Aboriginal population remained steady, the 'full-blood' population was in decline and the 'half-caste' population was on the increase (see Table 2.4). In 1883 the 'half-caste' population was only 27.7 per cent of the Aboriginal total population; by 1897 it had almost doubled to 51.7 per cent. Local authorities 'on the ground' made the determinations about Aboriginality. The Board required the classifications of 'racial mixture' – Aboriginal people need no such distinctions. The Board identified this 'change' and had been monitoring it each year. The 1898 Board report stated:

> The number of half-castes now exceed that of the full-bloods, there being a difference of 241 in favour of the former. Twelve years back the number of full-bloods was slightly more than double that of the half-castes. Since that time the full-bloods have decreased at the average annual rate of 100, against an average annual increase of 86 half-castes.[128]

---

125 Analysis of Board reports from 1883 up to 1897.
126 See all Board reports from 1890 up to 1897.
127 The Board was aware of many exclusions. At Gulargambone school 25 white children were removed from the school, leaving four Aboriginal children in the classroom. A local grazier convinced the Education Department that there were enough Aboriginal children in the district for a separate school; the minister excluded the Aboriginal children and all the white children returned. See Fletcher, *Clean, Clad and Courteous*, 66–68.
128 *APBR* 1898, 1.

The issue of the 'half-caste' population remained a 'problem' for the Board. Fosbery's Board offered the following evasive policy statement in its Board report of 1887–88:

> The difficulty in dealing with this latter class [the 'half-castes'] has by no means diminished, but it is hoped that whilst no special scandal arises from their presence in the community their absorption in the general population may at some future date be accomplished.[129]

Table 2.4: Board figures for the Aboriginal population from 1883 until 1897.

Year (ending Dec.)	'Full-blood'	'Half-caste'	Total
1883	6,126	2,345	8,471
1884	5,698	2,402	8,100
1885	5,362	2,662	8,024
1886	4,893	2,741	7,634
1887	5,042	2,860	7,902
1888	4,718	2,767	7,485
1889	4,652	2,877	7,529
1890	4,693	3,007	7,700
1891	4,458	3,015	7,473
1892	4,212	3,137	7,349
1893	3,982	3,273	7,255
1894	3,756	3,265	7,021
1895	3,660	3,386	7,046
1896	3,503	3,481	6,984
1897	3,422	3,663	7,085

Source: Analysis of all Board reports from 1883–84 to 1898.

In 1886 Victoria had found its 'solution'. Its parliament passed restrictive measures to exclude 'half-castes' from the managed Aboriginal stations. From 1886, the definition of an 'Aborigine', in Victoria, was: 'full-blood', 'half-caste' over the age of 34, female 'half-castes' married to an 'Aborigine', the infants of 'Aborigines' and any 'half-caste' who had permission from the Board to reside on a station.[130] Everyone else had to leave the

---

129 *APBR* 1887–88, 1.
130 Christie, *Aborigines in Colonial Victoria*, 197.

reserves.¹³¹ Richard Broome argues that the forced departures 'deprived the [reserve] communities of their muscle power which condemned them to economic oblivion'.¹³² Fosbery's view on the Victorian model in 1887 was unequivocal:

> I am opposed to the proposal to pass an enactment giving power to detain these people at Mission Stations as in Victoria. Knowing their habits well, their irrepressible desire to roam, I consider such a deprival of liberty would be cruel.¹³³

Fosbery's Board believed that 'to enforce the absorption of the half-castes into the general population' at present 'would be impracticable'.¹³⁴ Fosbery was not prepared to go down the Victorian path. A decade later, however, the Board had moved closer to restrictive measures. The regulations for the establishment of the local boards in 1896 discouraged the 'further introduction of half-castes [to the stations] which should be allowed only on the recommendation of the Local Board'.¹³⁵ Unlike in Victoria, these measures were discretionary and there were scores of unmanaged reserves where the policy could not apply.¹³⁶

Fosbery opted for 'soft restrictive policy' such as withdrawing the easy access to rail tickets to 'restrict them from idly wandering about from place to place'.¹³⁷ Richard Hill's influence may also have been in play here as it was highly likely that he agreed with Fosbery. Peter Read records Fosbery's policy of encouraging Aboriginal families to locate beside rivers and streams and suggests that he was a 'kindly man and his first policies were pursued with understanding'.¹³⁸ Read's assessment is in keeping with what had taken place over the first 15 years of the Board.

---

131 Christie informs that in 1886 there were 200 'half-castes' on various stations and their 'expulsion caused great hardships and is still today one of the Aborigines' bitterest memories'. Christie, *Aborigines in Colonial Victoria*, 201–2.
132 Broome, 'Victoria', 140.
133 This was part of Fosbery's reply to a report provided by education inspector Gerald O'Brien on the Warangesda School in 1887. Quoted in Fletcher, *Documents in the History of Aboriginal Education in New South Wales*, 81.
134 *APBR* 1887, 2.
135 *APBR* 1896, 11. Accessed via *Journal of LC*, Vol. 55, Part 1 (SLNSW).
136 In 1896 there were 105 reserves. *APBR* 1896, 2–12. There were only five managed stations: Cumeroogunga, Warangesda, Brewarrina, Brungle and Grafton Home.
137 *Aboriginal Mission Stations at Warangesda and Maloga (Report on Working Of.)*, New South Wales Legislative Assembly, 18 January 1883, 4.
138 Read, *A Hundred Years War*, 34.

2. POLICY DRIFT, 1883–1897

APA tensions 'had reached a crisis'

Perhaps contributing to the Board's policy drift was its inability to wrest control of the three most populous Aboriginal stations of Cumeroogunga, Warangesda and Brewarrina, operated by the APA. From the outset, in 1883, the Board reminded government of the difficulty of running parallel organisations, especially if it is was their intention to fund the APA in the future.[139] Premier Stuart was firm in his belief that the Board should play a secondary role and supplement the work of the APA. He considered that any money given to the APA should first pass through the Board and it should have a 'watchful inspection of and control over them'.[140] Yet the Board had no power to intercede if it suspected misuse of money or poor APA accounting procedures; it could only protest.

In the first few years, overall Board expenditure revealed the Board's problem. For the year ending 1885 the Board expended £2,975.6.5 on 846 Aboriginal people across the colony, or £3.5 per person. During that year it subsidised the APA by a total of £1,914.15.2 to fund the two missions at Maloga and Warangesda with a combined population of 225, or £8.5 per person. The APA had privately raised £959.7.8 to cover the full costs of both missions. So, in fact, the APA's total expenditure was £2,874.2.10 on 225 persons, or £12.77 per person – that is, more than three-and-a-half times that spent on non-APA locations.[141] This discrepancy was maintained over the remainder of the decade, and in 1890 the Board made the point that because the missions were almost entirely funded by government, control should be 'transferred from the Association to the Government'.[142] In the meantime, the Board insisted that the APA adhere to the rule that 'any expenditure beyond that for rations, clothing and necessaries must be submitted to the Board for approval'.[143] Uneasy with the Board's scrutiny of its finances, in October 1891 the APA tried to bypass the Board and sought funding directly from parliament, and also suggested a policy initiative that a Central Training Home for Aboriginal children be established.[144] In March 1892 the Board roundly criticised

---

139 *APBR* 1883–84, 3.
140 Quoted in the *APBR* 1885, 4.
141 These calculations have not included the shillings and pence but simply the pounds divided by the number of people.
142 *APBM*, 19 February 1891, Item 1.
143 *APBM*, 16 July 1891, Item 2.
144 *APBM*, 29 October 1891, Item 1.

the APA's many statements that were 'calculated to prejudice the public mind against the operations of this Board'.[145] In October 1892 the Board passed the following motion: 'in the opinion of the Board the time had arrived when the sole management of the aborigines should be vested in the Board'.[146]

Fiona Davis suggests that by 1894 the relationship between the two organisations had 'reached a crisis'.[147] In the same year the Board decided to send Fosbery and Board member W.H. Suttor to inspect Cumeroogunga and Brewarrina on the report of 'numerous persons' claiming mismanagement at both stations.[148] As a consequence of these inspections, the Board persuaded the colonial secretary to put in place Local Boards of Advice and Management for each Aboriginal station.[149] By 1897 the accumulated pressure applied by the Board and the APA's inability to raise private funds forced the APA to relinquish its hold on the three Aboriginal stations and they were transferred to the Board. However, right to the end, the APA tried to frustrate the Board by not handing over its books. The *Sydney Morning Herald* reported that the Board decided to inform the colonial secretary of the 'inconvenience caused by the delay in the transfer of books, etc., from the Aborigines Protection Association and urge that instructions be given to make the transfer'.[150]

The uneasy relationship between the Board and the APA had lasted almost 15 years. It demonstrated the Board's inability to control what it believed was its domain. Although there is no direct corollary that the APA stymied or prevented Board policy development, the situation was clearly unusual. The Board's impotency over this issue certainly caused it much irritation and may well have contributed to its policy drift.

In a holding pattern

In June 1883 the Board began cautiously. It soon realised the difficult task of supporting Aboriginal people across the far-flung colony, with the huge distances involved, and immediately accessed the services of the

---

145 *APBM*, 17 March 1892, Item 8.
146 *APBM*, 27 October 1892, Item 1.
147 Davis, *Australian Settler Colonialism*, 22.
148 *APBR* 1894–95, 3.
149 *APBR* 1894–95, 3.
150 *SMH*, 18 June 1897, 7.

New South Wales Police Force to undertake the distribution of the rations and organise the tenders for other supplies and equipment. With only one paid member, the secretary, all members were honorary: busy men with little time to spend on Aboriginal affairs and, like their Board chair, none appeared to actively pursue policy initiatives.

Under Fosbery's leadership, the Board never addressed various big policy issues: the exclusion of Aboriginal children from the schools, the greater numbers seeking assistance, and the increase in the 'half-caste' population. These questions appeared too difficult, and even perhaps worrying. Fosbery's policy drift allowed for comparative flexibility of movement between reserves and stations, but this would not be tolerated under new personnel. Peter Read reflects that the 'drift to greater force was not inevitable'. The Board could have allowed Aboriginal people to 'come and go as they pleased on unmanaged reserves which they had a hand in selecting'.[151] Fosbery's reluctance to follow Victoria's lead was a reprieve for the Aboriginal people of New South Wales. However, the policy void 'left the door open' for others to fill. Harsh policies would come, particularly concerning the 'quadroon' and 'octoroon' population and Aboriginal children.

Fosbery's initial vision of Aboriginal people quietly residing by riverbanks with their children in school was never going to materialise. The mere care of the old and infirm, the supply of boats, blankets, fishing tackle, huts and rations, would not be enough to assuage more pressing 'problems'. Men with more drive and tenacity to push through controversial policies would 'solve' the Board's dilemma of what to do with the Aboriginal people in the new state of New South Wales. In the first instance, it was afforded by George Edward Ardill, a single-minded Baptist evangelical who provided a policy impetus that would begin to reshape the Board.

---

151 Read, *A Hundred Years War*, 52.

3

The zealot from Parramatta

As we have seen, the first 15 years of the New South Wales Aboriginal Protection Board's existence were characterised by modest action and policy drift. Economic disruption had brought many more Aboriginal people within its purview, but the Board took a very minor role in resolving key policy issues of the period. However, a distinct change in Board activity and focus coincided with the appointment to the Board of George Edward Ardill in 1897. Ardill had been the secretary to the powerful Aborigines Protection Association (APA) and his presence on the Board provided an impetus for a shift in policy focus and a general increase in Board activity. Ardill became the *go-to* man. He was tasked with the resolution of some 'difficult' Board situations and provided the motivation for the increased removal of Aboriginal children from their communities. He was a fixer, a driver, an obsessive man spurred on by his evangelism and self-belief.

The evangelical activist

Born into a family of Baptists in 1857, George Ardill (Figure 3.1) completed his elementary education in the 1860s in Parramatta, and as a young man developed 'strict principles, was a teetotaller and a street preacher'. In his 20s, he decided to 'devote himself full-time to organising charities and to evangelism'.[1] In his biographical account of George Ardill, Bruce Thornton suggests that a pivotal event in his early life set Ardill on a path of 'rescue'.

---

1   Ramsland, 'Ardill, George'; Radi, 'Ardill, George Edward (1857–1945)'.

93

A woman approached him in 1882 asking for help and he agreed to meet her the next day where she lived, at 'the graveyard in Devonshire Street'. The following day, Ardill found a considerable number of men, women and children living among the tombstones with no shelter or any other facilities at all. It was close to the Benevolent Asylum where there were daily distributions of 'outdoor relief' and where one might pick up cast-off clothing. The 'atmosphere of hopelessness and utter despair' clearly had an impact on the young Ardill.[2]

Figure 3.1: George Edward Ardill.
Source: *The Rescue* 2, no. 10 (August 1882): 2. Mitchell Library, State Library of New South Wales.

He was not alone in his desire to rescue the poor. The concern for neglected and delinquent children was a worldwide phenomenon, which accelerated in the middle to later nineteenth century.[3] The New South Wales Government subsidised several charities as a major method of social welfare provision.[4] The Benevolent Society, founded in 1818, was the key driver in the establishment of asylums, the first of which was located in Pitt Street in Sydney. Ann O'Brien argues that the middle class felt responsible for proselytisation and philanthropy. Those in society who were already 'saved' and morally superior had to uplift those who were less fortunate; but there was also the view that 'financial assistance should be kept to a minimum' to place a strong emphasis on self-help.[5] George Ardill identified strongly with the sentiment of self-help and embraced the 'rescue' of children, an ideology inspired by British evangelicals in the 1860s and 1870s.[6] By his early 40s, Ardill was the director of 12 societies; he had created a mini-empire of institutions for the homeless and for neglected children in the Sydney region.[7]

---

2 Thornton, *Haste to the Rescue*, 16.
3 Parry, 'Such a Longing', 23. For a short and useful overview of charities from the early 1800s to the present, see O'Brien, 'Charity and Philanthropy', 18–28. For a broad overview see Dickey, *No Charity There*, Chapter 3. See also O'Brien's *Poverty's Prison*, Chapters 18, 19 and 20.
4 Horsburgh, 'Subsidy and Control', 64.
5 O'Brien, *Poverty's Prison*, 189–90.
6 Musgrove, *The Scars Remain*, 37.
7 Ramsland, 'Ardill, George'.

Ardill's Homes

In 1882, at the age of 25, Ardill formed the Blue Ribbon Gospel Army, a temperance organisation that provided for the destitute in Sydney. In 1884 he founded the All-night Refuge, which was an austere affair: a sparsely furnished Methodist shelter where he compelled inmates to attend his religious services. He established the Lying-In Hospital, known as the Home of Hope for Friendless and Fallen, which provided support for single pregnant women. He believed the 'fallen' should be encouraged to acquire skills that should fit them for a life of 'usefulness in the future' and residents were expected to do the 'washing, cooking and cleaning – while others took care of the children'.[8]

In 1886 he opened Our Babies Home and in 1887 Our Children's Home at Liverpool was established, followed by Our Boys Farm Home in Camden in 1890. He also founded, in 1890, the Sydney Rescue Work Society, which became the umbrella organisation for all his Homes. Children who were admitted to Ardill's Homes were those found on the streets who were either needy or friendless, or victims of vice, ill-treatment and neglect. Special officers from the Rescue Work Society, on the lookout across Sydney and in other places, picked up the children and took them to Ardill.[9] In some cases they were taken before magistrates as juvenile offenders and were committed to the care of Homes. Some children were brought to Ardill's Homes by their parents and surrendered as 'uncontrollable'.[10] Ardill also arranged for the adoption of children and there were regular advertisements in the official monthly newsletter of the society, *The Rescue*:

> Applicants are assured that no interference on the part of the mother of the child need be feared, indeed, in most cases, the address of the person adopting the child is not given to the mother, as she has full confidence in the judgment in the Director [Ardill] as to securing a good home.[11]

---

8   Thornton, *Haste to the Rescue*, 57.
9   The *Industrial Schools Act 1866* (NSW) allowed a child under 16 years to be committed to an industrial school if found 'wandering about' with reputed thieves. The police or 'any other person' could apprehend a child who was homeless or begging. Ardill's officers could do this and remain within the law. See O'Brien, *Poverty's Prison*, 146.
10 Thornton, *Haste to the Rescue*, 77.
11 *The Rescue*, 26 March 1902, 12.

Although these were well-publicised advertisements, there was a cloak of secrecy surrounding all the personal arrangements to preserve anonymity and confidentiality. There appeared to be little scrutiny into how Ardill's Homes were run. The protocols – if there were any – regarding parental consent, the selection of adoptive parents and the alteration of the child's identity all remain unknown. However, it is known that 'solicitors were very often involved' so there must have been some questionable practices.[12] The organisation and administration of all Ardill's establishments were undertaken by his own people within the Sydney Rescue Work Society. Our Boys Farm Home in Camden (Figure 3.2), set up in 1890 on the edge of Dharawal Country, was designed to apprentice out boys to local farms in the Camden district to acquire farming and work skills that would be useful for them in the future. It was still operating decades into the twentieth century, and from the two following accounts it was not a happy place.

Figure 3.2: Our Boys Farm Home, Camden. Two Aboriginal boys can be seen, second from the far right and one in front of the matron.
Source: Camden Historical Society Archives, Photo Files, CHS 0084.

---

12   Thornton, *Haste to the Rescue*, 78.

Mrs Wynne Stuckey, interviewed by Sylvia Hanson in February 2005, spoke of the time in the late 1930s when her father was the Methodist minister for Camden. She remembered 'Mr Ardill as dreadful man [and] to have the children for a meal they would have to go to him on bended knees to ask permission'. 'All the town knew the boys were half starved and only had syrup sandwiches for lunch'.[13] Eric (Slim) Johnson, born in 1927, who after six years in an orphanage in Baulkham Hills was transferred to Camden Boys Home, echoes Mrs Stuckey concerns. The home was run by two women, Matron Coulson and Sister Teasdale, who were very strict. Eric recalled:

> We were never allowed to make friends or talk or play games. We had to walk to school ... We were not allowed to wear shoes and I remember, in winter, on the way to school there would be cows lying in the fields. We would chase each [cow] away in turn to stand for a little while where they had warmed up the grass with their bodies ... the only time we were allowed to wear shoes was to church.
>
> One night, I had just got out of the bath when the matron came in carrying her four foot cane. She sent the boys outside and locked the bathroom door. I remember it vividly to this day. She said, So you like to sing Johnson? Well I'll give you something to sing about, and she laid into my bare body with her cane 78 times – I was about 12 years old at the time. (You were not allowed to sing at any time.)[14]

These instances were probably not isolated and reflect reports of institutional abuse of orphans that persisted well into the twentieth century.[15]

Ardill was a tireless worker who regularly conducted compulsory religious services for his inmates and believed that the 'fallen' could only be rehabilitated through the 'fear of God', and in the principles of obedience, honesty and industry. Ardill held to the view that laundry work for the

---

13   Mrs Wynne Stuckey, interviewed by Sylvia Hansen, February 2005, File: Camden Boys Home, Camden Historical Society Archives. It is unclear who had to go 'on bended knee' but the context suggests that it was probably the Methodist minister and his wife and not the boys from the Home.
14   Eric (Slim) Johnson to Paula Douglas, letter, 17 February 1914, File: Camden Boys Home, Camden Historical Society Archives.
15   Shurlee Swain has compiled a list of all the inquiries into child institutions, between 1852 and 2013. From 1990 up until 2013, some 234 separate homes and institutions, subject to investigation, resulted in many instances of various cases of child abuse. See Swain, *History of Australian Inquires Reviewing Institutions Providing Care for Children*.

'fallen' women was the way to 'cleanse the soul'.[16] He was a 'driven-man' who ruled through fear, within strict religious principles demanding the full compliance of his rules and regulations. John Ramsland portrays him as one who was 'absolutely certain of the validity of his notions'.[17]

Controversy and Ardill

Ardill's evangelism, fanaticism and perhaps even impropriety got him into trouble. In August 1890 he wrote a letter of complaint to the colonial secretary regarding harassment while conducting his regular religious services in the Sydney Domain. A large group of wharfies who were on strike accused Ardill of providing ex-prisoners from The Discharged Prisoners Mission (another of Ardill's Homes) to help break the strike. A local constable reported that 'several thousand people assembled' and Ardill instructed the police to arrest a man for disturbing his meeting. The crowd then closed around Ardill and the police had to escort him to a cab for safety.[18]

In December 1890, Ardill was attacked by the *Australian Workman* newspaper, which accused him of hypocrisy, mismanagement and exploitation concerning the House of Hope for Friendless and Fallen in 1890–91. Ardill was accused of using (11) rooms in the House of Hope to house his own family and 'took advantage of his position to perpetrate iniquity'. The paper had also accused Ardill of having a Maori girl who had become pregnant while in his employ.[19] Ardill sued the paper and publisher for libel and sought damages of £2,000 and defended all charges. He admitted that his family lived there but only occupied five rooms and not 11; that the girl in question was not Maori but a 'half-caste' Aboriginal girl; and that, while she was pregnant, he was not the father and had no inappropriate relations with her. The jury found in Ardill's favour. Despite his vindication Ardill's behaviour must have certainly

---

16 Parry, 'Such a Longing', 170.
17 Ramsland, 'Ardill, George'.
18 Extract of a report by Senior Constable Clarke of the incident that took place in the (Sydney) Domain, 31 August 1890, Colonial Secretary's In-Letters (hereafter CSIL), 5/5992, Item 90/10337, State Records of New South Wales (hereafter SRNSW).
19 *Evening News*, 3 July 1891, 6. The coverage of the trial appeared in the Melbourne *Age*. It reported that inmates sometimes 'went without'; the women in the Home 'received no wages' for their work in the laundry, complained of their treatment and had 'scaled walls to get out of the house': *The Age*, 7 July 1891, 5.

raised a few eyebrows among the philanthropic community in Sydney; the *Australian Workman* wrote that 'Ardill has long been suspected of hypocrisy and questionable honesty'.[20]

Ardill was involved in another scandal that concerned boys interned on the ship *Vernon* (Figure 3.3). The *Industrial Schools Act 1886* (NSW) was introduced to control children who were neglected and wandering the streets 'begging, abandoned or committing a crime'. The *Vernon*, a former merchant sailing ship, was purchased by the New South Wales Government in 1867, refitted as a public industrial school and moored between the Government Domain and Garden Island. Boys were placed on the ship (some as young as three) to be given 'moral training, nautical and industrial training and instruction and elementary schooling'.[21]

Figure 3.3: Naval Training Ship *Vernon*.
Source: SLNSW, c1888, bep_04427.1E1673451 Naval Training Ship 'Vernon' with cadets' washing between the masts – Sydney – IE1673452 – FL1673459 – Call no. At Work and Play – 04427.

---

20 *Australian Workman*, 7 March 1891, 2.
21 Dunn, 'Vernon Nautical Training Ship'. See also O'Brien, *Poverty's Prison,* 145–50, for a summary of what was expected of the boys on the ship and the underlying assumptions thereof.

In July 1890, the *Bathurst Free Press* stated that a Joe Bragg, and others, had produced a pamphlet that reflected poorly on the management of the *Vernon* and charged the boys with being guilty of 'abominable practices'. The issue was raised in parliament and Mr Carruthers MLA asserted that Mr Ardill was behind Bragg's accusations.[22] In debate, Mr Inglis MLA, who knew Ardill, was moved to say: 'I have looked upon that gentleman [Ardill] with a considerable amount of doubt for some time'. He intimated that the problem was a matter of honesty.[23] Bragg's pamphlet had accused the boys 'with every conceivable crime under the sun – bestiality, self-abuse, sodomy and everything else that is atrocious'.[24] The *Sydney Morning Herald* revealed that Joe Bragg had committed a string of serious criminal offences, knew Ardill well and had been working for him at the time of the publication. Ardill refuted all accusations regarding his role in the publication as well as Carruthers' claim that he 'was a philanthropist for the sake of gain'. Ardill's connection with the publication was never proven. Carruthers alleged, however, that he was an interested party; Ardill's Boys Homes (at Liverpool and Camden) were in competition with the *Vernon* and in the event of the *Vernon* closing he would receive many of the boys.[25]

This overall picture of Ardill is problematic. Ardill's personal scrapbooks suggest that he was obsessed with articles concerning 'fallen women', child abuse and pornography.[26] Anne O'Brien poses that Ardill not only saw men as 'despoilers' who 'basely deceived', he also saw women as having an 'aggressive desire to show their affection'.[27] Despite his strange proclivities, Ardill's character and actions should be viewed in the context of his fervent evangelicalism. He was undoubtedly a committed philanthropist, who wanted to help pregnant girls, ex-criminals and orphaned children. Ardill's Baptist upbringing, his strict adherence to temperance and his preaching were all embodiments of self-improvement and evangelicalism that emerged as energising forces in nineteenth-century Britain. These forces had their origins, as American historian Trygve Tholfsen has shown, in the turbulent early decades of the century when the working class, striving not to be ignored and marginalised, gave its 'unqualified allegiance to an ethic of improvement which exalted the intellectual and moral development of the

---

22   *Bathurst Free Press*, 12 July 1890, 5.
23   NSW, *Parliamentary Debates*, Legislative Assembly, 10 July 1890, 2025 (Inglis).
24   NSW, *Parliamentary Debates*, Legislative Assembly, 10 July 1890, 2019 (Copeland).
25   *Sydney Morning Herald* (hereafter *SMH*), 13 August 1890, 2.
26   Gapps, 'Mr Ardill's Scrapbook: Alternative Sources for Biography', 102. Stephen Gapps was a distant relative: Ardill was the brother of Stephen's grandmother's grandfather.
27   Quoted in O'Brien, *Poverty's Prison*, 121.

individual as the highest good'. The middle class adopted the same language and values and on 'every occasion' preached to the workers the gospel of 'improvement, social advancement, respectability and class harmony'.[28] These views were shared by many emigrant families and Ardill was immersed in these philosophies and driven by them. In 1901 the Evangelical Council of New South Wales sponsored large-scale interdenominational evangelism at outdoor meetings; one, held during November in Hyde Park, attracted 30,000 each night. John See (the Premier of New South Wales and Protection Board member) defended the right of the 'mission' to erect large tents in public places as it would 'benefit the conditions and improve the morals of the people'.[29] Ardill's religious focus on the uplift and salvation of the fallen was a mainstream middle-class activity.

Ardill's preoccupation with the need to regulate women and children helps explain the marked changes in Board activities after his accession in 1897. Under his dogged sway, the Board increased its activity in the removal of children – especially girls – without a legislative mandate.

The antagonist joins the Board

There was no doubt that Ardill was a controversial figure. Ardill's appointment to the Board on 18 October 1897 was result of the APA's 'forced' transfer of power over the Aboriginal stations at Cumeroogunga, Warangesda and Brewarrina in late 1897. Surprisingly, there was no apparent objection, from the Board, to his appointment. The Board was no stranger to Ardill. It had dealt with him for the last decade in his role as secretary to the powerful APA. As discussed in Chapter 2, the Board had had a fractious relationship with the APA and with Ardill over ongoing issues of funding and financial accountability. It seems strange that no protest was raised to Ardill's choice as a Board member. The 1898 Aboriginal Protection Board (APB) report gives some clues:

> The Council of the Aborigines Protection Association were given representation on the Board by their appointment of (Messrs Carpenter and Ardill) so that their work in connection with the religious instruction of the Aborigines might be continued.[30]

---

28 Tholfsen, 'The Intellectual Origins of Mid-Victorian Stability', 61–66.
29 Broome, *Treasure in Earthen Vessels*, 56–57.
30 *Protection of Aborigines: Report of the Board* (the APB Report: hereafter *APBR*) 1898, 3. Accessed via *Journal of the Legislative Council*, Q328.9106/7, *NSW Parliamentary Papers, Consolidated Index* (hereafter *Journal of LC*), State Library of New South Wales (hereafter SLNSW), Vol. 57, Part 1.

Perhaps the government (who appointed Board members) was genuine in the desire to maintain a 'religious connection'; or perhaps it considered that Ardill was easier to control by having him inside the tent as a Board member. Possibly, Ardill's and Carpenter's appointments were some form of inducement for the APA to relinquish control of its three Aboriginal stations, or perhaps it was a form of compensation for the APA's 'defeat'. Conceivably, Ardill insisted that the price of the APA's concession was a continuing presence for him and his colleague in Aboriginal affairs on the Board and he likely argued that his many Homes, already established, could provide immediate placement of Aboriginal children.[31] Some have suggested that the Board 'appeared to welcome' Ardill, even though he had been 'antagonistic' towards it in the past'.[32] However, considering his reputation, it seems just as likely that it was a cautious welcome indeed.

From the outset, Ardill made his presence felt in two ways: as a general 'fixer' and as a facilitator for the removal of Aboriginal children from their families. Unlike many on the Board, Ardill's name often appeared as the person to have carriage of issues. From October 1897 until the end of 1900, comprising 163 Board meetings, Ardill's name was mentioned in the minutes 13 times in the carriage of certain tasks; only one other Board member was tasked with a duty during that time.[33] Ardill was an active Board member. For instance, he offered to deal with a problem in August 1899 at Lake Illawarra where he had to 'warn' a Mr Vidler from the Aborigines' Mission to stay away from the Aboriginal people there. In August 1898 he was asked to investigate a long-running dispute at the Brungle Aboriginal Station (east of Gundagai) between the teacher-manager J. Ussher and the Aboriginal residents. Ussher was blamed for the problems, Ardill's version of events was accepted and Ussher dismissed.[34]

---

31 There is no evidence to suggest this, but his reputation for single-mindedly pursuing his agenda would clearly raise the possibility.
32 Parry, 'Such a Longing', 163.
33 APB Minutes (hereafter *APBM*), October 1897 to December 1900 (163 meetings were held during this period). All *APBM* accessed via: Minute Books (Aborigines Welfare Board), NRS 2, NSW Department of Aboriginal Affairs, Sydney.
34 The Board was unhappy with interference from Missionary Vidler in the Aboriginal camp at Lake Illawarra. Vidler wanted the camp moved to Port Kembla where it was not so isolated (*Evening News*, 21 July 1899, 3), but the Board disapproved and recorded: 'that prior to Vidler's visit the Aboriginals were happy and contented now they are unreasonable and discontented' (*APBM*, 24 August 1899, Item 1). There had been several complaints about J. Ussher from the Aboriginal residents and they often refused to work. Ussher was also 'agisting animals for his own gain on the Station'. See Read, *A Hundred Years War*, 40–41. After Ardill's visit, Ussher complained to the local Wagga Wagga police that he felt 'persecuted and ridiculed', Parry, 'Such a Longing', 172.

Ardill also sought to influence appointments to the APB. In November 1899, he wrote to the colonial secretary and urged the selection of a Mr Henry Trenchard to the Board, which was subsequently approved.[35] The Board had not had a member who so clearly dominated proceedings before.

'If a suitable girl can be found'

Ardill was ostensibly appointed to the Board to exert religious influence, but this was not where he found his niche. His focus became the placement of Aboriginal children into apprenticeships and sometimes into his own Homes. Prior to his membership of the APB, Ardill had already been involved with the placement of Aboriginal children into domestic situations. The first instance of Ardill, while secretary of the APA, placing an Aboriginal girl in service was in April 1892. He escorted girls to and from the mission at Warangesda, put them into service or into his own Homes in Sydney, and sorted out disputes with employers.[36] The Board had also put Aboriginal children into service well before it acquired legislative power to do so in 1909. During the 1890s the Board 'asked police to encourage young adults to "take service", but, because it had no power to apprentice children or youths, had to rely on families to make informal arrangements themselves'.[37] Or, as Peter Read writes, the Board resorted to 'threats and promises' if required. For example, after the Warangesda Dormitory was built in 1893 the Board offered the parents free rail trips home if they would leave their girls.[38] Members of the public also initiated removals. The Board minutes reveal many instances of public individuals requesting Aboriginal children to become domestic servants and labourers. In June 1898 when a particular resident of Gilgandra requested 'an aboriginal girl as a domestic servant' the Board's response was to 'request in the district ... if a suitable girl can be found in any of the camps, if not ... to see if [there is] one at Brewarrina'. The police at Gulargambone reported a month later that there was a 'suitable girl in the camp at that place' and the APB wrote to the resident at Gilgandra.[39]

---

35 Ardill to Colonial Secretary, CSIL, 1900, 5/6512, Item 99/22038 (SRNSW).
36 *Conservation Management Plan – Warangesda Aboriginal Mission & Station*, 21.
37 Parry, 'Such a Longing', 169.
38 Read, *The Stolen Generations*, 7.
39 *APBM*, 9 June 1898, Item 1; *APBM*, 7 July 1898, Item 2.

There was no apparent vetting process of the resident at Gilgandra by the Board nor any indication that the Board accessed official channels for these removals.[40]

After the appointment of Ardill to the Board there was a significant increase in 'removal activity'. Peter Read has been the only historian to venture that an estimated 300 Aboriginal children were removed during the period 1883 until 1909, a period when the Board had no specific legislative powers to do so.[41] Between these years no complete register or record was kept of such removals.[42] However, analysis of the Board minutes is useful in providing insight to this activity, as well as confirmation of increased removals after Ardill's arrival. The extant Board minutes from 1883 to March 1910 record 23 instances of discussions regarding the removal of children. However, the Board minutes are missing for 14 years and four months of this 27-year period.[43] Table 3.1 depicts the number of removals during the periods when the Board minutes are available. Periods 1, 2 and 3 represent times when the minutes are available prior to March 1910. Period 4 represents the first six-month period after legislation was enacted. I have included this period to draw an immediate comparison as a result of the Board's access to legislation.

---

40   The *Neglected and Juvenile Offenders Act 1905* (NSW) defined the powers of the Children's Court; providing that children (over 5 and under 16) were 'neglected or uncontrollable' they could be dealt with by the court. Up until 1905 there were a number of NSW Acts that dealt with the court's powers: the *Public Instruction Act 1880* allowed it to punish parents for not sending their children to school; the *State Children Relief Act 1881* let it 'board out' children and also created the State Children's Relief Board; the *Children's Protection Act 1892* enabled a magistrate to hand over a child to a home for destitute or neglected children; the *Reformatory and Industrial Schools Act 1901* made provisions for offenders under 16 and for vagrant and destitute children; the *Deserted Wives and Children's Act 1901* provided for legal custody of children; the State Children's Bill 1902 provided for a court to deal with criminal offences, paternity cases, assault and neglect and destitution and proposed to give it the power to commit children to the State Relief Board. Accessed via: childrenscourt.nsw.gov.au/Documents/History.
41   Due to a 'lack of records' for this period, Read only made an estimation: Read, *The Stolen Generations*, 11.
42   Technically, as journalist Keith Windschuttle points out, there are some records of children removed to Board institutions at Bomaderry, Singleton and Cootamundra from 1907 onwards. Windschuttle, *The Fabrication of Aboriginal History*, 75. See Chapter 6 for all details of removals from 1916.
43   Missing Board minutes: June 1883 to 25 September 1890 (7 years and 3 months); 4 July 1901 to 23 May 1905 (3 years and 10 months); 11 December 1906 to 17 March 1910 (3 years and 3 months).

Table 3.1: Numbers of Aboriginal children removed prior to, and following, Ardill's appointment to the Board during four periods (when minutes are available).

Periods of available Board Minutes	Number of removals recorded	Monthly average	Yearly average
September 1890 – October 1897 (85 months); Prior to Ardill's appointment	2	0.024	0.28
October 1897 – May 1901 (31 months); Ardill a Board member	18	0.58	7.0
June 1905 – November 1906 (17 months); Ardill a Board member	3	0.18	2.16
First six months under legislation: 2 June 1910 – 15 December 1910; Ardill a Board member	55	9.17	110

Source: APB minutes for appropriate years.

During the first period of just over seven years, and prior to Ardill's appointment on October 1897, there were only two removals recorded. However, from 1897, during the next 31-month period that Ardill was a Board member, there was a spike of 18 entries; and Ardill is specially mentioned in four of these removals.[44] In the third period there were only three removals recorded, but, importantly, in October 1906, the minutes suggest significant removal activity. The local board at Warangesda asked the manager to

> interview Parents *of all girls* [presumably in the district, my emphasis] to see if they will allow them to go into the Dormitory [at Warangesda] and any that object should be asked the reasons for their objection.[45]

We will never know how many removals took place in the years where Board minutes are missing – that is from May 1901 until June 1905 and from November 1906 until March 1910. However, if the Board's policy, from October 1906, of interviewing all parents was statewide, then the number of removals from 1906 to 1910 (a period of four years) may

---

44 In April 1900, the Board minutes record that 'Ardill agreed to receive "a half-caste" girl into his Children's Home at Liverpool as long as she was brought from Narrabri' (*APBM*, 5 April 1900, Item 1). A month later a minute entry read, that the 'girl brought from Narrabri from Sydney, by an officer of the Sydney Rescue Work Society; also, the Sydney Rescue Work Society brought a young Aboriginal boy from Moree who was admitted to the Benevolent Asylum' (*APBM*, 10 May 1900, Item 4). Ardill reported on a girl at Carisbrooke private hospital at Potts Point (*APBM*, 3 May 1900, Item 13).

45 *APBM*, 16 October 1906, Item 6.

have been higher than two per year as per the previous 17 months. There may of course have been removals that were *never* recorded. More telling perhaps was that after 2 June 1910, when the *Aborigines Protection Act 1909* (NSW) became law, there was an unprecedented spike in removals and 55 children were removed in just six months. This equates to 110 per year – an extraordinary increase.

The records are scant and incomplete, but there seems little doubt that the increase in removals coincided with Ardill's arrival on the Board. With Ardill's influence, even without legislative authority, the Board was becoming a powerful body. By the turn of the century it could refuse or withhold rations and equipment to force compliance, decline rail passes to stymie travel, determine land grants, hire and fire station managers, and remove children without a transparent process. However, the power of the Board was challenged. The Aboriginal residents at La Perouse, and its supporters, opposed the Board's intention to remove the community.

La Perouse: 'This camp should be broken up'

The Board's attempt to remove the Aboriginal community at La Perouse towards the end of 1900 was hubris. This was the Board's first attempt at overt coercive policy, and it failed. Unlike the mix of Aboriginal families and individuals who were removed by the police from the government boatshed at Circular Quay in 1881 (see Chapter 1), the La Perouse community had roots in the area reaching back beyond 1788. Like the boatshed residents, the La Perouse community was considered by the Board to be too close to the city and was attracting 'unsavoury elements'. However, the Board failed to recognise two major factors in its bid to remove the residents. First, the Aboriginal residents had developed strong ties with influential Sydney people such as high-profile parliamentarian and Board member Richard Hill and the establishment of the New South Wales Aborigines Mission at La Perouse in the mid-1890s contributed powerful allies who argued strongly for the community to remain.[46] Second, the Board failed to understand the degree to which Aboriginal

---

46 See Chapter 1 for reference to Richard Hill and the Sydney Aborigines Committee established in the 1840s with men such as Daniel Egan, Bob Nichols and George Hill. For more on Richard Hill, see also Irish, *Hidden in Plain View*, 71, 81, 116, 118–19, and 128–29.

residents could mobilise these networks against the Board. At another level, the attempt exposed the disparate nature of the Board. Some members acted alone, some opposed the policy position and, paradoxically, a Board member who was the current premier of New South Wales, as final arbiter, thwarted Board policy.

La Perouse is etched in the history of Australia. It stands as a reminder of both the presence of competing imperial players and their interaction with the local Aboriginal populations at the time of Australia's colonisation. As Captain Arthur Phillip sailed out of Botany Bay on 26 January 1788 for Port Jackson, two French ships – the *Bussole* and the *Astrolabe* – sailed in under the command of Jean-Francoise La Perouse. The French, under instructions to 'observe the new British colony', remained for six weeks on the northern headland of Botany Bay while Phillip established the site of Sydney.[47] La Perouse sailed out of Botany Bay in March 1788 and was never seen again, his ship lost at sea. Aboriginal people encountered both Phillip and La Perouse, as they had done with Cook 18 years previously. Today there are monuments to all three European men at Botany Bay, as well as structures and features of the landscape named after them.[48] However, there is no such obvious recognition of the original inhabitants. Perhaps markers are not needed, because the La Perouse community remains a vibrant, publicly engaged community to this day.[49] It is fitting then that the Aboriginal people of La Perouse inflicted the first setback for the APB.

Since 1883, as part of its function, the ABP had supplied Aboriginal families at La Perouse with rations and other essentials. From 1883 up to the beginning of the 1890s the population had never been large, fluctuating between the mid-teens and high 20s. However, from the 1890s the La Perouse Aboriginal community began to increase. The rise in numbers was generated by two factors. First, regular Board visits to Aboriginal locations/camps around the city to obtain statistical data and dispense rations applied a level of unwanted scrutiny. For example, Aboriginal groups had established themselves at the public reserve at Rushcutters Bay and the Board requested the police to move them on, but

---

47 Nugent, 'Botany Bay', 27.
48 These are the La Perouse Monument (1828), a public reserve on the southern side of Botany Bay at Kurnell (1899) dedicated to Cook's landing and a monument to the landing place of Arthur Phillip at Yarra Bay on the northern shores of the bay (1956). Local names include Captain Cook Drive, Phillip Bay, Frenchman's Beach and La Perouse.
49 Irish, *Hidden in Plain View*, 33 and 109.

they simply moved to other locations at Rose Bay and then returned in the evening. However, this increasing harassment made the 'security and stability' of the La Perouse community 'more attractive' and some moved there.[50] Second, the rising European population of suburban Sydney generated more calls for local Aboriginal people to be 'moved on'. In 1893 the Aboriginal group at Watsons Bay increased to over 15 and the local police determined they would be a nuisance to the European community. The Board requested that the police move them on and 'furnish requisites for their passages to the places from whence they came'. Two months later the camp was broken up.[51] Some of this group may well have moved to La Perouse, as there was a significant increase in the population in that year (see Figure 3.5).

Mission activity

In the early 1890s the La Perouse community became a focus for missionary endeavours. On 3 July 1893, 'four Christian Endeavourers' met at the vestry of the Petersham Congregational Church and held the first meeting of the 'Aborigines Committee'. A lantern evening was arranged (lantern and sheet for the slides provided by George Ardill) under the convenorship of a Miss J. Watson, with the expressed intention of raising funds to establish a mission at La Perouse.[52] Two months later the Petersham Congregational Christian Endeavour Society sought formal permission from the APB to erect a Mission House at La Perouse.[53] The Board initially rejected the appeal and determined it would be 'extremely undesirable to encourage any aborigine to La Perouse who do not belong to the place ... as they are constantly attracted to the city'.[54] The Endeavour Society persisted, and in October 1893 a further delegation that included George Ardill (as secretary of the APA, the body advocating the mission), put their case to the APB. This time the Board accepted the delegation's commitment that no 'new' Aboriginal people would be attracted to the community, welcomed an educational focus and agreed

---

50   Irish, *Hidden in Plain View*, 127.
51   *APBM*, 31 August 1893, Item 1; *APBM*, 5 October 1983, Item 3.
52   Telfer, *Amongst Australian Aborigines*, 12–13.
53   The Petersham Endeavour Society was part of a broad umbrella movement called the Australian Christian Endeavour Union. It produced a monthly journal published out of Melbourne that noted all the Christian 'endeavours' taking place in all the states and in New Zealand.
54   *APBM*, 14 September 1893, Item 8.

to erect a building.⁵⁵ The Christian Endeavour Society began a full-time mission at La Perouse in 1894 with Miss J. Watson as missionary.⁵⁶ Retta Dixon became the first resident missionary in 1897.⁵⁷

Figure 3.4: The Christian Endeavour Mission Church.
Source: Telfer, *Amongst Australian Aborigines*, 19.

The national body, the Australian Christian Endeavour Union, recognised the achievement in the December edition of its newsletter *The Golden Link*: 'It is with much pleasure that we record the fact that the long-talked of "Endeavour House" at La Perouse … is at last a reality'.⁵⁸ The La Perouse Aborigines Mission Committee was formally established in August 1895. Its members were crucial to the resistance against the removal of the community.

A few months prior to the establishment of Endeavour House, the Board and missionaries received some critical press attention. A lengthy piece in the *Bird O' Freedom* in June 1894 was scathing of the interaction between the Aboriginal residents and the white 'rough toughs and vagabonds' of the city. It heavily criticised the Board for not properly protecting the camp and preventing 'wild uncouth orgies', describing the

---

55   *APBM*, 14 September 1893, Item 8; *APBM*, 5 October 1893, Item 8.
56   Harris, *One Blood*, 554; Irish, 'Hidden in Plain View', 263–64.
57   Radi, 'Long, Margaret Jane (Retta) (1878–1956)'.
58   *The Golden Link* 3, no. 29, 1 December 1894, 58.

camp as a 'rendezvous for the pushes' and railing against the effects of alcohol on the Aboriginal population. It reminded readers that the soil at La Perouse 'was the undisputed property of their ancestors for … perhaps thousands of years' and accusingly concluded that the 'gentlemen philanthropists, members of the "missions", of the Aborigines Protection Board, and all others' were responsible for the appalling conditions at the camp.[59] Almost a year later, on 23 March 1895, a 7-acre reserve dedicated to the Aboriginal people at La Perouse was officially established. It is unclear who pushed for a reserve, but Richard Hill may have been behind the move to provide some security of tenure, or it may have resulted from the residents wishing to protect themselves from the encroachment of commercialism and missionaries.[60]

By the turn of the century, the La Perouse peninsula was attracting many tourists and Sydney weekenders. It had become a 'landscape of leisure' with daytrippers from the city. The tram from downtown Sydney to La Perouse brought tourists and outdoor enthusiasts, and promoted a local Aboriginal arts and crafts economy.[61] As Europeans rushed to La Perouse, the Board acted to stop the Aboriginal reserve from growing. In June 1896 the Board rejected a request by the La Perouse Mission to build additional housing for Aboriginal people as it would be 'injudicious to build more accommodation for Abs at La P. Especially for men not belonging to the place'. In late 1899 the Board reported 'unsatisfactory conditions' at La Perouse and recommended that the local Sergeant Bruce should 'continue oversight' to prevent non-Aboriginal people from entering the mission and 'warn off' Aboriginal people camping outside the reserve.[62]

Since European settlement the population at La Perouse had never been large and had fluctuated, reflecting Aboriginal movement (Figure 3.5). Its numbers were modest compared to the bigger stations such as Cumeroogunga, the population of which was 239 in December 1900.[63]

---

59 *Bird O' Freedom*, 23 June 1894, 4.
60 Irish, *Hidden in Plain View*, 129.
61 Nugent, 'Revisiting La Perouse', 127; Lambert-Pennington, 'What Remains? Reconciling Repatriation, Aboriginal Culture, Representation and the Past', 314.
62 *APBM*, 18 June 1896, Item 8; *APBM*, 21 December 1897, Item 1.
63 *APBR* 1902, 15. Accessed via *Journal of LC*, Vol. 64, Part 1, 6–7, 1101 (SLNSW).

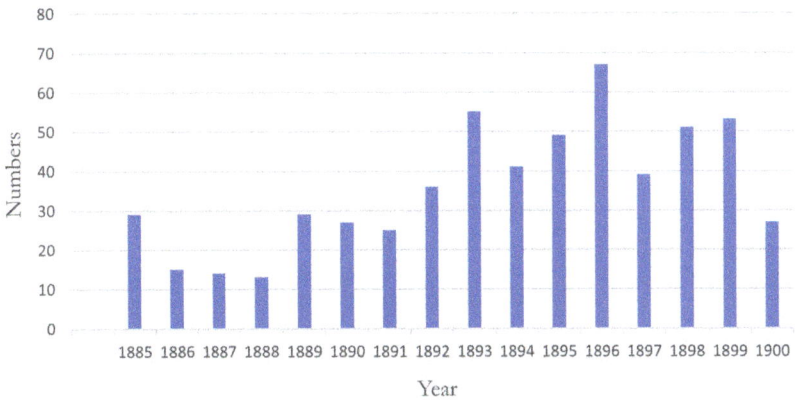

Figure 3.5: Aboriginal population at La Perouse, 1885–1900.
Source: Census as complied by the APB reports 1885 through to 1900.

Ardill's report on La Perouse

In the face of unwanted press attention and adverse police reports that reflected badly on the Board, Ardill was asked to prepare a report on the La Perouse reserve. Ironically, six years before, Ardill in another capacity had pressed the Board to establish the mission at La Perouse. He would now advocate for the removal of the community. His 16 September 1899 report was more a collection of observations and recommendations heavily laced with innuendo about sexual relations, predatory white strangers and the squalor of the camps than an objective appraisal. Ardill detailed the visits of a Mr De Santy and his contact with two young Aboriginal girls. On learning that De Santy had been seen 'out in bush' with the girls, 'ostensibly for the purpose of gathering flowers', Ardill recommended that De Santy 'be precluded from visiting the camp' and that Miss Dixon, the resident missionary, discourage visits from young men to the evening service.[64]

Ardill reported that those living in huts were comfortably housed, but those in tents 'lived in a wretched condition and provision should be made to erect suitable huts for them'. He declared that if new huts could

---

64 Inspection Report of La Perouse, 22 September 1899, *CSIL*, 5/6574, Item 00/23677, 1–3.

not be provided, then the residents should be 'induced' to remove to an inland or coastal station. He then recommended that the *whole* camp be removed:

> Few of the people [Aboriginal residents] are natives of the vicinity and it is my firm conviction that it is advisable that this camp should be broken up, and the people forced to locate at a much greater distance from the City, under proper supervision and with the possibility of some suitable employment ... I would here suggest the desirability of securing a central coast station to which several small groups of aborigines at La Perouse, Port Kembla, and other places could be transferred, and under proper management as at Warangesda, Grafton, Cumeroogunga and Brewarrina.[65]

Ardill had three more suggestions. First, he advised that while the camp remained open, a notice board should be erected at the front gates forbidding non-Aboriginal people to enter. Second, he was convinced of the importance of securing necessary legislation to 'deal effectively with aborigines', and suggested that the draft legislation already prepared by the secretary (of the APB) be dealt with by Board members and submitted to the colonial secretary as soon as possible. Third, he proposed that at least one inspector should be appointed to undertake regular inspections of the various stations and camps.[66]

Apart from his conclusion that the community should be removed, and that other groups should be gathered up and transferred to a central location, Ardill also raised the old white belief that these people did not belong. In the late 1870s, some 20 years before, when public calls grew for the government to *do* something about Aboriginal welfare, Aboriginal people in coastal Sydney were cast 'as migrants who did not belong'.[67] By characterising Aboriginal residents of Sydney as 'belonging to other places', the practice of removing them was justified.[68]

This representation was incorrect. Aboriginal families occupying La Perouse in the 1870s were the descendants of those who had encountered Cook, Phillip and La Perouse in the late eighteenth century. By the 1840s there were several Aboriginal camps in the Sydney area. Paul

---

65 Inspection Report of La Perouse, 1899, 3–5.
66 Inspection Report of La Perouse, 1899, 5–6.
67 Irish, 'Hidden in Plain View', 187.
68 Nugent, 'Revisiting La Perouse', 107.

Irish has confirmed settlements/camps in the Domain, at Woolloomooloo, Double Bay, Vaucluse, Camp Cove (North Head of Port Jackson), Rushcutters Bay, Darling Point, Botany Head (near La Perouse) and the Kurnell Headland.[69] George Thornton noted in his report of 1882 that Aboriginal people were at La Perouse, stating 'I found that some of them had settled at La Perouse, and were anxious to remain there'.[70] There is 'fragmentary evidence' to establish Aboriginal people of La Perouse well before 1870. A painting of 1864 of the north headland of Botany Bay shows the La Perouse monument and a group of 'Aboriginal people and their dogs in the foreground'.[71] Maria Nugent acknowledges that this is not irrefutable evidence as those depicted may well be figurative, but she draws on another painting that dates to 1819, of an Aboriginal man called Timbere in the area.[72] Nugent writes that after the unveiling of the monument to Arthur Phillip at Yarra Bay (in Botany Bay) in 1956, a local Aboriginal man named Robert Timbery presented the then governor of New South Wales with a boomerang. These individuals represented two powerful genealogical links: the governor as the 33rd in direct line from Governor Phillip and Mr Timbery as the 'oldest direct descendant at Yarra Bay of the tribe which was there when Captain Phillip arrived'.[73]

'Where no temptation existed'

The Board's paranoia about 'outside Aborigines' escalated in early 1900 when the Board was informed, via the Botany Police, that the camp at Coolangatta on the Shoalhaven River in southern Dharawal Country, was to be broken up and those Aboriginal people intended to come to La Perouse. The Board sent word to the Shoalhaven police to the effect 'that Shoalhaven Aborigines will not be permitted to reside at Botany'. Two weeks later the police at Berry on the south coast informed the Board that the Aboriginal people at Coolangatta had been warned they must not

---

69 Irish, *Hidden in Plain View*, 117.
70 Thornton, *Aborigines: Report of the Protector, to 31 December 1882*, 3. Also, newspaper reports demonstrated their presence. For example: a group undertook a fishing trip to Wollongong and then returned to Botany Bay, *SMH*, 20 April 1846; a gang of youths set upon a group of Aboriginal people heading for Woolloomooloo and pelted them, 'in a most mercilessly manner, with stones', *SMH*, 14 December 1842, 2.
71 Nugent, 'Botany Bay', 2003, 28.
72 The spelling of Timbere differs: Timbery and Timberely.
73 Nugent, 'Revisiting La Perouse', 73–74.

remove to La Perouse.⁷⁴ The Board's real concern was not so much about raw numbers but more about an influx of 'outside' Aboriginal people to the La Perouse reserve.

When pressed by the *Evening News*, Board Chair Edmund Fosbery provided four arguments for removal of the La Perouse community. First, there were too many children not being educated and 'learning to be idlers'; second, there was no manager to supervise the residents and a number of 'young girls' would be better 'away from the influences of the city'; third, the camp was a centre for 'undesirable aboriginals' to gain accommodation and visit Sydney; and lastly, the camp had lost privacy due to the many 'excursionists on Sundays'. Fosbery added that his concerns were justified by further details that were best kept from the public.⁷⁵ Fosbery's intervention is interesting, given the more 'hands-off' approach to Aboriginal affairs he favoured before Ardill's arrival. After 17 years as Board chair, Fosbery now seemed open to more restrictive measures.

The arguments variously referred to 'undesirables', the bad influence of the city and the allegations that many La Perouse residents did not 'belong' there. Yet there is no escaping that in the Board's perspective *no* Aboriginal people – regardless of where they came from – belonged in the new expanding city of Sydney. As Penelope Edmunds observes, this was not uncommon for the mid-nineteenth century. She argues the 'settler-colonial city was audaciously expansive' and it reached out over 'all Aboriginal land'. Edmunds remarks that the 'accelerated incorporation of town space' affected the attitudes towards Aboriginal people who were 'increasing viewed as inconvenient impediments to progress'.⁷⁶

Like the Lekwungen First Nation people of Victoria in British Columbia, the Kulin people of Melbourne and the boatshed squatters, the La Perouse community was suddenly 'too close' to Sydney. By November the Board had made the decision. Wallaga Lake, on the far south coast, had been

---

74 *APBM*, 1 February 1900, Item 2. The Coolangatta Estate was owned by Alexander Berry and he had employed many Aboriginal people, but at the end of 1890s the estate was broken up and the Aboriginal people had to move. John Hay, the new owner, wanted the Aboriginal families moved from Coolangatta across the Shoalhaven River to what would become Roseby Park Aboriginal Station; *APBM*, 15 February 1900, Item 5.
75 *Evening News*, 14 November 1900, 2.
76 Edmonds, 'Unpacking Settler Colonialism's Urban Strategies', 7–10.

chosen for relocation. At the end of the year the La Perouse reserve would be cancelled, rations stopped and the residents would be supplied with passes to Wallaga Lake.[77] The *Evening News* reported that the APB:

> had come to the conclusion that it is advisable that the aborigines at La Perouse be removed to a more suitable locality than one in the neighbourhood of a big city ... where many obstacles are interfering with the moral and physical improvement of those people.[78]

The same *Evening News* report noted that at Wallaga Lake 'huts would be erected', clothing and rations provided and that the 'young females, will be better under control ... and the children also will be more carefully attended to' as there was an excellent school there.

A coalition of support

However, the residents would not budge, and they had powerful defenders.

Figure 3.6: John Stuart Hawthorn.
Source: Parliamentary Archives, NSW Parliament Collection (HawthorneJS-136Web).

The plans to remove the settlement caused only a minor stir in parliament. John Stuart Hawthorne (Figure 3.6), who was member for the seat of Leichhardt, was a liberal reformist, temperance advocate and a member of the Church of England Synod. He asked the premier, John See, if it was correct that the La Perouse Aboriginal community was to be moved to 'some out-of-the-way place in the interior' and whether he would oppose any such move for those who have lived all their lives there and their ancestors before them. See replied that he had not agreed to any such transfer

---

77   *APBM*, 1 November 1900, Item 12.
78   *Evening News*, 10 November 1900, 3.

but would support such a move as he thought the camp at La Perouse was a danger to the 'poor unfortunate blacks, especially the women, and is a danger also to the morality of the community'.[79] The *Australian Star* reported on the exchange between See and Hawthorne and stated that the La Perouse community was to go to Brewarrina.[80] Apart from Hawthorne's question, there was little sympathy for the La Perouse community in the Legislative Assembly. In late 1900 John Rowland Dacey – member for Botany, foundation member of the Australian Labor Party and trustee of Cook's landing place at Kurnell – raised the issue. He claimed, 'it would be an advantage to the blacks themselves if it [the reserve] were removed to a more suitable location'.[81] Dacey may have had an ulterior motive. He had a commercial interest in the development of the La Perouse area and the removal of the Aboriginal residents would accommodate this.[82] He had also previously asked the Board for the residents to be removed.[83] Mr Chanter, member for Deniliquin and Board member, explained to the Assembly that for some 'considerable time the Board had been doing their best to remove the aborigines from La Perouse to the Wollongong district, where no temptation existed'.[84] These were hardly compelling arguments to remove a community yet no other parliamentarian voices opposed its removal.

However, other forces were stirring. First, the Aboriginal community had some very influential Sydney Christian leaders to aid their cause. And second, the Aboriginal residents themselves refused to leave. Thomas Edward Colebrook, a Methodist, alderman of Leichhardt, printer and publisher, was elected to the La Perouse Aborigines Mission Committee on 14 July 1899, and in that December became the secretary and then in 1902 was made president.[85] At the 1900 annual general meeting of the Petersham Christian Endeavour Society (the umbrella organisation), Colebrook was joined by the society's president: the coalminer, MLA and Minister for Mines John Lionel Fegan. Reverend Dr Thomas Roseby, a leading theologian, intellectual and chair of the Congregational Union of New South Wales, was also present. Four other reverends attended:

---

79 NSW, *Parliamentary Debates,* Legislative Assembly, 20 September 1900, 3100 (Stuart).
80 *Australian Star,* 21 September 1900, 5.
81 NSW, *Parliamentary Debates*, Legislative Assembly, 11 October 1900, 3891 (Dacey).
82 Dacey wanted to build a resort in the area and acquire a wine licence. See Nugent, 'Revisiting La Perouse', 131–32.
83 *APBM*, 16 August 1900, Item 5.
84 NSW, *Parliamentary Debates*, Legislative Assembly, 11 October 1900, 3891(Chanter).
85 Telfer, *Amongst Australian Aborigines*, 33.

S. Harrison, J.W. Holden, William Allen and J. Woodhouse. Fegan addressed the meeting proclaiming that Aboriginal people had 'rights and responsibilities which should be more generally acknowledged' and that these people needed 'solid help' and not the 'scanty tenderness and charity of the state'.[86] These were well-connected influential people who brought their experience and skills to support the La Perouse Aboriginal people. Colebrook argued in a letter to the editor in the *Evening News* that the decision to remove the community was harsh and unreasonable and that he doubted the 'justice of the proposal'.[87] He criticised the paper for previously saying the camp had been 'discredited' when there had been no reports to that effect and he challenged Ardill to deny that La Perouse was in fact better than many other stations controlled by the Board.

Figure 3.7: Lady Timbery, Queen of La Perouse.
Source: Photograph taken by author in the museum at La Perouse. Emma, Queen of La Perouse (Emma Timbery), Aboriginal shell-worker – portrait, 1895/ unknown photographer – Call no. P2/570. Mitchell Library, State Library of New South Wales.

On 12 November 1900, an open-air demonstration was held at La Perouse to support the community. The gathering included various church bodies 'embracing all shades of political opinions'. It was chaired by the president of the Mission Committee, Mr G.E. Bodley and was addressed by Reverends S. Harrison and J.W. Holden. The meeting opposed the removal of the Aboriginal people from La Perouse on the following grounds: the APB had not advanced sufficient reasons for the removal; the camp had been the recognised home for the Aborigines since the 'discovery of the Australian Continent'; the 'unceremonious method' adopted by the APB in removing 'Her Majesty's subjects against their

86 *SMH*, 20 July 1900, 8; *Australian Star*, 15 November 1900, 2.
87 *Evening News*, 10 November 1900, 3.

will'; and that it was a 'rendezvous' place for other visiting Aborigines. A petition that embodied the motion was made ready to present to the Legislative Assembly.[88]

The *Evening News* sent a reporter to La Perouse to get a first-hand look at the place and to meet the people. A lengthy article detailed the camp, its inhabitants and the strong sentiments of residents wishing to remain at La Perouse. The reporter described the camp as possessing 'a higher grade of respectability than some people might suppose' with about a dozen neatly constructed buildings and evidence of a certain 'amount of neatness, care, and attention'. The houses have 'ordinary boarded floors', 'comfortably lined' rooms and modest furnishings. Many of the men worked in the fishing industry and gained labouring work in the district. Most the children running about were 'clean and well-tended as any workman's children in the poorer neighbourhoods within the city limits' and 'pretty young half-caste girls … were … in clean and freshly-starched and ironed white or print dresses'. Mrs Timbery (Figure 3.7) and her family 'are said to be the only living descendants of the tribe of blacks who originally populated the neighbourhood'.

By way of appeasement, due to the increase in support for the La Perouse community, the APB had indicated that the Timbery family *could remain* due to their long connection to La Perouse, but Mrs Timbery would have none of it: 'I don't want to stop here if the others is all goin'.[89] As spokesperson for the 50 Aboriginal people at La Perouse Mrs Timbery said that they had only heard about the removal in the *Evening News* and that they didn't know why the Board wanted to 'shift us for'. She stressed:

> We're livin' quietly enough here, ain't we? Doin' no harm to nobody. 'Ere we've been all our lives, and 'ere we want to die – leastways I do, and a lot more of us too. Here they gave us seven acres of ground and they says here you can live and stop till you die … now they're goin' to clear us all out altogether. Have they got the power to do it? That's what I want to know. Ain't we free people in this country now? … I want to know if they can shift us if we don't want to go. Can they? Mister?[90]

88　*Australian Star*, 15 November 1900, 2.
89　*Evening News*, 14 November 1900, 2. It was recorded that Lady Timbery (Queen Emma of La Perouse) was in fact a vice-president of the Endeavour Society. Telfer, *Amongst Australian Aborigines*, 26.
90　*Evening News*, 14 November 1900, 2.

It was reported that Ardill interviewed the residents (after his report) and they 'absolutely refused to go', and when it was intimated that 'rations may be stopped' and their 'homes taken from them' the residents said they would not go and 'would camp on the beach as they had done in earlier days'.[91]

A deputation

In late 1900 a deputation to prevent the removal of the La Perouse community called on the premier and colonial secretary, John See. The group comprised: Thomas Colebrook, MLA John Hawthorne, six other members of the New South Wales Aborigines' Mission and three Aboriginal people from La Perouse. Hawthorn argued that the Aboriginal people had been living at this location well before white man came and that 'some of the descendants of those early blacks are here now'. Hawthorne argued that the government should not make exceptions: if it was right for a few to remain 'why is it not right to allow 50? There is no charge against them'. He also raised the issue of a possible conflict of interest. There had been an application for a licensed public house and See knew the man seeking the licence as the person who regularly hired out his boat for him to go fishing. While not accusing Premier See of wrongdoing, Hawthorne asked that if he knew of the proposed application for a public house, would he 'put his foot down to prevent it'.[92] Hawthorne also took a swipe at Ardill:

> I will guarantee there is no more misconduct at this station that the public have been informed has been the case at Ardill's Homes. I am astonished that men like Mr Ardill and Mr Carpenter lend themselves with others to try and get these people removed.[93]

Thomas Colebrook also took aim at Ardill, arguing that he had misrepresented the state of the settlement:

---

91 *Evening News*, 17 November 1900, 3.
92 Deputation to Colonial Secretary, 30 November 1900, CSIL, 5/6574, Item 00/23677 (no page numbers provided).
93 Deputation to Colonial Secretary, 30 November 1900, CSIL, 5/6574, Item 00/23677. Hawthorne was referring to Unni Carpenter, member of the APA, who had joined the Board along with Ardill in later 1897.

> We were told by Mr Fosbery that the moral and physical well-being of the Aborigines would be better looked after at Wallaga Lake … I challenge Mr Ardill, who has been the chief factor in the removal of these people, to deny that from every standpoint at La Perouse the condition of the people is better than ever it was before.[94]

Delegation member and president of the La Perouse Mission Committee Mr Dodley explained to See that while the Board chair, Edmund Fosbery, had claimed the Board was unanimous in its decision to close the reserve, Board member Henry Trenchard had in fact opposed the move.[95] A frustrated Dodley also noted that the APB claimed there were several reasons for removing the La Perouse settlement but would not publish them. Missionary Miss Retta Dixon explained to See that if the community was removed it would be more dependent on the government as there was no work at Wallaga Lake and the children received a good education La Perouse.[96]

John See (Figure 3.8) assured the gathering that there was no conflict of interest and that he opposed any licensed public house being erected at La Perouse. He also mentioned that as a member of the APB himself, he was aware of work done for Aboriginal people and was sympathetic to their cause.[97] He was concerned about the number of 'half-castes' and whites at the settlement: 'it is the white people who contaminate the Aborigines not the Aborigines who contaminate the white people'. He pointed out to the deputation that initially 'all the Aborigines consented to go' but soon afterwards they changed their minds, though he did not know why. He praised Board Chair Fosbery as a selfless worker for 'the aborigines', but he would go over all the 'papers very carefully' with Fosbery and reply through Mr Hawthorne.[98] John See would have been aware that the Randwick Municipal Council was also against the removal. At its November meeting in 1900 it resolved: 'That this council is in sympathy

---

94 Deputation to Colonial Secretary, 30 November 1900, CSIL, 5/6574, Item 00/23677.
95 *APBM*, 6 September 1900, Item 4. It was rare to have any recorded dissentions in the Board minutes but on this occasion, it was noted: 'Mr Trenchard objecting to the movement of the blacks from La Perouse'.
96 Deputation to Colonial Secretary, 30 November 1900, CSIL, 5/6574, Item 00/23677.
97 John See rarely attended Board meetings, for all intents and purposes he was a non-attender. From a possible 197 meetings he attended only 15, an attendance rate of 8.12 per cent. Arguably, he was not engaged in Board activity at any significant level. Analysis of *APBM* for relevant years.
98 Deputation to Colonial Secretary, 30 November 1900, CSIL, 5/6574, Item 00/23677.

with the Aborigines at La Perouse and protests against the action of the police … in removing them to another place'.[99]

Ten days after the deputation, Ardill – acting alone as usual – endeavoured to influence See's decision. He wrote to See and referred him to the report that he had written 15 months prior, 'flagging' his paragraphs that related to the breaking up of the camp, a new coastal Aboriginal station and possible legislation. Ardill wrote the letter on Sydney Rescue Work Society letterhead and not that of the Board's. He perhaps did not want the Board to know he had written the letter or felt that his Sydney Rescue letterhead would have more weight.[100]

Figure 3.8: John See.
Source: Parliamentary Archives, NSW Parliament Collection (SeeJ-4584).

No record of the subsequent discussion between See and Fosbery has been located. Trenchard was the only identified Board member who opposed the removal, while Ardill tried to influence the decision in favour of removal right to the end. There were two new Board members at this time. Frank Norrie, a solicitor from Grafton, joined the Protection Board in November 1899, but made no obvious contribution to the debate. Likewise, the views, if any, of Unni Carpenter – president of the APA who joined the Board at the same time as Ardill – could not be found. In the end, John See did not back the Board's proposal and there were no forced removals. In a strange twist, See, as a virtual non-attender of Board meetings, was perhaps distanced enough to see the injustice of the proposal.

---

99   Randwick Municipal Council Meeting, 20 November 1900 (no item number), *Randwick Municipal Council, Minute Books: May 1900 – Nov 1909*, Yv1532, CY 2933, Bowen Library, Randwick. However, six years later, the Council had changed its position and was in favour of removal. *APBM*, 30 October 1906, Item 2; 6 November 1906, Item 12; 20 November 1906, Item 1.
100 Letter from Ardill to Colonial Secretary, John See, 10 December 1900, CSIL, 5/6574, Item 00.24246.

The December deadline for revocation of the La Perouse lease passed. Eight adults with their families, 16 in all, willingly relocated to Lake Illawarra.[101] At the end of 1900, 27 people remained at La Perouse (Figure 3.5). The APB with all its posturing and deadlines about removals was, without government approval, unable to carry through its policy. It had no legislative mandate to force the issue, the lobby against removal was significant and most of the Aboriginal community did not wish to leave. The Board report for the year ending 1902 explained the La Perouse decision and in doing so acknowledged that it lacked the power to move the community: 'Strong representations were made by Mrs Timberley [sic] ... on behalf of the Aborigines themselves, and by others'. Although still of the opinion that it was not a suitable place considering the tram-link with the city and the approval of a licence for a hotel, the Board 'felt a difficulty in recommending that those who had been there so long should be deported to another place'. The Board acknowledged it had no power to remove the residents and that they 'absolutely' refused to 'leave the locality'. The Board recommended that the reserve not be cancelled, but in doing so 'no rations or other Government expenditure should be authorised in connection with those aborigines whose homes are in other parts of the state'.[102] The attempt by the Board to move the Aboriginal residents from La Perouse had failed. The La Perouse Aboriginal community remains today after repeated attempts, post 1900, to have its residents removed.[103]

---

101 *APBM*, 17 January 1901, Item 3. Figure 3.5 shows the decrease in population (1900) as a result of those departures for Lake Illawarra.
102 *APBR* 1902.
103 In late 1906 a Randwick Police report sought the removal of residents, but pressure to prevent the move came once more from the NSW Aborigines' Mission and the Board did not pursue the matter (*APBM*, 30 October 1906, Item 2; 6 November 1906, Item 12; 20 November 1906, Item 1). The Randwick Council tried again in 1928 urging the 'desirableness of removing the aborigines ... to a site where they could enjoy more privacy and where their presence would not militate against the progress of the district' (*APBM*, 23 March 1928, Item 2). The Aboriginal residents refused and, in a petition, stated: 'This is our heritage ... we feel justified in refusing to leave' (*SMH*, 4 April 1928, 24).

The die is caste

George Edward Ardill undoubtedly changed the dynamic of the Board. Arguably he was the most proactive member since its inception in 1883. His drive and persistence had an immediate impact in facilitating the removal of Aboriginal children and dealing with the Board's more difficult tasks. He was undeterred in the face of criticism and his influence in Aboriginal affairs was considerable: he helped create a climate that persisted well into the second half of the twentieth century that would promote and embrace harsh legislation towards Aboriginal people. A decade later, as vice-chair of the Board from 1910, he would have greater influence, but his tendencies to persist and demand would draw the attention of government.

Meanwhile, the Board's failed attempt to close the La Perouse reserve exposed its internal inadequacies. Its policy position could never be enforced as it lacked the power to remove, and any cohesive policy was hindered by members such as Ardill who often acted alone and by the non-engagement of others. Ironically, in this instance, it was an infrequent Board attender, the premier, John See, who overturned Board policy. At the same time, the event likely sharpened the Board's sense that it needed more formal powers to act in Aboriginal affairs. This sense would mature into draft legislation when another powerful figure arrived on the Board, which propelled it towards a legislative agenda with profound effects upon Aboriginal communities, particularly their children.

4

The 'almost white' children, 1904–1910

By the end of the first decade of the new century, all the state jurisdictions had forged their own special institutions to 'deal with' their Indigenous populations. As mentioned previously, Victoria was the first state to create a Central Board for Aborigines in 1860 and was the first to enact legislation concerning Aboriginal people in 1869, and later the very restrictive *Aborigines Protection Act 1886* (Vic) (commonly known as the Half-Caste Act 1886). In Western Australia the *Aborigines Protection Act 1886* established a Protection Board that could appoint honorary local protectors where and when required. Further legislation in 1897 abolished the Protection Board along with its protectors and established the Western Australia Aborigines Department. However, this legislation was deemed invalid (on funding grounds) and the positions of chief protector and regional protectors were re-established under the *Aborigines Act 1905*. The Queensland *Aborigines Protection and Restriction of the Sale of Opium Act 1897* provided for the appointment of protectors where required throughout the colony and later established the Chief Protector of Aboriginals Office in 1904. South Australia followed the Queensland model with the *Aborigines Act 1911* that established the position of chief protector and a system of regional protectors that remained in place until 1934. The Northern Territory came under South Australian law, which remained in force until changed by the Commonwealth after 1 January 1911.[1] Tasmania had no body or legislation that was like the

---

1   For all Acts concerning Indigenous Australians, see: 'Legislation', To Remove and Protect, Australian Institute of Aboriginal and Torres Strait Islander Studies (AIATSIS), aiatsis.gov.au/collections/collections-online/digitised-collections/remove-and-protect/.

other jurisdictions. However, the *Cape Barren Island Reserve Act 1912* (Tas) provided for a portion of land on the island to be set aside for the 'descendants of the Aboriginal natives' and the Secretary of the Department of Lands was responsible for the 'well-being of the residents'.[2]

All of these jurisdictions had enormous power over the Aboriginal people. The chief protectors were the legal guardians of Aboriginal children (despite having parents) in the case of South Australia, up to the age of 21 and in Western Australia up to the age of 16. Western Australia had laws that prohibited the marriage of an Aboriginal woman to a non-Aboriginal man unless with the express permission of the chief protector.[3] All had laws concerning the employment conditions of Aboriginal people and where Aboriginal people could live, and each had the power to remove Aboriginal people to a reserve.

After the New South Wales Protection Board's (APB) failure to remove the La Perouse Aboriginal community to the south coast at Wallaga Lake New South Wales, there was a new urgency to secure some legal control over Aboriginal people – it would no longer be content with the policy drift that characterised Edmund Fosbery's tenure. Peter Read observes that at the end of the nineteenth century the Board was concerned with Aboriginal mobility. Aboriginal people were not staying in the one place where Board oversight was more easily administered.

> The problem, quite unanticipated, was how to prevent the Aborigines from treating the stations and reserves as places where food and shelter were available when required, but which could be dispensed with if there was a desire to go somewhere else.[4]

If the Board acquired legislative backing it could force Aboriginal people to remain on the stations and reserves, exclude those who did not belong – especially those young men who did not work – and ensure that teenage girls remained in service.[5] George Ardill had raised the need for legislation in his 1899 report on La Perouse, but new impetus came when Robert Thomas Donaldson joined the Board in 1904.

---

2   'Tasmania', To Remove and Protect, AIATSIS: aiatsis.gov.au/collections/collections-online/digitised-collections/remove-and-protect/.
3   'Western Australia', To Remove and Protect, AIATSIS: aiatsis.gov.au/collections/collections-online/digitised-collections/remove-and-protect/.
4   Read, *A Hundred Years War*, 47.
5   Read, *A Hundred Years War*, 52.

Of all Board members (including George Ardill) none had more impact and left a more lasting legacy than Robert T. Donaldson. His Board membership and subsequent tenure as an inspector for the Board spanned 25 years, from 1904 to 1929. Donaldson voiced his opinions on Aboriginal affairs often, with authority, both in public and as a member of the New South Wales Legislative Assembly. Donaldson's time with the Board can be divided into three phases. His first period of influence spanned from the time of his arrival up to 1909 when he did much to prepare and promote the argument for the successful passage of the *Aborigines Protection Act 1909*. His second period of influence, from 1909 to 1915, witnessed the Board's successful *Aborigines Protection (Amending) Act 1915* that enabled it to remove Aboriginal children without court approval. Arguably, this was the most important and devastating piece of Board legislation. His last period of impact, as inspector for the Board, lasted from 1915 until his retirement in 1929. In this position he traversed the state checking on the reserves and stations, identifying and removing Aboriginal children to be placed into service or institutions. Heather Goodall concludes that, from an Aboriginal perspective, Donaldson was perhaps the most hated man on the APB in its latter period and gained a reputation throughout the Aboriginal community, as the 'Kid's Collector'.[6] Jack Horner also observed that Donaldson's focus on removing the children made him 'feared and hated among Aborigines'.[7]

This chapter focuses on Donaldson's first period of influence, the lead-up to the *Aborigines Protection Act 1909*. I argue that Donaldson differed from Ardill in that he was not overly religious, secretive or prone to public controversy. He was far more clinical and calculating. His background on the railways, and later as a mayor and as a member of parliament, shaped him as a dominant, no-nonsense performer. He was not a team player and the Board permitted him free rein. The Board allowed for 'lone-wolf' operators like Ardill and Donaldson to speak freely and to be unaccountable. Although he was a poor attendant of Board meetings, Donaldson's impact on policy was significant: he brought into sharp focus the removal of children, particularly girls, from Aboriginal families. This was his crusade: the removal of the 'almost white' children from the camps. It was Donaldson's persistent and targeted pronouncements in the public and parliamentary arenas that established the groundwork for the formal inclusion of child removal policies into the Board's legislative agenda.

6 Goodall, *Invasion to Embassy*, 1996, 123.
7 Horner, *Bill Ferguson*, 7.

POWER AND DYSFUNCTION

A formidable Irishman

Born in Ireland in 1851, Robert Thomas Donaldson (Figure 4.1) was brought to Australia by his family in 1863. He spent some years working on stations and prospecting in Queensland and then, after a brief period away in Britain, he returned to Queensland and was appointed inspector of railway construction.[8] It is unclear as to what qualification he obtained to undertake such a role.

Figure 4.1: Robert T. Donaldson.
Source: Third Australasian Catholic Conference, St. Mary's Cathedral Book Depot, Sydney, 1909.MG/1/U11/ (set) p. 480. Mitchell Library, State Library of New South Wales.

On moving to New South Wales, he became a contractor's manager for a firm that built the Cootamundra to Gundagai railway line. The Tumut valley 'appealed so much' that he purchased a butcher's shop and settled in Tumut.[9] In 1892, he became a local government council member, held that position for nine years, and was mayor for the years 1897 and 1898.[10] In July 1898, Donaldson was elected to the Legislative Assembly as member for Tumut and held the seat (renamed Wynyard) until 1913. Jack Horner, activist for Aboriginal equality and justice in the 1960s, described him as

> a big man, powerfully built, six-feet tall, with broad shoulders, and barrel chest supporting his short thick neck … His most memorable features were the keen, brown snapping eyes beneath bushy eyebrows flecked with white, a well-shaped nose, and large jaw thick and round as a soccer ball.[11]

---

8   Felton, 'Donaldson, Robert Thomas (1851–1936)'.
9   Hedley, *People and Progress*, 24.
10 Hedley, *People and Progress*, 24.
11 Horner, *Bill Ferguson*, 18.

His time as an inspector of railways, bridge builder, council member, mayor and parliamentarian provided him with a great deal of experience; he was comfortable with power and authority.

One incident points to Donaldson's dominant, forceful and less than even-handed character. It concerned rationing at Brungle Aboriginal Station (between Tumut and Gundagai) in July 1902. A heated exchange took place in the Legislative Assembly between Donaldson, as the member for Tumut, and Mr Norton, the member for Northumberland. Norton brought some rancid, unidentifiable meat into the parliament and claimed that this 'quality' of meat was provided as rations to the Aboriginal people at Brungle Station. Brungle was in Donaldson's electorate and, taken unawares, he took umbrage at the imputation that he was allowing such a practice to take place under his watch. Donaldson was further angered by the fact that Norton subsequently admitted that the meat 'had been carefully held back for four weeks' before bringing the rancid pieces into parliament.[12] Strong language was used, and Donaldson had to 'withdraw' on two occasions when he claimed that Norton revelled in 'anything putrid, disgusting and repulsive' and that he was a 'self-constituted scavenger'.[13] Donaldson launched a spirited defence of the APB, declaring that he had regular contact with the Aboriginal people at Brungle, that the residents knew him, and that he had supplied meat to them himself years ago. Donaldson attacked Norton for criticising the manager of Brungle, Mr Hubbard, and stated that the APB members were all 'respectable gentlemen' of well-known 'high reputation' and that the member should have waited until inquiries had been made before he 'besmirched the character of these people'.[14]

Norton claimed that the Aboriginal people were 'mal-treated and badly fed' not only at Brungle, but at the 'majority of other stations'. He deplored the situation whereby the 'aborigines [were] subject to harsh treatment' and that their 'rations [were] withheld' for supposedly trivial misdemeanours. Donaldson countered that the Brungle people had been stirred up by a 'half-caste' man called Clifford who was a 'notorious gambler' and therefore could not to be taken seriously. Norton stood by his claims.[15]

---

12 *Evening News*, 4 July 1902, 3.
13 NSW, *Parliamentary Debates*, Legislative Assembly, 3 July 1902, 962 (Robert Donaldson). This issue was reported in the press on 22 June 1902 in the *Truth* and the coverage did not conclude until 22 August 1902.
14 NSW, *Parliamentary Debates*, Legislative Assembly, 3 July 1902, 963 (Robert Donaldson).
15 NSW, *Parliamentary Debates*, Legislative Assembly, 3 July 1902, 964 (Norton).

In late August the Brungle residents were still refusing to accept the meat and stated that they would rather 'eat rabbit or possum than eat such stuff'.[16] In retaliation the Board stopped the meat ration to the 'disaffected ones' and suggested that as 'there are plenty of rabbits available they can trap them, if they must have animal food, or go without'.[17] Donaldson was not a Board member in 1902, so he could have taken a different view over this issue. He could have challenged the Board on the quality of its rations or its punitive approach to the Brungle residents, or asked questions about more funding for the APB in parliament. But instead he dismissed the concerns of the Aboriginal residents and defended the 'respectable' men of the Board: men, it transpired, that he planned to join.

The 'almost white' girls

Donaldson joined the Board in December 1904 after J. Waddell (premier of New South Wales from June 1904 to August 1904) wrote a short note to the premier, Mr Carruthers, recommending that he be appointed:

> There are a large number of Blacks in the Tumut District and Mr Donaldson M.P. takes a great interest in their welfare. I will be glad if you could have him appointed a member of the Aboriginal Board. I feel sure he will render good service.[18]

It is unclear whether Donaldson and Waddell had any conversation regarding the appointment and why Donaldson accepted a position on the Board. It would have been unlikely that he sought more power or needed an elevated profile; as a man of 53 years of age he had already achieved both. He had already been involved in supplying rations to Aboriginal families and, in view of the recent controversy at Brungle, he may have seen an opportunity to take a more active policy role in Aboriginal affairs. Perhaps this explains his support for the APB and not the Brungle residents in 1902.

In a speech to the Legislative Assembly in late 1906, Donaldson took the opportunity to speak on Aboriginal matters. He offered that Aboriginal people showed 'great reluctance to leave their old haunts' and that they

---

16 *Tumut and Adelong Times*, 22 August 1902, 2.
17 *Tumut and Adelong Times*, 22 August 1902, 2.
18 Letter from T. Waddell to J. Carruthers, 22 November 1904, Colonial Secretary's In-Letters (hereafter CSIL), 1904, 5/6817, Item 20897, State Records of New South Wales (hereafter SRNSW).

4. THE 'ALMOST WHITE' CHILDREN, 1904–1910

have a strong love for their 'native places' and, as a result, it was very difficult to move them. He thought the Board should always 'err on the liberal side' but at the same time there should be no waste in the camps, and that the able-bodied men should be encouraged to work and not 'loaf on surplus rations'. He acknowledged that it was harsh to order these men away from the camps but 'it had to be done'.[19] But he had another pressing concern, one that would define his 'contribution' to the Board. In December 1906, he couched it in the following terms:

> When the board went around to the schools, even at La Perouse, to Brungle … and other places, the question arose, what were we to do about the little boys and girls who were almost white? What was to be their future? Unfortunately, as they were growing up now, there was only one end for them. What could be done for their benefit? It was imperative to take them away from these camps.[20]

He informed the Assembly that Mr Ardill, a current Board member, 'took a great interest in these little children' and offered his strong support. If any permanent 'reformation was to be affected it was necessary to take these little white girls away from the camps'.[21] The member for Monaro, Mr Miller, asked Donaldson if the Board had recommended that such girls should be taken away. Donaldson's reply reflected his disconnect with the Board – he said he did not know! Donaldson had been on the Board for two years, was making some very bold statements about policy, and yet was unaware if the Board had made any recommendations. In fact, there was no such recommendation in the 1906 Board report. It merely included a short paragraph stating several girls had been sent out to service and the usual inquiries made as to the suitability of their placements.[22] Donaldson was advocating a policy to remove them all, not just a trickle, yet the Board had either not discussed the issue over the preceding two years or had done so when he was not present, and he was not informed. One member interjected, that it would be wrong to 'take them away from

---

19 NSW, *Parliamentary Debates*, Legislative Assembly, 6 December 1906, 4530–31 (Robert Donaldson).
20 NSW, *Parliamentary Debates*, Legislative Assembly, 6 December 1906, 4530–31 (Robert Donaldson).
21 NSW, *Parliamentary Debates*, Legislative Assembly, 6 December 1906, 4530–31 (Robert Donaldson).
22 *Protection of Aborigines: Report of the Board* (the APB Report: hereafter *APBR*) 1906, 4. Accessed via *Journal of the Legislative Council*, Q328.9106/7, *NSW Parliamentary Papers, Consolidated Index* (hereafter *Journal of LC*), State Library of New South Wales (hereafter SLNSW), Vol. 69, Part 1.

their mothers!' Donaldson responded only by saying 'it was a difficult thing to deal with'.[23] Donaldson was his own man – he spoke freely and did not need Board approval to make policy projections.

In November 1907 Donaldson maintained his focus on Aboriginal girls. In parliament he stressed that we 'educate them to a certain point', 'encourage them to be tidy' and then when they reach the age of 14 or 15 we 'leave them to their own devices'.[24] At a recent camp visit he noted that he found 'thirty-five children attending the Sunday School and half of them were white' with 'not a trace of aboriginal blood in them', and they were singing hymns 'as nicely as the children could sing them in any school in the city … Yet the inevitable end of most of these children is disaster'.[25] He claimed that there was only 'one way out of the difficulty, and that is to remove the children from the influence of the camps. There is no other way'.[26] Donaldson said nothing about the other Aboriginal children in the camps; he was only concerned with those who were 'almost white'. To Donaldson, it was apparently unacceptable that 'nearly white' children should remain in the camps, but it was acceptable for all the other children. He did not even argue neglect. On the contrary, he acknowledged that the children were being well cared for in the camps. His concern was that the 'almost white' adolescent girls might fall prey to white men who sought out the camps.[27]

In 1908, and without obvious approval from the Board, Donaldson wrote to the colonial secretary, William Wood, recommending that commission visit the major camps to consider the utility of removal. The full text is instructive of his matter-of-fact approach:

> You promised you would during the recess, have a report obtained re [sic] present condition of the half-caste children on the various Aborigines Camps and Homes – with a view of devising some plan to improve their chances of growing into respectable citizens. I believe the Insp. Gen. Mr Garvin is getting a return of the sex, ages, etc. of all the children in the Camps. When that is obtained I would suggest that a Commission (Honorary) be appointed to visit the larger Camps (if deemed necessary) confer with the

23 NSW, *Parliamentary Debates*, Legislative Assembly, 6 December 1906, 4531–32 (Unknown interjection).
24 *Bega Budget*, 23 November 1907, 5.
25 *Bega Budget*, 23 November 1907, 5.
26 *Bega Budget*, 23 November 1907, 5.
27 *Gundagai Times and Tumut, Adelong and Murrumbidgee District Advertiser*, 26 November 1907, 2.

managers. [sic] Obtain suggestions and finally drafting out a report recommending what action Parliament should take to give these children an opportunity to shake off the evil influences of the Camp surroundings. To give an idea of the decline of the full-blood, and the increase of the half-caste, I may tell you that at 4 of the Principal camps – there were on Nov. 30th last 9 full-blood children and 295 half castes or about 97 per cent on the white side. During the recess I will be only too glad to assist in every way to devise some scheme to better the prospects of these children. I look on it as an urgent matter and one we should not shirk from.[28]

Donaldson was persistent. In July 1909, rising to speak on the issue of a 'Graduated Land Tax' in the Legislative Assembly, he soon turned his attention to Aboriginal matters. He raised the issue of the increasing 'half-caste' population and spoke for over 30 minutes.[29] He recalled his time in northern and central Queensland where he interacted on many occasions with Aboriginal people. He proceeded to give the Assembly a history lesson regarding the missions at Cumeroogunga and Warangesda, the establishment of the Board, the reserves and stations, and the issue of rations and various supplies. Donaldson then described what was at the heart of the 'problem' for the Board:

> as the years rolled on, a new feature presented itself in the shape of a rapidly-semi-white population, for which these camps were never intended. The full bloods are racing along a track which leads to their inevitable extinction … but now we have thousands of their offspring, who have as much white blood as black in their veins. A large majority of their children are three-parts white; scores of them are seven-parts white.[30]

What was driving Donaldson? Donaldson did not explain his rationale but it likely reflected a view of the 'half-caste' Aboriginal people widely held by the white community. This perception was formed by two factors. First, there was white community debate about the 'worth' of the 'half-caste'. Henry Reynolds recalls a well-repeated saying by Dr Livingstone, of African fame, that 'God made the white man and God made the Black man, but the devil made the mulatto'.[31] The mulatto, a Spanish term, was

---

28 Letter from Donaldson to Colonial Secretary, W.H. Wood, 3 January 1908, CSIL 1909, 5/7030, 1-1200, Item 08.02 (SRNSW).
29 He spent half of his allocated time expounding on the issue of the 'half-caste' population. NSW, *Parliamentary Debates*, Legislative Assembly, 13 July 1909, 340–49 (Robert Donaldson).
30 NSW, *Parliamentary Debates*, Legislative Assembly, 13 July 1909, 346 (Robert Donaldson).
31 Reynolds, *Nowhere People*, 3.

half white and half black.³² Reynolds writes that many whites thought 'half-castes inherited the worst qualities of both parent races and the good qualities of neither'; they were considered to be morally and physically defective, unpredictable, unstable and degenerate.³³ When Jimmy Governor and his brother went on their rampage at the Breelong station in 1900, comments in the press pointed to Jimmy's 'half-caste' status as a basis for his infamy. In December 1900 the *Sydney Morning Herald* suggested interest in the case stemmed from the fact that the 'criminals were part aboriginal and part white'. The *Herald* reasoned that Governor resented his exclusion from white society and responded as a black man: the 'instinct of the mere savage broke out, and the blood-thirst of the infuriated aboriginal had its way'.³⁴ At the 1913 South Australian Royal Commission on the Aborigines, the then secretary of the New South Wales Board R. Beardsmore was asked if the 'half-caste' was a better man physically than the 'full-blood'? He replied:

> I do not think that either physically or morally the half-caste is as good a man as the full-blood. There is a very good reason for that. The fathers of the half-castes are naturally the most depraved white men, and if heredity counts for anything it must mean that those children are worse than the full blood children.³⁵

On another level, the 'half-caste' threatened the purity of race and even society itself. Anna Haebich notes that, at the time of Federation, racial theories 'endorsed the view that [Aboriginal people] were incapable of becoming modern citizens and fanned fears of an internal racial threat in a desired White Australia'.³⁶ They were a 'visible reminder' of the atrocities perpetrated on the frontier and after 'into which Aboriginal women had been drawn by the sexual desires of white men'.³⁷ The 'increasing number of "half-castes" reminded officials, doctors, and scientists of a moral violation of an officially forbidden intercourse between white men and Aboriginal women or girls'.³⁸

---

32   Reynolds, *Nowhere People*, 2. Reynolds refers to a 'table of terminology' in use in the Spanish colonies: a 'Mulatto', half black and half white; a 'Quadroon', three-quarters white and one-quarter black; a 'Sambo', three-quarters black and one-quarter white; a 'Mestizo' or 'Quinteron', seven-eighths white and one-eighth black.
33   Reynolds, *Nowhere People*, 3.
34   *Sydney Morning Herald* (hereafter *SMH*), 1 December 1900, 8.
35   Correspondence Files VPRS 1694/P0000/15, Question 2127, South Australian Royal Commissions, 1913, Public Records Office Victoria (hereafter PROV).
36   Haebich, *Broken Circles*, 132.
37   Haebich, *Broken Circles*, 134.
38   Kidd, quoted in Haderer, 'Biopower, Whiteness and the Stolen Generations', 9.

Yet, juxtaposed to this attitude was the Board's intention, right from the start, that those with a lesser 'admixture of Aboriginal blood' should be absorbed, or merged, into the mainstream community. Russell McGregor argues that, in the nineteenth century, 'absorption was more of an assumption than a strategy', with many settler Australians believing that the incorporation of the 'half-caste' would be a natural process. However, when this did not occur state administrations began to intervene in order to facilitate absorption.[39] Victoria was a case in point with the *Aborigines Protection Act 1886*. Patrick Wolf described three phases of Aboriginal policy: confrontation, incarceration and assimilation – the 1886 Act 'was the culmination of a shift from the second to the third'.[40] It was based on the premise that the able-bodied should be moved off the reserves to support themselves but it also 'accorded with the prevailing middle-class philosophy of self-improvement and self-reliance'. Coupled with this were social Darwinist ideas that 'encouraged different policies for those of "full-blood" and those of "mixed Aboriginal descent" who it was claimed were at 'different stages of acceptability' to the white community.[41] In other words, the 'half-castes' could be more 'safely absorbed' into white society.

However, the white construct of 'half-castes' together with terms like 'quadroons' and 'octoroons' were problematic administrative categories for the Board to deal with – a difficulty all of their own making.

Donaldson did not refer to any community discourse on the 'half-caste' population but his views were clear. The young 'near-white' children in the camps – the girls in particular – needed to be reclaimed by the white community. Donaldson was certainly fulfilling community expectations of individual self-improvement and self-reliance, and that 'near-white' children would have a better chance of merging into white society. He recognised that this policy would be harsh, yet he was uncompromising in its pursuit.

---

39   McGregor, '"Breed out the Colour"', 287.
40   Furphy, '"They Formed a Little Family as it Were"', 10.
41   Broome, 'Victoria', 139.

Drawing upon Board census figures, Donaldson told the Legislative Assembly in July 1909 that there were 2,700 'little Ishmaels, born in degradation, dragged up with all the vicious and bad surroundings of a camp'.[42] Using some colourful language, he submitted that the Board was hamstrung:

> The Board has no title to these reserves. It cannot sue for trespass. It cannot clear the camps of bad characters, the loafing adults, who prey like wolves upon the rations issued to the children, the human blowflies who haunt these places, always hovering with one object, and that is the pollution of the young children. The Board has no power to take charge of the orphans and neglected children, it cannot board them out, nor can it take them away from the evil influences ... The only solution ... is to take these children right away from the evil companionship and vicious surrounds of the camps.[43]

At the annual Catholic Congress held in Sydney October 1909, Donaldson explained his agenda further.[44] His 3,000-word address traversed reflections on Aboriginal people from Brisbane to Cape York, their customs, the pre-contact period; he assumed knowledge in all areas. He then turned his attention to the camps in New South Wales and introduced two new issues: he acknowledged that removing the children would be a delicate matter; but argued forcefully that the girls should *never* be permitted to return to their communities. He noted that there would be a great deal of opposition to removing children at the 'age of nine or ten from their mother's homes' because many of the 'mothers were almost white' and that they look after their children 'as well as their surroundings will allow'.[45] By inference, Donaldson drew the comparison that 'full-blood' mothers were not as connected or loving to their children. He pushed on with brutal clarity. The parents must not be allowed to stand in the way of the 'enormous and lasting benefits' of the removal of the children to be 'educated and fitted for domestic service' and apprenticed out to approved

---

42   NSW, *Parliamentary Debates*, Legislative Assembly, 13 July 1909, 347 (Robert Donaldson). This biblical reference concerns Abraham's wife Sarah who, at 75 years old, was considered barren (although she did subsequently conceive). Abraham, aged 85, required a son so Sarah offered her handmaiden, Hagar, to Abraham to conceive a child and Ishmael became Abraham's first son. Why Donaldson chose this analogy is curious; perhaps he saw Ishmael as the result of an unhealthy union.
43   NSW, *Parliamentary Debates*, Legislative Assembly, 13 July 1909, 347 (Robert Donaldson).
44   The proceedings of which were published as: *Third Australasian Catholic Congress, Held at St. Mary's Cathedral Sydney 26th September–3rd October 1909*.
45   *Third Australasian Catholic Congress*, 484–85.

4. THE 'ALMOST WHITE' CHILDREN, 1904–1910

homes. The girls should never be allowed to return to their camps and should sever all connection with family, their extended family and the community. He concluded with a short paragraph:

> In the course of a few years there will be no need for the camps and the stations; the old will have passed away, and their progeny will be absorbed into the industrial classes of the country.[46]

Did his Board colleagues agree?

No other Board member openly campaigned for policy change like Donaldson. It is difficult to know how other Board members felt about Donaldson's obsession with removing the girls. If they disagreed with him they were publicly silent. As we have seen, some Board members came and went with little impact. Board member William Charles Hill, son of Richard Hill, was one such member. He had absolutely nothing to say on Aboriginal affairs in the Legislative Council during his nearly 19 years as a member and, although spending 13 years on the APB, there is no evidence that he spoke on Aboriginal matters outside of the parliament either.[47] John Moore Chanter, mentioned in the previous chapter, made no obvious public statements on this issue and offered nothing in parliament on Aboriginal matters after 1900.[48] Members George Varley and Edward MacFarlane appeared silent on the issue.[49] Long-serving member Henry Trenchard, who had officially opposed the attempt to move the Aboriginal residents from La Perouse in 1900, may well have had a contrary view to Donaldson, but unfortunately his views on this issue are not known.

Edward Dowling (Figure 4.2), who joined the Board in 1901, had expressed views on Aboriginal matters well before his Board membership. Dowling was heavily involved in men's education, became the first secretary of the Board of Technical Education in 1883 and was also secretary of the New South Wales branch of the Australian Natives' Association.[50] He served on the Protection Board for nine years and was a regular attender. Mark Francis suggests that Dowling provided the 'intellectual support … for the Aboriginal Protection Board during the 1890s', but unfortunately

---

46 *Third Australasian Catholic Congress*, 485.
47 Doukakis, *The Aboriginal People*, 52.
48 Doukakis, *The Aboriginal People*, 157.
49 For brief details of these members refer to Appendix 1.
50 McMinn, 'Dowling, Edward (1843–1912)'.

provides no evidence for this. Dowling did have an interest in Aboriginal affairs. He addressed the 1892 Chicago World Columbian Exposition and presented a paper entitled *Australia and America in 1892: A Contrast*. It drew comparisons from every aspect of life between the two countries at the time. He observed:

> the aboriginal had considerable intelligence … was an admirable mesmerist … [had] some knowledge of astronomy and mythology … displayed considerable inventive power in the construction of the boomerang and a throwing lever for spear casting, and … [is] a superlative tracker in the bush.[51]

Figure 4.2: Edward Dowling.
Source: New South Wales State Archives & Records, 1843–1912, GPO 1-16186.

Dowling stressed that 'some atonement was needed for the treatment of the native races' and that they all may become extinct 'unless more care was taken'.[52] When on the Board he visited Brungle Station and recommended the merging of the Aboriginal school and the local public school, but the Minister for Public Instruction 'could not see his way to adopt the suggestion'.[53] His school merger proposal points to a liberal view, but it would be speculation to infer that he may have opposed Donaldson on the issue of removing the children from the camps. Peter Board, Director of Education, joined the Board in 1907 but made no public comment on the issue of removals.[54]

---

51 Dowling, *Australia and America*, 71.
52 Francis, 'Social Darwinism and the Construction of Institutionalised Racism in Australia', 99.
53 *Gundagai Times and Tumut, Adelong and Murrumbidgee District Advertiser*, 16 December 1904, 4.
54 Further discussion of Peter Board is found in Chapter 7 on the removal of Aboriginal children from schools.

4. THE 'ALMOST WHITE' CHILDREN, 1904–1910

Inspector-General of Police and new Board chair Thomas Garvin (Figure 4.3) raised no apparent objections to Donaldson's views. Garvin took over from Edmund Fosbery on 31 December 1903. He chaired the Board up to the end of 1911 but remained on the Board until early 1916. From police records, he was a 'capable and efficient police officer, patient, well-organised and unruffled in approach'.[55] He undertook his work on the Board with the same diligence and commitment.[56] Garvin was dedicated and tenacious. J.S. Ryan, writing for the Armidale Historical Society, stressed his 'drive and dedication', citing that in 1907, after his hip was broken by a tram, Garvin was within 10 days 'conducting the whole business of his huge department from his hospital bed'.[57] He received high praise from Fosbery for his efforts to secure the capture of several high-profile felons – including the 'Governor brothers' – and as an able rider in the mounted police.

Garvin was not without ego. Not everyone needs to praise themselves at their own retirement, but Garvin clearly did:

> It is well known that I have been a constant worker night and day, and that I have never spared myself … I pointed out [to the colonial secretary] that after continuous and arduous service for nearly 49 years I leave the force in the highest state of efficiency as an up-to-date service.[58]

He was a policeman first and foremost and made sure that the force remained central to the Board's work. When the Reverend Henry Nolan, member of the Local Aborigines Board for Gulargambone in north-central New South Wales, challenged the role of the police in Aboriginal affairs, Garvin would have none it. Nolan wrote a lengthy submission to the colonial secretary offering suggestions to be included in the 'forthcoming Bill', such as the provision of large reserves for all the Aboriginal people, special Board powers to keep the residents on the reserves, a separate department to deal with Aboriginal affairs as the 'Police Department is … most unsuitable … to manage the Aborigines', and the inclusion

---

55   Ryan, 'Thomas Garvin (CISO), 1843/1922', 63. Edmund Fosbery remained on the Board until 1905 (see *APBR* 1906, 1).
56   The available records between 1905 and 1916 indicate that he attended 303 Board meetings out of a possible 365, an attendance rate of 83 per cent: analysis of APB Minutes (hereafter *APBM*) from 1905 to 1916 (records missing between 1906 and 1909). All *APBM* accessed via: Minute Books (Aborigines Welfare Board), NRS 2, NSW Department of Aboriginal Affairs, Sydney.
57   Ryan, 'Thomas Garvin (CISO), 1843/1922', 89.
58   *SMH*, 9 November 1910, 8.

of the 'softening and elevating influence of religion ... on the reserves'.⁵⁹ Garvin informed the colonial secretary that Nolan's suggestion of reservations was totally impracticable and stressed that the 'Half-castes' now want to earn their own living and should be encouraged to do so, as the goal is to have them eventually 'absorbed' into the general population.⁶⁰ In a subsequent letter to the colonial secretary, Garvin insisted that the police were the best-placed organisation to run Aboriginal affairs.⁶¹

Figure 4.3: Thomas Garvin.
Source: Inspector-General of Police, Government Printing Office, 1-12252, New South Wales State Archives & Records.

Thomas Garvin did not oppose Donaldson on the removal of the children. In the light of his views on the absorption of the 'half-caste' population, is it more than likely that he would have approved.

Drafting the legislation

The first mention by the Board of its proposed legislation in the twentieth century was in its report for the year ending 1902:

> The Board ... feel that the time has arrived for the introduction of other much-needed legislation giving them power to extend their operations in the best interests of the aboriginal inhabitants of the State. Much has been done to improve their condition, but in the absence of necessary legislation ... the Board's powers are but limited.⁶²

---

59   Letter from Rev. Henry Nolan to Colonial Secretary's Department, 24 February 1908, CSIL 1909, 5/7030. 1-1200 (no item number) (SRNSW).
60   Letter from Garvin to Colonial Secretary, 16 March 1908, CSIL, 1909, 5/7030, Item 08.345 (SRNSW).
61   Letter from Garvin to Colonial Secretary, 20 March 1908, CSIL, 1909, 5/7030 (no item number) (SRNSW).
62   *APBR* 1903, 3. Accessed via 'NSW', To Remove and Protect, AIATSIS: aiatsis.gov.au/sites/default/files/docs/digitised_collections/remove/22888.pdf.

4. THE 'ALMOST WHITE' CHILDREN, 1904–1910

Unfortunately, from December 1906 until March 1910, the period in which the legislation was refined and drafted, the Board minutes are missing. However, when the minutes do 'reappear' in March 1910, George Ardill proposed an extensive range of further suggestions to improve Board procedures and to facilitate the new legislation – an indication that he may well have been heavily involved in the drafting phase.

One indicator of 'general involvement' was Board attendance. Figure 4.4 indicates attendance levels (from available records) of members for their entire time spent on the Board. The following were members on the Board during the lead-up to the legislation: Ardill (85.6 per cent) and Garvin (83 per cent) were the most regular attenders, followed by Trenchard (67.5 per cent) and Dowling (67.4 per cent). MacFarlane, Varley, Norrie, Chanter and Peter Board were very irregular, and parliamentarians Robert Scobie and Hill rarely attended. Another poor attendant, John See, had left by 1902. Donaldson attended just under a third of all meetings at 30.6 per cent.[63]

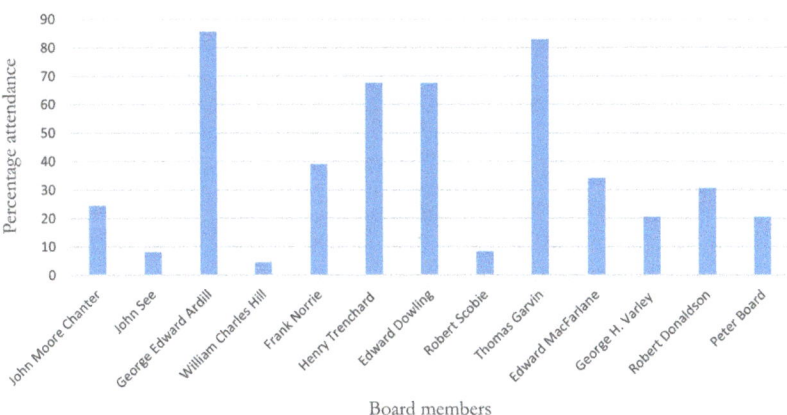

Figure 4.4: Board member attendance by percentage during the lead-up to the *Aborigines Protection Act 1909*.
Source: Author's analysis of Board minutes.

Trenchard, considering his history, may well have been a reluctant participant in forming restrictive legislation and it is unclear if Dowling may have offered to assist in the draft. Most likely, Garvin, Ardill, Donaldson and secretary Robert Beardsmore were responsible. Even with Donaldson's poor attendance rate, in the light of his regular public

---

63 See Appendix 1 for bibliographical notes and more detailed attendance information.

statements on the removal of children, it is inconceivable that he did not have some input into drafting the legislation. Moreover, he took a lead parliamentary role in the debate on the Bill (see below) because he knew more about the legislation than the colonial secretary.

Board Secretary Beardsmore prepared a brief to Premier Joseph Carruthers in 1907 that outlined the priorities for legislation. He mentioned two pressing points: the need to give the Board the power to remove girls from the camps, and for the provision of a paid inspector to visit all the stations. Beardsmore's brief appraised the premier of the Board's history and 'achievements', the honorary nature of the Board, and how it generally conducted its business.[64] After 24 years the Board was still an appendage to government.

As mentioned above, three colonies (Victoria, Western Australia and Queensland) had already acted on restrictive legislation before Federation in 1901. If New South Wales needed a blueprint for legislation, it had one in the Victorian model – Victoria and New South Wales had more in common, as their Aboriginal populations were not as remote as those of the vast expanses of outback Queensland and in Western Australia.

Victoria had passed three pieces of legislation by 1901: the *Aborigines Protection Act 1869*, the *Aborigines Protection Act 1886* and then the *Victorian Aborigines Act 1890*. The 1869 Victorian Act allowed for the removal of Aboriginal children to an institution if the children were 'neglected' by their parents or left 'unprotected'. However, the Victorian Board was unimpressed with the rate of the removals and introduced a regulation in 1899 that permitted the removal of *any* child of mixed descent over 14 years of age – not just those 'neglected'.[65] Richard Broome notes that under the 1890 Act, Aboriginal people were controlled by 40 regulations.[66] Some of these regulations sought to protect Aboriginal people from unscrupulous employers and to ensure assistance for the infirm, but many others were punitive. Overall, the impact of both the 1886 and 1890 Acts on Aboriginal people fell into four areas: a loss of freedom; removal from their homes; dividing kin and the removal of children; and the closure of reserves.[67]

---

64   Letter from APB Secretary R. Beardsmore to Under-Secretary of Colonial Secretary's Department, 9 July 1907, CSIL 1909, 5/7030, 1 -1200, Item 07.398 (SRNSW).
65   Broome, *Aboriginal Victorians*, 192.
66   Broome, *Aboriginal Victorians*, 187.
67   Broome, *Aboriginal Victorians*, 193. Many of the Victorian regulations, such as all clothing supplied to Aboriginal people belonging to the Board, penalties for supplying liquor to Aboriginal people and restrictions on who could enter reserves, were all part of the New South Wales regulations imposed by the Board after 1909. See Read, *A Hundred Years War*, 55.

While there was only sporadic contact between the Boards of Victoria and New South Wales, Jack Horner argued that the New South Wales Act was an almost word-for-word replica of the Victorian *Aborigines Act 1890*.[68] The main thrust of the Victorian Act was to merge the 'half-caste' population into white society. Chesterman and Galligan argue that Victoria, with its relatively small numbers of Aboriginal people (as few as 565 in 1891) could have been expected to take a more liberal or generous view towards Aboriginal people.[69] In fact, it was the reverse; the Victorian Board 'did not allow familial relationships to deter it from pursuing a rigid line of division between "Aborigines" and "half-castes"'.[70] All 'part Aborigines' aged 34 and younger were to leave the stations. Colin Tatz explains:

> all non 'full-bloods' and 'half-castes' under 34 years of age were forcibly expelled from missions and reserves, irrespective of marital or sibling status, of need, of ability to cope in the mainstream, of whether they had somewhere to go in the outside world. The penalty for returning was a £20 fine – the equivalent of about $20,000 in today's currency [1995].[71]

By 1907 a draft Bill had been submitted by the New South Wales APB for government consideration.[72] Peter Read notes that its aim 'was, in short, to drive as many Aborigines as possible into the white community'.[73] The definition of an 'Aborigine' was a key element. It defined an Aboriginal person to be:

> any full-blooded aboriginal native of Australia, and any person apparently having an admixture of aboriginal blood who applies for or is in receipt of rations or aid from the board or residing on a reserve.[74]

---

68   Horner, *Bill Ferguson*, 6. There is only the occasional reference to other jurisdictions in the Board minutes; for example, *APBM*, 18 February 1892, received a report from the Victorian Board; *APBM*, 7 September 1893, Item 7. Some correspondence on individuals took place; for example, the New South Wales Board contacted the Victorian Board about a 'half-caste' girl absconding from New South Wales into Victoria, VPRS 10768, P0000, 13 February, 1911, File no 73, PROV.
69   Chesterman and Galligan, *Citizens Without Rights*, 13.
70   Chesterman and Galligan, *Citizens Without Rights*, 24. In October 1910, the Victorian parliament passed a further Act that repudiated the 1890 Act. The parliament now saw *no need* to separate 'half-caste' from 'full blood' Aboriginal people: *Aborigines Act 1910* (Vic.), section 2. The Victorian premier at the time, John Murray, who had a long association with Aboriginal people, sought to formalise the aid that was being provided to the 'half-caste' population and allow them also to reside back on the reserves. See Broome, *Aboriginal Australians*, 198.
71   Tatz, *Obstacle Race*, 39.
72   *APBR* 1908, 7. Accessed via 'NSW', To Remove and Protect, AIATSIS: aiatsis.gov.au/sites/default/files/docs/digitised_collections/remove/22922.pdf.
73   Read, *A Hundred Years War*, 55.
74   *Aborigines Protection Act 1909* (NSW), Section 3.

Everyone else had to leave the reserves and stations. This left the Board with enormous discretion to exclude people or withhold rations. Read remarked that other people:

> regardless of their skin colour, culture, family or how long they had lived in the districts or on the reserves were no longer allowed to do so – because they were no longer held to be Aborigines![75]

The legislation proposed that the Board could remove any person 'who, in the opinion of the Board, should be earning a living away from the reserve'.[76] Section 14 would empower the Board to cause any 'aborigines, or any persons apparently having an admixture of aboriginal blood in their veins, who were camped or about to camp within or near any reserve, town, or township' to be removed away from such locations.[77] Section 11 provided for the apprenticing of any Aboriginal child who was 14 years or over (as Victoria had done in 1899), subject to the *Apprentices Act 1901*.[78] The proposed legislation also sought restrictive regulations upon Aboriginal people occupying the reserves and stations. Read asserts that it was designed to make Aboriginal people feel that life would be better 'amongst the whites'.[79]

Although never openly acknowledged by the New South Wales APB, there was significant crossover of ideas and legislative measures between the New South Wales proposed legislation and the many Victorian Acts up to the end of first decade of the twentieth century.

The passage of the *Aborigines Protection Act 1909*

The debate on the New South Wales legislation took place in the Legislative Assembly late at night on 15 December 1909.[80] The 'clause by clause discussion in committee was more concerned about the best means of "improving the existing machinery" of administration, rather than the future

---

75 Read, *A Hundred Years War*, 55.
76 *Aborigines Protection Act 1909* (NSW), Sections 8(1) and (2).
77 *Aborigines Protection Act 1909* (NSW), Section 14.
78 *Aborigines Protection Act 1909* (NSW), Section 11.
79 Read, *A Hundred Years War*, 55.
80 Anna Doukakis points out that most debates of Aboriginal matters were always late at night or in the early hours of the morning. Doukakis, *The Aboriginal People*, 54.

of Aboriginal people'.[81] Robert Donaldson advocated for the legislation because of his role on the Board and, as the colonial secretary noted, had read the 'official letters from Victoria concerning the proposed Act'.[82]

The legislation did not pass without debate. Mr Nielson, representing the people of Yass, was concerned that 'half-caste' Aboriginal people should be able to live just like Europeans and not be controlled. Nielsen wanted to be quite sure

> that aborigines, who elected to lead the life of white men, and to go out working for their living, should be quite independent of the board. He did not want to see the board interfere with a man who wanted to lead an ordinary decent life – a half-caste, for instance, who wanted to lead the life of a white man – who had nothing to do with the aborigines' camp.[83]

Donaldson responded that the Act only applied to Aboriginal people as defined in the Act and those who were receiving rations or applied for rations.[84] This was an expedient definition implying that Aboriginal people could opt out of the act. This was not true. In fact, all Aboriginal people came under some aspects of the Act such as its regulation on the sale of liquor, its provisions for the removal of children and its power to forcibly remove people from a reserve.[85] There was a lengthy exchange regarding the amount of money to be set aside for the Board to administer the Act, the value of installing telephones on the Aboriginal stations, the necessity to appoint inspectors, the supply of liquor and the health requirements for Aboriginal people. More notably, however, there was little further debate on the restrictive and controlling nature of the legislation.

Robert Scobie (Figure 4.5), member for Murray and a Board member, spoke on the issue of the amount of money granted to the Board each year. Scobie, a saddler and storekeeper by trade in Scotland, had moved to Australia around 1878 and established a business in Menindee. He moved to Sydney, joined the Australian Workers' Union and was elected to the seat of Wentworth in July 1901. He joined the APB in 1901. Anna Doukakis observes that

---

81 Horner, *Bill Ferguson*, 6.
82 Horner, *Bill Ferguson*, 6. Unfortunately, Horner did not leave a footnote as to the whereabouts of these letters. I have been unable to find them if they still exist.
83 NSW, *Parliamentary Debates,* Legislative Assembly, 15 December 1909, 4542 (Nielson).
84 NSW, *Parliamentary Debates,* Legislative Assembly, 15 December 1909, 4542 (Robert Donaldson). Technically correct, but an Aboriginal person had to convince the local policemen who supervised the reserves, or the manager who ran the Aboriginal station, that they required the rations.
85 *Aborigines Protection Act 1909* (NSW), Sections 9, 11 and 14.

he was asked to join the Board after he approached Premier John See (also a Board member) on behalf of his Aboriginal constituents who 'were in much worse condition than previously and no longer employed on the pastoral stations'.[86] Scobie's attendance at Board meetings was abysmal. This goes to the heart of one of the major failings of the Board: poor attendance did not disqualify ongoing membership. For the first seven years of available records Scobie only attended eight meetings – an average of one per year.[87] It would have been impossible for Scobie to engage in the work of the Board with such a poor attendance rate. Yet, he felt he could still speak confidently about Board matters.

Figure 4.5: Robert Scobie.
Source: Parliamentary Archives, NSW Parliament Collection (ScobieRobert-19P-1901).

The following two exchanges in the debate between Scobie and Donaldson (fellow Board members) are instructive as they reveal disagreement between the two. The first exchange concerned the 'Vote' (the amount of money) for the Board. Donaldson had formally moved that the Board would prefer a fixed annual sum of £20,000 instead of the variable amounts it had received from year to year. The opposing argument ran that the Board should be subject to the same yearly scrutiny as other statutory Boards throughout the state and that the parliament should decide on the annual amount. The colonial secretary, William Wood, countered by suggesting that a flat grant would be acceptable and that the Board would not abuse its power in dispensing with the money. Scobie opposed Donaldson. He said that 'Boards were all liable to go slightly wrong in their action' and there should be due scrutiny. Further, the Board may require more

---

86 Doukakis, *The Aboriginal People*, 108.
87 Over his last five years on the Board his attendance improved slightly. Overall, he attended only 33 meetings out of a possible 399, an average rate of 8.27 per cent. Author's analysis of *APBM* 1901 to 1916.

money, and it was therefore an unnecessary restriction.[88] Donaldson urged that the extra and regular (but capped) money was required to 'take charge of the neglected children'.[89] Scobie responded that the Board could always ask for 'an extra grant'. Donaldson did not pursue that matter; he either accepted the idea of an extra grant or that he had lost the debate. Donaldson's clause was rejected.[90]

The second exchange was over the provision of alcohol to Aboriginal people in case of sickness or an accident. Donaldson sought an amendment, that 'sickness' be omitted. He argued that there would be nothing to prevent:

> [a] half-caste, quadroon or octoroon, who possessed all the cunning of the lower class white men, from going into a hotel, and shamming a sudden attack of sickness in order to get grog.[91]

Scobie rejected this, pointing out that there might be

> [a] sick blackfellow on the station, whose horse had thrown him, and if the squatter gave him a glass of grog he would come under the penalty imposed by this act.[92]

Colonial Secretary Wood explained that an Aboriginal man, on the station, would not come under the Act.[93] Both exchanges reflect flawed Board processes and the lack of connectivity among members.

The Bill faced no opposition in the Legislative Council. John Hughes and Edmund Fosbery (former Board chair) were the only two speakers in the debate. Hughes opened with,

> I do not think hon. Members will require a very long explanation of this bill. It is a simple one for the protection of what is left of the aborigines of Australia.[94]

He outlined the clauses of the Bill and how each would facilitate the work of Board. He proposed no amendments or concerns.

---

88 NSW, *Parliamentary Debates*, Legislative Assembly, 15 December 1909, 4543 (Scobie).
89 NSW, *Parliamentary Debates*, Legislative Assembly, 15 December 1909, 4544 (Robert Donaldson).
90 NSW, *Parliamentary Debates*, Legislative Assembly, 15 December 1909, 4544.
91 NSW, *Parliamentary Debates*, Legislative Assembly, 15 December 1909, 4547 (Robert Donaldson).
92 NSW, *Parliamentary Debates*, Legislative Assembly, 15 December 1909, 4548 (Scobie).
93 Robert Scobie himself had little regard for the 'half-caste'. He has become infamous for his comments in 1915 when he offered in parliament that there were 6,000 'mixed blood' Aboriginal people growing up in New South Wales and that 'it is a danger to us to have people like this amongst us, looking upon our institutions with eyes different to ours'. Quoted in Goodall, *Invasion to Embassy*, 2008, 142.
94 NSW, *Parliamentary Debates*, Legislative Council, 17 December 1909, 4654 (John Hughes).

Fosbery's contribution is important as it provides the first window into his views since 1883. He began in similar fashion, 'It is not my intention to delay the House many moments in making a few observations regarding this bill'. He recalled that four of the first Board members were all once members of the Legislative Council (King, Hill, Suttor and Foster) and that they all devoted themselves 'with great assiduity to the task of removing the disabilities under which the unfortunate race was suffering'. He outlined some of the changes that had taken place over the last 27 years, indicating that back in 1884 the numbers of 'full-blood aborigines' were between 6,000 and 7,000 and that now they were around 2,000 and that the necessity for extra money should therefore diminish. The 'object of the Board, no doubt is, and always has been', that those people living on the reserves, who are 'half-castes, quadroons and octoroons, should merge as soon as possible into the general community'. He explained that the object of the stations had been to provide for those who were 'crippled, aged, and infirm, and, above all, to provide some education and training for the children, in order that they may be apprenticed out'.[95]

Then he changed tack. He urged that the Bill was well overdue and had been 'earnestly sought' by the Board for a long time – a strange phrase to use when there was no evidence that he actively pursued the legislation during his tenure. Yet his speech clearly disagreed with the Bill's core premise. Fosbery presented a confusing picture that put him at odds with the legislation and exposed deep-seated views that had prevented him from proposing such legislation when he was chair of the Board. He recalled how the predicament of Aborigines in the 'old times was a standing historical disgrace', and that he had found them wandering about like 'pariah dogs seeking for scraps and bones' and that they had no clothing or shelter and disease was prevalent. He believed that most Aboriginal people living on the reserves and stations were good people, many were 'total abstainers' but there were 'intruders', who would not leave. Fosbery acknowledged that there was a great affinity within Aboriginal families 'which prevents them from parting from anyone of their blood, even if they are only quadroons'. He explained to the Legislative Council that they could not be forcibly removed, as was the case in Victoria. He also offered that you could not put all the Aboriginal people on one station as they 'will not remove' from where they have been living for years.[96] Despite this deep disagreement,

---

95 NSW, *Parliamentary Debates*, Legislative Council, 17 December 1909, 4654 (Edmund Fosbery).
96 NSW, *Parliamentary Debates*, Legislative Council, 17 December 1909, 4654 (Edmund Fosbery).

he urged the Council to pass the Bill without delay.[97] In 1909 at the age of 75 Fosbery was reflective, clearly torn and perhaps considering his legacy. Read remarks, 'Fosbery's peaceful vision of self-sufficient riverside communities was entirely swept away [after the Act]'.[98] The *Aborigines Protection Act 1909* passed in late December 1909 and became law in July 1910.

The Board had no time for Fosbery's sentiments. It moved quickly and circulars where issued to all stations seeking particulars of residents, especially the 'half-castes', 'quadroons' and 'octoroons'; the particulars of girls and boys above the age of 14; details of 'respectable' householders 'desirous of securing the services of aboriginal apprentices'; and particulars of 'orphan children in the various camps'.[99] A suite of restrictive measures had been established to control Aboriginal people of New South Wales and would remain for the life of the Board and beyond.[100]

A direction forged

Robert Donaldson's regular and targeted policy pronouncements laid the groundwork for the successful passage of the *Aborigines Protection Act 1909*. In the lead-up to the legislation he established himself as the most forceful public figure on the Board. Just as Ardill had provided an impetus for a hard-edged approach to Board policy at turn of the century, Donaldson did the same with his single-minded focus on the removal of girls and determination that they would never return to their families. Ardill had targeted children before Donaldson's accession to the Board, but Donaldson turned illicit action into state policy. His public advocacy shaped the position of the Board and the legislatures and cleared a path that led to the systematic removal of Aboriginal children that continued well past the middle of the twentieth century. The government and the Board, collectively, were responsible for the passage of restrictive legislation that affected only one section of Australian society, but it was Donaldson who galvanised the Board to remove the 'almost white' girls from the camps.

---

97 NSW, *Parliamentary Debates*, Legislative Council, 17 December 1909, 4654 (Edmund Fosbery).
98 Read, *A Hundred Years War*, 55.
99 *APBM*, 14 July 1910, Item 1.
100 Restrictive legislative measures remained for 60 years until the end of the Aborigines Welfare Board in 1969.

Donaldson's success in achieving his goals was also a reflection of the Board's inherent weaknesses. The APB allowed for lone wolf operators to speak on policy without Board approval. It permitted members to independently lobby the government and it tolerated very poor attendance at Board meetings. These failings persisted throughout its tenure. Donaldson's rise to power was only beginning. The Board soon realised that it still did not have enough power to remove the children – it wanted to bypass the courts. Over the next five years, with Donaldson's imposing presence and persistent policy proposals, the Board would achieve that goal.

5

Enter the bureaucrats, 1916

By 1916 the New South Wales Aboriginal Protection Board (APB) had functioned for 33 years and 37 members had served.[1] Apart from *The Report from the Select Committee on the Condition of the Aborigines* in 1845, commissioned by the New South Wales Parliament, the New South Wales Government did not undertake a major inquiry into the status or the needs of its Aboriginal population up to the establishment of the Board in 1883.[2] After the creation of the Board, this path of indifference continued well into the twentieth century and the Board carried out its operations with little interference or oversight.

Historically this was unusual. Victoria had its first Select Committee 'into Aborigines' in 1859, followed by a Royal Commission on 'Aborigines', and then a report on the Aboriginal settlement at Coranderrk in 1882. Queensland provided a Select Committee report into the 'Native Police and Aborigines' in 1861, there were two more reports into the condition of Aboriginal people at Mackay (1874 and 1876), and a Select Committee on the 'Aboriginals of Queensland' held in 1896. Western Australia had no fewer than 11 Select Committees and reports on the 'Aboriginal Natives' up to 1904, with a full Royal Commission in 1905. South Australia had its first Select Committee on 'The Aborigines' in 1860, a second one in 1866 on the 'Management of Northern Territory Expedition' and a Royal

---

1   See Appendix 1 for full list of Board members and short profiles.
2   *The Report from the Select Committee on the Condition of the Aborigines, with appendix, minutes of evidence, and replies to a circular letter*, commissioned by the New South Wales Parliament, Legislative Council in 1845, was mainly in response to the failed Port Phillip Protectorate. The only other Select Committee was in 1858, but with a narrow focus on the murders of whites by Aborigines on the Dawson River.

Commission on 'The Aborigines' in 1913.³ In stark contrast, New South Wales had no official major inquiries.⁴ The 'mother state' would wait until 1937 and 1938 to have its first official inquiries undertaken by a Select Committee and then by the Public Service Board, respectively, into the New South Wales APB. Put another way, from 1859 to 1916 there were 23 significant inquiries concerning Aboriginal populations across Australia, but *none* were staged in New South Wales. To press the point a little further, the opinions of the secretary of the New South Wales APB, Robert Henry Beardsmore, on Aboriginal people and policy direction are found, not in any New South Wales archive, but between questions 2118 and 2144 of the 1913 Royal Commission 'on the Aborigines' in South Australia.⁵

There is a paradox here. Although other jurisdictions had many inquiries into 'Aborigines', this did not mean that Aboriginal people in other states had better outcomes. On the contrary, Victoria, the first to undertake such inquiries, was in fact the first colony to impose the most coercive legislation: the *Aborigines Protection Act 1886*.⁶ The very fact that no major inquiries took place in New South Wales may have helped cocoon its Aboriginal population from an early onset of punitive legislation. As Heather Goodall notes, the Aboriginal people of New South Wales had successfully acquired 31 reserves (for their own use) between 1861 and 1864, whereas by 1869 the Victorian Board had strict management control over *all* six Aboriginal reserves.⁷ John Chesterman and Brian Galligan remind us that after Federation Aboriginal people 'had no share in the rights and entitlements that ordinary citizens enjoyed'.⁸ State scrutiny brought more control, not less, over Aboriginal people.

---

3   These reports, select committees and Commissions, are found on the Australian Institute of Aboriginal and Torres Strait Islander Studies (AIATSIS) website, 'To Remove and Protect': aiatsis.gov.au/collections/collections-online/digitised-collections/remove-and-protect.
4   Thornton's Report, in 1882, was significant in the NSW context but it was mostly statistical and, in part, a defence of his own policies. The Fosbery/King two-page report on Maloga and Warangesda, 1882, was the result of the opinions of two people only, both of whom became inaugural Board members.
5   Correspondence Files VPRS 1694/P0000/15, Question 2127, South Australian Royal Commissions, 1913, Public Records Office Victoria (hereafter PROV), 107–10.
6   Christie, *Aborigines in Colonial Victoria*, 178–204.
7   Christie, *Aborigines in Colonial Victoria*, 179–80.
8   Chesterman and Galligan, *Citizens Without Rights*, 2–3.

Just like the absence of any inquiries into its own Aboriginal population prior to the establishment of the Board in 1883, for the next 33 years there had been no official analysis or inspection of the Board's functionality or effectiveness. The Board's only requirement was an annual report to the colonial secretary, which it produced diligently, but the reports, and the Board's overall policy directions, were never questioned.

However, the government suddenly intervened in 1916. Virtually overnight, without warning, it replaced all the private individuals on the Board with a membership predominately composed of senior public servants. The events leading up to the restructure and the ramifications of the government's decision to do so is the subject of this chapter.

Ardill's elevation to vice-chair

The *Aborigines Protection Act 1909* (NSW) came into force on 1 June 1910. Robert Donaldson had done much of the promotional work, regularly articulating his views in public and through the parliament. George Ardill, on the other hand, focused on the administrative work of the Board and his enthusiastic approach in the carriage of his duties was rewarded with his rise to the vice-chair, a position made available under the new Act on 23 June 1910.[9] Donaldson may have been an obvious choice for vice-chair but his sporadic attendance and role as a parliamentarian may have excluded him. Perhaps he did not want the position. He preferred to be his own boss, expressing his views freely. Ardill, the always-present fixer, was better suited to the position. In August 1910, Ardill presented a minute to the Board outlining a reorganisation of the office. He suggested the appointment of an 'Inspector and Secretary', a 'competent Clerk', a typist, a 'Home finder and a superintendent of Apprentices'. He raised the issue of apprenticing children and advocated the removal of all able-bodied 'Quadroon' and 'Half-castes' from the Board's stations and reserves. This was the first major policy articulation recorded in the available Board minutes since 1883. The Board accepted his proposal about the clerk and typist but postponed indefinitely all other issues.[10] Why the other Board members present did not accept all his

---

9   APB Minutes (hereafter *APBM*), 23 June 1910, Item 1. All *APBM* accessed via: Minute Books (Aborigines Welfare Board), NRS 2, NSW Department of Aboriginal Affairs, Sydney.
10 *APBM*, 11 August 1910, Item 1.

suggestions is unclear. They may have felt that he was being too forceful too early in his tenure as vice-chair, or they needed more time to consider the more important issues of his proposals.

Ardill opened on another front: he recognised that the *Aborigines Protection Act 1909* still did not allow for the easy removal of children. An entry in the minutes of a late July Board meeting in 1910 flagged the problem for the Board. A Mrs Bain had requested an Aboriginal apprentice and the Board response was 'Instruct the manager [of the Aboriginal station] to endeavour to persuade the girl's mother to allow her to accept the situation'.[11] The Aboriginal girl was under the age of 14 so the Board had to either cajole the mother to release her or apply to the courts to have her removed. Ironically, now that the Act was in place, the Board felt more pressure to operate within the bounds of the law. As mentioned previously, informal removal 'arrangements' had taken place for years, with scant consideration for age or anything else, but now that the Board had legislation it was constrained to work within it. Ardill realised that nothing less than a full legislative mandate to remove all children, regardless of age or reason would be acceptable.

In November 1911 Ardill raised the issue again and presented to the Board a comprehensive array of policy recommendations. He proposed the appointment of an inspector and a homefinder; the establishment of a training home for Aboriginal girls and boys; wider powers to control Aboriginal children; the transferral of government money from the Department of Instruction to the APB; the Board to appoint all teachers to its stations; the closure of the smaller reserves; and the forced removal of able-bodied 'half-castes' and 'quadroons' from all reserves after 12 months' notice.[12] The Board again deferred almost everything that Ardill had proposed. But it did agree to

> wait upon the minister and urge the appointment of an inspector ... [and approve] the steps being taken to induce the aborigines on smaller reserves to remove to larger reserves where there are managers and teachers.[13]

Ardill had not achieved all he wanted, but, importantly, he was given licence to proceed with his suggestions and to draft changes to the Act.

---

11   *APBM*, 21 July 1910, Item 7. (It is unclear as to which Aboriginal station the minutes referred.)
12   *APBM*, 30 November 1911, Item 11.
13   *APBM*, 30 November 1912, Item 11.

He responded quickly and in early 1912 presented several changes, which all were carried by the Board. His proposals were extensive. Over the last three decades of the life of the Board this was the first instance where such a detailed program for change had been tabled in the Board minutes.[14] As far as Aboriginal children were concerned, Ardill recommended that the Board should have full control and custody of the child of 'any aborigine', that the Board have discretion to make its own terms and conditions and not abide by those of the NSW *Apprentices Act 1901*, that if any child refused a Board placement then the Board could remove that child to any home or institution, that any child absconding from a placement by the Board would be dealt with as a 'neglected child' under the *Neglected Children and Juvenile Offenders Act 1905* (NSW), that the Board have control over the finances and appointment of teachers, and that a training home for 'the lads' be established at the earliest possible date.[15]

In April 1912, all these points were accepted by the Board and Ardill's proposals formed the basis of policy. John Ramsland declared: 'on a single day he turned the Aborigines Protection Board into a ministry of fear' by advocating a rigid 'prison like universe for all Aboriginal adults who were unfortunate to be living on the state's Aboriginal Reserves and Stations'.[16] Ardill and Donaldson were given the task of framing policy and preparing regulations in connection with the amending Act. They were unlikely bedfellows – two dominant men with quite different personalities – but their shared focus on child removals led to productive collaboration. After Ardill and Donaldson's deliberations, a deputation called upon Fred Flowers MLA to put the Board's case for changes to the 1909 Act – chiefly to increase its powers to remove children.

The Board formally met with Fred Flowers on 13 May 1912.[17] The deputation comprised Mr Ernest Day, Police Commissioner (APB chair), Robert Scobie, George Ardill, Robert Donaldson and R.H. Beardsmore (secretary). The Board sought a paid inspector to visit the stations, reserves and camps to provide a consistent approach across the state; the

---

14   There may have been an equally extensive submission in the lead-up and drafting of the *Aborigines Protection Act 1909* (NSW), but unfortunately the minutes are missing for that period.
15   *APBM,* 18 April 1912, Item 2.
16   Ramsland, 'Ardill, George'.
17   Fred Flowers was not the colonial secretary (he had been, but for only 19 days in 1911); in May 1912 he was not even a minister, although he was Minister for Public Instruction for a brief period up to February 1912. It is curious that he – and not the current colonial secretary, James McGovern – met the deputation. However, the Board may have felt Flowers would be more sympathetic to their agenda.

establishment of a homefinder position to secure domestic situations for the Aboriginal children; and the power to remove children from the camps.

Apart from Beardsmore, each member made a submission. Day informed Flowers that the Board wanted an inspector to visit all the stations and reserves so that the 'treatment of aborigines throughout the whole of the state [would] be uniform'. An inspector could launch snap visits that would have a 'salutary effect'.[18] He also requested the establishment of a female 'Homefinder' who could obtain 'particulars of suitable children' and 'find suitable homes in which to place them'.[19] Ardill conflated several issues. He admitted that many of the camps 'had not been visited by the Board', that visits had been 'haphazard', and the condition of some of the camps 'reflected credit on neither the Board or the Government'. He proposed that the Board should be able to apprentice children from the age of 12 and that the Board should have 'full control over the children'.[20] Ardill also advocated for Board-directed Aboriginal education, and stated that Aboriginal children 'need not be educated right up to the standard of the white population'.[21] Robert Scobie presented a more humanitarian, even progressive, perspective. He declared that 'aborigines were not given the same privileges and rights that they should get in this democratic country'. Education was vital, but once educated 'there was no opening for them in the white population of the country'.[22] He then fell in with the prevailing Board views regarding the 'deplorable state of the aboriginal communities' and he feared for the children exposed to the 'low class white population'.[23] Donaldson remained focused on the children. He claimed that the camps were established 25 years previously to provide 'relief to the old darkies, but they had gradually drifted into breeding grounds for half-castes'. The only way 'out of the trouble was to take the white children away and merge them into the general population'. If the girls were removed from the camps it would reduce the financial burden on the

---

18   APB Deputation to the CS, 13 May 1912, Colonial Secretary's In-Letters (hereafter CSIL), 1913, 5/7165, 1-2100, Item 12.134, 1–2, State Records of New South Wales (hereafter SRNSW).
19   APB Deputation to the CS, 13 May 1912, CSIL 1913, 5/7165, 1-2100, Item 12.134, 3 (SRNSW).
20   APB Deputation to the CS, 13 May 1912, CSIL 1913, 5/7165, 1-2100, Item 12.134, 4 (SRNSW).
21   APB Deputation to the CS, 13 May 1912, CSIL 1913, 5/7165, 1-2100, Item 12.134, 4 (SRNSW).
22   APB Deputation to the CS, 13 May 1912, CSIL 1913, 5/7165, 1-2100, Item 12.134, 5 (SRNSW).
23   *Maitland Daily Mercury*, 13 May 1912, 5.

state and eventually the camps could be abolished.[24] Fred Flowers found the whole discussion a 'revelation … especially those [points] made by Mr Scobie and Mr Donaldson'.[25]

Cracks appear between the Board and government

Flowers agreed to bring the matters before Cabinet and to have their statements typed up and sent to every minister of the Crown.[26] However, the necessary funding was rejected by Colonial Secretary James McGovern, citing the 'need for economy'.[27] Soon after, the Board sought funding to cover the costs of their own members to carry out the inspections.[28] The minutes of 14 August 1913 record that the new colonial secretary, William Holman, refused permission for Board members to visit the stations and reserves, would not consider any payment of members and had not responded to the Board's entreaties on the matter.[29] In the past the police had undertaken the bulk of inspections, so the colonial secretary could argue that it was unnecessary for members to duplicate that state-funded role. Interestingly, as Naomi Parry remarks, Ardill was the only Board member without a salary and 'was in financial strife' from operating his various Homes across Sydney.[30]

The Board, exasperated by continued funding rejections, reacted dramatically, Ardill proposed:

> That in view of the discourtesy shown … by the minister in failing to reply to the request [to visit] Stations and Reserves to secure necessary information … without which … the Board cannot judiciously or satisfactorily deal with the conditions

---

24 APB Deputation to the CS, 13 May 1912, CSIL 1913, 5/7165, 1-2100, Item 12.134, 6 (SRNSW).
25 APB Deputation to the CS, 13 May 1912, CSIL 1913, 5/7165, 1-2100, Item 12.134, 6 (SRNSW).
26 *Sydney Morning Herald* (hereafter *SMH*), 14 May 1912, 7.
27 *Protection of Aborigines: Report of the Board* (the APB Report: hereafter *APBR*) 1913, 3. Accessed via 'NSW', To Remove and Protect, AIATSIS: aiatsis.gov.au/sites/default/files/docs/digitised_collections/remove/23014.pdf.
28 *Daily Telegraph*, 11 October 1913, 13.
29 *APBM*, 14 August 1913, Item 1; James McGowen (Labor) was colonial secretary from 27 November 1911 to 29 June 1913.
30 Parry, 'Such a Longing', 281.

prevailing ... and the further discourtesy shown ... in failing to reply ... the Board decline to proceed with any further business until the minister has made a suitable reply.[31]

The Board went on strike. The matter was noted across the border in Victoria, where *The Age* wrote:

> The Board for the Protection of Aborigines has passed a resolution declining to proceed with any further business until some notice is taken of its action to visit the aborigines' reserves ... The [Board] sought Ministerial authority for an expenditure of £25 in connection with [the] proposed visits but this was declined.[32]

The *Richmond River Express and Casino Kyogle Advertiser* explained that Board members were purely 'honorary', attended 'weekly meetings and gave a large amount of time on matters submitted to them' and that the only costs to the government for recent visits to the reserves and stations were 15 shillings per day allowance and train fares. In response to the strike the colonial secretary said that he 'was perfectly willing to receive the deputation' but only when the 'current session of parliament is over'.[33]

It is unknown whether the Board was happy with the colonial secretary's guarantee but Ardill and the APB returned to work. However, Board member Dr Walter Hull handed his resignation to the chair on the following grounds:

> That the Minister has refused to authorise without giving any reason the payment of disbursements incidental to the inspection of Aboriginal Stations under the control of the Board and has not suggested any other means of inspection.

> That the Board is not justified in attempting to manage these stations unless it is able to inspect them from time to time as it considers the necessity of doing so arises.[34]

Medical doctor Walter Hull had replaced retiring Board member Dr Robert Paton on 10 April 1913. Hull had only spent seven months on the Board before he resigned over the stand-off on inspection payments. From 28 meetings he attended 23, an attendance rate of 82 per cent, so he appeared to be an interested replacement and felt the issue important

---

31 *APBM*, 13 October 1913, Item 1.
32 *The Age*, 13 October 1913, 10.
33 *The Richmond River Express and Casino Kyogle Advertiser*, 17 October 1913, 6.
34 *APBM*, 20 November 1913, Item 1.

enough to resign over.³⁵ Notwithstanding the deputation, the government in 1913 held firm; it was unprepared to fund the role of an inspector or pay members to undertake inspections.³⁶ The government never paid members to inspect the stations. The issue over funding had seen the first real 'crack' in the relationship between the Board and the government.

Full control of the children

In 1914 the Board put forward an amendment to the *Aborigines Protection Act 1909* (NSW) to allow the removal of Aboriginal children from their families without referral to the courts. If the Act was passed, the Board could remove any Aboriginal child, with no age restriction, as it saw fit. The managers of stations, or police, or any agent of the Board, could decide to remove a child. Aboriginal people would have redress to the courts only after the event.³⁷

In the Legislative Council, Fred Flowers introduced the amendment as a 'small alteration of the law with the object of dealing with the younger members' under the *Aborigines Protection Act 1909*.³⁸ Flowers was so impressed with Donaldson's submission in 1912 that he quoted directly from it. He informed the council that currently there were 'five half-castes for every two full-bloods'. In seeking increased powers to remove biracial children, the Board planned 'to put things in train on lines that would eventually lead to the camps being depleted of their populations and finally the closing of the reserves and camps altogether'. Consequently, the 'charge upon the State would disappear'. This would only be possible if the 'children were removed from the low surroundings of the camps and placed in a position where they would be sought after for healthy occupations'. In this way, the 'children would be saved and the camps abolished'.³⁹

---

35 Analysis of *APBM* for Hull's tenure on the Board.
36 Refusing members permission to visit the reserves and stations is curious. It is unclear if the colonial secretary had any other concerns about Board members visits but it can only be assumed that financial constraints were the issue.
37 *Aborigines Protection Amending Act 1915* (NSW), Section 4. New South Wales would have been aware of Victoria's move to yet again pass another Aborigines Protection Act in late 1915. However, the Victorian focus was not on the removal of children. It consolidated the repeal of the Aborigines Acts of 1890 and 1910, but it spawned some 56 regulations in 1916 that 'extended the Board's coercive powers over the lives of Aboriginal people' and mirrored many of the New South Wales regulations already in place. See Broome, *Aboriginal Victorians*, 202.
38 NSW, *Parliamentary Debates*, Legislative Council, 24 November 1914, 1353 (Fred Flowers).
39 NSW, *Parliamentary Debates*, Legislative Council, 24 November 1914, 1353 (Fred Flowers).

Flowers apprised the Legislative Council that the Board was requesting to become 'parents to the children' and that from 'whatever age' they could be removed from the 'civil influences of the camps, and apprenticed out or adopted as is thought fit'. He reminded members that currently the Board could only remove children over 14 and under 21 to be apprenticed but only with the permission of the 'child and its parents or guardians'. He advised that determining neglect can be 'unnecessarily cumbersome and ineffective' and that when actions had been instigated 'parents have removed children across the border into Victoria … [defeating] … the object of the Board'.[40]

He pointed out that a 'Home Finder' should be appointed to the Board and that 'this lady' (Miss Alice Lowe) had already undertaken visits to the camps encouraging mothers to give up their children. The mothers had refused, raising 'frivolous objection and withheld their consent'. Flowers pressed that the Board was now 'compelled' to push for change that would give them

> absolute control in *loco parentis* over every aboriginal child whose moral or physical welfare is, in the opinion of the Board, being imperilled by remaining, as they are to-day, under the influences of camp life.

Flowers again stressed the difficulty of proving neglect and the need to bypass the courts, saying that the 'difficulty of proving neglect where children are fairly clothed and fed is insurmountable'.[41] The crusade that Donaldson began in 1904 was coming to fruition.

Though Edmund Fosbery, as chair of the Board, had supported the removal of Aboriginal people from La Perouse in 1900, in 1914 he got to his feet to defend the camps. He did not consider that Flowers had been very fair in his depiction of them and encouraged fellow members to visit them for themselves, saying they would find that the 'moral condition of the camps has been in no respect neglected'. He informed members that there were schools and 'instruction classes for the female children' and other 'suitable employment for the male children'. But he could hardly argue against the amendment when it was he who proposed the measure

---

40   NSW, *Parliamentary Debates*, Legislative Council, 24 November 1914, 1354 (Fred Flowers).
41   NSW, *Parliamentary Debates*, Legislative Council, 24 November 1914, 1354 (Fred Flowers).

back in 1883, some 32 years prior.⁴² He added, 'it had always been the intention of the Board to almost entirely … absorb these half-castes and quadroons into the general community'. In a word of caution, he alerted members to the impending difficulties of the removal of Aboriginal children from their families. He stressed that there was a 'fervent and strong affection between the parents and relations of these half-caste and other children – an affection quite as strong as that exists amongst any of the white population'. He warned that Aboriginal parents would resist any attempt to remove their children, but claimed the only 'one proper way' to do this was to give the Board the authority to do it.⁴³ As in 1909, Fosbery was in two minds: he probably felt the need to defend his own legacy but had always been opposed to punitive measures. Though he had planted the seeds for removal three decades ago, it seems that he found the reality unpalatable.

The debate in the Assembly was much more robust. Colonial Secretary J.H. Cann introduced the amendment.⁴⁴ Although the voices of dissent were few, it was immediately attacked by Mr McGarry (member for Murrumbidgee) who interjected that the Act would 'steal the children away from their parents'.⁴⁵ McGarry's electorate took in the southern central part of New South Wales where there were significant numbers of Aboriginal people, including the long-established Aboriginal station of Warangesda. Cann defended his position by stating that it was not a question of stealing but of 'saving them' from immorality and placed the blame on Aboriginal women by innuendo, saying that a 'young girl of 13 may be an asset to an Aboriginal woman'. Cann concluded that the removal of the children would give them a fair chance in life and they would be 'reared in such a way as will enable them to merge into citizens amongst the white people'.⁴⁶

McGarry continued at length and his arguments best reflected the limited opposition to the amendment. He stressed that current legislation to prove neglect was available and that the Board should be satisfied to

---

42   The very first Board report sought control, as in *loco parentis*, of the children. *APBR* 1883–84, 2. Accessed via 'NSW', To Remove and Protect, AIATSIS: aiatsis.gov.au/sites/default/files/docs/digitised_collections/remove/22818.pdf.
43   *NSW, Parliamentary Debates*, Legislative Council, 24 November 1914, 1355.
44   John Cann became colonial secretary from 29 January 1914, so perhaps he had assumed carriage of this amendment before taking up his official position (i.e. he was speaking in the debate two days before his appointment).
45   NSW, *Parliamentary Debates*, Legislative Assembly, 27 January 1915, 1951 (McGarry).
46   NSW, *Parliamentary Debates*, Legislative Assembly, 27 January 1915, 1951 (J.H. Cann).

invoke it if needs be. He then spoke of the injustice of separation: 'I have heard of a measure of this kind talked of for years, but I never expected to see it submitted to parliament'. We have 'over-run their country and taken away their domain. We now propose to perpetrate further acts of cruelty upon them by separating the children from their parents'.[47] He reminded members that it would be almost impossible for an Aboriginal parent to fight the removal of a child through the court system as 'who will listen to her?' He agreed that the children should be controlled but that the 'child should not be separated from the mother' and made the point that society would 'never improve the child by taking it away from the parent'.[48] He concluded his major speech with another serve at the unscrupulous:

> We are going to hand over these children to merciless, grasping, cruel people, who are looking for cheap labour all the time.[49]

McGarry had exposed what had been happening for many years: the use of Aboriginal labour, both adult and child, without appropriate remuneration and indeed with cruelty. He even suggested that policemen may be 'in league' with squatters who sought absolute control of a child to 'use him as a slave'. He also raised the issues of prejudice from Board officials in dealing with the matters of child separation and suggested that managers and teachers on the stations were of limited ability or worse. He was certainly correct about the latter, as Tracey Bell's research has shown.[50]

Robert Scobie, member for Murray and a Board member, opposed the amendment too, but his contribution was muddled and contradictory. He did not believe the Board should have such powers, that 'these people' [the Aborigines] should be under the control of the Inspector-General of Police, then, confusingly, suggested a 'Protector' should be appointed, and complained that the parliament did not provide enough money to the Board.[51] He opposed the summary removal of Aboriginal children.[52]

---

47 NSW, *Parliamentary Debates*, Legislative Assembly, 27 January 1915, 1952–53 (McGarry).
48 NSW, *Parliamentary Debates*, Legislative Assembly, 27 January 1915, 1952–54 (McGarry).
49 NSW, *Parliamentary Debates*, Legislative Assembly, 27 January 1915, 1955 (McGarry).
50 Bell, 'A Benevolent Tyranny – The Role of Managers on Aboriginal Stations in New South Wales 1880–1965', 141. Bell reveals how the responsibilities of managers of Aboriginal of stations were far too broad and not all could be carried out competently.
51 NSW, *Parliamentary Debates*, Legislative Assembly, 27 January 1915, 1964–65 (Robert Scobie).
52 Doukakis, *The Aboriginal People*, 109.

The member for Naomi, George Black, raised several concerns. There were risks in leaving such decisions in the hands of ordinary Board officials. He expressed concern that the nation had neglected its duties towards the 'aboriginal owners' of the country and that Australia fared unfavourably to the comparative treatment of the original owners of New Zealand and America.[53] He stressed that the whole system of boarding-out the Aboriginal girls was wrong as many were left alone on isolated stations amongst young white men with obvious consequences. He also thought it was an act of 'cruelty to deprive a mother of her daughters'. Mr Fern, member for Cobar, agreed with Black, citing that he had many requests from people in his district for a young girl to be apprenticed to them but that he noted, in the case of a 'black child', she is 'generally hooked on to a plough or swings an axe' and nobody 'cares what becomes of her'.[54] Black was equally concerned that the police had to act on many things and one could not expect them to always act with 'humanitarian feelings'. He agreed with McGarry that they should 'return them to their original territory', with their families intact and supported 'to make a good living'.[55] Strangely, Black voted for the amendment but, as Naomi Parry points out, as a Cabinet government member, he was obliged to vote with the government.[56]

Scobie, Fern and McGarry voted against the amendment and there were 35 votes in favour.[57] All three men were 'rural Labor men who knew Aboriginal people well'.[58] Once again, as in the debate over the *Aborigines Protection Act 1909*, Board member Scobie voted against Board policy. Though he hardly ever engaged with the Board over his 16 years as a member, attending only 33 meetings from a possible 399 (see Appendix 1), he took a stand on key issues.

In the end it made no difference. The clear majority supported the amendment either because they firmly believed that it was right for the Board to be able to remove Aboriginal children without reference to the courts, or through indifference. The 1915 amendment gave the Board unprecedented powers.

---

53   NSW, *Parliamentary Debates*, Legislative Assembly, 27 January 1915, 1957 (George Black).
54   NSW, *Parliamentary Debates*, Legislative Assembly, 27 January 1915, 1962–63 (Fern).
55   NSW, *Parliamentary Debates*, Legislative Assembly, 27 January 1915, 1958 (George Black).
56   Parry, 'Such a Longing', 277.
57   NSW, *Parliamentary Debates*, Legislative Assembly, 27 January 1915, 1967.
58   Parry, 'Such a Longing', 276.

POWER AND DYSFUNCTION

Ardill pushes to expand Board jurisdiction

With the Board's new-found powers, an ever-vigilant Ardill recognised that the identification, removal and placement of young Aboriginal girls and boys into service required increased Board activity. He put forward a motion to the new colonial secretary, George Black, suggesting that due to an 'increased workload' the 'time had arrived' to pay members for their attendance at Board meetings.[59] While George Black ruminated over the request, Ardill pushed for Board control over the education of Aboriginal children on reserves and stations. On 15 July 1915, he put forward a motion to a special Board meeting:

> it is not deemed necessary by the Board that the full schedule of lessons laid down by the Department of Public Instruction should be given to these children, and as the Board is desirous of placing managers in charge of these various reserves, they wish to have the full control of all employees, so that such managers may also be appointed as school teachers, thus occupying the dual position.[60]

The Board had always considered that Aboriginal children should only require a basic education. The 1894 Board report stated:

> The usual standard for Public School is scarcely applicable for schools for Aboriginal children, at the suggestion of the Board, the subjects now taught are confined to reading, writing, dictation, and arithmetic.[61]

Ardill's motion sought full control by the APB of the curriculum and the appointment of teachers. Inherent in this proposal was that because the manager had to run the station, they would only need to teach a limited curriculum. The Board maintained that because Aboriginal children were only ever going to be domestic servants and labourers they were in no need of any higher education.[62] Ardill's motion also included a clause that asked that all moneys given to the Department of Education for the

---

59   *APBM*, 24 June 1915, Item 1. George Black (Labor) was colonial secretary from 15 March 1915 to 15 November 1916.
60   *APBM*, 15 July 1915 (special meeting), Item 23.
61   *APBR* 1894, 3. Accessed via 'NSW', To Remove and Protect, AIATSIS: aiatsis.gov.au/sites/default/files/docs/digitised_collections/remove/22879.pdf.
62   Fletcher, *Clean, Clad and Courteous*, 100.

teaching of Aboriginal children be transferred to the Board.[63] In another instance of Board friction, Henry Trenchard dissented from Ardill's motion on education.[64]

These were extraordinary requests. The Department of Education had allowed the Board to build the schools on stations and reserves, but the teaching component was its domain. Peter Board, the Director of Education (and previous APB member from 1907 to 1911), and James Dawson, chief inspector of schools, were unimpressed by Ardill's push for complete control. Both men were

> convinced that for historical reasons Aboriginal education was a government responsibility and a professional field which should not fall into the hands of men or boards who had not given adequate thought to the proper education of such children.[65]

However, as we shall see, Peter Board's commitment to Aboriginal education wavered over time. Ardill's insistent requests in an area considered outside the Board's brief added another point of tension between government and Board.

Donaldson loses by one vote

Although it failed in its bid to exercise more power over education, and the government was silent on payments for Board members, the Board finally convinced government of the need for an inspector.[66] The appointment, however, drew considerable controversy and most certainly contributed to the decision to reconstitute the Board. The Board considered that a full-time paid inspector, who would be free from weekly meetings and other work commitments, could focus fully on visiting all the stations and reserves around the state and provide a consistent policy approach. The duties, drawn up by Ardill and Board chair Garvin, were varied and broad: the inspector would visit and inspect all reserves, camps and stations; provide a full inventory regarding population, health, sanitation and buildings; examine the station manager's books; afford opportunities

---

63   *APBM*, 15 July 1915 (special meeting), Item 23.
64   *APBM*, 15 July 1915 (special meeting), Item 23.
65   Fletcher, *Clean, Clad and Courteous*, 100.
66   Requests for the appointment of an inspector can be found in the following Board reports (all accessed via AIATSIS: aiatsis.gov.au/collection/featured-collections/remove-and-protect): *APBR* 1912, 3; *APBR* 1913, 2; *APBR* 1914, 2; *APBR* 1915 (a deputation to the colonial secretary), 2.

for local boards and residents to state any complaints; provide appropriate advice to managers; enforce the Act regarding removal and guardianship of children; from 'time to time' visit each apprentice; endeavour to interview each resident on the reserve and station; enquire into the employment and treatment of Aboriginal people; receive no inducements; account for all expenses; and attend the Board office each day when in Sydney.[67]

The advertised position drew, incredibly, 511 applications, one of which was from Board member Robert T. Donaldson. A Board subcommittee (Ardill, Garvin and Alfred Hill) dealt with the applications and reduced the list to 24.[68] After interviews, the 10 remaining applicants underwent an exhaustive ballot by the full Board.[69] Mr A.L. Swindlehurst of Goulburn secured the position over Robert T. Donaldson by one vote.[70] It was astonishing that Donaldson did not win the ballot by a significant margin. He had been on the Board for the last 11 years, was instrumental in securing the passage of both the *Aborigines Protection Act 1909* and the amendment to the Act 1915, had been a policy driver and was conversant with operations on the ground. Swindlehurst was a complete outsider. At the time of his appointment he was the shire engineer in the Goulburn district, a prominent member of the St Saviour's Catholic Council and choir and a member of the Prisoners' Aid Society. A press release noted he would be greatly missed in many circles in Goulburn.[71] It is certainly interesting that he was chosen over Donaldson. One can only speculate that at least half of the Board did not embrace either Donaldson's views on Aboriginal matters or his 'operational style', or both.

George Black, colonial secretary in the Holman Labor Government, opposed Swindlehurst's appointment and wanted the Board to reconsider.[72] The Board passed a motion maintaining its position to appoint Swindlehurst and reminded Black that the Board had the power to do so. But there was also division within the Board. The new Board chair, James Mitchell (who joined in late 1914), and Robert Scobie (with a rare appearance on the Board) dissented from the motion.[73] Swindlehurst, recognising that

---

67 *APBM*, 24 June 1915, Item 1.
68 Alfred Hill had joined the Board in January 1914.
69 *APBM*, 24 June 1915; 22 July 1915, Item 1; and 28 July 1915, Item 1. The minutes reveal that there were eight applicants on 22 July, but another two were added at the Board meeting of 28 July.
70 *APBM*, 28 July 1915, Item 1.
71 *Goulburn Evening Penny Post*, 11 September 1915, 4.
72 *APBM*, 12 August 1915, Item 1.
73 *APBM*, 19 August 1915, Item 1. It is interesting that Scobie dissented, indicating that he was in fact a supporter of Donaldson, or that he felt the colonial secretary had the right to overturn a Board decision.

Black preferred Donaldson, was clearly uncomfortable with the whole situation and wrote to the colonial secretary, but the content of the letter is unknown.[74] A proactive Ardill broke the deadlock and suggested two appointments be made, and that Donaldson, who was second in the ballot, be appointed along with Swindlehurst.[75] The colonial secretary agreed. It appeared that George Black was prepared to fund two positions – in times of financial constraint – to secure his desired candidate. The outcome, however, was expensive, and relations between the Board and the colonial secretary must have been at breaking point. Fuelling this tension was the fact that George Black owned the newspaper the *Australian Workman,* which had campaigned against George Ardill's use of women laundry workers and alleged improprieties within his Homes.[76]

During the inspector furore, there was further friction within the Board. Henry Trenchard, not averse to dissent, voiced his opposition to Board practices regarding the appointment of Board subcommittees. He did not specify but he may have wanted to be considered for one. Subcommittees were appointed from time to time. For example, Ardill and Garvin drafted the duties of the inspector. Trenchard wrote to the Board and claimed that he had also sent a copy to the colonial secretary.[77] Uneasy with this situation, the new Board secretary, Walter Charles Pettitt, wrote to the minister's department inquiring about Trenchard's letter.[78] Whether Trenchard sent the letter to the colonial secretary is unclear.[79] At the first APB meeting in January 1916, in Trenchard's absence, the Board passed a resolution to the effect that all 'remarks of ill treatment' by Trenchard were 'quite unwarranted'. But in the same resolution the Board offered a more conciliatory gesture; it conveyed its regret in connection with Trenchard's recent illness and advised him that the 'business transacted at to-day's meeting was of a general nature and that all the sub-committee's recommendations are submitted to the full Board for ratification or amendment'.[80]

---

74 *APBM*, 2 September 1915, Item 5. His letter was tabled at this Board meeting, but the content was not revealed, and it could not be located in the colonial secretary's correspondence.
75 *APBM*, 14 September 1915, Item 1; Read believes that Donaldson probably convinced the Board to have two positions: Read, *A Hundred Years War,* 62.
76 See Chapter 3.
77 *APBM*, 16 December 1915, Item 1. The content of Trenchard's letter was not recorded in the minutes.
78 APB to colonial secretary, 17 December 1915, CSIL 1915, 5/7324, Item 15.162 (SRNSW).
79 The letter could not be located in the colonial secretary's correspondence.
80 *APBM*, 6 January 1916, Item 15.

The upshot of these continuing strains within the APB and the overarching ambition of Ardill, combined with the atmosphere of general financial restraint due to the war effort, was that the government reconstituted the Board in February 1916.

The reconstitution

At the beginning of 1916, the Board carried on as usual, apparently unaware of the pending government action. From the Board's perspective, it had achieved much. The Board's usual promotion of its 'achievements' were on show in the report for the year ending 1915. It boasted that it had finally achieved the appointment of two inspectors when it had only sought one; it had secured two pieces of legislation; the homefinder had 'placed 80 girls in situations' over the year and 'all were enjoying the comfort of good homes'; the 'progress of the children at school was satisfactory'; and 20 local Protection Boards across the state assisted the station managers in the carriage of their duties.[81] On 6 January 1916, George Ardill was again unanimously elected vice-chair, and all appeared normal. For the next month of meetings, no changes appeared to be imminent except that its most regular attender, Ardill, was missing for two weeks. Then at the 17 February Board meeting members were informed that the resignations of George Ardill, Thomas Garvin and Alfred Hill had been accepted by the colonial secretary. The three members had either got wind of the coming changes or had been asked to resign by the colonial secretary.[82] Naomi Parry observes that the government 'extracted Ardill's resignation in February 1916'.[83] Incredibly, over the next six weeks the remaining members carried on as normal or, most likely, some had been informed of the reconstitution and were asked to remain until new members were appointed. We learn that when Henry Trenchard attended the 30 March meeting, the reconstitution was complete but he had not been informed.[84] The minutes record that Mr Trenchard 'not being aware of the completion of the re-constitution of the Board attended the meeting'.[85]

---

81 *APBR* 1916, 1–8. Accessed via *NSW Legislative Assembly: Aborigines Report of Board for the Aborigines 1915–1922*, Q572.991 N, State Library of New South Wales (hereafter SLNSW).
82 I have researched widely to locate the resignations letters but without success. They may not have survived or have been put in an obscure location, or they were never written. Alfred Hill had joined the Board in July 1914.
83 Parry, 'Such a Longing', 281. The circumstances around these resignations remain very uncertain.
84 Doukakis, *The Aboriginal People*, 112.
85 *APBM*, 30 March 1916, Item 1.

It must have been an embarrassing moment for Trenchard. The three members in attendance – James Mitchell, Robert Scobie and T.H. Abbott – passed a resolution thanking Trenchard for the 'great assistance' he had given the Board over the 17 years and for the interest he had 'always manifested towards the Aborigines generally'. It was a messy affair. Jim Fletcher remarks that the 'reconstitution of the Board came at the end of a nine-month battle … between the Board and the colonial secretary, which led to the resignations in protest of Ardill, Garvin and Hill'.[86] A minimal reference to the reconstitution appeared in the Board report: 'In March 1916, the Board as previously constituted was disbanded.'[87]

On 6 April 1916 the reconstituted Board sat for the first time. Its members were James Mitchell, chair and Inspector-General of Police (he was retained, carrying on the long-held tradition of the top policeman as chair); James Dawson, Chief Inspector of Schools; Hugh Ross, inspector, Department of Agriculture; Robert Paton, Director-General of Health (second time on the Board); and Edward B. Harkness, the Under-Secretary of the Colonial Secretary's Department. Both politicians, William Millard and Robert Scobie – one from each side of politics – were retained. Robert Scobie died later in 1916 leaving only six members on the Board in 1917. Hugh Ross attended one Board meeting but never appeared again, with no explanation given.[88] A.W. Green, president of the State Children's Relief Department, had been appointed by June 1917. The Board was now almost entirely populated with high-ranking public servants.

Publicly, the government used financial constraints as the pretext to dissolve the Board. George Black informed the Cabinet that recent requests had been made that 'fees should be paid' to the non-salaried Board members, that the Board had been increasing its staff during the last few years and expenditure had been mounting.[89] A snapshot of Board expenditure between 1909 and 1915 does not entirely support Black's claims and strengthens the argument that other reasons were also important.

---

86 Fletcher, *Clean, Clad and Courteous*, 101.
87 *APBR* 1916, 1. Reference to the new Board also appeared in the *APBM*, 6 April 1916, Item 1.
88 *APBM*, 6 April 1916.
89 *SMH*, 23 February 1916, 12.

Table 5.1: Board expenditure for years 1909–1916.[90]

Year ending	Overall expenditure	Secretary & staff component
1909	£24,744.6.9	£150.11.2
1910	£24,899.12.0	£315.0.0
1911	£24,565.5.6	£330.0.6
1912	£28,579.4.4	£336.13.7
1913	£28,777.2.10	£312.13.10
1914	£21,009.12.1	£377.2.10
1915	£24,805.16.11	£497.2.0
1916	£27,629.8.0	£1,821.0.0

Source: Author's analysis of *APBR* from 1909 to 1916.

As Table 5.1 indicates, George Black did have a valid argument in that the salary component increased by more than 30 per cent for 1915. The overall financial picture, however, was not too disturbing. The irony was that in reconstituting the Board the government sought to save money on salaries and staff, but by allowing two inspectors positions (costing £800) and other obvious increases, the salaries bill at the end of 1916 had blown out from £497 to £1,821, an increase of 266 per cent from the previous year.

Nevertheless, money had been an issue prior to 1916. The government may have considered that pressure to pay Board members was going to be a perennial one. Sacking the Board and putting their own salaried men in their place would prevent the problem re-emerging in the future. A *Sydney Morning Herald* report mentioned nothing of the Board controversies but simply noted that Cabinet had decided 'to substitute a board of men already receiving salaries from the Government for the present board'.[91] It was a nice piece of lateral thinking by the government. Also, decision-making would be easier with such high-level bureaucrats who directly represented their respective departments. However, Jim Fletcher points out that 'Department Board members' were now compromised. If they did not agree with a Board or government decision, it would be difficult to challenge it as paid public servants. Thus, the new Board 'lost much of its earlier independence of thought and action'.[92] This suited the purposes of the government; it had sought compliance and had achieved that goal.

---

90   All figures from *APBRs* for those years ending are found in the appendices of Board reports.
91   *SMH*, 23 February 1916, 12.
92   Fletcher, *Clean, Clad and Courteous*, 101.

Although the government had successfully reconstituted the Board and transformed it into a compliant body, it had not foreseen that the bureaucratic members would have little to do with Board policy direction and daily operations. The one main constant in the whole structure was Robert Donaldson, who remained an inspector. Heather Goodall observes that Donaldson was 'now in a position of unchallenged power'. The old-style philanthropists were gone.[93]

Susan Greer asserts that the new Board was designed to engage several government departments more directly in the governance of Aboriginal people in order to assimilate them more rapidly. The additions of the under-secretary to the colonial secretary, the president of the State Children's Relief Department and the departments of Education and Health all strengthened the bureaucratic input; A.W. Green's appointment provided extra focus on the removal of children.[94] Whether the government had such specific intentions is unclear. A more compliant Board was perhaps uppermost in the government's mind and the Cabinet had never formally prepared (to the author's knowledge) any policy advice to the Board. However, the reconstitution certainly changed the nature of the Board. Board meetings were now dominated by public servants used to delegating. This is exactly what happened. An environment was created where a small group of non-Board officials could control the day-to-day running of the Board. A severe reduction in the number of Board meetings and less reporting of Board activities increased the 'distance' between the public servant Board members and events on the ground. This had a profound impact on the Aboriginal communities of New South Wales.

A cabal

Whether by design or convenience the primary functions of the Board fell to the secretary, the two inspectors, the homefinder and, to a lesser extent, Board member and under-secretary E.B. Harkness. Within six months the Board had been transformed, not by chair James Mitchell, or by the collective wisdom of the Board public servants, but mostly by secretary Arthur Charles Pettitt. Former prominent member Robert Donaldson, having resigned as a Board member to become an inspector, was now

---

93 Goodall, *Invasion to Embassy*, 2008, 147.
94 Greer, 'Governing Indigenous Peoples', 57.

totally committed to his statewide inspectorial role with a strong focus on the identification of Aboriginal children to be sent to institutions or to service. He and the second inspector, Swindlehurst, along with the homefinder, Miss Lowe, were the three most important people on the ground. This cabal carried on the day-to-day functions of the Board.[95] The full Board met so infrequently that appropriate oversight and awareness of the issues by Board members was severely limited, if not totally out of reach.

These officials became the drivers of the Board's agenda. Secretary of the Board Arthur Charles Pettitt came out from England as a child and spent most of his youth in Inverell. On coming to Sydney, he went to Fort Street Model School and sat the public service exam.[96] Pettitt had had no contact with Aboriginal people up until the time of his appointment as a junior clerk to the Board in March 1910 on a salary of £65.[97] He was appointed as secretary on 1 July 1914 and remained in that position until the end of the Board, and then served the new Aborigines Welfare Board for two years. Effectively, he dealt with Board matters for 32 years – longer than any Board member or other official. Pettitt's position as secretary became increasing powerful. He determined the agenda of meetings, filtered information to Board members, dealt with the day-to-day running of the Board and was intimately involved in policy issues. When Jim Fletcher interviewed Pettitt in 1977, he did not disagree with Fletcher's proposition that he, Donaldson, Swindlehurst and Lowe got together and 'thrashed out a new policy'.[98]

Edward Burns Harkness (Figure 5.1) the under-secretary to the colonial secretary, was elected vice-chair of the new Board and remained in that position for the life of the Board.

The duopoly of Pettitt and Harkness was the longest of any personnel combination throughout the entire 57-year life of the Board. All APB matters, of any significance, went to the Colonial Secretary's Department via E.B. Harkness. Harkness had the bureaucratic skills to deal with myriad issues emanating from many government departments. The Protection Board was only one small function of his role.

---

95   Goodall, *Invasion to Embassy*, 2008, 147.
96   A.C. Pettitt, interview by J.J. Fletcher, 1977, J01-018426, PMS 5380, AIATSIS.
97   Appointment of A.C. Pettitt as a clerk to the Board, 11 March 1910, CSIL, 1910, 5/7073, Item 10.93 (SRNSW).
98   A.C. Pettitt, interview by J.J. *Fletcher*, 1977, J01-018426, AIATSIS.

Figure 5.1: Edward Burns Harkness.
Under-secretary to the colonial secretary, New South Wales Government. Seen here as the returning officer for the liquor referendum, at his desk, New South Wales, September 1928.
Source: National Library of Australia, picture obj.162031836.

Although Harkness dealt with all major Board issues and was the conduit between the Board and the colonial secretary, his knowledge of the day-to-day Board operations was questionable. In 1934 (18 years after the reconstitution) an exchange took place between Harkness, Pettitt and Joan Kingsley-Strack that exposed Harkness' ill-informed position. Some details of this exchange are instructive. Kingsley-Strack had an Aboriginal girl in her care as a domestic servant under the Board's apprenticeship scheme.[99] This domestic servant had been physically assaulted in a public park and the perpetrators had not been arrested. Mrs Kingsley-Strack had called upon the Deputy Police Superintendent William MacKay, who advised that the matter would be investigated in time. Unhappy with MacKay's response, she was advised (by vice-president David Stead of the Association for the Protection of Native Races) to call upon vice-chair of the Board E.B. Harkness.[100] In speaking with Mrs Kingsley-Strack, Harkness was curious to hear what she thought of Homefinder Miss Lowe as he had heard 'she might not be the best person'. Kingsley-Strack told Harkness she had a very poor opinion of Lowe. Surprisingly, Harkness revealed that he had never even met Miss Lowe who had been in the Board's employ for 20 years. Upon hearing Mrs Kingsley-Strack's very negative reports regarding her performance, he suggested that 'there was a bit of a dictatorship going on here'.[101] Harkness summoned Pettitt, and, in Mrs Kingsley-Strack's presence, had a frank exchange with him. He castigated Pettitt for being 'in the pocket' of this Miss Lowe and not insisting that she treat the girls in a 'humane and kindly manner'.[102]

The exchange could be viewed in two ways. Kingsley-Strack had been a persistent 'thorn in the side' of the Board. She accused the Board of stealing girls' wages, taking poor care of them and failing to investigate allegations of abuse.[103] Harkness, meeting Joan Kingsley-Strack in person, may have been intimidated by her and sought to sheet the blame home on Pettitt; or Harkness could have feigned surprise and annoyance at Pettitt for the benefit of Mrs Kingsley-Strack to get her off their back. Pettitt had to simply endure the dressing down until she left the meeting. This last explanation holds some water as Harkness did not deliver on promises of redress made to Kingsley-Strack and dismissed her later complaints about

---

99   Joan Kingsley-Strack was an active feminist and campaigner for Aboriginal rights. After taking on the Aboriginal girls as apprentices (like many other North Shore upper-middle-class women), she became alarmed at the Board's withholding of their wages and by its general lack of 'duty of care'. She fought a long campaign to redress many issues faced by such girls. See Haskins, *One Bright Spot*.
100 Haskins, *One Bright Spot*, 117.
101 Haskins, *One Bright Spot*, 117.
102 Haskins, *One Bright Spot*, 118.
103 Joan Kingsley-Strack Papers, MS 9551, Series 7, Folders 5 and 6, National Library of Australia (hereafter NLA).

two policemen arriving late in the evening with a 'warrant' to put the Aboriginal girl on a train back to her home.[104] Two weeks later, irritated with her persistence, Harkness quipped:

> I'm sorry Mrs Strack, I can't do anything – you must not go against these people, now be sensible or you will be in serious trouble you had better let her go [home] I only saw you because Mr Childs [Inspector-General of Police and Board chair] was away ... you'd better see Mr Childs now this is a matter for him.[105]

It is also interesting that Harkness referred to them as 'these people'. As vice-chair of the Board he had the power to direct all matters regarding Aboriginal people. He now intimated he had nothing to do with such events. This episode reveals Harkness's complete indifference to events as they occurred on the ground and adds weight to the fact that the other Board members probably knew even less of Board matters. The fact that E.B. Harkness had never met Miss Lowe reflected the nature and structure of Board operations in place for 18 years. The complete disconnection is compounded by the fact that Harkness, over his time on the Board, had four Aboriginal boys apprenticed to him! In his closing remarks to a station managers' conference in January 1938, Harkness said:

> We all know the Aborigines ... I have had Aborigines indentured to me, I have one now. During the last fourteen or fifteen years I have had three boys trained by Mrs McQuiggan, and the boys are typical of the work that Matrons are doing throughout the country.[106]

The exchange between Harkness and Kingsley-Strack cannot be completely understood but, generally, it typifies the Board's disengagement, arrogance, tardiness, readiness to cover up, and lack of compassion and understanding of the impact of its policies during the last two decades of its life.

Little is known about Miss Lowe, even though she spent 24 years in the employ of the Board and undertook one of its most controversial functions. Anna Cole notes that Miss Lowe or the 'Homefinder' was the 'first direct employee of the Board, hired to "find" girls for training and

---

104 Haskins, *One Bright Spot*, 120.
105 Joan Kingsley-Strack Papers, MS 9551, Series 7, Folder 5 (Doris Henry) (iii) (NLA).
106 Bate, 'Conference on the Plight of the Aborigines 1938', 24–26 January 1938, JaHQ 2014/1905, 84, Mitchell Library (hereafter ML).

domestic service'.[107] In doing so she was required to act as a go-between between the Board and Aboriginal parents and help secure the 'consent' of the latter.[108] From her appointment in 1912 until 1915, the Board could gain custody of children by two means. First, it could obtain a magistrate's order under the *Neglected Children and Juvenile Offenders Act 1905*; second, if it obtained the consent of the parents, it could remove a child under the conditions of the *Apprentices Act 1901*. Miss Lowe did not hesitate to apply pressure to Aboriginal families to give up their children. After the 1915 amendment that gave the Board power to remove without reference to the courts or the parents, her job was made easier. Alice Lowe moved quickly into her role. Naomi Parry observes that Miss Lowe had 'been given *carte blanche*' to take speedy action on the girls.[109] The 1915 Board report summarised her efforts:

> This Officer continues to do excellent work, and has been successful in placing many girls in situations during the year, in addition to securing the transfer of several others to Cootamundra homes. Sixty-two (62) girls are now enjoying the comfort of good homes, and are being kept under strict supervision, the Home-Finder visiting them at frequent intervals to ensure that they are being properly cared for ... These will not be allowed to return to their former associations, but will be merged into the white population.[110]

The Board's rosy picture was far from the truth. Life at the Cootamundra Training Home for Girls was harsh and unpleasant.[111] Many girls were forcibly removed to Cootamundra and significant numbers absconded from their domestic situations.[112] When girls absconded the police were informed, and when 'captured' the Board was notified; Miss Lowe would then pay the girl a visit and advise the Board of appropriate action. Her 'detached' style and approach are reflected in a report from an Aboriginal station to the Board.[113] Her abrupt style was matched by her meanness. Mrs Kingsley-Strack's diaries and notes portray Lowe as a ruthless operator who lacked any compassion and humanity for the Aboriginal

---

107 Cole, 'The Glorified Flower', 69.
108 Cole, 'The Glorified Flower', 69.
109 Parry, 'Such a Longing', 277.
110 *APBR* 1915, 6.
111 Kabaila, *Home Girls*.
112 Walden, 'That was Slavery Days' provides a detailed analysis of the privations and difficulties faced by Aboriginal domestic servants.
113 *APBM*, 14 January 1915, Item 3.

girls. One entry records, that Alice Lowe lectured one of Kinglsey-Strack's apprentices who was desperately ill, threatening that if she 'didn't eat she would be sent to an asylum'.[114] Miss Lowe would have been an imposing and frightening figure among the Aboriginal families of New South Wales and indeed among some of the white families who apprenticed the girls. Joan Kingsley-Strack's diary entry noted that she and the 'public in general' thought that Miss Lowe '*was* the board!'[115]

Inspector A.L. Swindlehurst was only four years in the job; he never gained a reputation like Donaldson. In fact, it is hard to find many references to him. He was mentioned on a few occasions in the press. The *Yass Courier* noted that he was on a visit to Yass on 'dusky' business.[116] In 1917 he visited the Cumeroogunga Mission Station and found everything in 'good order'.[117] Swindlehurst resigned his inspectorial position in March 1921.[118] With Swindlehurst's departure, the position was advertised, but never filled. The Board informed the minister that it 'was never the intention of the Board that more than one inspector should be appointed'.[119] It is strange that the Board opposed a replacement – why would it not embrace more resources? Most likely, the cabal/Board did not replace Swindlehurst because Robert T. Donaldson was a dedicated officer but not a team player.[120] He preferred to act alone.

Rounding out the cabal was Robert Donaldson (Figure 4.1). With no parliamentary responsibilities he devoted himself fully to his inspectorial duties. For the next 14 years he travelled the state. Considering some places were hundreds of miles from Sydney, it was a gruelling task; in some cases, it took up to a full week to achieve one inspection. Donaldson was up to the challenge. Goodall describes Donaldson's work ethic as

> a relentless routine of travels around the State, selecting children for removal. Known as the 'Kid's Collector' [sic], he was feared and hated by Aboriginal people more than any other.[121]

---

114 Haskins, *One Bright Spot*, 84.
115 Haskins, *One Bright Spot*, 117.
116 *Goulburn Evening Penny Post*, 14 October 1916, 4.
117 *Echuca and Moama Advertiser and Farmers Gazette*, 5 June 1917, 4.
118 *APBM*, 2 March 1921, Item 2.
119 *APBM*, 5 October 1921, Item 1. J.P. Cochran applied for the position but was not deemed suitable by the Board and then the Board withdrew the position.
120 See Chapter 4.
121 Goodall, *Invasion to Embassy*, 2008, 147.

In 1924 Donaldson spread the same message about the need to remove girls from the camps, as he had done prior to the *Aborigines Protection Act 1909*. In his inspection report of the Purfleet Reserve (Taree), as recorded in the *Northern Champion*, Donaldson stated that it was 'no use educating a girl until she reached the age of 20, and then allowing her to drift back on to the reserve to become a common gin'. He explained that the girls were not allowed to return to the reserve, while in service, unless for serious illness of a relative, or exceptional circumstances. He extolled the virtues of the Home at Cootamundra that trained the girls to be 'useful domestics, to observe cleanliness, to speak the truth, and to respect property', and he was pleased to record that the Board held over £800 in wages from the girls who had been working in home placements. He also held firm to the view that the camps would eventually not be required, as the 'full-bloods' would 'die out' and the girls continued to be removed.[122]

He applied himself to the task of inspecting, selecting children for removal and ensuring consistent policy implementation across the state. Perhaps his rigorous run of inspections had taken its toll, on 1 February 1929, Donaldson resigned due to ill health. The Board accepted his resignation 'with much regret' and conveyed to him the Board's 'sincere appreciation of his energy, honesty of purpose and loyal service'.[123]

At a special function in May of the same year, Secretary Pettitt presented Donaldson

> with an easy chair, a wallet of notes on behalf of the head office staff, the managers and matrons of the various Aboriginal stations, and teachers of Aboriginal schools throughout the State, together with gifts from the Aborigines and Aboriginal children.[124]

Pettitt had the greatest admiration for him, remarking:

> [Donaldson] said what he thought ... he was a fine character and a very close friend of mine, he had a convincing manner ... Full of Irish wit, you know, a delight to be in his company.[125]

---

122 *Northern Champion*, 13 September 1924, 8.
123 *APBM*, 1 February 1929, Item 3.
124 *Gundagai Times and Tumut, Adelong and Murrumbidgee District Advertiser*, 14 June 1929, 2.
125 A.C. Pettitt, interview by J.J. Fletcher, 1977, Audio-tape J01-018426 and 018427, PMS 5380, AIATSIS.

At his farewell function, Pettitt recalled how 'universally his departure would be regretted' and Donaldson remarked how he had 'loved his work' that he had always 'endeavoured to conscientiously carry out'. He noted that 'although at times it was necessary for him to deal firmly with them, he was still able to retain their affection and regard'. The residents at Brungle Station 'forwarded a fountain pen and a redwood tray made by a boy attending the school'.[126]

There is a complete disconnection here but an obvious one. The Board's praise for Donaldson is understandable as he was the one who had the will, the determination, the drive and the tenacity to carry out the Board's policies on the ground. Yet there was clearly another perception of Donaldson. Apart from his positive recollections of the inland tribes he spoke of at the Catholic Convention in 1910 (see Chapter 4), most of his recorded comments about Aboriginal people and the camps were negative. He continually spoke of the vile and evil surroundings of the camps, the idleness, the immorality and the degradation. He never mentioned, in the public arena, any aspects of Aboriginal culture, family life, farming endeavours or individuals in a positive light. By inference he blamed Aboriginal people for their predicament. Goodall asserts that Donaldson was a man

> repelled by Aboriginal social and cultural life … and he took up the goal of gaining power over adolescent girls as a crusade [and that he] made no mention of any positive aspect to life on Aboriginal reserves or farms.[127]

Jack Horner, himself close to many of the Aboriginal activists as secretary to the Sydney-based Aboriginal Fellowship during the 1950s, said of Donaldson:

> Nobody doubted his admirable sincerity; the trouble was he could never see the Aboriginal point of view. To send a girl by train from a mean humpy to a job in Sydney, hundreds of miles away, was (as far as he was concerned) a change for her own good. But the Aboriginal parents did not understand this view, and, judging for themselves what became of these girls, came to distrust him.[128]

---

126 *Gundagai Times and Tumut, Adelong and Murrumbidgee District Advertiser*, 14 June 1929, 2.
127 Goodall, *Invasion to Embassy*, 2008, 145.
128 Horner, *Bill Ferguson*, 11.

Donaldson was the personification of the arrogant, paternalistic crusader who largely prosecuted his own agenda across the state of New South Wales. It was upon his insistence that the removal of girls from the camps became the primary focus of the Board. The effects were devastating for hundreds (if not thousands) of Aboriginal families across New South Wales. The reconstitution of the Board was the perfect platform for Donaldson's vision to be implemented. Haskins maintains:

> the restructuring of the Board reflected a definitive move away from a missionary-style preoccupation with the 'moral' reclamation of fair-skinned Aboriginal girls towards a rigorous secular policy aimed at the most effective dismantling of the reserve populations.[129]

Donaldson was initially replaced by Thomas Austin, on probation, in July 1929; two months later, Austin was replaced by the permanent appointment of Ernest Charles Smithers.[130] Smithers had been the manager of an Aboriginal station for the last 14 years. Like Donaldson, he was also a controversial character, as witnessed through the findings of the 1937 Parliamentary Select Committee Inquiry into the Board (discussed further in Chapter 8).[131]

A streamlined Board

Arthur Charles Pettitt set the tone early and from April 1916 the Board operated in a very perfunctory manner. Pettitt prepared all agenda items and insisted on précised reports, that all questions be submitted in writing in advance of meeting and that all minor matters be dealt with by the secretary.[132] The frequency of Board meetings were dramatically reduced from close to 50 per year (i.e. weekly) to an average of only nine per year from 1917 onwards (Figure 5.2).[133] In 1930, only five meetings were held. Who made this important decision is unclear, but there may have been a prevailing view that it was unnecessary to 'drag out' the highly paid public servants once a week when Pettitt and the inspectors could carry on the work of the Board.

---

129 Haskins, *One Bright Spot*, 32.
130 *APBM*, 26 July 1929, Item 1; 28 September 1929, Item 1.
131 Smithers was heavily involved in the forced relocation of the Aboriginal people from Angledool to Brewarrina in 1936, intimidating the residents by carrying a gun. See Goodall, *Invasion to Embassy*, 2008, 243–45.
132 *APBM*, 6 April 1916, Item 1.
133 Analysis of minutes from relevant years. From 1917 to 1939: 207 meetings divided by 23 years is nine per year.

5. ENTER THE BUREAUCRATS, 1916

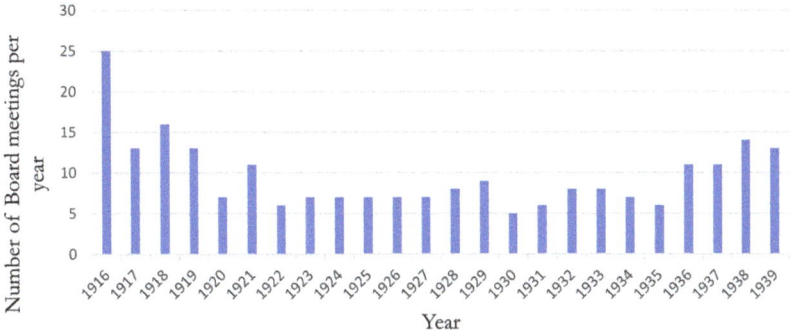

Figure 5.2: Number of Board meetings held each year by the 'new' Board from 1916 to 1939.
Source: Analysis of Board minutes for the appropriate years.

As can be seen in Figure 5.2, the 'new' Board, for its entire existence (1916 to May 1939), met for a total of 232 times. Contrast this record with that of the 'old' Board, which, over an equivalent 23-year period, met for a total of 1,128 times.[134] The reduction in meetings sent a clear message: less commitment to, and engagement with, Aboriginal people.

Another indication of the growing disconnection with Aboriginal people were the yearly Board reports. After 1916, each contained far less information and provided little detail. A typical report *before* the reconstitution comprised general comments about Board appointments; minor reports from local Protection Board committees;[135] census, revenue and expenditure summaries; breaches of the Act; mission work; general health of the Aboriginal population; an educational summary furnished with extensive reports by inspectors from the Education Department on every Aboriginal school; lists of improvements to reserves and stations; a list of inspection visits by Board members (after 1909); and sizable reports from each Aboriginal station. The appendices included every census location across the state (over 200) and an expenditure analysis at every location point including medical outlays, and expenditure outlays

---

134 From 1883 to 1916, during the 12 full years of available records, the 'old' board met 589 times; an average of 48.9 times a year. Therefore, 589 established meetings (over 12 years) plus a further 11 (years) x 49 (rounded average) = 539 + 589 = 1,128 (*APBM* for all recorded meetings).
135 Local Board reports first appeared in the *ABPR* of 1896. They were comprised of interested local people of the district (approved by the Board) and served to help with the overall management of the Aboriginal station and reserves in the district. *APBR* 1896, 3. Accessed via *Journal of the Legislative Council*, Q328.9106/7, *NSW Parliamentary Papers, Consolidated Index* (hereafter *Journal of LC*), Vol. 55, Part 1 (SLNSW).

at each Aboriginal school and station. The annual reports generally ran upwards of 20 dense pages. Although rich in statistical information, the reporting lacked any critical appraisal of the Board's performance or policy, had no Aboriginal input or perspective, and contained generous doses of Board 'spin'. Despite the obvious spin, on reading, one gets a sense of the Board's desire to report across the state, attention to detail and an overall 'interest' in what was happening on the ground.

The annual reporting post-1916 contrasted starkly to the preceding 33 years. The report for the year ending 1916 comprised only 11 pages, about half the length of the average report before the reconstitution. It contained similar obligatory summary information on inspections, census, employment, revenue, new buildings on reserves and stations, information on the Cootamundra Training Home for Girls and appendices on expenditure, stations, medical and school outlays – but all with much less detail.[136] Subsequent reports became even less informative, almost worthless. The reports from 1923 to 1938 averaged three pages. For the last two decades of the Board their annual reporting was totally inadequate. No one reading these reports could gain any detailed knowledge or understanding of what was happening to the Aboriginal population under the Board's control. By any measure, they were a totally inadequate account of the Board's interaction with Aboriginal people for any given year.

One can only speculate as to why this gross negligence occurred. At best, perhaps the Board members did not feel the need to meet so often, and report in detail, as its vice-chair – under-secretary E.B. Harkness – was the direct link to the Colonial Secretary's Department. Also, as members were high-ranking public servants, their first responsibility was to their departments – the Board commitment was likely an unwanted extra for these men and were indifferent to Board accountability. Further, the Board parliamentarians were historically poor attenders and with only two permitted on the Board after 1916 there was a reduced exposure to the parliament.[137] At worst, there was a clear intention, either by the cabal and/or some Board members, to keep matters regarding conditions on the stations, the removal of children and the holding of the moneys of apprentices in trust concealed from the public. Or overall indifference, negligence and incompetence.

---

136 *APBR* 1916.
137 For example, for the year ending 1911 there were four parliamentarians on the Board, *APBR* 1912. Accessed via: aiatsis.gov.au/sites/default/files/docs/digitised_collections/remove/23014.pdf.

Board policy curtailed by the parliament

In 1917 the Board pursued even greater authority. It sought to change the definition of an 'Aborigine' to include 'any full-blooded or half-caste aboriginal who is a native of New South Wales'.[138] In other words, all those classed as 'quadroons' and 'octoroons' would not be considered 'Aborigines'. By law they would be expelled from the reserves and stations.[139] The Board had emulated the Victorian *Aborigines Protection Act 1886*. Although under the Victorian legislation, those who had to move into the general community could, at least, apply for rations, clothing and blankets for seven years to assist in the transition into the wider community.[140] The New South Wales version was far more drastic: all 'quadroons' and 'octoroons' were to be removed with no transitional period and no ability to receive rations. The Board had already gained powers in this area in 1915 when Regulation 28 of the Act was changed to read: 'Anyone persistently refusing to work … shall be liable to be removed from the station'. Regulation 28a allowed a fine of up to £10 for 'entering and remaining' on a reserve or station without permission. And a new Regulation 28c required all 'quadroon', 'octoroon' and 'half-caste' men 18 years or over to leave the Board's stations and reserves on or before 31 May 1915.[141] But it wanted more.

The Board was driven by two factors: finances and the quest to enforce assimilation. The Board minutes of July 1916 were the first indication that a change was underway:

> The Secretary was instructed to write to the Crown Solicitor and request him to furnish the Board with the definition of the words 'Aboriginal' and 'Half-Caste' in an enactment which would be designed with a view to cutting off from the assistance of the Board, all persons of less than half-caste Aboriginal blood.[142]

It is unclear who drove these changes. Secretary Pettitt had joined the Australian Infantry Forces in late 1916 and was in Europe, so presumably had little influence on the preparation of the amendment.[143] Although

---

138 *Aborigines Protection (Amendment) Act 1918* (NSW), Section 2(1)a.
139 Read, 'The History of the Wiradjuri People of NSW 1909–1969', 112–13.
140 McGrath, ed., *Contested Ground*, 139–40.
141 *NSW Government Gazette*, No. 97, 2 June 1915, Management of Stations, 3072–73 (SLNSW).
142 *APBM*, 13 July 1916, Item 9.
143 S.A. Maddocks was appointed secretary on 2 November 1916 but resigned soon after, for by 17 February 1917, T.J. Foote was appointed acting secretary to the Board. CSIL 1917, 5/7483, 1-845, Items 17.42 and 17.65 (SRNSW).

Donaldson's name does not appear in the promotion of this change, there is little doubt of his input as he was in close contact with the stations and reserves. In 1916 he was responsible for the expulsions of 12 boys from Brungle Station in a single day.[144] However, the financial imperative, compounded by the war effort, was a key factor in prosecuting the amendment. E.B. Harkness, in advice to the Department of Attorney General and Justice, stated:

> while the full bloods and half castes should receive every possible assistance, the board should have the power to determine what others who may have aboriginal blood are to receive ... This is rendered even more necessary owing to the present financial conditions.[145]

Peter Read asserts that the amendment was designed to toughen up the expulsion orders. The Board recognised a weakness in the 1909 Act: 'there was no-one to police the unmanaged reserves, there were administrative bungles, and the Aborigines resorted to tricks like using false names'.[146] The Board wanted increased powers to exclude more Aboriginal people. Read points out that the 'Government's answer to everything was the "considerable economy" that would follow when the reserves, and ultimately the managed stations, were closed'.[147] Read observes:

> The people now excluded from hotels on the grounds that they were Aborigines were now to be excluded from the reserves on the grounds that they were not.[148]

Although the New South Wales Parliament agreed to a change in the definition of an 'Aborigine', the potential summary expulsion of several thousands of Aboriginal people from their homes was a step too far for parliament.[149] The parliament passed its own amendment that gave the Board power to 'permit any member of quadroons or octoroons, if they

---

144 Donaldson expelled the boys because they 'should be earning a living away from the station': *APBM*, 21 January 1916, Item 8.
145 E.B. Harkness to Under-Secretary Department of Attorney General and Justice Department, 14 May 1917, CSIL 1918, 5/7956, 1-800, Item 17.93 (SRNSW).
146 Read, *A Hundred Years War*, 62–63.
147 Read, *A Hundred Years War*, 63.
148 Read, *A Hundred Years War*, 63.
149 For the year ending 1918 the Board determined that there were 5,041 men, women and children who were 'half-castes'. It was from this sizable group that individuals could be forced off the stations and reserves. *APBR* 1919, 2. Accessed via aiatsis.gov.au/sites/default/files/docs/digitised_collections/remove/23673.pdf.

see fit, to still remain on the reserves'.¹⁵⁰ While this amendment did not limit the power of the Board absolutely, it deliberately did not extend powers to exclude. Rather, parliament insisted that agents of the Board have discretion to exercise a little more humanity.

In the parliamentary debate, member for Allowrie and former 'old' Board member Mark F. Morton was uneasy with the 'new' Board. He stated, 'I am not satisfied that the members of the present board carry out this work quite as sympathetically as the members of the old board did', but was comforted by the amendment.¹⁵¹ William Millard, the member for Bega and current Board member, took offence at Morton's comments about the 'new' Board and assured the Assembly that the 'civil servants [on the Board] are just as sympathetic to these unfortunate people as the old board were'.¹⁵²

The subsequent amendment had placed the onus on the Board not to be too harsh. The Board appeared to be cognisant of this but seemed more concerned with potential criticism than the well-being of those it sought to exclude. The APB minutes record:

> Suggestion that the [census] returns be handed to the Inspectors with instructions that action be taken, with a view to discontinuance of aid to quadroons and octoroons, and their removal from Reserves, was approved, – each case, however, being dealt with on its merits to ensure that no undeserved hardship be inflicted, thus obviating the possibility of any criticism for harshness.¹⁵³

Despite the apparent willingness to comply with the parliament's more compassionate amendment, expulsions were a regular occurrence. According to the Board's minutes from 1916 until May 1940, there were 255 expulsions. Sixty-seven per cent – 171 expulsions – occurred between 1919 and 1930. There was a drop-off from 1930, which coincided with Donaldson's retirement in 1929.¹⁵⁴

---

150 NSW, *Parliamentary Debates*, Legislative Council, 5 February 1918, 2392.
151 NSW, *Parliamentary Debates*, Legislative Assembly, 5 March 1918, 3256 (Mark Morton).
152 NSW, *Parliamentary Debates*, Legislative Assembly, 5 March 1918, 3256 (William Millard).
153 *APBM*, 14 July 1920, Item 1.
154 Analysis of Board minutes for that period. It must be noted that not all expulsions may have appeared in the minutes.

A free hand to intrude

At the turn of the century the direction of the Board had been predominately set by George Ardill and Robert Donaldson. The restrictive measures of the *Aborigines Protection Act 1909* and the amendment of 1915 had cemented that course. As Bain Attwood notes, the 'reshaping' of Aboriginal people had begun.[155] Even if the Board had not been reconstituted, there was no indication that this path would have varied. Most alarming was the fact that the 'old' Board foundered, not because the government held it accountable for failing Aboriginal people or imposing harsh measures on the population, but for its own lack of cohesion, government irritation and impatience with its persistent demands, and a controversy over the appointment of a Board inspector. The restructure had nothing to do with the welfare of Aboriginal people.

With fewer independent thinkers and a lack of accountability due to severely reduced yearly meetings and token reporting, the Board seemed more disconnected from Aboriginal people than ever before. Unsurprisingly, and yet ironically, this detachment ushered in the most destructive and intrusive period (1916–40) for Aboriginal families across the state. Perhaps unwittingly, but culpable nevertheless, the government's reconstitution of the Board enabled the worst excesses upon the Aboriginal communities of New South Wales.

The only 'brake' applied to the Board came from the parliament. Its efforts to temper the 1918 legislative amendment showed clear disquiet with the Board power to remove all 'quadroons' and 'octoroons' from the reserves and stations. But the amendment created a discretion for the Board to act with constraint – it was not a requirement. Alarm bells should have alerted the government, but there was no collective will to reassess the direction of Aboriginal affairs.

For the next two decades after 1916, the newly shaped Board acted as it pleased. With no external examination of its operations, the Board bureaucrats attended the less than monthly meetings, and the cabal carried out the day-to-day operations unhindered. It is interesting to note that the Victorian Board was also reconstituted in 1916, although for different reasons. Richard Broome explains that Victorian Board membership

---

155 See Chapter 2.

had dwindled to three, was run by the secretary alone, had not met for two years and had not issued any reports to parliament for four years. The reconstruction saw parliamentarians who had an Aboriginal reserve in their electorate placed on the Board. The performance of both Boards says much about governments, and the public, that allowed these bodies to be very much unaccountable and secretive.[156]

The focus for the next chapter explores the Board's most invasive impact on Aboriginal communities: the increased removal of Aboriginal children from their families. However, it also highlights another Board policy failure.

---

156 Broome, *Aboriginal Victorians*, 206.

6

The girls return

Doug Nicholls – Aboriginal activist, pastor, Australian Rules football star for Fitzroy, and Governor of South Australia – was eight years old in 1914. At the time he was living on Cumeroogunga Station on the New South Wales side of the Murray River and it was then that he had the 'fear of the police instilled in him'.[1] As a young lad he knew nothing of the world outside Cumeroogunga Station nor did he understand that there were different laws for Aboriginal people and white people. He does remember though how the police would come to the station 'at night, or at odd times looking under the beds and behind the sheds for those who were meant to be … living among the white people'. He soon understood that 'all half castes or less, over fourteen years, must leave the reserves'; they were no longer eligible for rations and had to make their way in the white community. As an eight-year-old he learned something else: the police were after his 16-year-old sister Hilda. Anticipating trouble, the manager of Cumeroogunga Station had organised for all the Aboriginal men to leave early in the day, to cut timber. When the men were gone, two police cars arrived. Doug, standing at a distance on an elevated position with other youngsters ready for school, watched a policeman push open the door of his mother's home, enter unannounced and emerge

---

1 Clark, *The Boy from Cumeroogunga*, 31. Jack Horner refers to this incident in *Bill Ferguson*, 13. Horner puts the date at 1918, whereas Clark puts it at 1914 (Doug Nicholls was born in 1906 and, according to Clark, the incident took place when he was eight in 1914). There was a lot of unrest at Cumeroogunga around 1918–19: a riot had occurred at Barmah when a policeman tried to shoot at a group of Aboriginal men, an outbreak of influenza resulted in heavy restrictions on the Aboriginal community's ability to move about and there was deep unrest about the taking of girls from the station by the Board. The school teacher, Thomas James, had written several letters to the Education Department, and in April 1919 he telegrammed: 'No attendance today police seized some girls parents with children fled across river situation serious'; see Davis, *Australian Settler Colonialism*, 35–37.

dragging his sister Hilda firmly by the hand. His mother, Florence, ran after them protesting loudly: 'You can't take her!' The policeman shouted that he was, and if she did not stop her 'caterwauling' he would 'take all her kids'. Florence turned quickly in Doug's direction and screamed: 'Run, Dougie, run!'[2]

The two police cars left with six girls, along with Hilda's mother who had whacked the policeman with a wooden stake and fought her way into the car with the girls only to be bundled out 20 kilometres up the road to walk home. The Cumeroogunga community spoke of the events for 'days and weeks and months and years afterwards'. Doug knew the adults were 'angry and afraid'. He didn't understand what had happened; but he knew 'that the police had frightened his mother, taken his sister and threatened to take him'.[3]

The Board's prosecution of the removal of young Aboriginal girls and boys from the camps, reserves and stations has been extensively discussed and written about over the last three decades. In his speech to the parliament, prime minister Kevin Rudd acknowledged and apologised for the removal policies that were enforced across all of Australia. Rudd spoke to the nation:

> We apologise for the laws and policies of successive parliaments and governments that have inflicted profound grief, suffering and loss on these our fellow Australians.
>
> For the pain, suffering and hurt of these stolen generations, their descendants and for their families left behind, we say sorry.
>
> To the mothers and the fathers, the brothers and the sisters, for the breaking up of families and communities, we say sorry.[4]

Rudd's words broke a long period of silence; the previous federal government under John Howard had been unable to say 'sorry' for 11 years (and still refuses to this day).

In 1916, there were no such regretful sentiments from the Board for the parlous position of many Aboriginal people across the state of New South Wales. The policies directed at Aboriginal people had hardened during

---

2   Clark, *The Boy from Cumeroogunga*, 33.
3   Clark, *The Boy from Cumeroogunga*, 35.
4   Quoted in Raynes, *The Last Protector*, ix.

the first decade of the twentieth century with the passing of the *Aborigines Protection Act 1909*, but in the second decade of the century the Board had entered a new phase. Inspector Robert Donaldson, and colleague A.L. Swindlehurst, freed from the regular Board meetings, were able to travel across the state and identify Aboriginal girls and boys suitable for training. These were sent to the Cootamundra Training Home for Girls, to the Kinchela Home for boys on the Macleay River (from 1924) or directly into service.

The Stolen Generations

Aboriginal child removal in New South Wales is now a well-told story.[5] The Stolen Generations has become part of the Australia's historical consciousness since historian Peter Read coined the term in 1981 and produced a pamphlet for the New South Wales Ministry of Aboriginal Affairs.[6] Read estimated that in New South Wales between 1883 and 1969 some 5,625 children were removed from their families.[7] In a later publication, *A Rape of the Soul so Profound*, he revised the figures to an estimate of 10,000.[8] Read's estimates have been challenged – along with the works of other well-known Australian historians – by journalist Keith Windschuttle in his third volume of *The Fabrication of Aboriginal History*.[9] Windschuttle claims that Read, in his first analysis of removals from New South Wales in 1981, had exaggerated some estimates, inflated figures and double counted. He revised Read's assessment of 5,625 down to 2,600.[10] Windschuttle contests that the whole concept of the Stolen Generations is totally unwarranted and that 'Aboriginal children were never removed from their families in order to put an end to Aboriginality or, indeed, to serve any improper government policy or

---

5   There are several volumes that depict the stories of those removed. Mellor and Haebich, eds, *Many Voices*; Human Rights and Equal opportunity Commission (HREOC), *Bringing Them Home*; Edwards and Read, eds, *The Lost Children*; Read, 'Fathers and Sons'; Read, 'A Rape of the Soul so Profound', 23–33; Simon, *Through My Eyes*; Tucker, *If Everyone Cared*; Haskins, *One Bright Spot*; Miller, *Koori: A Will To Win*; Rintoul, *The Wailing*; Woodrow, *One of the Lost Generation*; Clark, *The Boy from Cumeroogunga*; and Matthews (as told to), *The Two Worlds of Jimmie Barker*.
6   Read had initially used the term 'The Lost Generations', but Jay Arthur, according to Read, proposed 'The Stolen Generations'. See Windschuttle, *The Fabrication of Aboriginal History*, 73.
7   Windschuttle, *The Fabrication of Aboriginal History*, 61. Read revised that figure to 6,225 in *The Stolen Generations*, 11.
8   Read, *A Rape of the Soul so Profound*, 27.
9   Windschuttle, *The Fabrication of Aboriginal History*.
10 Windschuttle, *The Fabrication of Aboriginal History*, 102.

program'.[11] This became part of a heated debate at the highest level of politics, which began with the 'History Wars'.[12] Windschuttle escalated the discussion in a determined attack on many historians in the field of Aboriginal history. His first volume, which challenged the claims made by historians of the Australian frontier wars, was heavily criticised, primarily in Robert Manne's publication of *Whitewash: On Keith Windschuttle's Fabrication of Aboriginal History*.[13] Windschuttle's third volume on the *Stolen Generations 1881–2008* has not been rebutted in the same way. Historian Bain Attwood has some suggestions as to why this may be so. Attwood offers several ways to respond to Windschuttle, one of which is not to! Attwood argues that Windschuttle's work 'is a form of denialism' and historians should not 'engage in such work' because 'seeking to rebut' his work only draws attention to it.[14] Attwood contends that the 'truth' for Windschuttle is not a complex or complicated affair: 'Truth is black or white; there are no greys'. He argues that Windschuttle does not make 'fine distinctions' but reduces 'historical truth' to a 'matter of facts' and that when historians claim 'a truth' based upon 'interpretation and perspective', Windschuttle feels as though he has been 'misled' or even 'duped'.[15] Windschuttle's simplistic views on the truth and history are challenged below with his assertions concerning the removal of Aboriginal children.

Peter Read laments the fact that old established ground still needs to be defended. He argues that historical research should instead be breaking new boundaries and deepening our understanding of the impact upon Indigenous Australians by the various jurisdictions that controlled their lives.[16] Read contends that there are 'larger' and 'smaller' truths in history. For example, in the Australian colonial context, a 'larger truth' is the dispossession of Aboriginal people by the British resulting in the deaths by frontier violence of – according to Henry Reynolds – up to 30,000

---

11   Windschuttle, *The Fabrication of Aboriginal History*, 17.
12   Attwood, *Telling the Truth about Aboriginal History*, is essential reading regarding the 'History Wars'; Mark McKenna provides an instructive background to the development of the 'Black Armband' view of Australian history (a term first coined by Professor Geoffrey Blayney) and canvasses the proponents on both sides of the argument. See McKenna, 'Different Perspectives on Black Armband History'.
13   Manne, ed., *Whitewash*.
14   Attwood, *Telling the Truth about Aboriginal History*, 3–4.
15   Attwood, *Telling the Truth about Aboriginal History*, 69.
16   Read, 'Clio or Janus?', 54–60.

Aboriginal people.[17] Over time, historians wrote of 'smaller truths'; for example, that some Aboriginal people 'betrayed or led neighbouring clans to their deaths, that some pastoralists protected bush people against their neighbours [and] that some Aboriginal people committed massacres of their own'. At the same time, other historians reinforced the central truth of dispossession with examples supporting the 'big' truth. Read argues that these 'local qualifications, of which there were many, did not seem to disturb the central fact of dispossession-by-violence'.[18]

Read's thesis is pertinent in the context of exploring child removals. The important 'big truth' was the fact that Aboriginal children in New South Wales were removed from families in vastly increased numbers after 1916. They were targeted because they were Aboriginal and particularly if they were 'half-castes', 'quadroons' or 'octoroons'. However, by 1995 Read had decided not to write any further of those who had been separated because the previous 20 years had produced 'volumes of oral testimony', 'blanket media coverage' and extensive postgraduate research, so that the Stolen Generations had 'become part of the fabric of Australian history'. It was now time to research or write about the qualifications, the regional variations, the 'smaller truths'. Smaller truths included stories of some Aboriginal children who received a good education and loved their white parents, of some Aboriginal parents who had abandoned their children or of others still who asked the Board to look after their children. Other 'small truths' include the fact that Aboriginal mothers had a 'blanket thrown over their legs in childbirth to prevent them seeing their babies even once', that 'hardly anyone from the Kinchela Boys Home reached the age of fifty-five', and that 'officials looked forward to the day when there would be no identifying Aboriginals remaining in the whole of southern Australia'. But Read argues these histories cannot be told if the central truth is continually challenged. The quandary for the historian, Read suggests, is 'how can we tell little truths if the big truth is so under attack that its future in the mainstream narrative is imperilled?'[19]

---

17 Reynolds, *The Forgotten War*, 134. The figure of 30,000 is a revision of his earlier work *The Other Side of the Frontier*, 121. To calculate the numbers of Aboriginal people who died in the conflict, Reynolds considers the estimates by Ryan in Tasmania (800), Green in one area of Western Australia (102), Prentis in the Northern Rivers region of NSW (100), Christie in Victoria (2,000) and Reynolds in Queensland (between 8,000 and 10,000). Reynolds made an educated assessment: for the 'continent as a whole it is reasonable to suppose that at least 20,000 Aborigines were killed as a result of conflict with settlers' and that 'somewhere between 2,000 and 2,500 Europeans in the course of the invasion and settlement of the continent' died (121–22).
18 Read, 'Clio or Janus?', 54–55.
19 Read, 'Clio or Janus?', 56–59.

The declared objectives of the Aboriginal Protection Board (APB) were to remove Aboriginal children from the influence of their communities, to train them as domestic servants, to take their place in mainstream Australia as part of the labouring classes, and for them *never* to return to their families or communities. The corollary is that Aboriginal families lived in constant fear of losing their children. The exact number removed is important but will never be known precisely – yet not knowing does not displace the 'larger' truth of systematic removal. Intellectual endeavour and intelligent estimation allow some conclusions to be drawn.[20]

The Board's intentions and the identification for removal

As noted, the removal of Aboriginal children from their families and placement in apprenticeships had been in the mind of the Board since 1883.[21] Fosbery and King had advocated the same in their 1883 report to the colonial secretary on the Maloga and Warangesda missions. Their recommendation to first target only those children without parents and then to consult with the parents so as to obtain their consent suggests a modicum of understanding of the severity of the policy. The report also acknowledged that the feelings of the parents and relatives should be taken into consideration.[22] There were no such niceties from 1916.

The focus on the girls

As revealed in Chapter 4, Robert Donaldson and the Board had convinced the colonial secretary that those children with a less than half of an 'admixture of Aboriginal blood' needed to be removed from the camps, reserves and stations. Although both sexes were targeted for removal, the policy focused strongly on girls. This is demonstrated by the fact that Cootamundra Training Home for girls was established in 1912,

---

20   Reynolds, *The Other Side of the Frontier*, 121.
21   Aboriginal child removals had, of course, occurred well before the Board existed. Richard Johnson, the chaplain on the First Fleet, and his wife Mary, took in a young Aboriginal girl named Araboo in 1789: see Harris, *One Blood*, 41. In 1814, Lachlan Macquarie's Native Institution removed Aboriginal children from their communities: see Harris, *One Blood*, 52.
22   *Aboriginal Mission Stations at Warangesda and Maloga (Report on Working Of.)*, New South Wales Legislative Assembly, 18 January 1883, 4.

well before an equivalent home for boys at Kinchela in 1924.²³ Moreover, Heather Goodall's research shows that from 1912 to 1921, '81 per cent of the children removed were girls' and for the whole period up to 1928, 'girls made up 72 per cent of all the 12 and over children who were taken'.²⁴ All 'half-caste', 'quadroon' and 'octoroon' boys were required to leave the stations and reserves to find work, while the girls at the same age had either to accept domestic work or be taken to Cootamundra Training Home.

The Board's unequivocal policy on the removal of girls, as adopted on 6 April 1916, stated:

> All girls on reaching the age of 14 years ... shall leave the Reserves. In order to affect this result, the mothers shall be given the option and opportunity of themselves placing their girls out in situations to the satisfaction of the Board's Officers. If they fail to do this within a period of one month, after being notified, the Board's Inspectors shall have power to despatch such girls to Sydney or to Cootamundra Home for a period of training, as arranged by the Secretary.²⁵

It was not a question of neglect or having no parents; the APB compelled all mixed-race girls, regardless of their circumstances, to leave. The month's grace given to the parents to find a placement for their female children could be viewed, at worst, as an exercise in saving the Board's time and resources or, at best, a weak attempt to allow girls to be placed at a location of her or her parents' choosing. It was no coincidence that the identification process began at age 14. Goodall argues that the apprentice system was 'quite explicitly directed at removing girls reaching puberty from the Aboriginal community'. The intention was to 'intervene in the rising Aboriginal birth-rate by constricting and controlling young, fertile Aboriginal women's sexual activity'.²⁶

The Board had two clear and related objectives: to hasten the closure of the stations and reserves; and to 'absorb' all Aboriginal girls of marriageable age into white society. Katherine Ellinghaus contends that politicians, in the south-eastern states, 'tried to engineer the "disappearance" of

---

23   Cole, 'The Glorified Flower', 65.
24   Goodall, 'Assimilation Begins in the Home', 81–82.
25   APB Minutes (hereafter *APBM*), 6 April 1916, Item 1. All *APBM* accessed via: Minute Books (Aborigines Welfare Board), NRS 2, NSW Department of Aboriginal Affairs, Sydney.
26   Goodall, 'Assimilation Begins in the Home', 81.

their Indigenous populations by physically dividing Aboriginal people from one another, removing families and individuals from reserves, and removing children from their families'.[27] Ellinghaus suggests that New South Wales was unique in its 'blatant and single-minded focus on absorbing the Aboriginal population by means of removing children from their parents'.[28] Victoria Haskins declares that, through the apprentice system, the APB intended to reduce the numbers within the reserves and stations to bring about their eventual closure and – moreover – to 'breed out the race'.[29] Her conclusion is chilling:

> The New South Wales Aborigines Protection Board colluded in, condoned and indeed encouraged the systematic sexual abuse and impregnation of young Aboriginal women in domestic apprenticeships with, I contend, the ultimate aim of eradicating the Aboriginal population.[30]

The Board's language was circumspect. It did not use words such as 'breeding out', 'intervening in the birth rate', 'engineering' or 'eradicating', but its intent was the same. It frequently used the terms 'merging' and 'absorption' coupled with the belief that the 'full-blood' population would soon die out; the unstated conclusion was that the Aboriginal 'problem' would soon be solved.

To strengthen the argument that the Board's intent was to 'breed out the race', Haskins explains that the apprenticing of white girls was common during the nineteenth century but was on the decline. By the 1920s the practice was almost obsolete. Implicit in the state's decision not to apprentice white girls was the acknowledgement that 'their sexuality could *not* be controlled'.[31] Yet, it was during this period that the Board began to ramp up the removal of Aboriginal girls into indentured situations. Arguably, the intention was not to 'protect them' from 'present surroundings' but to place them in an environment where they would more likely find white husbands or partners.

---

27 Ellinghaus, 'Absorbing the "Aboriginal Problem"', 183–207.
28 Ellinghaus, 'Absorbing the "Aboriginal Problem"', 195.
29 Haskins, 'A Better Chance?', 35.
30 Haskins, 'A Better Chance?', 53.
31 Haskins, 'A Better Chance?', 37.

Identification of available girls

By 1916 the Board had created 19 Aboriginal stations across the state.[32] Each was staffed by a manager/teacher and his wife who looked after the needs of the women and girls. The managers of stations were also required to identify children for removal and inform the Board. Also, under the Act local officers in charge of police had responsibility for the unmanaged reserves and therefore undertook the task of identifying Aboriginal children for removal.[33] Towards the end of 1914 the Board had expressed frustration that some station managers were tardy in reporting children for removal. A Board circular to all managers began with: 'It is feared that some of the Managers do not understand what is required in connection with [Circular No. 18] regarding youths and girls'. The Board reminded managers to comply.[34] Perhaps some managers were reluctant to identify individuals for removal. Also, in April 1916 a circular went out to all superintendents of police (stationed at Sydney, Armidale, Goulburn, Depot (sic), Bathurst, West Maitland, Tamworth, Deniliquin, Bourke, Albury) requesting that they provide the Board with particulars of all orphaned or neglected children under the age of 18 'on the various reserves in his district'. It also advised the superintendents to provide:

> particulars of children who were *not* [my emphasis] neglected, but who were living under circumstances which, in the opinion of the Police, are likely to endanger their future moral or physical welfare, should be shown separately at the end of the Return, giving the fullest details ... In every case a definite recommendation should be made as to whether the child should be removed from its present surroundings.[35]

Other institutions also initiated removals. A Board minute entry reads: 'indenture between Aboriginal Girl "Y" and the Australian Aborigines Mission'; Board response: 'Approved'.[36] However, on this occasion, Board

---

32 *Protection of Aborigines: Report of the Board* (the APB Report: hereafter *APBR*) 1916, Appendix A. Accessed via *NSW Legislative Assembly: Aborigines Report of Board for the Aborigines 1915–1922*, Q572.991 N, State Library of New South Wales (hereafter SLNSW).
33 Under the *Aborigines Protection Act 1909* (NSW), Regulation 28c gave the police authority on the unmanaged reserves.
34 APB Circular No. 1, 10 November 1914, Copies of letters sent 1914–27, 4/7128, Reel 1853, State Records of New South Wales (hereafter SRNSW).
35 APB Circular No. 67 to Superintendents, 1 April 1916, Copies of letters sent 1914–27, 4/7128, Reel 1853, (SRNSW).
36 *APBM*, 2 August 1916, Item 15.

secretary Robert Beardsmore wrote to Mrs L.W. Long of the Aborigines Inland Mission, stating the Board's mild displeasure at not being 'kept in the loop'. His letter also reveals how 'ad hoc' the removal process could be:

> A case has recently come under my notice in which Mr Smith of the Singleton Home has arranged to send out a girl to service. While the Board are [sic] always willing to accept your recommendation for the placing of girls from Singleton Home in suitable situations, might I suggest the desirableness of instructing Mr Smith to, in future, communicate with this office when he has a girl ready to send out, and stating where he suggests she should go.[37]

Another example of a removal likely initiated by an institution is told by Dharawal men Les Bursill and his cousin Bryan Smith. It relates to the placement of one of their relatives, an eight-year-old Aboriginal girl at a convent in Tempe. Les was told it occurred just before the First World War when the girl was taken by the police 'in a horse drawn wagon' and removed to the convent; neither men could say if the girl's mother knew of the impending removal. At age eight, she was far too young to be apprenticed – usually the girls went straight to Cootamundra Training Home until they were 14. Most likely, a request had come from the convent to the Board for an Aboriginal domestic servant. The girl worked in the convent for the next six to seven years. Her job was to 'push down the clothes into boiling vats of soapy water – she was a laundry maid, ironer, and starcher'. At the end of it all 'she was given a florin'. Bryan Smith remarked that she was 'a slave in that place'. At the age of around 18, and without any notice, she was returned, unannounced to her mother by the police.[38]

---

37 Letter from Robert Beardsmore to L.W. Long, 15 March 1914, Aborigines Inland Mission, Records, 1904–1988, MLMSS 7895, Folder 1905–1923, Correspondence primarily from the NSW Office of the Board for the Protection of Aborigines, Mitchell Library (hereafter ML). The Singleton Home, run by the Aborigines Inland Mission, was for Aboriginal boys and girls from birth until 14 years of age. The property was bought by the Board around 1918. See also: www.findandconnect.gov.au/guide/nsw/NE01616.

38 Les Bursill and Bryan Smith, interview by the author, 12 July 2017, at Worrigee (near Nowra). There is no record of this girl in the Board minutes or the Ward Registers. The vast majority of girls went into domestic service in residential homes but the placement in a convent was unusual. As seen in Chapter 3, many requests for domestic servants came to the Board. Both men said that she was taken around the age of eight years old; however, if Olive was at the convent for seven years, she would only be 15 and not 18 when she returned home. She may well have had another placement after the nunnery of which they were unaware.

Aboriginal pushback

The Board regularly employed strategies to encourage compliance. Homefinder Miss Lowe was often tasked with explaining to Aboriginal mothers the benefits of 'giving up' their girls.[39] If persuasion failed then the Board withheld 'aid' to the girls and directed the family 'to secure suitable situations locally to the satisfaction of police, within a period of [a] month'.[40] If they declined to do so then the Board made the 'suitable' arrangement. In some cases when the Board met with stiff resistance it seemed reluctant to use its own powers. In 1919, the mother of a 14-year-old 'half-caste' girl at Brungle Station refused to allow her daughter to be removed to Cootamundra Training Home for Girls. The Board minutes record that proceedings to 'be instituted under the Neglected Children and Juvenile Offenders Act in the event of the mother persisting in her refusal to allow the child to be transferred to Cootamundra Home'.[41] This course of action was not necessary. The Board chose not to enforce its own powers under the 1915 amendment to the *Aborigines Protection Act 1909* (NSW). Perhaps the Board believed that the removal of a child from Brungle by the police would create a negative public reaction. To hide under the state's *Neglected Children and Juvenile Offenders Act 1905* may have been a more palatable approach.

A similar situation developed at Bulgandramine Reserve (just north of Parkes). Inspector Donaldson had recommended the removal of two sisters but the parents refused to let them go. The Board instructed the police to interview the girl's parents 'with a view to … persuade them to consent'; in the event of their failing to acquiesce, it advised that the parents should be 'warned the children will be brought before the court'.[42] There is no further mention of this incident, but clearly the parents were reluctant to give their children up and the Board tended to avoid any public incidents. In later life, Board Secretary Pettitt reflected in an interview that there were 'some instances where there was trouble getting the girls away very naturally' and he admitted to the use of force:

---

39   Cole, 'The Glorified Flower', 70.
40   *APBM*, 14 September 1916, Item 15.
41   *APBM*, 15 October 1919, Item 20.
42   *APBM*, 12 November 1919, Item 9.

> I mean to say there was a lot of hostility and some of these circumstances where I suppose, they were unavoidable but in some cases, I believe that girls were taken away when there was an uproar on the station because of their forcible transfer.[43]

After three girls 'were seized and sent to Cootamundra' from Cumeroogunga Station on the Murray River in 1919, there was a fear of further removals. Sixteen Aboriginal families fled to the safety of Victoria and would not return until they were guaranteed a fair court hearing.[44]

The APB, sensitive to negative publicity, held the view that it would 'adhere to its current practice of bringing children to the courts ... rather than summarily removing them under the provisions of the Aborigines Protection Act'.[45] Due to parental resistance and the subsequent movement of Aboriginal families away from the stations, summary removals had to be tempered. In 1922, to prevent families from leaving the stations, the APB sent out a circular to all managers and teachers to 'dissuade them [Aboriginal families] from leaving the stations to the reserves where there is no supervision'.[46]

The record of removals

Significant difficulties face researchers of records concerning Aboriginal child removals in New South Wales from 1883 to 1940. The Ward Registers 1916–28 are the only surviving archive that records the names and relevant details regarding the placements of young Aboriginal girls and boys who were removed by the Board.[47]

The archive contains the records of 800 children removed between 1916 and 28. It is the most important archive of the period. Even so, the archive remains challenging due to its fragmentary, unclear and ambiguous nature. Some names and places are difficult to decipher. As a result,

---

43   A.C. Pettitt, interview by J.J. Fletcher, 1977, Audio-tape J01-018426, Australian Institute of Aboriginal and Torres Strait Islander Studies (hereafter AIATSIS) Library, Canberra.
44   *Daily Herald* (Adelaide), 28 April 1919, 2; and the *Albury Banner and Wodonga Express*, 2 May 1919, 35.
45   *APBM,* 13 September 1922, Item 4.
46   *APBM,* 13 September 1922, Item 4.
47   Aborigines Welfare Board – Ward Registers, 18 January 1916 – 2 June 1926; 28 May 1924–27 and December 1928, NRS 26, Original location 4/8553 and 4/8554; Reel 2793 (SRNSW) (hereafter referred to as Ward Registers, 1916–28).

researchers can differ in their interpretation of the number of children recorded therein. For instance, I found six double entries while Naomi Parry found seven duplicates.[48] Generally though, historians who have looked at this archive have agreed that 800 children (approximately 570 girls and 230 boys) were removed between 1916 and 1928.[49] There is a second archive, called the Index to Ward Registers, 1916 – c.1938, but this Index only lists the names of the children who were made wards, with no other details regarding their removal.[50] It does include the names of the 800 children detailed in the Ward Registers. The Index also records the names of 654 additional children removed. In a third archive there are the names of a further 128 children are listed but with no details.[51] Together, these registers document the removal of 1,582 individual Aboriginal children in New South Wales.

Each entry in the Ward Registers is filled out on a template – called a 'Register form' – with the following headings: entry number, date at beginning of entry, name of child, age, birthday, place of birth, religion, reason for the Board assuming control, father's name and occupation and address, mother's name and address, other relatives, how many brothers and sisters with names and ages, previous placements in other situations, where placed and for how long, further particulars (where living during childhood and in whose care), to which institution sent and when, the certificate of admission and the relevant 'disposal'. The 'disposal' section of the files records where the children were initially placed and their subsequent placements. The name of the person/household where the child was sent, the location and the date are consistently recorded. There are, however, many gaps in the information under each heading; for example, no birthdate or place of birth, no details for the mother or siblings, and so on. In some cases, information is indecipherable. These gaps can lead to potential misreading of the evidence, or assumptions made, leading to the minor statistical differences drawn by researchers viewing the same file. Table 6.1 below lists a sample of some of the reasons the Board recorded for removal.

---

48   Ward Registers, 1916–28, Nos 166 and 130; 538 and 681; 676 and 550; 677 and 549; 678 and 548; 604 and 669. Parry, 'Such a Longing', 285.
49   Read, *The Stolen Generations*, 10; Parry, 'Such a Longing', 285–90; Walden, 'That Was Slavery Days', 196; Haskins, 'A Better Chance?', 43; Windschuttle, *The Fabrication of Aboriginal History*, 76.
50   Index to Ward Registers, 1916 – c.1938, NRS 27, location 4/8555–56, Reel 1649 (SRNSW).
51   Windschuttle, *The Fabrication of Aboriginal History*, 76.

Table 6.1: Reasons recorded by the Board for the removal of children, organised under four categories.

Training	Situation	Age	Other
to send to service from surroundings of camp life	abandoned by her mother	attaining school age	aboriginal
to train for domestic service	orphan	to attend school	at own request
to send to service and give a better chance in life	neglected child	past school age	transferred to the State Children's Relief Department
to fit for situation	death of mother	having attained the age of 14 years	–
to train for a situation	parent's dead; neglected	too old to stay longer at reserve (aged 14)	–
apprenticed	parents unable to support, living destitute	–	–
to be apprenticed	living on mission camp and not under proper care of parents	–	–
to have him trained	likely to lapse into career of vice	–	–
to have advantage of proper training and protected against the risk of going to the bad	to better her conditions & take from surroundings of Aboriginal Station	–	–
to send to service as not to lead idle life on reserve	to improve conditions of living; living under conditions that would lead her to a career of vice and crime	–	–
for domestic service	–	–	–

Source: Ward Registers, 1916–28.

It is interesting to note how Keith Windschuttle has interpreted the Ward Registers. To support his argument that the Board acted appropriately, he concluded that a total of 526, or 65.75 per cent of the 800 children, were removed for what *he asserts* were reasonable motives. From the record he determined that the Board removed: 173 on the grounds that they went 'into apprenticeship or employment'; 113 who were deemed 'neglected'; 73 for being 'orphaned'; 62 to 'improve the child's condition of living'; 52 to 'go into education or training; and 53 at the request of the State Children's Relief Board.[52] But what Windschuttle ignores is that the Board had *absolute discretion* to determine whatever reason it chose to remove the children. There was no independent scrutiny or oversight of the Board in this matter, thus making a mockery of Windschuttle's breakdown of reasonable motives.

The *reason* could have been provided by either of the two inspectors, a local policeman, the manager of an Aboriginal station or an officer of the APB acting on information from the stations and reserves. As can be seen in Table 6.1, many of the reasons are insufficient to justify the removal of a child or adolescent from their family or community. Herb Simms was born at La Perouse in 1926 and was sent to Bomaderry Aboriginal Children's Home at three years of age. After six years he was transferred to Kinchela Boys Home. Years later, Herb recalled as a young lad how the police and station managers had extraordinary powers:

> we were mindful … that the police themselves could go in and drag Aboriginal kids out and take them all without question from their homes. There would be the manager of the Aboriginal settlement who could do the same thing.[53]

Naomi Parry argues that the Board threatened parents with neglect proceedings if they did not give up their children: this was blatant intimidation. But also points out that the rate of parental surrenders was very low at 5 per cent, like that among white families. Parry found only two cases of 'surrender' and both were short-term placements. One mother applied to the Board for respite from her 18-year-old daughter for a few months; and a Moonacullah (north-west of Deniliquin) woman who had been 'deserted by her husband' reclaimed her four children after 'securing housing and employment'.[54] This would suggest that almost all removals were resisted.

---

52 Windschuttle, *The Fabrication of Aboriginal History*, 93–94.
53 Herb Simms, interview by Fred Maynard, 7 April 2001, La Perouse, Bib ID: 950973, ORAL TRC 5000/263, National Library of Australia (hereafter NLA).
54 Parry, 'Such a Longing', 287.

The removal of Aboriginal children into apprenticeships

The following analyses calculate the number of children removed from numerous communities and sent into apprenticeships across the state. Also, by tracing the movements of the apprentices from Dharawal Country, I endeavour not only to personalise the removals but also to demonstrate the vast distances that many travelled, and the number of placements they endured.

The statistics are solely derived from the Ward Registers 1916–28, and it must be stressed that they are far from complete for this period. Therefore, there are limitations to the analyses that follow. First, the Index to the Ward Registers (listing 654 Aboriginal children removed) is not mentioned below because there are no details about the children removed. Second, as Board reporting was so tardy, particularly after 1916, no researcher could be confident that all Board reporting was accurate, let alone comprehensive. Third, the Board was totally unaccountable to any person or authority in compiling its statistics. Fourth, as already mentioned, there are differences of accounting among historians who have viewed this archive. Furthermore, Aboriginal families across New South Wales will be able to attest to children being removed from locations that do not appear below.

Aboriginal girls removed

In the absence of any consistent historical regional reporting by the Board, I have used the current New South Wales Aboriginal Land Council (ALC) boundaries to represent the regions throughout New South Wales (Figure 6.1).[55]

The ALC has nine regions: North Western, Wiradjuri, Northern, Mid-North Coast, North Coast, Central, Sydney/Newcastle, Western, and South Coast.

---

55   The Board reports provided census figures based on individual locations across the state. From 1883 until 1911 (28 years) it listed the census locations, usually in alphabetical order, as detailed by the local police officer in the district. From 1911 until 1915 (5 years) the Board then divided its census report into nine regions: metropolitan, northern, southern, eastern, western, north-eastern, north-western, south-western, and Murray. For the next 24 years the Board failed to report any breakdown in its census figures. Without any consistency of reporting from the Board, I have therefore chosen more recent Aboriginal Land Council boundaries to reflect the spread of removals.

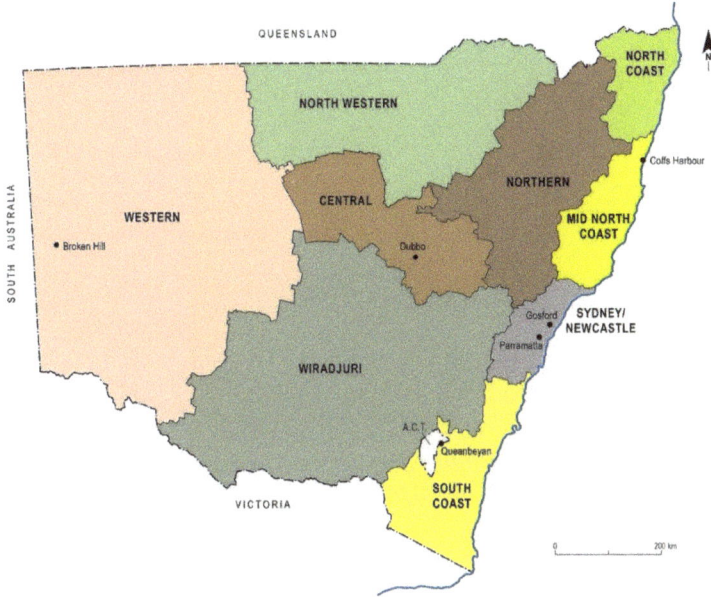

Figure 6.1: Map of New South Wales Aboriginal Land Council boundaries.
Source: alc.org.au. Cartographer: Peter Johnson, Cordeaux Heights, NSW.

The archive records the placement of 501 girls into apprenticeships by the Board. This number is short of the accepted figure of 570 only because some girls were placed by the State Children's Relief Board, some into George Ardill's Homes and others into hospitals/asylums. The figures below only represent those girls who were apprenticed.

The greatest number of girls (438) removed and subsequently placed into domestic service were from regional locations across New South Wales, while 11 more were taken from Sydney and Newcastle (Figure 6.2). Seven more girls were removed, but the locations from where they were taken could not be determined. An additional 41 girls were placed in domestic situations after being removed from New South Wales institutions. This latter group is represented separately because we do not know from which region the girls originally came. There were also four girls from interstate placed into apprenticeships in New South Wales (see Appendices).[56]

---

56   Inara Walden records that 570 girls were removed (Walden, 'That Was Slavery Days', 96). Victoria Haskins records a total of 570 girls removed and identifies 514 wards who were apprenticed. (Haskins, 'A Better Chance?', 43); Keith Windschuttle concludes that it is possible to identify the sex of 781 files, of which 557 were female and 224 were male (Windschuttle, *The Fabrication of Aboriginal History*, 76). The discrepancies reflect the difficulty in reading the files; sometimes the records are illegible, and some entries are open to interpretation.

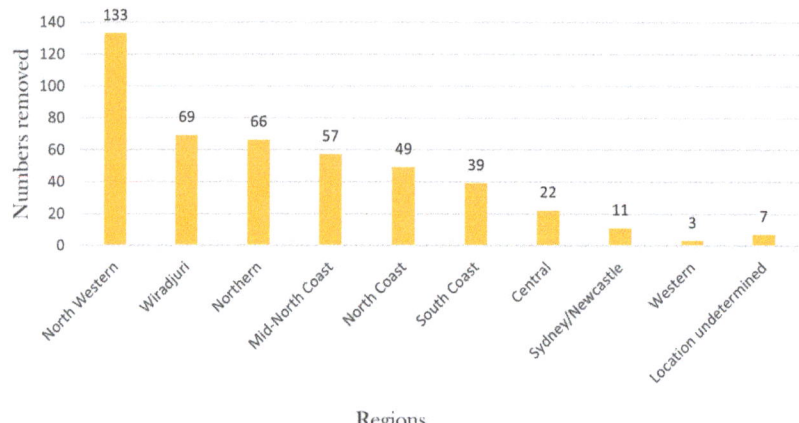

Figure 6.2: Numbers and regions from where Aboriginal girls were removed and subsequently placed in apprenticeships (1916–28). Total: 456.
Regions are based on the current New South Wales Aboriginal Land Council boundaries.
Source: Author's summary of Ward Registers, 1916–28.

Figure 6.2 demonstrates two interesting findings. First, the removal of Aboriginal girls among New South Wales regions was uneven. Second, one region, the North Western, bore the brunt of the removals with 133 out of 449 girls, or 29.6 per cent, coming from this area of the state. Also, data on removals within each region, shown with further graphs in the Appendices, demonstrates that some Aboriginal stations and reserves bore a disproportionate burden of removals: the highest numbers of girls removed from each region were drawn from Aboriginal stations or reserves, but it should be noted that girls were also removed from towns that had no appended stations or reserves, including Barmah, Blayney, Forbes, Tamworth, Armidale, Broke, Stanthorpe, Gloucester, Nambucca Heads, Tweed Heads, Kiama, Port Kembla, Mudgee, Bowral and Cabramatta. Aboriginal families living independently of the Board were not immune to the *Aborigines Protection Act 1909*. Section 11(1) stated: 'The board may … by indenture bind or cause to [be] bound the child of *any* [my emphasis] aborigine … to be apprenticed to any master'.[57]

Moreover, of those 133 girls, who were removed from the North Western region, 78 or 58.6 per cent came from just three locations: Brewarrina, Angledool and Pilliga (Figure 6.3).

---

57 *Aborigines Protection Act 1909* (NSW).

Figure 6.3: Numbers of Aboriginal girls removed from locations within the North Western region (1916–28). Total: 133.
Source: Author's summary of Ward Registers, 1916–28.

These three locations also play a similar role, but even more predominantly, in the removal of Aboriginal boys.

Aboriginal boys removed

The removal of Aboriginal boys was similarly most concentrated in the North Western region (Figure 6.4). A total of 152 Aboriginal boys were removed from identifiable locations and placed in apprenticeships; seven locations could not be identified. Fifteen boys were removed directly from Aboriginal Boys' Homes, making a total of 174 boys removed and placed in apprenticeships between 1916 and 1928. As with the Aboriginal girls who were removed, fewer boys were taken from institutions. Of the 174 boys removed, more than 91 per cent were from stations and reserves. A breakdown of each region can be found in the Appendices.

As with the girls within the North Western region, Brewarrina, Angledool and Pilliga are over-represented in the removal data. Of the boys removed in this region 51 of 84, or 60.7 per cent, came from these three locations (Figure 6.5).

POWER AND DYSFUNCTION

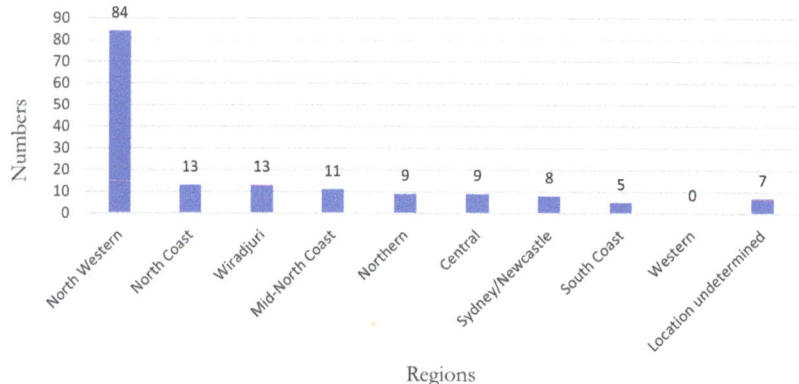

Figure 6.4: Numbers and regions from where Aboriginal boys were removed and subsequently placed into apprenticeships (1916–28). Total: 159.
Regions are based on the current New South Wales Aboriginal Land Council boundaries.
Source: Author's summary of Ward Registers, 1916–28.

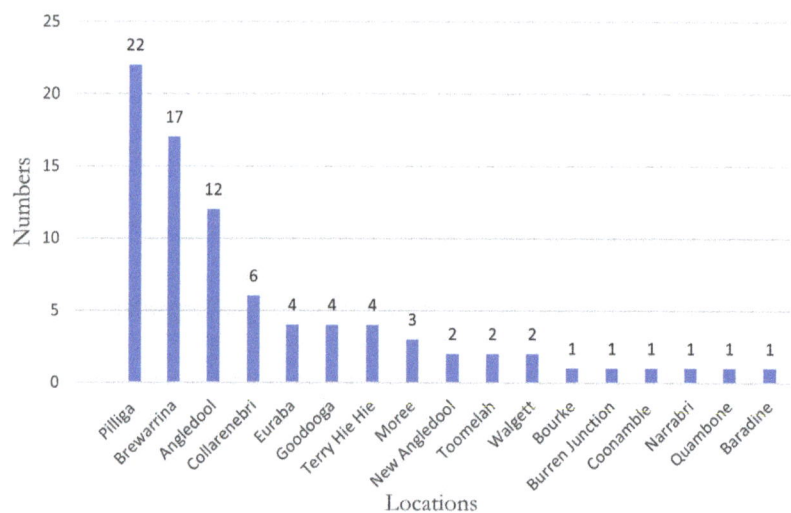

Figure 6.5: Numbers of Aboriginal boys removed from locations within the North Western region (1916–28). Total: 84.
Source: Author's summary of Ward Registers, 1916–28.

In summary, this *limited record* suggests that 675 Aboriginal children (501 girls and 174 boys) were placed into apprenticeships between 1916 and 1928. The obvious question is why did most of child removals come from the North Western region? Of the 675 children/adolescents placed into apprenticeships, 217 (133 girls and 84 boys), or 32 per cent, came

6. THE GIRLS RETURN

from this region. Moreover, in the breakdown of removals within the North Western region, three main centres – Brewarrina, Angledool and Pilliga – stand out as locations from where 129 children (51 boys and 78 girls) were removed. This figure represents 19 per cent of the removals from across New South Wales. No other location point had higher raw numbers of removals than these three.

Some observations can be made about these three locations. First, Angledool and Pilliga were not major Aboriginal population centres, but Brewarrina was. Figure 6.6 represents population levels of just 17 location points, not necessarily a station or reserve, over the five-year period from 1911 to 1915, with an Aboriginal population close to or above 100.[58] Brewarrina, Angledool and Pilliga (far right) have been included to show a direct comparison.

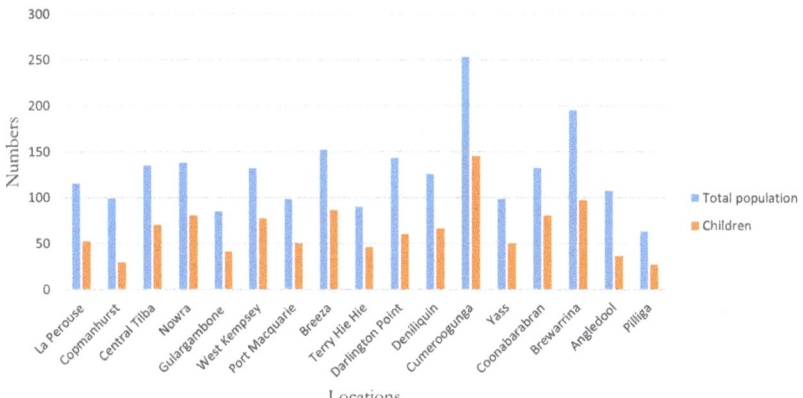

Figure 6.6: Mean total Aboriginal populations at major Aboriginal concentration centres from 1911 to 1915. Numbers of children are included in the total population columns and are also represented separately.
Source: Author's summary of *APBR*, 1911–15.

Brewarrina was a significant population centre; in fact, it was the second largest in the state after Cumeroogunga. Angledool was close to the mean population of other main centres while Pilliga was at the lower end of numbers. Cumeroogunga clearly had the largest population of both adults and children in 1915, so you would expect significant removals

---

58 As outlined in Chapter 5, the APB reduced its reporting after 1916. After 1915 and for the next 24 years, the Board failed to produce *any breakdown* census figures for the various regions and stations as it had done prior to 1916.

from here. Yet, only nine girls were removed from Cumeroogunga under the period under discussion (see Appendices). There were other locations with lower populations and from where more girls were removed: Burra Bee Dee (near Coonabarabran), Warangesda (Darling Point) and Roseby Park (near Nowra) all had populations approximately half that at Cumeroogunga, yet the number of girls removed from these locations were higher (18, 16 and 10, respectively) (see Appendices). Therefore, the overall population of centres or stations was not the predominant factor in determining removals.

Second, the children targeted for apprenticeship were generally *not* 'full-bloods' *but* 'half-castes', or those children with 'less than an admixture of Aboriginal blood'.[59] So you would expect to see locations with a higher concentration of 'half-caste' children to be targeted for removal. However, an examination of the breakdown of 'full-blood' and 'half-caste' children at the locations from where more than 10 girls were removed does not support this (Figure 6.7).

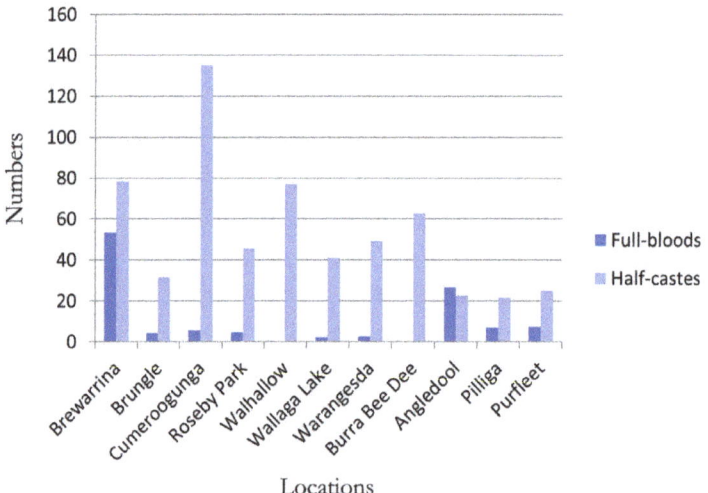

Figure 6.7: Numbers of 'full-blood' and 'half-caste' children at location points between 1911 and 1912 from where 10 or more girls were subsequently removed.[60]
Source: Author's summary of *APBR*, 1911–15.

---

59 There are numerous references to the Board targeting children classified as 'half-caste' or 'quadroons' and 'octoroons'. See Chapter 4.
60 The Board statistics are only consistent, for the breakdown of children on this basis, for these two years.

Both Brewarrina and Angledool had the highest percentage of children who were classified as 'full-bloods'. Arguably, then, you would *not* expect to see large numbers removed from Brewarrina or Angledool. Brewarrina *did* have a large 'half-caste' population, but in comparison to other locations, Angledool and Pilliga did not, and should not have been overly targeted. Heather Goodall argues that the 'full-blood' children and adolescents were targeted just as much as those with a 'lesser admixture of Aboriginal blood', so this may not be a valid distinction. The Board did allow for the removal of 'full-blood' children but stipulated that they should not be sent too far away from their communities.[61] The main thrust of Board policy was the removal of the 'half-caste', 'quadroon' and 'octoroon' population. However, it may not have been implemented on the ground and poor reporting on the status of each child in this regard removes the opportunity to check this.[62]

From 1916, only three Board reports indicated where the inspectors travelled during those years. A situation may have arisen whereby the inspectors concentrated on the North Western region for some reason in the other years.[63] A further examination of the archive to ascertain any trends of spikes or troughs in removals for each year from 1913 to 1929 did not provide any clear evidence to that end; the only clear trend was a reduction in removal activity in 1928, which coincides with Inspector Donaldson's retirement through ill health.[64] One can only speculate as to what caused this intense interest in this area to remove Aboriginal children. Perhaps the North Western region had a cluster of overzealous managers or local police. One thing, though, is clear. The newly reconstituted Board from 1916, primarily run by the trio of Secretary Pettitt, Inspector Donaldson and Miss Lowe, had carriage of these removals. I would suggest that the Board's actions were arbitrary, but also influenced by compliant managers and local police. In addition, the degree of Aboriginal resistance may also have influenced Board removal activity. Significant press coverage of the

---

61   *APBM*, 6 April 1916, Item 1.
62   The Ward Registers, 1916–28, sometimes record whether a child was a 'full-blood' or 'half-caste', but these data are too infrequent.
63   *APBR* 1916, 2; 1918, 1; 1921, 1. Accessed via *NSW Legislative Assembly: Aborigines Report of Board for the Aborigines 1915–1922*, Q572.991 N. (SLNSW). No other reports specifically listed their visitations. In a recent email conversation, Heather Goodall suggests that the north-west was targeted after early locations like Cumeroogunga. She also points out that for inland locations like Brewarrina and Pilliga it was difficult to 'escape' the Board, unlike Cumeroogunga or Toomelah on the Victorian and Queensland borders respectively. Also, she notes that in the north-west there was significant opposition from Aboriginal families to the removal of their children. Email correspondence, 3–5 July 2017.
64   Ward Registers, 1916–28.

16 Aboriginal families fleeing across the Murray River from Cumeroogunga to avoid possible child removals appears to have influenced the Board to stay clear, arguably to avoid public scrutiny.[65] Heather Goodall notes that age, sex 'and proximity to the Board's inspectorial routes of travel' were the only reliable predictors of removal.[66] Further intensive investigation is required to provide a satisfactory explanation to this interesting finding of disproportionate removals from Brewarrina, Angledool and Pilliga.

Placement of Aboriginal girls and boys into apprenticeships across New South Wales

Girls

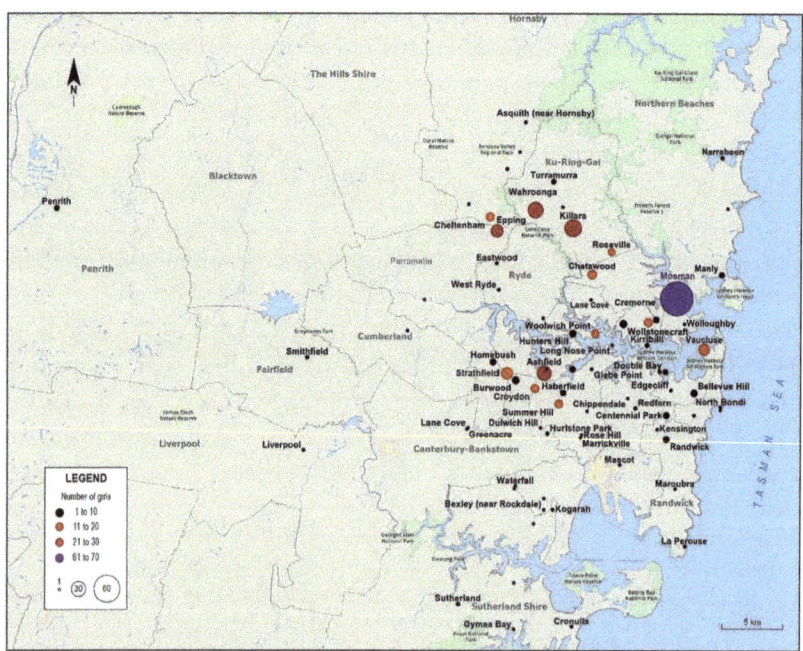

Figure 6.8: Location points in Sydney for the placement of Aboriginal girls who had been removed from their communities.
Source: Ward Registers, 1916–28. Cartographer: Peter Johnson, Cordeaux Heights, NSW.

---

65   This incident was widely canvassed in the press. See Davis, *Australian Settler Colonialism*, 36.
66   Goodall, 'Assimilation Begins in the Home', 82.

6. THE GIRLS RETURN

Overall, there was a total of 1,184 placements of Aboriginal girls into homes across the state of New South Wales. There were six more placements with details that could not be clearly determined making a total of 1,190. Just under half of the 1,184 placements, 535, were in suburban Sydney. With 501 girls involved overall, clearly, many had several placements.

In the Sydney region, Mosman had 64 placements and was the location that received more Aboriginal female domestic workers than anywhere else (Figure 6.8). Research revealed that there were 33 separate residents in Mosman who took in Aboriginal domestic servants and many of these residents took multiple placements of girls. One Mosman resident used five different girls.[67] Homefinder Alice Lowe was tasked with the job of securing homes for these girls; but with such a concentration of Aboriginal girls in the suburb of Mosman, some networking by the Mosman residents with apprentices – to circulate the girls – may well have occurred.

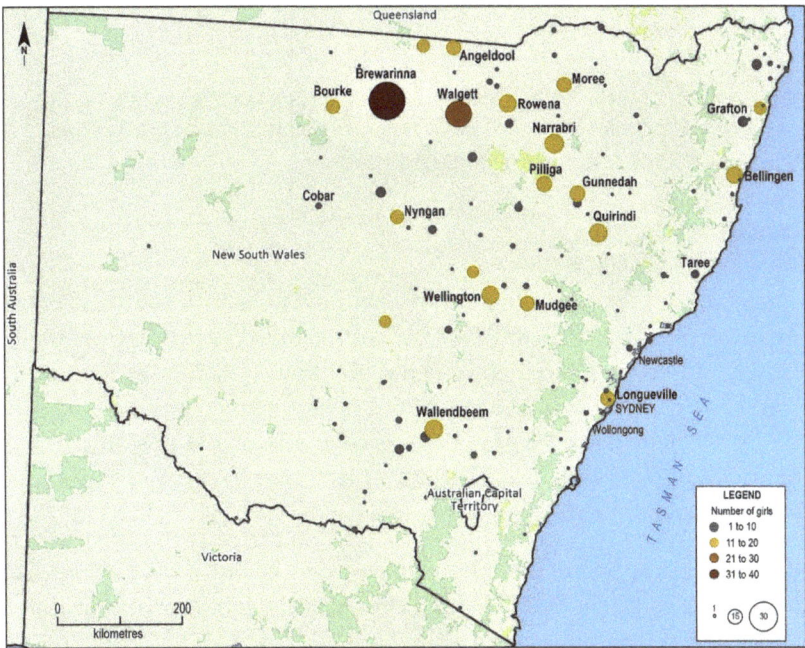

Figure 6.9: Location points in rural New South Wales for the placement Aboriginal girls who had been removed from their communities.
Source: Ward Registers, 1916–28. Cartographer: Peter Johnson, Cordeaux Heights, NSW.

---

67 Ward Registers, 1916–28.

POWER AND DYSFUNCTION

In rural New South Wales, Brewarrina was the highest recipient of female domestic workers with 39 placements. Another finding is that many of these locations in both the city and rural areas had only one Aboriginal female domestic worker, a situation that further increased the isolation of these young girls (one small dot on the map represents just one placement).

When examining the top 30 locations for the placement of Aboriginal girls into domestic service across the state (Figure 6.10), this cheap labour was sought in the cities, towns and remote rural areas.

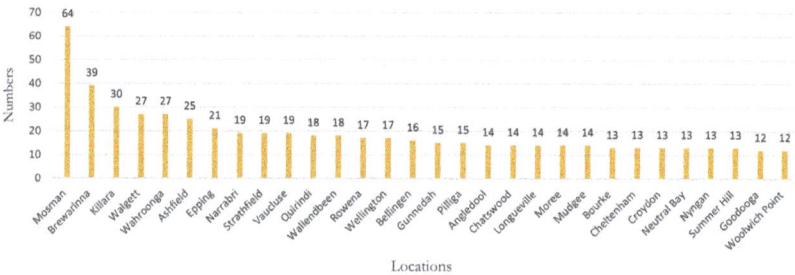

Figure 6.10: The top 30 location points across New South Wales for the placement of Aboriginal girls removed from their communities.
Source: Author's summary of Ward Registers, 1916–28.

Boys

There were 286 placements of Aboriginal boys (two placement destinations were unidentifiable but are included in the overall total). In contrast to the placement of girls, the boys were almost exclusively placed in rural areas. Thirteen boys (or 4.5 per cent) were placed in suburban Sydney and 273 or 95.5 per cent were placed in country New South Wales.[68] As with the girls, several placements comprised of only one boy, at a remote location (Figure 6.11).

Brewarrina was by far the most frequent destination for boys who had been removed by the Board, with 34 placements, followed by Gunnedah with 16, and then Pilliga with 12 (Figure 6.12).

---

68   This figure is close to that of Victoria Haskins, who determined that 98 per cent were in placed in country areas. Haskins, 'A Better Chance?', 43.

6. THE GIRLS RETURN

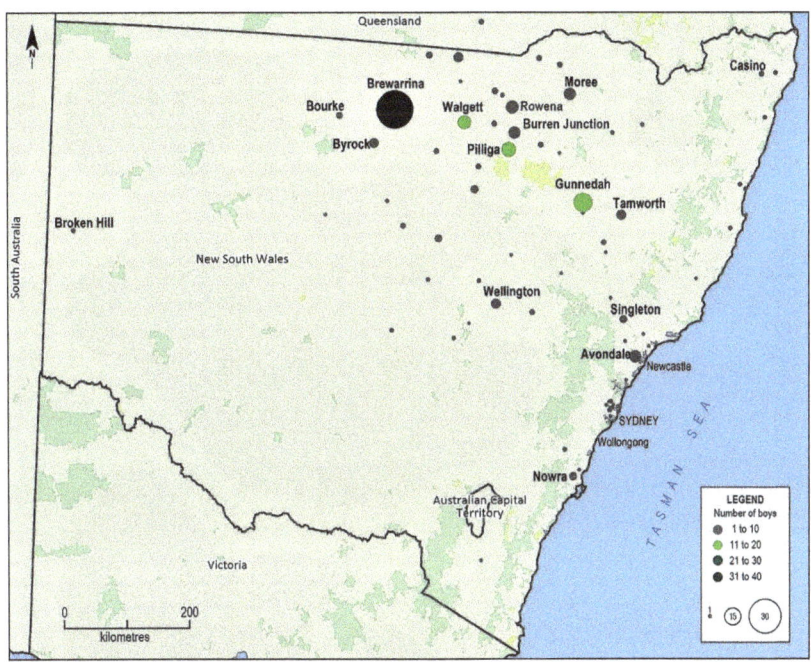

Figure 6.11: Location points across New South Wales for the placement of Aboriginal boys.
Source: Author's summary of Ward Registers, 1916–28.

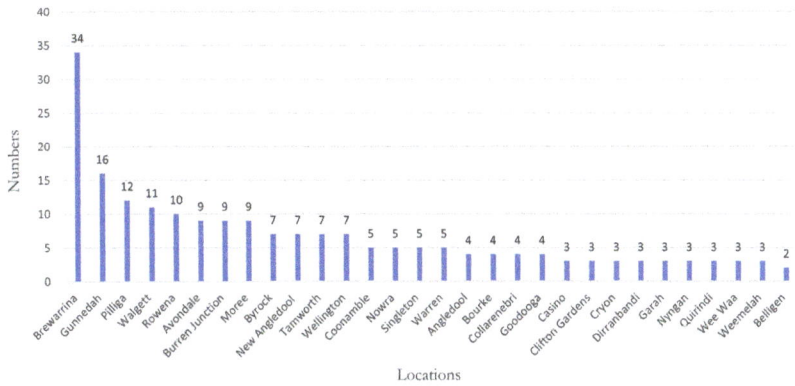

Figure 6.12: The top 30 location points across New South Wales for the placement of Aboriginal boys removed from their communities.
Source: Author's summary of Ward Registers, 1916–28.

The high number of Brewarrina placements, of both boys and girls, may support the policy of not sending 'full-blood' children too far away from their communities. It is also likely that the fact that some parents, realising their children would be removed, arranged their own placements close to home before the Board made its own decision to place them in more distant locations in Sydney and elsewhere. If parents felt they could not resist the Board due to possible retribution, the practice of 'getting in before the Board' may have occurred on many occasions.

Dharawal Country and multiple placements

The following data, drawn from Dharawal Country, demonstrates the number of placements some Aboriginal children were forced to endure, and the impact of those apprenticeships on them. It is impossible to determine the number of children within Dharawal Country who were removed to institutions and domestic placements during the period of the first Board (1883–1940) using the extant written records. The only sure way of determining this would be to canvass oral history from Dharawal families. Nevertheless, the Ward Registers reveal that there were 31 children with obvious connections to Dharawal Country who were removed over the 12 years.[69] They were either born in Dharawal Country or were located within Dharawal Country at the time of their removal. For example, a child may have been born in Kempsey but living permanently with a parent at La Perouse when removed. From a Board perspective, the two main Aboriginal population centres within Dharawal Country were the reserve at La Perouse and the managed Aboriginal station (from 1906) at Roseby Park, opposite Greenwell Point east of Nowra. Most of the girls (19) and all the boys (8) who were removed and placed into service by the Board came from these two centres (Figure 6.13).[70]

---

69   Ward Registers, 1916–28.
70   There were of course, within Dharawal Country, other Aboriginal population centres. At the year ending 1915, population centres within Dharawal Country were: La Perouse: 124; Nowra:123; Roseby Park: 66; Port Kembla: 60; Mittagong: 31; Burragorang: 21; Kiama: 20. *APBR* 1916, 6, 10 and 11.

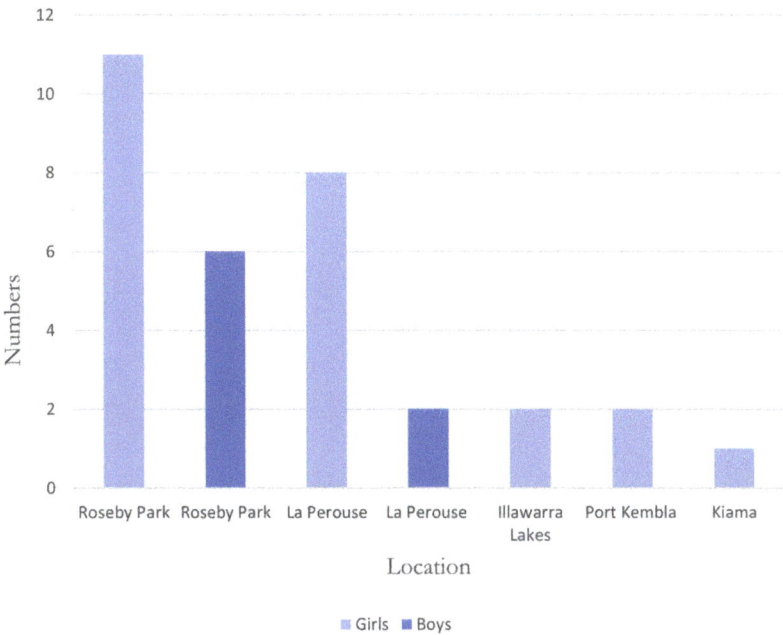

Figure 6.13: Numbers of children removed from Dharawal population centres (1916–28).
Source: Author's summary of Ward Registers, 1916–28.

At Kiama, one girl went into service independently of the Board and has not been included in the figures below as being removed, but this may well have been a result of Board pressure to either do so or face such consequences such as a court referral.

Many of the Dharawal children put into service across New South Wales had multiple placements during their apprenticeships. The 23 girls removed from Roseby Park, La Perouse, Illawarra Lakes and Port Kembla collectively had a total of 94 placements, an average of 4.1 each.[71] The eight boys from Roseby Park and La Perouse collectively had a total of 22 placements, an average of 2.75 each. Of the 31 apprentices from Dharawal Country, 13 absconded at least once from their placements; this demonstrates that many were clearly distressed in their situations. Only the children themselves and their families know the real pain and anguish associated with these removals. Many children undoubtedly endured long

---

71 Two of the girls had 'a number of placements' written on their forms, but the placements were unidentified. Therefore, the overall placements of the 23 Dharawal girls would have been even higher.

periods of suffering through loneliness, separation, rejection, humiliation and abuse. A significant number of girls fell pregnant while in service. Victoria Haskins records that 17 per cent of girls apprenticed to urban situations at some time became pregnant during that time.[72]

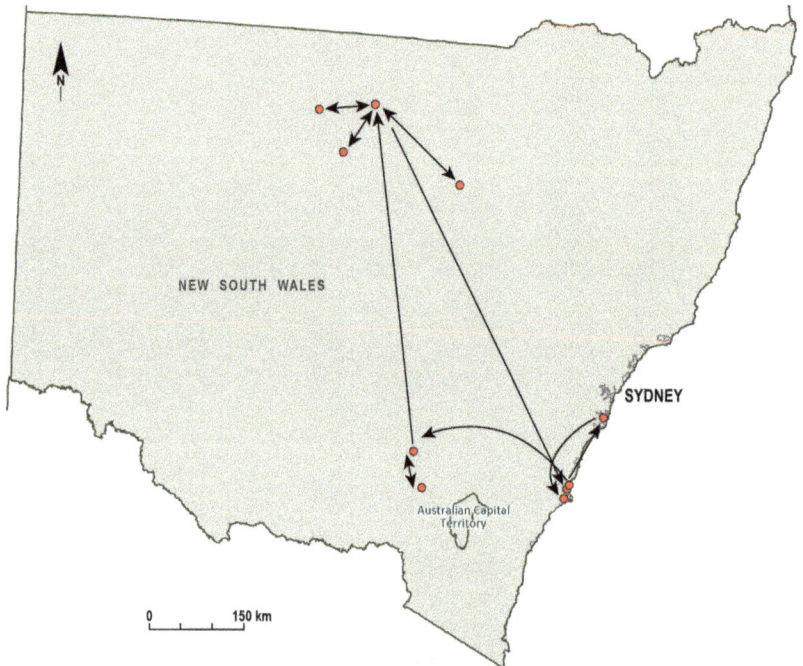

Figure 6.14: Domestic placement history of one Dharawal apprentice.
Source: Ward Registers, 1916–28. Cartographer: Peter Johnson, Cordeaux Heights, NSW.

Figure 6.14 depicts the placement history of one Aboriginal apprentice that took place over a period of 14 years. From the age of eight this child was placed in 10 different locations across the state, with a total of 14 separate placements, and was not free of the Board until their early 20s.

The words of Aboriginal people as documented in the *Bringing Them Home: National Inquiry into the Separation of Aboriginal and Torres Strait Islander Children from Their Families*, best reflect the impact.

---

72 Haskins, 'A Better Chance?', 42.

From the Bomaderry Home near Nowra:

> If we got letters, you'd end up with usually 'the weather's fine', 'we love you' and 'from your loving mother' or whatever. We didn't hear or see what was written in between. And that was one way they kept us away from our families … We were all rostered to do work and one of the girls was doing Matron's office, and there was all these letters that the girls had written back to their parents and family – the answers were all in the garbage bin.[73]

From a girl placed into service:

> The thing that hurts the most is that they didn't care about who they put us with. As long as it looked like they were doing their job, it just didn't matter. They put me with one family and the man of the house used to come down and use me whenever he wanted to … Being raped over and over and there was no-one I could turn to.[74]

Reflections of Wagga Wagga Elder Isabel Hampton:

> We were coming home from school [North Dubbo] one day when a truck pulled up and asked us, 'Did we want a ride back home?' We got on the back of the truck but it didn't go home. He took us to the police station where they put us in the cells overnight. They had nowhere else to put us at the station. Some missionaries came and talked to us hoping to get us out. They were unable to do that. The next day we were put on a train to Sydney. I think we went to the Aborigines Protection Board Office to sign forms or something. Jack was sent to Kinchela Boys Home and Betty and I were sent by train to Cootamundra. The day Jack left on the train for Kinchela was the last time I ever saw him … Betty and I spent nine years at Coota.[75]

The impact of the Board's policies as they related to the removal of Aboriginal children and adolescents is incalculable. The fact that some of their voices have now been heard and listened to may well have brought an element of healing. The Board removed children at will, for a range of spurious reasons, relocated them when placements 'broke down', had no apparent regard for the welfare of the children, and left them to the whims of masters and mistresses across the state. Board secretary Arthur

---

73 HREOC, *Bringing Them Home*, 155.
74 HREOC, *Bringing Them Home*, 168.
75 Kabaila, *Home Girls*, 49–50.

Pettitt, at the 1937 Canberra conference of Commonwealth and State Aboriginal Authorities, confirmed the total neglect of the Board. In reply to statements 'made about aboriginal girls in domestic service becoming pregnant', Pettitt remarked, 'we throw the responsibility on the employer for the physical and moral well-being of the apprentices'.[76] Board inspections of the girls in Sydney were 'sporadic and superficial' and in the rural areas they were limited to inquiries by the 'Board, managers or police'.[77] And, as Victoria Haskins has recorded, if the Board did find out about a pregnancy while in domestic service, the Board invariably blamed the girl, subjected her to a 'stern, even vituperative lecture', moved her on to another posting, and then supplied the client with another girl.[78] When one considers that hundreds of Aboriginal children were left in situations, far from any independent scrutiny, some of which were clearly dangerous, then the whole apprentice system could only be seen as completely out of control. It is a terrible indictment of successive governments that allowed this small administrative body to act with such cruelty, negligence and impunity.

Not only were Aboriginal girls to be removed, but the Board insisted that after their apprenticeships they *should never be allowed to return* to their families and communities. Thankfully, the Board was unable to fully implement this pillar of its agenda.

A failed Board policy

Of the 23 girls from Dharawal Country who were removed it can be determined that nine girls returned to their communities and the records suggest that of those nine, six married into their communities. Seven were married away from their communities, but it is unclear whom they married. It is also unknown whether the five girls who did not return married. Sadly, one girl died in Long Bay goal and one more remained incarcerated there.[79] At least half the girls, across the state, returned to their place of origin and many married back into their community.[80]

---

76 *Aboriginal Welfare: The Initial Conference of Commonwealth and States Aboriginal Authorities, April 1937*, Q353.53499/10 (ML), 16.
77 Haskins, 'A Better Chance?', 48.
78 Haskins, 'A Better Chance?', 51.
79 Ward Registers, 1916–28.
80 Haskins, 'A Better Chance?', 41.

This was against Board policy. In 1915, as outlined above, the Board was 'quite open' in its determination that the girls were never to return to their communities; they would be 'merged' into white society, live like white people and perhaps marry white men.[81] The Board did not seek legislation to enforce a 'no return policy', nor did it dabble in marriage control at the legislative level. If the vociferous debate in the New South Wales Legislative Council on the 1915 amendment (see Chapter 5) was any indication, any legislative measures that sought to control the marriages of Aboriginal women would have been rejected. Russell McGregor argues that the policy of 'breeding out the colour', although widely endorsed and pursued at the national level, was undertaken primarily by 'senior members of the bureaucracy' and not by 'parliament or minister'.[82] Politicians, particularly in the northern states, did not want to be too closely associated with 'absorption' as they came under fire from 'southern welfare bodies and academics'.[83]

Even when passed, marriage laws in the 'frontier' administrations – although employed – were ineffective.[84] Chief protector A.O. Neville in Western Australia had the power to stop 'undesirable marriages' but he could not compel 'desirable' ones. The only 'desirable' interracial ones were 'half-caste' women marrying white men and this gender-specific nature of absorption posed insuperable problems. Protector Cecil Cook fared no better in the Northern Territory – in 11 years he achieved fewer than 50 'desirable' marriages.[85] Although Queensland mirrored the policies of the Northern Territory and Western Australia, after the 1914 appointment of John W. Bleakley as chief protector the state switched to favouring marriages within their own race. Bleakley 'went out of his way to rid Queensland of its mixed-descent population by absorbing it into the Indigenous population rather than the white'.[86] Whether the New South Wales Board was aware of these policies prior to the 1937 Canberra conference of Commonwealth and State Aboriginal Authorities is unclear – the Board minutes and the Board reports show no evidence of any serious discussion of policies employed by other states with the possible exception of Victoria.

---

81 Haskins, *One Bright Spot*, 29.
82 McGregor, '"Breed out the Colour"', 288.
83 Austin, 'Cecil Cook, Scientific Thought and "Half-Castes" in the Northern Territory 1927–1939', 115.
84 The term 'frontier administrations' was used by Victoria Haskins in 'A Better Chance?', 50.
85 McGregor, '"Breed out the Colour"', 289.
86 Ellinghaus, 'Absorbing the "Aboriginal Problem"', 200.

The Board did not develop a policy mechanism to prevent young Aboriginal women from returning to Country after their apprenticeships were complete. It did, however, employ two strategies to pursue its 'no return policy'. First, whenever the girls absconded from their placements the Board was quick to have them apprehended and returned to the same situation, back to Cootamundra or to another placement. Marjorie Woodrow, born in 1922, was taken to Cootamundra Home on the premise that she was 'uncontrollable'. She recalled:

> It was hard for me there because my mind was placed elsewhere, to get back to where I belonged. I always had that I must go back to my people … where my destiny was. I got away a couple of times but got caught and brought back.[87]

Inara Walden states that most girls were caught within a day of absconding and some 'dispatched immediately to another employer' or institutionalised.[88] The second strategy involved retaining all wages earned during apprenticeship in a trust account managed by the Board. Consequently, the girls had no means of saving money to have any semblance of independence, or funds to return home more easily. Board regulations stipulated the wages for each year of apprenticeship and the employer signed an agreement that required payment in quarterly instalments:

> First Year: 1s 6d per week with 3 pence as pocket money.
> Second Year: 2s 6d per week with 6 pence as pocket money.
> Third Year: 3s 6d per week with 6 pence pocket money.
> Fourth Year: 5s per week with 1s pocket money.[89]

These wages were well under the standard rates for white domestic servants who, in 1910, received between 10s and 20s per week.[90] Without the advocacy of their employer, the girls were highly unlikely to retrieve any of their money while working as an apprentice and, even with it, there was no guarantee of success. There were some employers who recognised that the Board's tactics. Sydney resident Joan Kingsley-Strack (mentioned in Chapter 5) had several Aboriginal apprentices and in one case she refused to pay her wages to the Board. Kingsley-Strack thought it scandalous that

---

87 Woodrow, *One of the Lost Generation*, 13.
88 Walden, 'That Was Slavery Days', 204.
89 Regulation 41 of the *Aborigines Protection Act 1909*: *NSW Government Gazette*, No. 92, 8 June 1910 (SLNSW).
90 Walden, 'That Was Slavery Days', 200.

6. THE GIRLS RETURN

the girls were refused access to money that was rightfully theirs and were unable to spend it as they wished. Instead, she paid the money directly to her apprentice.[91] The Board pursued her. Secretary Pettitt wrote:

> With reference to the wages of the Aboriginal girl … in your employ, I beg to draw your attention to the fact that the account is now nearly twelve months in arrears, the account due being £11.2.9. I would ask that you give the matter immediate attention, otherwise I shall be reluctantly compelled to place the matter in the hands of the crown solicitor.[92]

Joan Kingsley-Strack was a formidable advocate for justice in this matter and had many influential connections in the Feminist Club, members of the Association for the Protection of Native Races, the Salvation Army and among members of parliament. The fact that the Board had not acted for the previous 12 months perhaps reflected a reluctance to take her on. One of Joan Kingsley-Strack's former apprentices who was now 'free' of the Board, revealed how difficult and intimidating it was for the girls to retrieve their wages even *after* they had completed their apprenticeships and had returned to their communities. She wrote to Kingsley-Strack:

> Pettitt doesn't send it strait through the post to me he sends it to the police and gets them to ask me what I want it for anyone with common sense would know what I want it for only now its my money and I should get it without telling them anything my sister is going to the hospital soon and she has no-one to look after her two little children so I said I would mind them for her. I wanted to write for more money to get a dress for the show but I am two frighten. The policemen said to me Mr Pettitt not boss over you now I am and if you don't get some work I will send you back to the board do you think he can boss me Mrs Strack I'm nearly twenty now don't you send me any money Mrs Strack love all and yourself.[93]

With such restrictive and threatening practices employed by Pettitt and local authorities it was no wonder that the trust fund continued to grow. The Board reported on 31 December 1918 that there were '170 girls

---

91 Letter from Joan Kingsley-Strack to the Board, 4 November 1933, Joan Kingsley-Strack Papers, MS 9551, Series 7, Folder 3, National Library of Australia (hereafter NLA).
92 Letter from Secretary Pettitt to Joan Kingsley-Strack, 8 January 1934, Joan Kingsley-Strack Papers, MS 9551, Series 7, Folder 4 (1933–40) (NLA).
93 Letter from former apprentice to Joan Kingsley-Strack, no date. Joan Kingsley-Strack Papers, MS 9551, Series 7, Folder 4 (1933–40) (NLA).

in situations, all enjoying the comfort of good homes and learning the general duties of housework, fitting them in time to come to be useful citizens' while the 'amount at deposit with the Board representing wages earned on the 31st December 1918, was £2,775 14s. 6d'.[94] For the next 20 years the Board failed to mention this accumulated amount of moneys held in trust in its yearly reports. As noted previously, the Board's overall yearly reporting after 1916 was severely curtailed, but in this case it may well have felt there would be some scrutiny of an ever-increasing fund that was not being dispensed to apprentices as they left the Board's services.

Despite the Board's coercive tactics, its attempts to prevent girls from returning to their communities failed. Legally, the Board had no further control over the girls or the boys once they reached 18 years of age. Walter Henry Childs, chair of the APB from 1929 until 1935, informed Colonel Campbell of the Salvation Army (who was inquiring on behalf of Joan Kingsley-Strack about a girl) that he 'had no jurisdiction … as she was 18 years old'.[95] The apprentices usually went into service at 14 and finished at 18. The Board did not inform Aboriginal apprentices that their time of service had expired (as witnessed by the Dharawal examples) and treated any appeals by them with 'suspicion and in cases refused to release them'.[96] Yet, just under half of the girls apprenticed returned to their communities.

By early 1920 the Board recognised that this part of its policy had failed and decided to adjust its approach. Secretary Pettitt sent a Board circular to all managed stations:

> I am writing in connection with an aspect of the Board's work which is beginning to create a considerable amount of anxiety, i.e. the disposal of girls who have been out in domestic service for a number of years and have reached a marriageable age …

---

94   APBR 1919, 3. Accessed via *NSW Legislative Assembly: Aborigines Report of Board for the Aborigines 1915–1922*, Q572.991 N (SLNSW).
95   Letter from Joan Kingsley-Strack to Joseph Jackson MLA, October/November 1934, Joan Kingsley-Strack Papers, MS 9551, Series 7, Folder 3 (NLA). There is some confusion surrounding the finishing date. Inara Walden, puts the 'release' age at 21, see 'That Was Slavery Days', 205. This is borne out by the fact that the 1940 amendment to the *Aborigines Protection Act 1909* (NSW), which constituted the Aborigines Welfare Board, reduced the completing age of apprenticeships to 18 years; see Section 11(2). Peter Read, however, states that the Board was legally unable to hold them after they were 18, see Read, *The Stolen Generations*, 15. This is also confirmed by Parliament of New South Wales, *Aborigines Protection: Report and Recommendation of the Public Service Board of New South Wales*, 4 April 1940 (SRNSW); *NSW Parliamentary Papers*, Session 1938–40, Vol. 7, 18.
96   Haskins, 'A Better Chance?', 40; Read, *The Stolen Generations*, 22.

> It is noticed that at the age of 19 or 20 years they naturally become restless and refuse to remain in their situations unless they have a visit home, which is quite natural. They also express a wish to marry and settle down … It would appear therefore the only solution … is to allow them upon attaining the age of 20 years to return to the station [to allow] them to marry. This result might very largely be brought about by the sympathy and co-operation of the managers.[97]

Heather Goodall argues that, to a large extent, it was the 'resistance of Aboriginal girls and their families' that forced the change in Board policy.[98] When the girls were old enough, they were clearly demanding to return home. Also, the issue of Aboriginal girls and marriage began to receive intense media scrutiny in the mid-1920s. Reports claimed that 'Aboriginal girls locked up in private households were being prevented from meeting and marrying potential husbands'.[99] In 1924 the *Sydney Morning Herald* alerted its readers with this opening paragraph:

> That the aborigines of the State are doomed to extinction we have been told often enough, but, if this be their unfortunate fate, should the processes that are operating towards this end be accelerated by the Aborigines Protection Department itself? The answer, of course, must be no.

It further stated that the 'segregation of the sexes is making it difficult for any more [Aboriginal children] to be born'. It noted that they should not be denied the 'same opportunities for love, courtship, and marriage among their own kind'. It explained to its readers that the girls were taken to Cootamundra for training (usually up to the age of 14) then sent out as domestic servants where they were generally confined to quarters. As a result, the 'matrimonial prospects of these girls are not very bright' and it is not 'creditable to us to have the passing of the race accelerated in this way'.[100]

In the face of criticism, the Board report of 1926 was an admission that it needed to alter its policy to promote marriages back into Aboriginal communities. The Board conceded that 'these young people should not

---

97 APB Circular No. 1050, 2 June 1920, Copies of Letters Sent 1914–27, 4/7128, Reel 1853 (SRNSW).
98 Goodall, 'Assimilation Begins in the Home', 82.
99 Haskins, 'A Better Chance?', 39.
100 *Sydney Morning Herald*, 29 October 1924, 12.

be deprived of the opportunity to marry and settle down' and determined that they should return to their community for a holiday to facilitate 'meeting young people of their own colour'. Under pressure from the girls themselves and the from criticism in the press, the Board had done a complete 'backflip' on its initial policy. The report stated that during the prior 12 months 'over thirty suitable marriages have resulted'. Arrangements were made for the Board's managers 'to take charge of them and to take an interest in their welfare'.[101]

However, placing some of these girls under the supervision of the managers was problematic. Isabel Flick, an Aboriginal woman born in Goondiwindi in 1928, who spent four years at school on the mission at Toomelah, recalled:

> There's one thing I remember very clearly. There was a mass wedding, it was about six couples married at once ... you just couldn't fall in love [all at once] there had to be a reason ... As the managers kept changing, some of the girls were more favoured by certain managers and it always makes me think you know ... it's happened in other places where managers have had their fling with the girls ... got afraid that they might be pregnant and so set them up with their mates and married them off.[102]

From her interviews with Aboriginal people in the north-west of the state, Heather Goodall records:

> Aboriginal people remember these hastily arranged marriages, some with bemusement, as they recall how as young children they could not understand how so many people could decide to marry all at once, others with bitterness, as they recall their own lives blighted by inappropriate marriages forced on themselves or their loved ones.[103]

Goodall does not see the Board's policy change as a capitulation but rather as another way of achieving the same goal: when the girls returned to their communities, trained in the skills of domestic service, they would become

---

101 *APBR* 1926, 3. Accessed via aiatsis.gov.au/sites/default/files/docs/digitised_collections/remove/23866.pdf.
102 Flick and Goodall, *Isabel Flick*, 29–30.
103 Goodall, 'Assimilation Begins in the Home', 83–84.

the 'trainers of their future nuclear families' and they could help train other Aboriginal women to be, like 'Trojan horses, the bearers of white culture and lifestyle into the heart of Aboriginal families and community life'.[104]

However, Robert Donaldson's crusade to ensure that all apprenticed girls would never return was unsustainable. Over half the girls returned to their communities, with many making their own decisions about whom to marry.

A damning legacy

Arguably, the period between 1916 and 1928 was one of the most destructive and intrusive periods of the Board as it imposed further into the lives of New South Wales Aboriginal communities. It was no coincidence that it occurred after the restructure of the Board in 1916. The new Board, comprised largely of public servants, was less accountable and its agenda was primarily determined by Secretary Pettitt, Inspector Donaldson and Homefinder Miss Lowe. This cabal drove a regime that sought to separate Aboriginal children from their families in the misplaced belief that they would sever their Aboriginal connections and live like white people. It was an attempt to eradicate the Aboriginality of those with less than half an 'admixture of Aboriginal blood': it was an attempt at cultural genocide. Collectively, the Board, and the cabal, saw no worth in Aboriginal culture, family ties, kinship or lore.

The data pertaining to the locations from which Aboriginal children were removed suggests that the Board lacked a considered implementation plan. All Aboriginal children, not just mixed-race children, were targeted. Some large Aboriginal population centres were not among the primary targets, while others were targeted for no obvious reason. In the absence of evidence about inspectors' yearly movements across the state, particularly that of Donaldson over a period of 15 years, there is so far no way of telling, from the written evidence, why some areas became the focus of removals. This muddled picture reflects several things: the arbitrary nature of the Board's implementation of this policy, the Board's lack of oversight and the indifference from Board members. The skewed statistics suggest that Aboriginal communities lived at the whim of the Board's core trio. Their decisions were likely influenced by managers with varying

---

104 Goodall, 'Assimilation Begins in the Home', 83.

degrees of compassion, by local authorities and by the desire to avoid locations that might present more resistance than others. However, it also demonstrates the strength of individual communities to challenge the removal of their children.

There is no doubt that the intent of Board policy was to 'merge' or 'absorb' the lighter-skinned Aboriginal population into the mainstream Australian community while it waited for the 'full-blood' population to die out. The APB's needless removal of thousands of Aboriginal children from their families across New South Wales by the Aborigines Protection Board was cruel and tragic. The trail of apprenticeships of Dharawal children and young adults described above provides a disturbing picture. For many, if not most of the apprentices, the separation from family, the isolation from community, the extreme loneliness, the uncertainty of not knowing why they had been removed and when they could return home, and the abuse that many had no choice but to endure would have been an unbearable burden. For many of the girls, the unwanted sexual attention by males in the household of their employ was an added torment with disastrous consequences. The Board's policy left most of the apprentices isolated and some confused about their Aboriginality, mentally scarred and struggling to resume a normal life. The scale of this tragedy makes the determined resistance by Aboriginal families and the young Aboriginal women who, despite significant hurdles, returned to their communities, even more remarkable. It was small comfort that the Board failed to achieve a key plank in its removal policy.

7

If the 'white parents object'

In 1920 an Aboriginal girl, Barbara Timbery, was expelled from the school at Roseby Park Station.[1] She had refused to pick up fresh cow dung to put on the manager's strawberry patch at his residence (Figure 7.1). The manager/teacher at the station had regularly asked Barbara to do this distasteful job but she had decided that she did not want to do it anymore. As punishment, the manager excluded her from the school.

Figure 7.1: The manager's house at Roseby Park Aboriginal Station.
Source: Photograph album of New South Wales Aboriginal reserves, c.1910, presented by the Department of Youth and Community Services, PXB 492. Mitchell Library, State Library New South Wales.

---

1   Roseby Park Aboriginal Station (now known as Jerringa) was established on the Crookhaven River some 15 km west of Nowra on the south coast of NSW in 1906. For background to the establishment, see: *Cullunghutti: The Mountain and its People*, 220–29; Bennett, 'For a Labourer Worthy of His Hire', 217–20.

Barbara continued her education at the local public school at Greenwell Point that was located across the Crookhaven River – a rough crossing of some 150 metres (Figure 7.2). Each day, Barbara rowed a small boat in a difficult manoeuvre across the fast-moving river that ran between two peninsulas. To negotiate the dangerous return crossing, her father, standing on high ground, used hand signals to instruct her as to when to 'pull in' or 'stay out' according to the currents. This was a formidable start and end to the school day.[2]

Figure 7.2: View from Greenwell Point across to Orient Point (Roseby Park); this was the punt journey for young Barbara Timbery to attend school.
Source: Author, September 2016.

---

2   Sonny Simms (a Bidigal man, from La Perouse Aboriginal Reserve, now living in Nowra), interview by the author, 28 June 1916, Norwa.

This incident raises several issues concerning the education of Aboriginal children in New South Wales, not least of which was the unfettered powers of the manager/teachers who controlled Aboriginal stations throughout the state (in 1920, there were 21 such stations).³ More important still is what the incident reveals about Aboriginal access to education.

The Timbery family remained at Roseby Park and Barbara attended Greenwell Point Public School. In this case, an Aboriginal girl excluded from an Aboriginal school was now enrolled at the local public school. This was the exception to the rule, for across the state the reverse was happening. From the end of the nineteenth century and well into the twentieth, Aboriginal children were being excluded from the local public schools when white parents complained about their presence in the classrooms. Consequently, the Board established separate Aboriginal schools on their stations and reserves.

The New South Wales Aboriginal Protection Board (APB) could not have envisaged that, by 1900, 13 Aboriginal schools would be required, mostly because of the forced exclusions of Aboriginal children from the state system, and that there would be 41 separate schools by 1915. Exclusion of Aboriginal children from public schools continued for the life of the Board. Indeed, the exclusions continued even when the government embraced the policy of assimilation under the new Aborigines Welfare Board after 1940 and the Department of Education took full responsibility for the education of Aboriginal students.⁴ When the Board was established in 1883, there was no clear understanding between it and the government as to who had control over Aboriginal education – the Education Department or the Board? To what level would Aboriginal children be educated? What did the law say in relation to the education of Aboriginal children? Were Aboriginal children to be educated separately or within the white community? As with other Board matters, there were just vague guiding principles and assumptions.

---

3   *Protection of Aborigines: Report of the Board* (the APB Report: hereafter *APBR*) 1920, 2. Accessed via aiatsis.gov.au/sites/default/files/docs/digitised_collections/remove/23673.pdf. Most managers were 'self-made' men with only a basic education; teaching was secondary to running the station. See Bell, 'A Benevolent Tyranny', 42–50.
4   Fletcher, *Clean, Clad and Courteous*, 171–93.

'Amongst the industrial classes'

The *Public Instruction Act 1880* (NSW) introduced by the Parkes–Robertson Government required all children between the ages of six and 14 to attend school. From 1880, all children of school age, living within a 2-mile radius of the local school, had to attend at least 70 days every half year. Inadvertently, the government had made it mandatory for Aboriginal children to attend school. The Act did not specify Aboriginal children – but then it did not identify Chinese, German or Irish children living in New South Wales either. In the second reading of the Bill, Premier Henry Parkes emphasised the fairness of compulsory education. It sought to establish a 'splendid system in throwing open the doors of our schools to all children of all sects ... inviting all to sit side by side'.[5] Parkes probably felt no need to mention Aboriginal children, as there was a strong community belief that Aboriginal people would soon die out.[6] Just as likely though, he did not even consider them in the same context as the Chinese, Dutch, Irish or German children; Aboriginal people were viewed as being *apart* from society and not *of* it. Educational historian Alan Duncan concludes that it was obvious that 'Aboriginal and part-Aboriginal children were not included in the meaning of the Act'.[7] Also, Heather Goodall observes:

> Townspeople regarded [Aboriginal] reserves as always being 'somewhere else', where Aborigines rightly 'belonged' and to which they should be 'sent back'. Aboriginal people were seen to have no automatic right to a domestic dormitory area for themselves within the town boundaries nor any rights to access ... the hotel, the stores, the school or the very streets.[8]

In 1883, the Board could have demanded, with the full backing of the law, that all Aboriginal children attend local public schools. But the Board never considered that Aboriginal children would, or indeed should, be integrated into the school system on an equal basis with white children. Instead, a report on the two mission stations at Maloga and Warangesda in early 1883 advocated segregation and determined that Aboriginal children would 'take their places amongst the industrial classes' and as

---

5 NSW, *Parliamentary Debates*, Legislative Assembly, 20 November 1879, 274 (Henry Parkes).
6 As discussed in Chapter 1.
7 Duncan, 'A Survey of the Education of Aborigines in New South Wales', 224.
8 Goodall, *Invasion to Embassy*, 2008, 109.

domestic servants and rural labourers.[9] The policy was not to nurture Aboriginal children's potential but to prepare them for menial jobs. Preferably, they would be taught a limited program, away from white children in separate Aboriginal schools. The Board hoped that Aboriginal families would move to 'quiet calm river banks' or by the coast in numbers significant enough to justify a school.[10]

Providing separate schools was, however, a burden on the Board's limited funds. To mitigate the cost, the Board created a second policy. The Board hoped that Aboriginal families living close to towns should be able send their children – if few in number – to the local public school. This would reduce the number of separate Aboriginal schools to be built. The Board considered that if the children were 'decently clad and sufficiently fed', there could be 'no serious objections' to their admission.[11] It is noteworthy that in the late nineteenth and early twentieth century many *white* children were barred from public schools due to their 'rowdy behaviour, dirty or untidy appearance and their parent's inability to pay the smallest fees'.[12]

The early education policy of the APB did foresee the possibility of complaints about Aboriginal children enrolling at public schools from 'parties chiefly interested' and signalled that it would accept 'reasonable' objections.[13] Its resolve was soon tested. The Board faced its first occurrence of Aboriginal exclusion from a public school in June 1883 at Yass. White parents had objected to 15 Aboriginal children from the local 'camp' attending the school and threatened to withdraw their children if the Aboriginal students were not removed.[14] The APB had asked Premier Alex Stuart to intervene because excluding the Aboriginal children was contrary to the department's guidelines as per the 1880 Act, but the premier suggested the Aboriginal children go to either Warangesda or Maloga (some 500 km away!).[15] The Minister for Education, George Reid,

---

9   *Aboriginal Mission Stations at Warangesda and Maloga (Report on Working Of.)*, New South Wales Legislative Assembly, 18 January 1883, 3.
10 *APBR* 1883–84, 3. Accessed via 'NSW', To Remove and Protect, AIATSIS: aiatsis.gov.au/sites/default/files/docs/digitised_collections/remove/22818.pdf.
11 *APBR* 1883–84, 3.
12 The issue was one of poverty and neglect. Ragged Schools, originating in late eighteenth-century Britain, took hold in Sydney with the first school in 1862 in Sussex Street. The aim was to provide free education for the poorest of the poor who were not accepted in other institutions. Henrich, 'Ragged Schools in Sydney', 50.
13 *APBR* 1883–84, 3.
14 *Goulburn Evening Penny Post*, 2 June 1883, 4.
15 Warangesda and Maloga were the only two Aboriginal schools at the time. Fletcher, *Clean, Clad and Courteous*, 62.

ordered the Aboriginal children out of the school. The APB considered the prospects of setting up an Aboriginal school in Yass, but the local Catholic School of St Augustine's defused the situation by taking in the Aboriginal students.[16]

The incident prompted the Department of Education to formulate a policy platform on the education of Aboriginal children. The Board noted the department's new policy:

> The Minister is of [the] opinion that in all localities where a sufficient number of aboriginal children can be grouped together for instruction it would be advisable to establish a school for their benefit exclusively; but in places where there are only a few such children, there will be no objection offered to their attending the nearest Public School, provided they are habitually clean, decently clad, and that they conduct themselves with propriety both in and out of school.[17]

This policy fitted neatly with the Board's own dual policy. From a department and Board perspective, it was 'always best' to educate Aboriginal children away from whites, but where there were few Aboriginal children in a locality they could attend the local school.[18] Yass was an aberration because an alternative solution was found. However, by 1893, due to successful pressure from white parents to remove Aboriginal students from local schools, mainly on the north coast, no fewer than 13 Aboriginal schools had been established.[19] Eight of those schools were in walking distance of the local public schools. In other words, they had been created because of exclusions. Jim Fletcher contends:

> This meant that facilities and teachers were being duplicated and a separate system of schools was emerging, contrary to the Board's policy of educating in local schools those Aboriginal children who lived on the outskirts of white settlement.[20]

---

16   *The Burrowa News*, 21 September 1883, 2.
17   APBR 1885, 2. Accessed via aiatsis.gov.au/sites/default/files/docs/digitised_collections/remove/22813.pdf.
18   Fletcher, *Clean, Clad and Courteous*, 64.
19   APBRs 1883–93: Maloga and Warangesda (1883); Brungle (1889); Brewarrina (1889); Wallaga Lake (1890); Barrington (1890); Pelican Island in the Macleay River (1890); Wauchope (1890); Forster (1890); Rollands Plains (1890); Cabbage Tree Island (1893); Cowra, later called Erambie (1893); and Grafton (1893).
20   Fletcher, *Clean, Clad and Courteous*, 69.

The Board's dual policy was under pressure and separate schools were being established much faster than the Board had anticipated and could afford. The level of Board frustration was evident in its report for 1892–93:

> The Board continue their efforts to secure the attendance at public schools of children of Aborigines camped near European settlements. A large number do attend but in a few places it has been found necessary to withdraw them, owing to the objections from the parents of the European children, not that they were not clean or decently clad, but simply because they were aboriginal children.[21]

The Board's apparent indignation is curious. In 10 years, the Board had never argued for racial equality, yet now it objected to the fact that children were being excluded because they were Aboriginal. It had foreseen the exclusions but now complained about them. Was the Board demanding racial equality or was it more concerned about the additional cost that exclusions incurred? The answer most probably lies somewhere between. It was evident, however, that the Board had little influence in these disputes.

The Board's level of annoyance was voiced publicly in early 1898, at Wollar, a small town near Gulgong in the central west of New South Wales. The Minister for Education expelled seven Aboriginal children because they were a 'health risk'. But the grounds for removal were contradicted by both the local police officer and the teacher. The *Evening News* reported that Edmund Fosbery, Inspector-General of Police and chair of the APB, took the policeman's word, described the expulsions as 'an absolute disgrace' and said he 'wished the Minister was present and he would tell him so'. He added that 'through the country there was no difficulty with regard to these children, who were well behaved, cleanly, and intelligent'.[22] Why Fosbery decided to make this stand in 1898 is a matter of conjecture. But Fosbery was clearly frustrated and most likely reasoned that it was unfair for Aboriginal children to be barred from schools and financing separate Aboriginal schools had become costly.

---

21   *APBR* 1892–93, 3. Accessed via *Journal of the Legislative Council*, Q328.9106/7, *NSW Parliamentary Papers, Consolidated Index* (hereafter *Journal of LC*), Vol. 50, Part 2 (SLNSW).
22   *Evening News*, 4 February 1898, 3.

The depth of mistrust between the department and the Board surfaced in May 1898 when the Board requested the original documents of complaints from the white parents. The Department of Education refused. The Board remonstrated, declaring that it was in the public interest that all the facts should be made available, but the department held firm.[23] The department was under no official obligation to reveal anything to the Board and the Board was unable to gain any leverage.

'They must be excluded'

The exclusion of Aboriginal children slowly came to the attention of others. In early February 1902, Mr Thomas Colebrook, the secretary of the New South Wales Aborigines Mission (who had led a deputation to prevent the removal of the Aboriginal community at La Perouse in 1900), protested to the Department of Education about the general exclusion of Aboriginal students across the state.[24] On the reverse side of Colebrook's letter is a small, seemingly insignificant, entry from the Minister for Education John Perry. Perry's directive – encapsulated in one short sentence – consigned Aboriginal education to a second-class entity for decades to come (Figure 7.3):

> Inform – and instruct all teachers that if white parents object to the black children's admission to school they must be excluded
> JP 6.3.2.

Minister Perry ignored Colebrook's protestations. Perry sought a simple policy instrument that would be clear and effective: it was 'exclusion on demand'. Perry's instruction went out to the 2,800 teachers across the state of New South Wales.[25] In effect, it only required the objection of one white parent – *regardless of the grounds* – to exclude *all* Aboriginal children from a school. The APB's secretary, Robert Beardsmore, was disappointed, and wrote: 'Board note the Minister's decision and desire to express their extreme regret thereat, no objection having been raised at other Public Schools'.[26] It was of course dishonest for the APB to say that

---

23 *Evening News*, 20 May 1898, 2.
24 Letter from T. Colebrook to Department of Education, 2 February 1902, Euroka School Files, 5/15854 (Bundle A), Item 14572, State Records of New South Wales (hereafter SRNSW).
25 Fletcher, *Clean, Clad and Courteous*, 78.
26 Note from Secretary of APB, Beardsmore, Euroka School Files, 5/15854 (Bundle A), Item 08319 (reverse side) (SRNSW).

no objections had been raised at any other schools – many had – but the Board was clearly trying to protect its finances and the access of Aboriginal children, if few in number, to local schools. The department's decree was extraordinary to say the least and blatantly racist. Premier John See, who oversaw this edict, made no obvious objections to the instruction, despite being a Board member himself.[27]

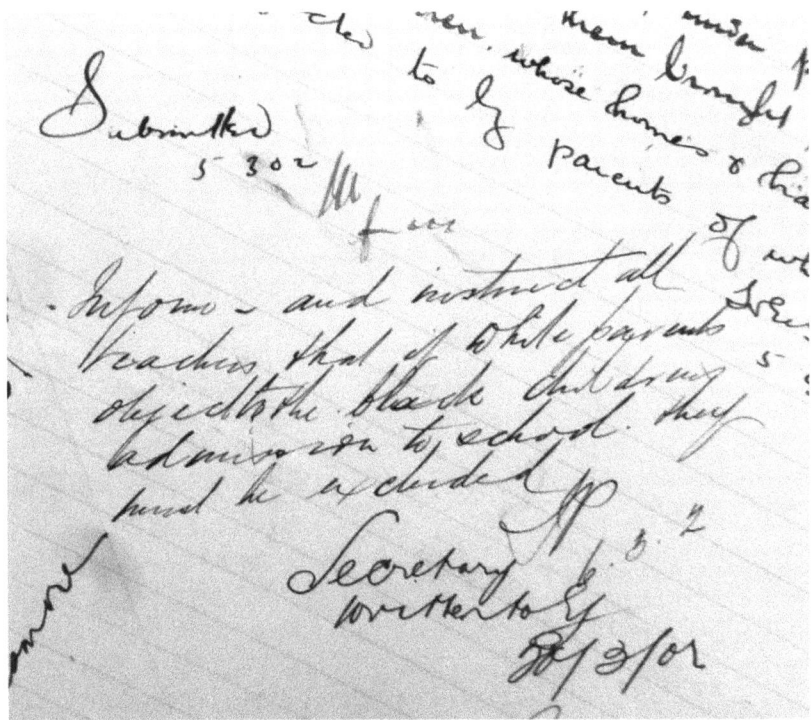

Figure 7.3: Internal note from Minister for Education, John Perry, 6 March 1902.
Source: Euroka School Files, 5/15854 (Bundle A), Item 14572. State Records of New South Wales.

---

27 John See (Progressive Party) was premier from 28 March 1901 to 14 June 1904 and was a Board member from 1897 until 1904. I have been unable to discover any correspondence between Perry and See over the issue of 'exclusion on demand'.

POWER AND DYSFUNCTION

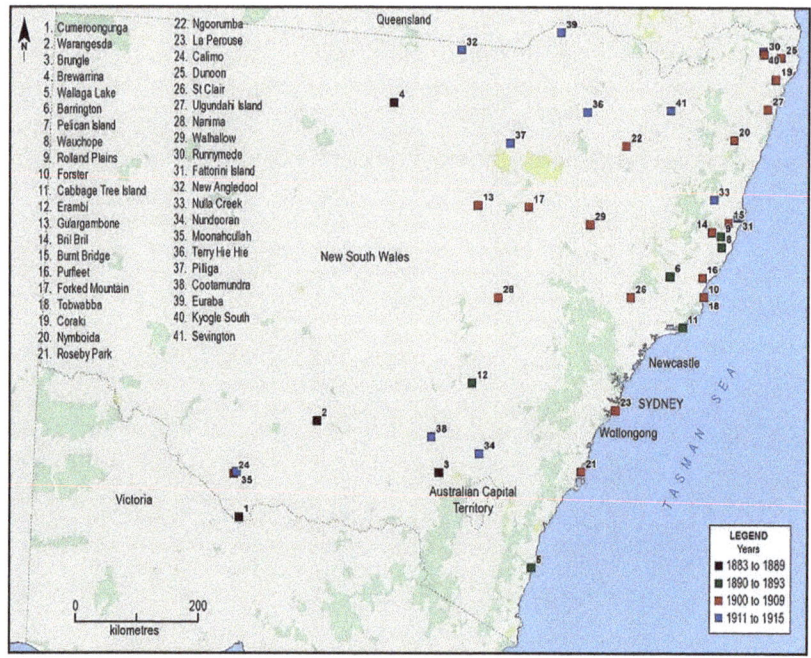

Figure 7.4: Aboriginal schools established between 1883 and 1915.
Source: APB reports from years 1883–1915. Cartographer: Peter Johnson, Cordeaux Heights, NSW.

The APB had a policy dilemma: it was being 'squeezed' by white parents and the Department of Education, and had limited funds and no real influence. Further exclusions of Aboriginal children were now made easier by Minister Perry's decree. The number of Aboriginal schools slowly but surely increased (Figure 7.4). By the time the Board had been reconstituted in 1916 nearly 30 additional Aboriginal schools had been established since 1900.[28]

---

28 Schools added since 1900: Gulargambone (1900); Bril Bril (Rollands Plains) (1905); Burnt Bridge (Kempsey) (1906); Purfleet (Taree) (1906); Forked Mountain (Coonabarabran) (1907); Tobwabba (near Forster) (1907); Coraki (1908); Nymboida (Clarence River) (1908); Roseby Park (near Nowra) (1908); Ngoorumba (near Bundarra) (1908); La Perouse (1908); Calimo (near Deniliquin) (1909); Dunoon (near Lismore) (1909); St Clair (Singleton) (1909); Ulgundahi Island (Maclean) (1909); Nanima (Wellington) (1909); Walhallow (near Quirindi) (1909); Runnymede (Stony Gully) (1909); Fattorini Island (Macleay River) (1911); New Angledool (1911); Nulla Nulla Creek (Bellbrook) (1911); Nundooran (Edgerton, near Yass) (1911); Moonahcullah (west of Griffith) (1911); Terry Hie Hie (1912); Pilliga (1912); Cootamundra (1912); Euraba (Boomi) (1913); Kyogle South (1914); Sevington (1915). *APBRs* 1899–1916.

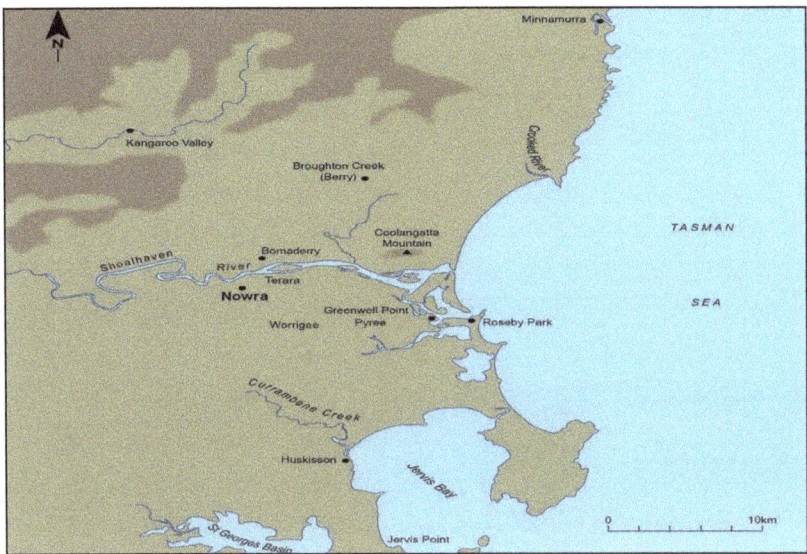

Figure 7.5: Map of the Shoalhaven.
Source: Peter Johnson, cartographer, Cordeaux Heights, NSW.

The restructure of the Board in 1916 provided it with no new powers with respect to the education of Aboriginal children. However, as noted, the reconstituted Board (see Chapter 5) enabled a trio of Board officials to undertake the day-to-day running of the Board and to initiate policy. This made the Board even less able to respond in a coherent or coordinated way to the continued exclusions. Also, in a strange twist, under the restructure, a high-ranking education bureaucrat always had a position on the Board. So, any discussions about exclusions invariably involved a Board member acting in his capacity as spokesperson for the Department of Education – a clear conflict of interest.

The long history of exclusions, up to this point, had already placed the Board and the Education Department at odds. Post-1916, the potential for a conflict of interests was real. That conflict played out very clearly in the Shoalhaven, in the southern portion of Dharawal Country – a region that has always been home to a large Aboriginal population.[29] As noted above, Roseby Park Aboriginal Station (see Figure 7.5) was established

---

29 The last Board report that provided population figures for districts was 1916. The population for the Nowra area was 123: *APBR* 1916, 11. The Aboriginal population at Roseby Park Station for the year ending 1915 was 66: *APBR* 1916, 6. Accessed via *NSW Legislative Assembly: Aborigines Report of Board for the Aborigines 1915–1922*, Q572.991 N (SLNSW).

in 1906 and was the only Board station in the Shoalhaven, and indeed in all Dharawal Country. In 1921 the Roseby Park population was 100 residents (16 'full-bloods' and 84 'half-castes') with a school roll of 24 children.[30] Greenwell Point was the closest township to Roseby Park. The following two examples of the exclusion of Aboriginal children from Greenwell Point School and Huskisson North School demonstrate the marginalisation of the Board in the disputes, the conflict of interests of some Board members, contradictory policies of the Education Department and Aboriginal parent pushback.

Greenwell Point Public School: 'Of learning their antecedents'

On 5 March 1919, a petition was received by Augustus James MLA, the education minister, from residents and parents at Greenwell Point complaining about the admittance of Aboriginal children to the local school. The 27 petitioners simply stated: '[we] respectfully protest against the admission of aboriginal children to this school. The aboriginals have a local school [Roseby Park] and we contend their children should attend it'.[31] From April until August a battle between the white parents and the Department of Education was waged over the exclusions.

On 19 April 1919, acting Board secretary T.J. Foote wrote to Board member James Dawson in his capacity as the Education Department's chief inspector of schools. He requested all the relevant information concerning the petition at Greenwell Point School and stated that it was a matter of 'serious consequences'.[32] Glaswegian James Dawson had taken up a teaching position at Sydney Grammar School in 1880. At age 25, he was appointed as a school inspector, and in 1905 was elevated to chief

---

30   *APBR* 1921, 3. Accessed via *NSW Legislative Assembly: Aborigines Report of Board for the Aborigines 1915–1922*, Q572.991 N (SLNSW).
31   Petition from parents to Minister for Education, 5 March 1919, Greenwell Point School Files, 5/16146.2 (Bundle B), Item 12778 (SRNSW).
32   Letter from APB to Chief Inspector, 12 April 1919, Greenwell Point School Files, 5/16146.2 (Bundle B), Item 22981 (SRNSW). The Board did not elaborate but may have feared a wider inquiry into its affairs. A month later, Roseby Park Aboriginal Station Manager Mr Burns alerted the Board to a possible inquiry into the matter. Telegram from Burns to the APB, 20 May 1919, Greenwell Point School Files, 5/16146.2 (Bundle B) (SRNSW).

inspector.³³ Peter Board, Director of Education (1905–22), described Dawson as 'a dour Scot with a pawky wit, a friendly manner [and someone who] proved himself a "very able inspector"'.³⁴

In response to the situation at Greenwell Point School, the Department of Education sent three letters at the end of May 1919: one to Mr Weichman, the teacher at Greenwell Point School; one to Mr Wilson, the author of the petition; and one to secretary T.J. Foote of the APB – all stating that the Aboriginal children had been officially excluded.³⁵ An internal departmental report from James Dawson outlined the reasons for the exclusion. He claimed that the residents at Roseby Park Aboriginal Station 'are eccentric … some of them quarrel with the manager or get a distaste for Station life, and then they want to send their children to another school'. Dawson stated that the 'white parents complain that the coloured children are not clean, and say they have an "itch" which is contagious. Mr Weichman says he sees no sign of it'. Dawson concluded that there is 'no doubt that in many ways it is objectionable to have the white and coloured children in the same school', especially when there was an Aboriginal school close by.³⁶

The Cruikshanks and Lonesboroughs, two Aboriginal families whose children had been excluded, wrote to the local MP, Mark F. Morton, in protest at the exclusions. Mark Morton was born at Numbaa near Nowra and became a stock and station agent and auctioneer in the late 1880s. He moved into politics in 1901, representing the seat of Shoalhaven and was a member of the parliament until his death in 1938. He was regarded as the 'Father of the House' and had 'endeared himself to the people far and wide in this State'.³⁷ Morton had also been a Board member for five years from June 1910. Whether the Cruikshanks and Lonesboroughs knew of his previous association with the Board is unclear. However, their letter provoked Morton to intervene by way of a letter to the department in early June.³⁸ His correspondence gained traction. Suddenly and with no reason provided, the decision to exclude the children was overturned – but only for the children from the Cruikshank and Lonesborough families. In an internal departmental note (that echoed the words in Morton's letter), James Dawson noted that both Lonesborough and Cruikshank were

---

33   *Goulburn Evening Penny Post*, 12 February 1935, 2.
34   Crane and Walker, *Peter Board*, 291.
35   Greenwell Point School Files, 5/16146.2 (Bundle B), Items 17572 and 17573 (SRNSW).
36   Greenwell Point School Files, 5/16146.2 (Bundle B), Item 37616 (SRNSW).
37   *Camden News*, 29 September 1938, 1.
38   Letter from Morton to the Department, 1 June 1919, Greenwell Point School Files, 5/16146.2 (Bundle B), (no item number) (SRNSW).

white men married to 'half-caste' women 'of the very best of character' and that these fishermen were good workers, and that 'they have never received government rations and … their children have never attended the Aboriginal school'. Dawson explained that the policy was only designed to exclude those children who had come from the Aboriginal school at Roseby Park, or whose parents had received or were receiving government rations.[39] But Dawson then added a caveat: the department would accept the children of Cruikshank and Lonesborough 'until it is seen whether the residents will raise any objection, when the matter can be re-considered'.[40]

Mr Wilson, the author of the original petition, found this second decision 'inexplicable' and reminded the department that the original objection was that the white children had fallen ill from what he described as the 'black-itch', which was 'brought to the school by the aborigines'.[41] On 2 August the department advised that 'due to further protest' (presumably from Wilson), it was reversing its revised decision and excluding the students once more.[42]

Undeterred, the families of Cruikshank and Lonesborough organised a meeting with chief inspector James Dawson when he visited Nowra. Dawson wrote of the meeting:

> I had the opportunity of seeing the children and of learning of their antecedents. They show no trace of aboriginal descent although my investigations show that through a very remote relationship there is some native blood in their veins.
>
> No reasonable objection can be taken to the attendance of these children at the Greenwell Point Public School, and I promised the parents that their children would be readmitted on application.[43]

---

39   It is unclear where this 'nuanced' policy that Dawson articulated came from. Exclusion on demand, regardless of the circumstances, was still operational in 1919.
40   Internal departmental note from Chief Inspector Dawson, 10 June 1919, Greenwell Point School Files, 5/16146.2 (Bundle B), Item 19116 (SRNSW). See also a precis of Morton's letter prepared by Peter Board, Under-Secretary to the Minister, 10 June 1919, Greenwell Point School Files, 5/16146.2 (Bundle B), Item 46376 (SRNSW).
41   Letter from Mr Wilson to the Department of Education, Greenwell Point School Files, 5/16146.2 (Bundle B), Item 51719 (SRNSW).
42   Letter from Under-Secretary to Morton MLA, 2 August 1919, Greenwell Point School Files, 5/16146.2 (Bundle B), Item 23679 (SRNSW).
43   Internal Departmental letter from Chief Inspector Dawson, Greenwell Point School Files, 5/16146.2, (Bundle B), 20 August 1919, (Item number visible but not clear). (SRNSW). It is unknown how this meeting was arranged.

Unfortunately, there is no further correspondence in the school files to confirm the outcome of the last reinstatement and there was no apparent press coverage of these events. However, this example demonstrated the fickle nature of the department's policy, its acquiescence to political pressure and the determination of Aboriginal families to fight the exclusions.

Huskisson North School: Policy reversals and Aboriginal protest

In early December 1921, secretary of the Huskisson Progress Association T.A. Cahill wrote in conjunction with the Parents and Citizens Association to the Education Department to demand the exclusion of Aboriginal children from North Huskisson School. Mr Cahill's letter noted the recent influx of Aboriginal and 'half-caste' children from Roseby Park and Greenwell Point.[44] Cahill stated that these children were 'brought up under disgusting circumstances' and that the children attended school 'in a dirty, verminous condition and are a menace to the local white children'.[45] However, a report by the teacher Mr A.E. George supported the Aboriginal children. George explained that there were 10 Aboriginal children attending in very cramped conditions but the 'white children don't mind sitting with them'. He informed the inspector that the Aboriginal children were generally well-mannered, their conduct satisfactory and that their attendance was likely to be permanent while the parents were able to 'eke out' an existence.[46]

The Department of Education, appropriately, endorsed the teacher's view. The school was informed that the Aboriginal children should not be excluded, that a larger classroom should be built, and that the teacher already had the power to exclude any child under the Infectious and Communicable Diseases regulations.[47] But, by late January 1922, the decision not to exclude had been reversed and the Aboriginal children were to be excluded. The Huskisson Progress Association had obviously pressed the department again after the first ruling. In February 1922, the department informed the school, Mr Cahill and the Board of its decision.[48]

---

44 Roseby Park and Greenwell Point are only 1 km apart but separated by the Crookhaven River. They are about 15 km east of Nowra and approximately 15 km from Huskisson (see Figure 7.5).
45 Cahill to Education Department, 2 December 1921, Huskisson North School Files, 1919–1939, 5/16348.1, Item 93167 (SRNSW).
46 Huskisson North School Files, 1919–1939, 5/16348.1, (no item number) (SRNSW).
47 Huskisson North School Files, 1919–1939, 5/16348.1, (item number unclear) (SRNSW).
48 Huskisson North School Files, 1919–1939, 5/16348.1, Items 4917, 4916 and 4919 (SRNSW).

The letter from Peter Board on behalf of the Department of Education informed the APB that the Aboriginal children had been excluded and requested that the Board 'kindly make suitable arrangements for the education of the students concerned'.[49] On this occasion, the department's under-secretary acted as the spokesperson. Perhaps to avoid a perceived conflict of interest, W.G. Armstrong (the department's representative on the Board) does not appear in the correspondence. Under-secretary Peter Board (Figure 7.6) had also been an APB member under the old structure from 1907 until 1911 and would have been familiar with Board processes and its concerns over exclusions during that period. Peter Board has been described as an outstanding educationalist, intellectual, humanitarian and visionary with a 'deep sympathetic interest in delinquent and neglected children'.[50] His biographers, Alan Crane and William Walker, claim that to 'many he was an educational oracle, and an administrator by divine right and a born reformer'.[51] His quiescence about Aboriginal exclusions is noteworthy. Minister Perry's 1902 decree imposing 'exclusion on demand' was by now 20 years old. Who better to review it than someone like Peter Board? His failure to do so reinforced the ever-widening chasm separating Aboriginal people from mainstream Australia. Aboriginal people faced an impenetrable barrier to social mobility.

The APB did not object to the department's ruling and informed the department that the children would be sent to Roseby Park Aboriginal School.[52] It did so without any obvious consultation with the Aboriginal parents. The Board assumed, with some encouragement from the police, that the Aboriginal families would pack up their possessions,

Figure 7.6: Peter Board.
Source: Crane and Walker, *Peter Board*, iii.

---

49   Letter from P. Board to APB, 22 February 1922, Huskisson North School Files, 1919–1939, 5/16348.1, Item 4919 (SRNSW).
50   'Peter Board, M.A., C.M.G', by E. Williams, Peter Board Papers, 1872–1944, MLMSS 1095, Part 3, 29, Mitchell Library (hereafter ML).
51   Crane and Walker, *Peter Board*, 319.
52   Letter from APB to Department of Education, 9 March 1922, Huskisson North School Files, 1919–1939, 5/16348.1, Item 15190 (SRNSW).

leave their employment, accept the loss of income, sever ties with the community and move to Roseby Park without complaint. Their assumption was incorrect.

Mr John Carpenter and Mr A. Penrith, both Aboriginal men whose children had been excluded from Huskisson North, sent a letter of complaint to Mr Austin Chapman, the federal member for Eden-Monaro. They pointed out the injustice of the situation and stressed that they were independent families receiving no rations:

> Dear Sir,
>
> As I know you take a great interest in your constituents in this part of the State I make bold to bring before your notice a case of injustice on behalf of the School Board in stopping my Children and Grand Children from attending the Public School at Huskisson Although we are Half Casts we are earning our own living and receive no help from the Government and I think it is very hard that our children should be debarred from receiving an education at the nearest school to their house trusting that you may be able to do something to help us,
>
> We remain your reply,
> Mr J. Carpenter Mr A. Penrith[53]

In March 1922, another parent, Aboriginal father Mr T. Campbell, wrote to the Minister for Education. He sought the reason for his children's exclusion, reported that the police had harassed him and suggested the white children were just as 'filthy' as the Aboriginal children were accused of being. He made known that the local police officer had come to his house instructing him to 'shift to Wreck Bay … some 12 or thirteen miles distant'. Campbell challenged the policeman's authority in this matter:

> I would like to know what he has to do with instructing anybody as to where they are to send their children to school I suppose he thinks that I am a fool like a few more of the coloured folks about here [to] run away and leave the town but as I have my work here I do not intend to leave so if there cannot be something done in the matter will only have to do the best I can with the teaching of the children my-self … I have been reared here … It comes very hard to think that our children are turned away from the school

---

53   Letter from J. Carpenter and A. Penrith to Austin Chapman, MHR, 7 March 1922, Huskisson North School Files, 1919–1939, 5/16348.1, (no item number) (SRNSW).

> my father who cleared the timber off the land so as the school could be erected in 1883 and he had six of us attend the same school ... he was paying weekly for our Education as we are some of the oldest inhabitants of Huskisson.[54]

J. Moore, from the Huskisson Parents and Citizens Association, restated the white parents' objections in another letter to the inspector of schools, claiming that it was 'impossible to keep their children clean', that there was insufficient room at the school to cater for the Aboriginal children, and that the Aboriginal children should be taught at Aboriginal stations.[55] The Huskisson Progress Association offered that 'it was obvious' why the Aboriginal children should not be attending the public school.[56]

However, the white community was not united. The local Sunday school teacher Mr Bannister wrote to the school board in late April 1922 and complained of the exclusions, stating that the Aboriginal children were always well-dressed and as clean as 'the parents means would allow' and that they should be admitted to school.[57] His protestations came to nothing. In May 1922, Mr T. Campbell received a letter from department under-secretary, Peter Broad stating that his children would not be admitted to the school, and that

> very real objections have been raised by the white population to the attendance of coloured children at the school. In the circumstances the Minister regrets that he has no alternative but to sanction the exclusion of such children from attendance at Huskisson Public School, which is the procedure adopted in similar instance across the State.[58]

It would have been hurtful, humiliating and annoying for Mr Campbell that the department did not provide any specific reasons for the exclusion of his children, other than that it was policy applied elsewhere in the state. Another letter from John Carpenter (using a surprisingly, under

---

54 Letter from T. Campbell to Minister for Education, 22 March 1922, Huskisson North School Files, 1919–1939, 5/16348.1, (no item number) (SRNSW). This letter, in full, is found in Fletcher, *Documents in the History of Aboriginal Education in New South Wales*, 124–25.
55 Letter from J. Moore to Inspector of Schools, Braidwood, 18 April 1922, Huskisson North School Files, 1919–1939, 5/16348.1, (no item number) (SRNSW).
56 Letter from Huskisson Progress Association to Inspector of Schools, 8 April 1922, Huskisson North School Files, 1919–1939, 5/16348.1, (no item number) (SRNSW).
57 Letter from Bannister to Secretary of the School Board, 25 April 1922, Huskisson North School Files, 1919–1939, 5/16348.1, Item 25899 (SRNSW).
58 Letter from P. Broad to Mr T. Campbell, 15 May 1922, Huskisson North School Files, 1919–1939, 5/16348.1, Item 14424 (SRNSW).

the circumstances, respectful tone) to the Minister for Education, Mr Bruntnell, in June 1922, represented the frustration of Aboriginal parents:

> As our children have been stopped from attending the public school at Huskisson through some report that was sent to the school board from the white residents of this place we would beg of you to enquire into the matter for us, and kindly let us know the reason and also who made the complaint as our children had been attending the school and we are all working in the district for some time, hoping you will be able to help us in this matter, we are respectfully yours, John Carpenter (Aboriginals).[59]

The minister replied to Carpenter in the same vein as he had to Campbell and the original complaints from the white parents were kept off-limits to the Aboriginal parents.[60]

In 1923, the APB intervened dramatically. Having previously claimed that it would relocate the Aboriginal families to Roseby Park, it now sought to absolve itself of all responsibility for the education of those excluded from Huskisson. It explained to the department that because the APB had already provided educational facilities at Roseby Park for Aboriginal children then 'responsibility for providing for those living outside is really one for your Department'.[61] Having failed to move the families, the Board now considered that the department needed to solve the problem of educating these children. After almost 40 years of operation, the APB (and the department) had no clear understanding of who had responsibility for the education of Aboriginal children excluded from public schools. For the first time since Edmund Fosbery's outcry over the exclusion of Aboriginal children in 1898 at Wollar, the Board had thrown the responsibility of educating 'excluded Aboriginal children' back onto the Education Department.

Over the course of the next two years the department received complaints about the Huskisson exclusions from a teacher at Methodist Ladies College in Burwood (Sydney) and from the president of the New South

---

59 Letter from John Carpenter to Minister for Education (Bruntnell), 15 June 1922, Huskisson North School Files, 1919–1939, 5/16348.1, (no item number) (SRNSW).
60 Letter from Minister for Education (Bruntnell) to John Carpenter, no date, Huskisson North School Files, 1919–1939, 5/16348.1, (no item number) (SRNSW).
61 Letter from Pettitt, Secretary of the APB, to the Education Department, 29 May 1923, Huskisson North School Files, 1919–1939, 5/16348.1, Item 8608 (SRNSW).

Wales Teachers Federation.[62] These interventions may have had some effect. In March 1925, the teacher at Huskisson North, Mr Dunlop, received instruction from Mr H.D. McLelland, chief inspector of primary schools and Board member, to admit the local Aboriginal and 'half-caste' population if the children were clean.[63] Three months later in early June, bizarrely, and with no explanation, the decision was overturned and the children were excluded once more.[64] It is unclear what happened to the Aboriginal children after this last exclusion but it appears they remained barred from the school.

Years later, in 1935, an officer of the Government Printing Office named Mr Jenkins wrote to the APB after a holiday visit to Huskisson, requesting that Aboriginal girl Fay Carpenter (daughter of John Carpenter) be admitted to the Huskisson School.[65] Education Department Inspector White offered that she be admitted as 'a one off', that it was not to set a precedent, and that the decision would be reviewed.[66] When the APB was informed, it agreed with the decision, and suggested that the whole issue may settle down as it believed that the white protestors had left the district.[67] However, once more the department fell back on its policy of exclusion. A letter from G.R. Thomas, Director General of Education and Board member, to Mr Jenkins in July 1935 regretfully indicated that the child could not be admitted to the school. In a final insult, enclosed were enrolment forms to the Education Department's Correspondence

---

62 Letter from Under-Secretary, Education Department to Rev. Frederick Potts of Methodist Ladies College, 5 December 1923, Huskisson North School Files, 1919–1939, 5/16348.1, Item 46655 (SRNSW). Fletcher, *Clean, Clad, and Courteous*, 119–20. Fletcher outlines this exchange but does not provide any sources.

63 Letter from McLellan to Dunlop, 27 March 1925, Huskisson North School Files, 1919–1939, 5/16348.1, (no item number) (SRNSW).

64 Letter from Under-Secretary to APB, 4 June 1925, Huskisson North School Files, 1919–1939, 5/16348.1, (no item number) (SRNSW). A departmental report sheds some light on the general situation. In May 1927 a report from school attendance staff officer Mr Robertson indicated that the Campbell children should be able to attend school but provided no specific reason. Robertson's report also fleshed out what might have been, in part, behind the exclusions. The white families feared competition from Aboriginal workers in the town and a felt that a 'further influx of other black families ... would compete against the white fishermen'. This may well have been a factor, but there can be little doubt that the exclusions were racially motivated. Huskisson North School Files, 1919–1939, 5/15348.1, Item 60813 (SRNSW).

65 Letter from Jenkins to APB, 20 May 1935, Huskisson North School Files, 1919–1939, 5/15348.1, Item 046103 (SRNSW).

66 Letter from Inspector White to Jenkins, Huskisson North School Files, 1919–1939, 5/16348.1, Item 046103 (SRNSW).

67 Letter from APB to Under-Secretary, Department of Education, 21 May 1935, Huskisson North School Files, 1919–1939, 5/16348.1, Item 3817 (SRNSW).

School, which came highly recommended.[68] Tragically, over the course of 15 years, Aboriginal families were unsuccessful in seeking a public education for their children. Yet Aboriginal families persisted in politely seeking answers of the department in attempts to have their children reinstated in school. Their protest provoked high-level action, even if they ultimately failed.

These two disputes, at Greenwell Point and at Huskisson, raised several issues. First, the Board was unable to provide any leverage and, in the end, abrogated all responsibility for the education of 'excluded Aboriginal children'. Second, during the disputes the Education Department had adopted contradictory positions. It excluded Aboriginal students on the basis that families were receiving Board assistance, or that they came from an Aboriginal school, or on health grounds. Then it decided to include some Aboriginal children based on degrees of whiteness or the likelihood of complaints, and purposely withheld information from Aboriginal families. Its policy was unworkable. Third, Aboriginal families caught up in the disputes were resourceful and went to considerable lengths to have their children reinstated. However, the generally 'silent' power of the white parent lobby was considerable, and the Education Department was complicit. Aboriginal children could not go to a public school. Lastly, it was apparent there were other groups and teachers who supported the Aboriginal parents and spoke out against the exclusions.

By the mid-1930s the Board was under severe pressure on a whole range of policy fronts as witnessed in the following chapter. One of these pressure points, the mobility of Aboriginal people, is the focus of this next example.

Bomaderry: 'Invited to co-operate'

The exclusion of Aboriginal children at Bomaderry School exposed a broader issue confronting the Board in the mid-1930s. The Board regularly expelled Aboriginal people from the reserves and stations, only to have the municipal authorities of towns to where they relocated demand their removal back to Board locations.[69] An exclusion controversy at Bomaderry School brought this issue to a head.

---

68   Letter from Thomas, Director of Education, to Mr Jenkins, 18 July 1935, Huskisson North School Files, 1919–1939, 5/16348.1, (no item number) (SRNSW).
69   Read, 'A Rape of the Soul so Profound', 23–33.

Across the state the Board faced pressure from local municipalities and white residents to remove many Aboriginal groups congregating on the fringes of towns. This situation had developed partly as a result of the Board's own dispersal policy of removing Aboriginal people who were classified as 'quadroons' and 'octoroons' from stations, reserves and camps and by the Board's general expulsion policy for misdemeanours.[70] Moreover, the economic downturn due to the Great Depression had caused considerable dislocation in both the white and Aboriginal communities with many labour lay-offs, and Aboriginal people sought refuge back on the reserves and stations. White activist for Aboriginal equality Jack Horner observed that

> hundreds [of Aboriginal people] turned to the Board's rations for sustenance, pocketing their pride. If houses on reserves and stations could not accommodate them, they pitched tents outside and defied the police to send them away.[71]

Many Aboriginal people, though, refused to return, choosing instead to be free of the police and the strictly controlled life on the stations. These groups, or 'fringe dwellers', lived on 'uncontrolled' camps on the edges of country towns to avoid supervision by authorities. Richard Broome describes them as 'cultural warriors, refusing to surrender Aboriginal ways'.[72] Tension over fringe camps was exacerbated by the outbreak of the eye disease gonococcal ophthalmia in some Aboriginal reserves and stations. This led to pressure to have Aboriginal camps removed from white communities so as to avoid 'contamination'. The colonial secretary, Captain Chaffey, generated a sense of fear and panic when he suggested, wrongly, that while it was not too destructive to Aboriginal people, this disease would be devastating within white communities as it caused blindness.[73]

This issue of removing Aboriginal people from rural towns drove the dispute over the Aboriginal children at Bomaderry School. The inspector of schools, Mr H. Campbell, filed a report on 16 October 1935 that the public school at Bomaderry was 'fully taxed' with an enrolment of 141 and only three classrooms. Since there were 41 children of 'aboriginal blood', it would 'appear preferable to transfer these to a separate school

---

70 The 1918 amendment changed the definition of the word 'Aborigine'. From 1918, an Aborigine was 'any full-blood or half-caste who is a native of NSW'. It meant that 'quadroons' and 'octoroons' were now 'not Aborigines' and had to leave the reserves and stations. See Chapter 5.
71 Horner, *Bill Ferguson*, 23.
72 Broome, *Aboriginal Australians*, 2010, 196.
73 *NSWPD*, Legislative Assembly, 18 June 1936, 4750.

for aborigines in locality'. This would relieve the pressure upon 'existing accommodation for white children'. He urged that the matter be taken up with the APB immediately.[74]

In November 1935 the Nowra Municipal Council had already discussed the matter of removing Aboriginal people from the municipality. J.J. Carrall, the health inspector, recommended to council that it seek the cooperation of the APB to 'have all the aboriginals removed to the camps provided for them'.[75] Also, in the same month, G.R. Thomas (no longer a Board member but now the Under-Secretary of the Department of Education) wrote to the APB urging 'early consideration' in providing some separate schooling alternative for the Aboriginal children at Bomaderry.[76] APB Secretary Pettitt explained to the Department of Education that the removal of the families concerned would probably be difficult as 'my Board does not at present possess the necessary powers to compel these people to remove to an Aboriginal Reserve'. Pettitt suggested a way around the issue. Perhaps the local municipal councils of Berry and Nowra could be 'invited to co-operate' by exercising their powers under 'ordinances & insanitary conditions' to remove the Aboriginal families.[77] Pettitt submitted that if this avenue did not prove successful, then it must wait until a proposed Bill to amend the *Aborigines Protection Act 1909* (NSW) had become law. The Department of Education raised no opposition to Pettitt's proposal.

The APB's proposed amendment sought considerable powers. The Board had signalled its intention to change the Act in its report of 1932–33:

> Apart from the stations, there are a large number of reserves situated at various centres … Unauthorised camps have also been formed at many places, in most instances adjacent to a town, which presents certain attractions to the Aborigines concerned … The Board contemplates … certain amendments of its Act, which will enable it to remove these camps and concentrate the residents thereof on to stations where they, and particularly the women and children will be housed, and encouraged to live, under better conditions.[78]

---

74 Internal departmental note – extract from Inspector of Schools, 31 October 1935, Bomaderry School Files, Pre-1939, 5/14993 (Bundle B), Item 710 (SRNSW).
75 Health Inspector's report to Nowra Council, Nowra Council Minutes, 11 November 1935, *Nowra Council Minute Book* (November 1933 to December 1935), Shoalhaven City Council, Nowra.
76 Letter from Thomas to Secretary of the APB, 29 November 1935, Bomaderry School Files, Pre-1939, 5/14993 (Bundle B), Item 108827 (SRNSW).
77 APB Minutes (hereafter *APBM*), 5 February 1936, Item 7. All *APBM* accessed via: Minute Books (Aborigines Welfare Board), NRS 2, NSW Department of Aboriginal Affairs, Sydney.
78 *APBR* 1934, 2. Accessed via 'NSW', To Remove and Protect, AIATSIS: aiatsis.gov.au/sites/default/files/docs/digitised_collections/remove/23911.pdf.

The amendment had several features but the main thrust was to seek various powers to apply to the courts to remove Aboriginal people to a 'reserve or other place controlled by the board', to authorise medical examinations of Aboriginal people, to remove Aboriginal people from employment positions if the Board felt necessary and to direct the wages of Aboriginal people in employment directly to the Board.[79]

The *Shoalhaven Telegraph* was more revealing about Pettitt's suggestion inviting the councils 'to co-operate'. It reported that the 'Inspector of aborigines [Mr Smithers] had recently been to Nowra and in conversation with him [Health Inspector Carrall] asked the co-operation of Council and adjoining Councils to stop aborigines camping in municipal areas'. The *Telegraph* further informed readers that the idea was to have the Aboriginal people moved to Roseby Park, and Mr Smithers would arrange for the men – who were wanted on farms for pea-picking – to be brought in daily and returned home to the station in the afternoon. Alderman Stewart opposed the motion. He offered that most of the men were 'well conducted, as were their women folk. They did no harm, and were useful to many farmers'. Smithers disagreed with Stewart and argued that the APB was 'anxious to have these people brought under proper control, which he thought would be to their own interest and the interest of the community generally'.[80] The *Nowra Leader* fleshed out more details: Smithers wanted the men to work Monday to Friday and then be returned to Roseby Park for the weekend and the farmers would have to accommodate them during the working week.[81]

In mid-November 1935, the Nowra Town Clerk requested the Berry Municipal Council to have the Aboriginal families transferred to Roseby Park and put under control of the APB. Aldermen Barham and Knapp agreed with the proposal, but the Mayor of Berry Council felt they should remain in the community. He noted that some of these men were an 'asset to local farmers'. They were 'well conducted and good at certain classes of farm labour'.[82]

---

79   *NSWPD*, Legislative Assembly, 18 June 1936, 4749. See also *Aborigines Protection (Amendment) Act 1936* (NSW), Sections 2(c), (i) and (j). The Amendment successfully passed the Parliament in July 1936. Heather Goodall notes that the amendment was known as 'the Dog Act'. Brewarrina resident Henry Hardy explained: Aboriginal people 'felt that now they could be penned up and shifted around just like animals'. Goodall, *Invasion to Embassy*, 2008, 230.
80   *Shoalhaven Telegraph*, 13 November 1935, 5.
81   *Nowra Leader*, 15 November 1935, 1.
82   *Berry Council Minute Book* (1928–1936), 20 November 1935, Item 19, 505, Shoalhaven City Council, Nowra; *The Shoalhaven News and South Coast District Advertiser*, 23 November 1935, 1.

Both councils decided against imposing any orders, agreeing in the end that Aboriginal workers were of use to local farm workers. In early April 1936, the Board let the matter rest. Pettitt informed the Department of Education that there had been no direction from the Berry or Nowra municipal councils and that the Aboriginal families at Bomaderry did not wish to remove to Roseby Park due to the 'distance from their work' and their current ability to 'secure relief work'.[83] The Board's endeavours to influence local authorities to move Aboriginal families had failed and Smithers's solution that local farmers house the men up for five days and then to arrange transport to Roseby Park on a Friday night did not resonate with anyone. The Aboriginal people were never removed. Even after the amendment was passed in July 1936, there were no mass removals in the Shoalhaven, unlike in other areas in New South Wales.[84]

Because of the Board's failure to remove the Aboriginal families, the situation at Bomaderry School remained as it was. On 19 August 1937, the minister, D.H. Drummond, urged that the matter of overcrowding be ended quickly. Drummond's impatience was perhaps driven by the fact that he had been publicly embarrassed by a group of Aboriginal parents whose children had been refused entry to another local school and he sought to avoid a similar situation.[85] In early October 1937 the Parents and Citizens Association from

---

83   Letter from Pettitt to Education Department, 2 April 1936, Bomaderry School Files, Pre-1939, 5/14993 (Bundle B), Item 032501 (SRNSW).
84   The residents at Angledool Aboriginal Station on the Queensland border were forcibly removed to Brewarrina by the APB on the grounds of inaccessibility in the wet season and an outbreak of trachoma. The Yuwalaraay (Angledool residents) did not want to move where they would be among strangers and with less prospect of work. The APB forced the move, stripped their houses, burnt the remains, trucked them to Brewarrina and placed them in two-roomed tin shacks, 10 feet by 20 feet, with no windows or doors. See Goodall, *Invasion to Embassy*, 1996, 203–5.
85   Minister Drummond was generally sympathetic to the concerns of white parents and supported the exclusions of Aboriginal children; he had expressed a view, unsolicited, that relationships between white and black were 'embarrassing and may be harmful'. In July 1937, 44 white children were withdrawn from Woolbrook School due to the presence of 15 Aboriginal children. The Aboriginal community demanded of the department that the white parents should be prosecuted for not sending their children to school. The press became involved and Drummond acted – he instructed the principal to exclude all the Aboriginal children. The Aboriginal parents threatened legal action and they refused to allow their children *not* to attend. The principal closed the school for a week. When it reopened, only white children attended and their parents said they would send their children to nearby Walcha Public if the Aboriginal children returned. Some Aboriginal parents and five of their 'excluded children' intercepted Drummond at an official function. Drummond was embarrassed – he saw that the children were well-mannered, clean and almost unrecognisably Aboriginal! He immediately overturned his decision, threatened the white parents with prosecution if their children did not attend school and refused them admission to another public school. His concession to the white parents was that no children with 'marked Aboriginal characteristics' would be enrolled until approval was given by his department. See several press reports between 15 July and 11 August 1937 (available through the National Library of Australia's Trove service: trove.nla.gov.au); Fletcher, *Clean, Clad and Courteous*, 141–43.

Bomaderry School changed tack – it now sought to remove the children on health grounds. The association had arranged health checks at the school and a Dr van Someren, who conducted the checks, had advised the association that some of the 'coloured children were suffering from scabies and pediculi [lice] and also that other children [white] were liable to become infested by using the same latrines seats or lavatory basins'.[86] Some of the more overzealous white parents had deliberately misrepresented Dr van Someren's findings, suggesting he had referred to 'dangerous' conditions and that the 'coloured' children may have been suffering from venereal disease. In a report to the Education Department on the Bomaderry situation, the Principal Medical Officer ignored the specious claims of venereal disease. He advised the Department of Education that scabies and lice were common in 'any type of school in New South Wales' and could not be considered a danger to other children, and that such conditions would 'certainly not be considered to be sufficient ground for the permanent exclusion of the children'.[87]

The district inspector of schools in Wollongong, C. Harrold, wrote on 23 September 1938 about the Bomaderry situation:

> In view of the Medical Officer's report, I recommend that the request for the exclusion of Aboriginal children from the school be declined. The matter has not been discussed by the P & C [Association] since my investigation. I suggest that no communication on the subject be forwarded to the P & C Association unless a further request is made for the exclusion of the coloured children.[88]

The Department of Education was on firmer ground with health concerns: if a child was unwell or infectious, they could be excluded until they were well again. When the complaint was based on Aboriginality, the department's policy was found wanting. The Aboriginal children remained at school. However, District Inspector Harold's recommendation *not* to contact the Parents and Citizens Association and 'let sleeping dogs lie' demonstrates the department's continued unease about requests to remove the Aboriginal children.

---

86 Letter from Principal Medical Officer to the Under-Secretary of the Department, 6 October 1937, Bomaderry School Files, Pre-1939, 5/14993 (Bundle B), Item 102975 (SRNSW).
87 Letter from Principal Medical Officer to the Under-Secretary of the Department, 6 October 1937, Bomaderry School Files, Pre-1939, 5/14993 (Bundle B), Item 102975 (SRNSW).
88 Internal departmental note from C. Harold, District Inspector Wollongong, 23 September 1938, Bomaderry School Files, Pre-1939, 5/14993 (Bundle B), Item 094006 (SRNSW).

By early 1938, Berry Municipal Council had not resolved the issue of Aboriginal removals. The moderating voice of the mayor stated that these

> coloured people have citizens' rights provided they live as citizens. They have bought certain land, and as far as council is concerned, if they comply with the housing condition … and build to the requirements … they are all right.[89]

So the Board's attempt to use council regulations to move Aboriginal families backfired. The Berry and Nowra councils were clearly split over the removal of the communities because Aboriginal labour was crucial to local agriculture and Aboriginal families had every right to reside if their land had been acquired appropriately. Perhaps realising the possibility of opposition from several quarters, the Board did not utilise its new-found powers acquired in 1936.

Trapped in a mire of hypocrisy

The Board hoped that some Aboriginal students would be able to slip under the radar of white rural parent opposition and sit in classrooms across New South Wales. When the racially based exclusions occurred, its dual policy became unsustainable. The Board had little leverage in the local public school disputes as it had no moral authority – it had never argued that all Aboriginal children were entitled to a full public education. When it did defend the right of some students to attend local schools, it often displayed weakness in its response to exclusions, employed coercive strategies towards Aboriginal families to relocate, criticised the Department of Education, colluded with municipal bodies and, when all else failed, disengaged.

Fosbery, in 1898, was probably genuine in his criticism of the Education Department for allowing Aboriginal children to be barred on the basis of skin colour, but there was no serious retreat from the Board's initial preferred position. It had always held that Aboriginal children, in large numbers, were better educated apart from white children. Compounding the Board's inability to solve some of the disputes about integrated schools was the reconstitution of the Board in 1916. The fact that one

---

89   *Nowra Leader*, 25 February 1938, 6.

Board member was always a high-ranking bureaucrat from the Education Department – and often the department's representative in these disputes – ensured that the Board's voice was ineffectual.

On any level, the role of the Department of Education was indefensible. Its defined policy of 'exclusion on demand' was a complete capitulation to the white parent lobby. But when confronted with 'almost white' children being excluded, it had no appropriate policy response other than to reverse decisions previously made. Even the progressive educationalist Peter Board, as Director of Education, could not provide a sensible policy, or indeed any security for the education of Aboriginal children.

Significantly, the examples reveal the tenacity of Aboriginal parents who engaged different strategies to fight the exclusion of their children from schools. In doing so they fought to remain in their homes, continue their connection with the district, and maintain employment opportunities. They found support among interested educational groups and from some teachers; a sign of things to come. However, even after 1940 when the Department of Education assumed complete control of schooling for Aboriginal children, the entrenched preference for separation was still apparent. David H. Drummond, the Minister for Education from 1932 to 1941, held the view that Aboriginal people were a 'child-like' race and those children with a predominant 'admixture of Aboriginal blood' should not be schooled alongside white children.[90]

Yet change was on the way. By the mid-1930s deep cracks had appeared in the Board's façade. Uncomfortable questions about the Board's processes and management of the reserves and stations were raised by emerging Aboriginal activists and white civil rights advocates. The Board's moribund structure, enshrined in the reconstitution of 1916, had run its course; scrutiny that had been absent during the 1920s was now being applied. Slowly but surely the foundations crumbled while an increasingly paranoid Board resisted to the end.

---

90   Department of Education policy statement, 6 August 1936, Premiers Letters Received 1927, File No. A27/915, Premiers Special Bundles, File No. 62/1515 (Part 1), Item 560 (SRNSW).

8

Winds of change

In late January 1938 the New South Wales Board for the Protection of Aborigines (APB) convened a three-day Sydney conference of all its managers and matrons of Aboriginal stations throughout the state.[1] This was the first time, after 55 years of the Board's existence, that its managers and matrons (or any staff for that matter) had gathered together. A crisis point had been reached and the Board felt the need to assemble its agents to reassure them that all was well. However, the tone of the opening addresses was far from reassuring. Colonial Secretary of the Government Captain Chaffey began proceedings. He reminded his audience that they were tasked with 'very grave responsibilities'. Chaffey praised the men of the Board individually and reassured the assembled office holders that they were in very good hands. He also underlined the need for loyalty and 'honourable service'. Recently voiced criticism of the Board, although not identified by Chaffey, prompted this somewhat alarmist and disjointed plea:

> Now this is what you have got to guard against, and what I have got to guard against, and what the Members of the Board have got to guard against. There are elements in the community and every part of the world, with a psychology and atmosphere, whose one objective is discord, disintegration, disruption and destruction or anything when it comes to real responsibilities of life.[2]

---

1   The conference was held 22–25 January 1938. Bate, 'Conference on the Plight of the Aborigines 1938', 24–26 January 1938, JaHQ 2014/1905, Mitchell Library (hereafter ML). (The dates conflict in the title and for the transcript. The transcript records proceedings from Saturday 22 January until Tuesday 25 January at 5 pm.)
2   Bate, 'Conference on the Plight of the Aborigines 1938', 2–3.

Figure 8.1: B.C. Harkness.
Source: Royal Australian Historical Society, Inspectors of Schools, PXA 1538, 2039/24. Mitchell Library, State Library of New South Wales.

Bertie Clarence Harkness (Figure 8.1), long-term Board member (and brother of E.B. Harkness), followed Chaffey.³ Harkness had joined the APB in January 1931. Born in Grafton, he became a teacher and took posts in several country centres before his elevation to inspector of schools in 1923, with further promotions to chief inspector of schools and Deputy Director of Education in 1933.⁴ Harkness reassured the assembled listeners that recent criticism of the Board was unfounded and malicious. He insisted that the Board was functioning properly, but emphasised the importance of fidelity and solidarity:

> the idea of this conference occurred spontaneously from the Board itself. It was not stimulated to do this by any criticism from without or any feeling that something was going to happen … I am very glad he [the minister] emphasised the need for 'perfect loyalty' … if there is not this you are against us. I am not suggesting that you are against us. If you have anything to say, it is a very good thing to say it in the right quarter.⁵

It was an interesting welcome. As a member of the conference on a hot January Sydney day you could be forgiven for moving uneasily in your chair. Conference chair (and Board member since 1929) Henry John Bate MLA (Figure 8.2) was next to address the meeting. Bate had been a long-time participant in Aboriginal affairs on the south coast at Wallaga Lake Aboriginal Station. He acknowledged the hard work of the managers in their various locations and assured them that, although members of the Board were all busy public servants, they still found time once a month to meet on Board matters and had only the 'welfare of the Aborigines' at

---

3 Horner, *Bill Ferguson*, 29.
4 *Daily Examiner*, 15 October 1951, 2.
5 Bate, 'Conference on the Plight of the Aborigines 1938', 4.

heart. Bate's concluding remarks added to the discomfort: 'If there is ever an occasion when you think someone is a spy, we ask you to let us know'.[6] This was a highly charged opening to the conference and possibly even a paranoid one.

The conference had nothing to do with spontaneity, as Harkness alleged. What had prompted this gathering was a successful, and unexpected, motion put by opposition Labor MP Mark Davidson on 9 November 1937 to establish a Select Committee inquiry into the Board and its practices. The inquiry was still underway when the Board convened its conference. The Board had gathered its personnel, not to thank everyone for their services, but to secure solidarity and loyalty, and to weed out any likely internal critics before mounting a last-ditch attempt to stare down its detractors.

The Board's problems had begun well before 1937. Andrew Markus reflects that the 1930s saw:

> the beginnings of a change of policy towards Aborigines. Aboriginal spokespersons, and by the late 1920s, a small group of whites, including clergymen, academics, female philanthropists, businessmen, and politicians, urged governments to accept that … it was possible for Aborigines to 'advance' towards 'civilisation' with appropriate guidance.[7]

The APB had neither facilitated nor even acknowledged this shift. As described in Chapter 5, it had become insular, reactionary and negligent, and was run by a small cabal. Its unaccountability made it impervious to change. After the Great Depression it faced a barrage of criticism from both black and white activists that it could not withstand.

Black and white protest groups challenge the Board

Aboriginal people have 'always resisted colonialism in Australia'.[8] From 1788, the 'clans fought the invasion of their lands' across the frontier, initially in New South Wales and Van Diemen's Land and then eventually across the continent. After the frontier wars abated, resistance took on

---

6 Bate, 'Conference on the Plight of the Aborigines 1938', 13.
7 Markus, *Blood from a Stone*, 4.
8 Attwood and Markus, *The Struggle for Aboriginal Rights*, 7.

other forms. A powerful tool of resistance was the petition. Ann Curthoys and Jessie Mitchell observe that petitioning by Indigenous peoples has a long history.[9] The earliest known example in Australia was in the mid-1840s in Van Diemen's Land.[10] Perhaps the best known example in Victoria comes from Diane Barwick's account of the fight by the Kulin, near Healesville, north-east of Melbourne, who regularly used petitioning to their advantage.[11] As Curthoys and Mitchell observe, Aboriginal people 'learned where the power lay, and they never lost sight of those authorities closest to them, seeking to draw them into patterns of mutual and personal obligation'.[12] Jessica Horton has given weight to the numerous political letters written, particularly by Aboriginal women in Victoria, in the latter part of the nineteenth and early twentieth centuries. Horton notes how the manager at the Lake Condah Aboriginal Mission complained to the secretary of the Aborigines Board in that state, about 'discipline problems caused by the residents writing letters' to Protection Board members about the disrepair of housing on the mission, that their men were away fighting in the First World War and concern about rumours that the mission would soon close.[13] A collection of letters from 80 Indigenous women, edited by Patricia Grimshaw, Sandra Smith and Elizabeth Nelson, suggests that Aboriginal women wrote far more than Aboriginal men and were more equipped to do so, having greater access to education than the men.[14] Horton notes a number of Aboriginal women such as Bessy Cameron, a Nyunger from Albany in Western Australia, Mary Ellen McRae from Gippsland, and Emily Milton Stephen also from Gippsland, who all wrote about political matters ranging from child removals, conditions on the missions and grievances. The letter-writers, both women and men, were not 'community leaders but people who were determined to influence the decisions of authorities regarding their lives and to bring about change

---

9   The 'influence of petitioning stretched throughout Britain's empire' and was 'widespread in the American colonies in the seventeenth and eighteenth centuries': Curthoys and Mitchell, 'Bring this Paper to the Good Governor', 185.
10   The Aboriginal people of Van Diemen's Land, who were 'encouraged' to move onto Flinders Island with their 'protector' George Augustus Robinson, were misled. Their new establishment, called Wybalenna, was substandard and many died while others suffered from malnutrition. The Aboriginal residents employed their literary skills and 'humanitarian principles' gained from Robinson and the missionaries to write letters of protest and petition Queen Victoria; see Attwood and Markus, *The Struggle for Aboriginal Rights*, 37–41. See also Reynolds, *The Fate of a Free People*, 7–26; and Ryan, *Tasmanian Aborigines*, 240–52.
11   Barwick, *Rebellion at Coranderrk*; see also Barwick, 'A Little More than Kin', 101–9; Curthoys and Mitchell, 'Bring this Paper to the Good Governor', 193; Attwood, *Rights for Aborigines*, Chapter 1; Broome, 'Victoria'; and Christie, *Aborigines in Colonial Victoria*, 182–99.
12   Curthoys and Mitchell, 'Bring this Paper to the Good Governor', 198.
13   Horton, 'Rewriting Political History', 158.
14   Horton, 'Rewriting Political History', 167–68.

for the better'.[15] By the time Aboriginal political activity increased in the 1920s in south-eastern Australia, it had been preceded by a rich history of letter-writing and petitions from both Aboriginal women and men seeking change at a local level and wider level.

In New South Wales during the late 1920s and 1930s, several black and white organisations formed during this period to challenge the government policies directed at Aboriginal people. The efforts of these organisations and individuals ensured that, from the early 1920s, the level of public scrutiny began to increase. The Board responded to these groups with suspicion, scepticism and indifference.

The Australian Aborigines Progressive Association (AAPA), established in 1924 by Aboriginal waterside worker Fred Maynard, was key among these.[16] Richard Broome notes that Maynard's organisation was the first 'Aboriginal political group' in Australia.[17] Fred Maynard was born in 1879 at Hinton in New South Wales and was of both Aboriginal and African-American descent. After his mother's death in 1884, he and his five sisters were brought up under the strict discipline of a protestant minister in Maitland and Fred read widely. He worked as a bullock-driver and drover before becoming a wharf labourer on the Sydney docks in 1914.[18] John Maynard (Fred's grandson) observes that Fred Maynard's activism began in 1907 when the black American boxer Jack Johnson fought in Sydney and Maynard formed a connection with the Coloured Progressive Association.[19] Tim Rowse asserts that Maynard's deep association with black Americans gave him 'a blueprint' to develop his own principles.[20] Maynard, 'angered by the NSW government's handing over … of reserve land to returned non-Aboriginal servicemen' after the First World War, formed a chapter of the Universal Negro Improvement Association founded by Marcus Garvey.[21] From there, Maynard formed the AAPA, guided by Garvey's call for 'pride in culture, solid economic base and strong association to the land of birth'.[22]

---

15   Horton, 'Rewriting Political History', 180.
16   Attwood and Markus, *The Struggle for Aboriginal Rights*, 58.
17   Broome, *Aboriginal Australians*, 2010, 204.
18   Goodall and Maynard, 'Maynard, Charles Frederick (Fred) (1879–1946)'.
19   Maynard, 'Fred Maynard and the Awakening of Aboriginal Political Consciousness', 105–33. See also Goodall, *Invasion to Embassy*, 1996, 149–70; and Attwood and Markus, *The Struggle for Aboriginal Rights*, 58–61.
20   Rowse, *Contesting Assimilation*, 33.
21   Rowse, *Indigenous and Other Australians Since 1901*, 188–89.
22   Quoted in Rowse, *Indigenous and Other Australians Since 1901*, 189.

The first indication that the Board would have to deal with a growing public interest in Aboriginal affairs was an approach made by Elizabeth McKenzie Hatton, a white missionary, who was an important supporter of the AAPA.[23] In late 1923, Elizabeth McKenzie Hatton sought funding from the APB to establish a home for Aboriginal girls who had 'run away from their white employers because of maltreatment, abuse and molestation'.[24] Because of the implied criticism of its policy of removals, the Board refused her request for financial assistance and viewed her proposal as a serious challenge to its authority. Board Secretary Pettitt immediately began inquiries into the work that McKenzie Hatton had undertaken in Victoria.[25] In January 1925 the Board had been alerted to McKenzie Hatton's girls' home at Homebush – a 12-roomed house named 'Comorques' – and was waiting upon a police report on her activities.[26] In March of the same year, the Board instructed the police to 'maintain surveillance' and ruled that her application to visit the reserves was denied.[27] McKenzie Hatton and the AAPA were undeterred. In early 1925, McKenzie Hatton and Fred Maynard, with the aid of the Nambucca Heads community, removed from a household a girl who was under the Board's control.[28] The Board was outraged and in July 1925 it sought advice from the Crown solicitor as to what action it could take against McKenzie Hatton, as well as the AAPA. The Crown solicitor informed the Board that they could take no action 'at the present time'.[29] These events revealed the extent to which the Board was prepared to go to prevent and frustrate any challenge to its affairs.

---

23 Well-known social worker Elizabeth McKenzie Hatton had spent 16 years in Queensland working with South Sea Islanders before moving to New South Wales in 1923. For an understanding of her significant influence on AAPA policy and the energy she brought to her role in the organisation, see Maynard, 'Fred Maynard and the Awakening of Aboriginal Political Consciousness', 142–225. John Maynard corrects the record that McKenzie Hatton was not the secretary of the AAPA – all office holders were Aboriginal.
24 Maynard, 'Fred Maynard and the Awakening of Aboriginal Political Consciousness', 146.
25 APB Minutes (hereafter *APBM*), 14 December 1923, Item 10: all *APBM* accessed via Minute Books (Aborigines Welfare Board), NRS 2, NSW Department of Aboriginal Affairs, Sydney; Maynard, 'Fred Maynard and the Awakening of Aboriginal Political Consciousness', 147.
26 *APBM*, 23 January 1925, Item 10. McKenzie Hatton had tried to secure a house previously but had run into financial difficulties, but she persevered and acquired a year's lease on a second home, 'Comorques', to which the Aborigines' Inland Mission contributed £22 towards the first month's rent. The first Aboriginal girl, Emily Melrose, was admitted in 23 January 1925. See Maynard, 'Light in the Darkness', 8.
27 *APBM*, 6 March 1925, Item 10; see also Huggonson, 'Aborigines and the Aftermath of the Great War', 7.
28 Maynard, 'Fred Maynard and the Awakening of Aboriginal Political Consciousness', 156. The girl 'held' on Stuarts Island in the Nambucca River was the daughter of Fred Buchanan, an Aboriginal activist who had recently been dispossessed of reserve land. See Goodall, *Invasion to Embassy*, 2008, 184.
29 Maynard, 'Fred Maynard and the Awakening of Aboriginal Political Consciousness', 156.

A proposal for the AAPA to become a registered company had come to the notice of the Board at its meeting of 23 October 1925. The Board strongly opposed the application:

> on account of the unfitness of the promoters who, with the exception of Mrs Hatton, are all Aborigines, certain available particulars re the character of whom we are to be furnished [sic] and also because many of the objects set forth in the articles of Association of the proposed company are already included among the duties imposed upon the Board by the Aborigines Protection Act.[30]

The Board was concerned that if the AAPA became a registered company it could interfere with some of the functions of the Board. The Board saw any Aboriginal lobby as impertinent; from its perspective, Aboriginal people had no place in any decision-making process.

The Board was now under scrutiny – not only from Aboriginal groups but from white organisations and the press as well. John Maynard suggests the 'Board … for the first time was beginning to feel the heat of the public's gaze'.[31] Newspaper reports were challenging the practices of the Board, particularly the removal of Aboriginal girls. As noted above in Chapter 6, in late 1924 several articles appeared in the press on the decline of the Aboriginal 'full-blood' population.[32] The *Sydney Morning Herald* accused the APB of accelerating the extinction of the race. The Board's policy of sending Aboriginal girls into service – and subsequent separation from their communities – resulted in these Aboriginal girls having little chance of marrying young men of their own race.[33]

The *Sydney Morning Herald* asserted that because of this separation 'many of these luckless girls must dismiss all thoughts of matrimony'. Further, while serving their apprenticeships, the girls remained entirely dependent on the Board because it held onto their money – it 'restrains [them] from going back to the bush'.[34] To be accused of contributing to the extinction of the very people in your care would have provoked, one

---

30 *APBM*, 23 October 1925, Item 1A.
31 Maynard, 'Fred Maynard and the Awakening of Aboriginal Political Consciousness', 147.
32 *Northern Star*, 26 November 1924, 12; *Sydney Morning Herald* (hereafter *SMH*), 22 April 1924, 8; *Inverell Times*, 16 December 1924, 6.
33 *SMH*, 29 October 1924, 12.
34 *SMH*, 29 October 1924, 12.

would think, some reaction from the Board. But none was forthcoming. The criticism did not appear to worry the Board; over the course of 1925, and eight Board meetings later, no mention of the article was noted.

In March 1926 the 25th annual conference of the Sydney-based Australian Natives Association (ANA) called for a Royal Commission into the 'conditions among aborigines'.[35] J.J. Moloney, ANA member and strong advocate for Aboriginal people as editor of the Newcastle's *Voice of the North*, spoke forcefully about how Aboriginal people 'have been kicked into the wilds to starve [to live] under petrol tins and old bags' and reported that 'Aboriginal boys are apprenticed to farmers at 6d a week' with the bulk held in trust until they are 21.[36] In response to Moloney's press release, Secretary Pettitt prepared a brief for Mr Lazzarini, the chief minister, to reply.[37] Mr Lazzarini's response, aired in the press, stressed that the children were not removed unless 'in cases of gross neglect' and the average credit for each apprentice was £25.[38] Most likely, he would not have been told that children were removed for many spurious reasons and would have been unaware that the Board held onto their wages well beyond the length of apprenticeships and then made them extremely difficult to retrieve.[39]

More pressure was applied on the Board when the ANA called on the federal government to appoint Sir John Murray as a permanent commissioner to replace all existing authorities and 'to arrange for the repatriation of the Australian people upon their own land'.[40] In May 1927, Mr J.J. Moloney again petitioned the Board about the maltreatment of Aborigines across the state.[41]

---

35 The ANA was formed in Melbourne in 1871 and membership was restricted to white males born in Australia; the New South Wales chapter was formed in 1900 and in 1926 it boasted 11,031 financial members and 73 branches across the state. *The Age* (Melbourne), 8 March 1926, 10.
36 *Daily Examiner*, 8 March 1926, 5.
37 *APBM*, 19 March 1926, Item 2. Carlo Lazzarini (Labor) was appointed June 1925.
38 *Daily Examiner*, 30 March 1926, 5.
39 Haskins, *One Bright Spot*, 118–19 and 160–61.
40 Letter from ANA to Jack Lang, 31 July 1925, Premiers Department Correspondence (hereafter PDC), 1927, A27/915, Box 9/1957, Item A26/1251, State Records of New South Wales (hereafter SRNSW). Sir John Murray was the colonial administrator in New Guinea: adb.anu.edu.au/biography/murray-sir-john-hubert-plunkett-7711.
41 *APBM*, 13 May 1927, Item 3.

The July 1927 APB meeting dealt with a formal communication from the premier and the colonial secretary regarding the proposal for a Royal Commission into the status and general condition 'of aborigines including half-castes throughout Australia'. The Board's response was arrogant. It politely dismissed the idea; it believed the

> control and care of the Aborigines in NSW has been successful as circumstances would admit, and having in view the time and trouble involved the Board doubts that the appointment of a commission to inquire is called for, so far as this state is concerned.[42]

Applying further pressure, Fred Maynard wrote to Premier J.T. Lang in May 1927, petitioning for 'early alteration to the laws relating to aboriginals'. He requested that capable Aboriginal people to be given land, that Aboriginal family life to be held sacred, that the old and infirm to be cared for and that a management Board be comprised of 'capable educated Aboriginals' under a chair appointed by the government.[43] The matter was referred to the APB. E.B. Harkness replied to Maynard in patronising tones and stated that all proposals were 'impracticable'. Harkness claimed that the Board only intervened regarding children if their parents did not organise apprentice positions. Ignoring the obvious racial and financial barriers, he suggested that Aboriginal people were free to make their own land purchases if they so desired.[44] Maynard persisted. He wrote to the premier and referred to the response he received from Harkness. Maynard informed the premier that Harkness 'appears to be perfectly satisfied with the inference of inferiority of our people, but we accept no condition of inferiority'. Maynard stressed that, at the time of 'invasion by Europeans … we called no man "master" and we had no king', but since then, 'we have accepted your system of government and are now striving to obtain full recognition of our citizen rights on terms of absolute equality with all other people in our own land'. Maynard reminded the premier of the calls from London and elsewhere for a Royal Commission to inquire into the 'conditions under which the native people live in this State'.[45]

---

42 *APBM*, 8 July 1927, Item 2.
43 Letter from Maynard to Lang, 28 May 1927, PDC, A903-1342, Box 9/1957, Item A27/3319 (SRNSW).
44 Letter from E.B. Harkness to Fred Maynard, 23 September 1927, PDC, 1927, A903-1342, Box 9/1957, Item A27/3319 (SRNSW).
45 Letter from Fred Maynard to Premier J.T. Lang, 3 October 1927, PDC, 1927, A903-1342, Box 9/1957, Item A27/3319 (SRNSW).

Late in 1927, E.B. Harkness provided advice to the chief minister on Maynard:

> From personal knowledge of the writer (F. G. Maynard) combined with a recognition of the difficulties inseparable from the aborigine question, I have no hesitation in recording the view that the representations of Mr Maynard, who is not altogether a disinterested party, should not be allowed to unduly occupy the Premier's time. Mr Maynard is a full blooded black (either American or South African) whose voluble manner and illogical views are more likely to disturb the Australian aborigines than achieve for them improvement of conditions.[46]

In his clear attempt to discredit Maynard, Harkness misleads on Maynard's descent, and imputes ulterior motives to create unrest. John Maynard asserts, '[Fred Maynard] … became the central focus of the Board's vicious attacks as they attempted to destabilise the support and momentum that the AAPA had generated'.[47] The Board even tried to implicate him in a sexual scandal when it published a letter Maynard had written to an Aboriginal girl who had been sexually abused in her apprenticeship situation at Angledool. Maynard sought the 'particulars of the assault' from the girl in order that the perpetrator could be prosecuted. The Board doubted his intentions and published the letter to discredit him. It had the reverse affect; Maynard's reputation, once he had exposed the supervisory neglect of the Board, was enhanced.[48] However, the constant harassment by the police – instigated by the Board – wore Maynard down. His children agree that threats were made against their father and themselves.[49] In Sydney, Maynard kept his family close and virtually went underground. He was frightened to leave his children alone with their mother. His son Mervyn was picked up and threatened by the police in Bankstown. Jack Horner notes that Fred Maynard and his group 'were hounded by the police officer' acting for the Protection Board.[50] Other AAPA members went to ground for fear of reprisals against their children.[51] In the early 1930s, while he was working on the wharves, Fred Maynard fell victim to a large container accident under suspicious

---

46   Harkness advice on Maynard, 9 November 1927, PDC, 1927, A903-1342, Box 9/1957, Item A27/6809 (SRNSW).
47   Maynard, 'Fred Maynard and the Awakening of Aboriginal Political Consciousness', 226.
48   Maynard, 'Fred Maynard and the Australian Aboriginal Progressive Association (AAPA)', 7.
49   Maynard, 'Fred Maynard and the Australian Aboriginal Progressive Association (AAPA)', 11.
50   Horner, *Bill Ferguson*, 27.
51   Maynard, 'Fred Maynard and the Awakening of Aboriginal Political Consciousness', 333–34.

circumstances. Fred spent six months in hospital. With his ongoing medical problems and diabetes he could not survive the amputation of his leg and he passed away in 1946.[52]

With Maynard and his group driven underground, the Board had a short reprieve from public attack. Then, in 1934, William Cooper – who formed the Australian Aborigines League (AAL) in 1932 – sought Board permission to secure signatures for a petition to the Australian Government regarding the 'betterment of Aborigines'. Yorta Yorta man William Cooper was born in 1861 at the junction of the Murray and Goulburn rivers. He is best known for his 1887 petition to the governor of New South Wales seeking 100 acres of land for every Aboriginal man 'capable of and wishing to farm himself'. He organised another petition in September 1933 to King George V to prevent the extinction of the Australian Aborigines and to grant them representation in the Federal Parliament.[53] Surprisingly, the Board had no direct objection to Cooper seeking signatures for a petition but requested that 'nothing is done to cause dissatisfaction among the Aborigines residing on the Board's stations and reserves'.[54]

Over the next three years, a steady stream of interested parties sought policy change in Aboriginal affairs. Wiradjuri man William Ferguson – born in 1882 at Waddai, Darlington Point, schooled at the Warangesda Aboriginal station, and later a shearer and shed-organiser for the Australian Workers Union – became a persistent campaigner for Aboriginal rights.[55] Ferguson had identified the problem at a Christmas gathering in 1923:

> That Board in Sydney has a complete control over us; they can do anything. One day we will have a full inquiry into these activities of the Protection Board … I have been a member of the Labor Party since 1916 … I have my faith in the Labor movement to help us … but we need to collect more information about this Board.[56]

---

52 Maynard, 'Fred Maynard and the Awakening of Aboriginal Political Consciousness', 345–47.
53 Markus, *Blood from a Stone*, 7. See also Attwood and Markus, *Thinking Black*, 27.
54 *APBM*, 13 April 1934, Item 14.
55 Horner, 'Ferguson, William (Bill) (1882–1950)'. See also Horner, *Bill Ferguson*, Chapter 1.
56 Horner, *Bill Ferguson*, 21.

Nursing sister Helen Baillie had formed the Aboriginal Fellowship Group in 1932, which focused on the education of the broader community in the 'right understanding of these natives'. Baillie was also connected with the Victorian Aboriginal Group, the Association for the Protection of Native Races in Sydney and the Aborigines Protection Society in London.[57] Baillie became a life member of the AAL and provided transport for many of its members involved in the Day of Mourning in January 1938.[58] In March 1935, William Ferguson and Helen Baillie sought permission by the chair of the Board to visit the reserves and stations.[59]

Figure 8.2: William John MacKay.
Source: Lindsay, *True Blue*, 143.

Around the time of Ferguson and Baillie's request to visit the stations and reserves, police commissioner William John MacKay (Figure 8.2) took over from Walter Henry Childs as chair of the Board. The dour Scotsman MacKay had policing in his blood. The son of a Glaswegian police inspector, he migrated to Sydney in 1910, joined the New South Wales police and rose rapidly through the ranks to lead the Darlinghurst division. During the Depression he was responsible for directing police action towards the unions' political unrest and in suppressing the New Guard; he became increasingly involved in 'political surveillance as unemployment and dissent' became more widespread.[60] Although one of the Force's 'great reformers', he was criticised for his autocratic methods. He fell out badly with the Police Association over a pay dispute. The Police Association's secretary, Charles Cosgrove, stated that Mr MacKay believed

---

57 Attwood, *Rights for Aborigines*, 56.
58 Egan, 'An Analysis of White Organisations', 16.
59 *APBM*, 13 March 1935, Item 10. William Cooper had been granted permission a year earlier but only on condition 'that he did not cause dissatisfaction among the Aborigines', *APBM*, 13 April 1934, Item 14. Sometime after April 1934, permission was required from the Board chair.
60 Cain, 'MacKay, William John (1885–1948)'.

'he should have complete control over the police force without any right of appeal against any decision'.[61] The pay dispute worsened, and MacKay had Cosgrove sacked. But MacKay had overstepped; colonial secretary Bill Sheehan likened MacKay's actions as akin to 'principles that have been introduced under the Gestapo of Hitler and his puppet Mussolini'.[62] Nevertheless, MacKay held his job.

MacKay was clearly a formidable character. It is hard to imagine that as Board chair he would have welcomed any intervention or advice from Aboriginal 'agitators' or interfering white humanitarians. Campaigner Joan Kingsley-Strack had a run-in with MacKay over police reluctance to fully investigate assault and stalking allegations of one of her Aboriginal domestic servants. The altercation demonstrated MacKay's quick temper and his patronising and dismissive attitude to outspoken women. He demanded that she not 'come in here *insisting* on anything'. The exchange descended into a 'shouting match' leaving Mrs Kinglsey-Strack severely shaken but not defeated. She said she would fight to the end for legal protection of the girl. MacKay suggested she would need a lot of money for a lawyer.[63]

In December 1935, six months after MacKay took over the chair of the Board, he wrote to the Colonial Secretary's Department seeking the relocation of all APB staff to his office. He sought to consolidate the Board's administration under his immediate control. In keeping with his dictatorial style, he advised the colonial secretary that, in the interests of efficiency and economy, the

> Secretary of the Board and his staff [should] be more closely under my personal supervision … [and it would be] much better if the staff of six officers were located at Police Headquarters where clerical work will be absorbed in the routine of the Department and the staff and work be subject to the same systematic oversight and control as is applied to the staff of this office.[64]

However, Pettitt and his clerical team did not move into the Police Department. Three months later, it appeared that MacKay had pulled back from this level of oversight of Board matters. In a letter to Mr Harkness,

---

61 Lindsay, *True Blue: 150 Years of Service*, 142.
62 Lindsay, *True Blue: 150 Years of Service*, 149.
63 Haskins, *One Bright Spot*, 124–26.
64 Letter from MacKay to Under-Secretary to the Colonial Secretary's Department, 10 December 1935, Colonial Secretary's In-Letters (hereafter CSIL), 1937, 9/2420, Item 68517/2 (SRNSW).

MacKay queried the need for him to sign the large volume of Protection Board correspondence and gave his opinion that it did not 'warrant its transmission from the Chief Secretary's building to this Department and back again'. He requested of Harkness to 'relieve [him] of the necessity of signing quite a number of papers of a purely routine character'.[65] Harkness said he 'was delighted to fall into line with the suggestion'. He assured MacKay that all papers would be 'safely and expeditiously dealt with' and that the chair 'will not be "blind-sided" in any case'.[66] A follow-up note in May 1936 from Harkness stated that all administrative work of the APB seemed to be 'proceeding smoothly'.[67] This administrative change further compounded the disconnection between Board activities and Board members.

In late 1936 and early 1937, pressure on the Board was mounting from many directions. Indirect pressure came in November 1936 in the form of an invitation from the Australian Government to its proposed 1937 national meeting on Aboriginal affairs. In a typical demonstration of its indifference, the Board was reticent to attend.[68] The notion of a national conference was a sign that the whole country was now beginning to focus on Aboriginal affairs. It would be the first time that all the states would gather to discuss Aboriginal policy. Other pressures soon followed. In December 1936, Professor A.P. Elkin and Mrs Caroline Tennant Kelly from the anthropology department at Sydney University attended a Board meeting with various proposals 'in connection with the control of aborigines'. After a lengthy discussion, the APB decided to appoint a subcommittee to consult with Elkin and Kelly.[69] A month later the APB received advice that William Cooper's AAL was meeting the premier of Victoria with the purpose of 'urging improvement to the conditions' at the New South Wales Aboriginal Station at Cumeroogunga.[70] And, during the early months of 1937, William Ferguson (having secured permission) undertook visits to six Aboriginal stations.[71] He recorded inadequate schooling, the brutal treatment by managers, the withholding of rations as punishment, regular expulsions and the receipt of wages well under

---

65   Letter from MacKay to Harkness, 16 March 1936, CSIL, 1936, 12/7533, Item S.897/2 (SRNSW).
66   Letter from Harkness to MacKay, 20 March 1936, CSIL, 1936, 12/7533, Item S.897/2 (SRNSW).
67   Internal note from Harkness, 6 May 1936, CSIL, 1936, 12/7533 (no item number) (SRNSW).
68   *APBM*, 4 November 1936, Item 4.
69   *APBM*, 2 December 1936, Item 3.
70   *APBM*, 6 January 1937, Item 14.
71   Horner, *Bill Ferguson*, 34–35.

the award rate. Ferguson was convinced that the time had come to 'fight openly at last'.[72] He organised a public meeting at the Masonic Hall in Dubbo, held 27 June 1937, and successfully passed the following motion:

> That the meeting form an Aborigines' Progressive Association, with the object of advocating the abolition of the Aborigines protection board, and full citizen rights for Aborigines, with direct representation in parliament similar to that of the New Zealand Maoris.[73]

Michael Sawtell, a member of the Association for the Protection of Native Races, concluded by August 1937 that the APB was 'an anachronism' and highlighted a major failing of the Board. He observed that

> country newspapers were full of the details of the shameful and unjust manner in which the board treats the aborigines. The main cause of all this unjust and unsympathetic treatment is that the Board members are busy government officials, who have neither the time nor perhaps the inclination to study the aborigines' way of life.[74]

In the same month the Reverend Canon J. Needham, chair of Australian Board of Missions, registered his complaints regarding the Board's policies. Needham referred to allegations that Board managers were 'withholding' rations as discipline. The Board offered to meet with Needham to discuss his complaints and quickly issued a directive to all managers that under no circumstances 'should aborigines be deprived of rations as a means of punishment'.[75] In November 1937, William Ferguson called on the Board to stop the apprenticing of Aboriginal boys and girls, discontinue the expulsions of Aboriginal people from the reserves and stations and provide cash to Aboriginal women for their endowment payment. Pettitt informed Ferguson that his demands could not be actioned.[76] The calls for change had reached fever pitch and it was the New South Wales Parliament that took the initiative.

---

72   Horner, *Bill Ferguson*, 35.
73   Horner, *Bill Ferguson*, 37.
74   *Labor Daily* (Sydney), 27 August 1937, 6.
75   *APBM*, 5 August 1937, Item 16; 1 September 1937, Item 1.
76   *APBM*, 3 November 1937.

A Select Committee inquiry into the APB

Mark Davidson (Figure 8.3), a staunch Labor man, had been 'everything from a deckhand to a farm worker, miner, tank sinker and shearer'.[77] He was elected to state parliament in 1918 to represent the huge electorate of Cobar that stretched from the northern and western borders of the state to Cobar and Nyngan. Davidson believed that Aboriginal people should be left alone and not made to 'conform to European conditions of life', but he also believed that they should be 'protected from exploitation' and cared for.[78] By 1936 he was a bitter critic of the Board. By law, Aborigines were debarred from the Old Age Pension and the Maternity Allowance because they received rations from the government, but Davidson claimed the 'meat ration was never issued'.[79]

Figure 8.3: Mark Davidson.
Source: Parliamentary Archives, NSW Parliament Collection (DavidsonMA – 25P-1920).

Davidson was also a friend of William Ferguson. Both had discussed the abolition of the Board. Mr Roy Brain, the manager at Brewarrina, had been dismissed by the Board from his position on 30 November 1936.[80] Neither man liked Brain, nor did the Aboriginal people of Brewarrina. But Davidson and Ferguson knew that Brain was ready to unload on the Board because he was unable to seek an appeal for his dismissal. Both men saw a possible *cause célèbre* to pressure the Board. Davidson and Ferguson decided that an inquiry into the Board, with Brain giving evidence, could work in their favour.[81]

---

77 Horner, *Bill Ferguson*, 12.
78 NSW, *Parliamentary Debates*, Legislative Assembly 18 June 1936, 4750 (Mark Davidson).
79 Read, *A Hundred Years War*, 86.
80 *SMH*, 15 September 1937, 10.
81 Horner, *Bill Ferguson*, 42. See also Parry, 'Such a Longing', 306.

Davidson put a motion to the Legislative Assembly to establish a Select Committee into the administration and practices of the Aborigines Protection Board. He proposed:

> I am submitting this motion because I have received numerous complaints from various mission stations concerning the treatment that has been meted out to what remain of the natives of this country.[82]

Davidson remained on his feet, uninterrupted (apart from one question), for 45 minutes. He explained that the managers of stations, who had to double as the teacher, were often not sufficiently trained, that the rationing was inadequate and that the accommodation was in many cases unsuitable. He cited a recent transfer of Aboriginal people to Menindee where the temperatures were 110 or 112 degrees[83] and the Aboriginal people had 'to live in tin huts like sardines'.[84] Davidson argued that the Board, 'owing to want of wisdom or lack of knowledge of the customs of these people' forced different Aboriginal 'tribes' together as when the Goodooga Aboriginal people had to move to Brewarrina.[85] He raised the recent dismissal of the manager at Brewarrina, Mr Brain. He acknowledged he was not privy to all the facts but felt there had been an injustice in that Mr Brain had not been allowed to defend himself before the Board. He was at a loss to know why the police commissioner was the chair of the Board and questioned whether the Board ever met, as it was always tardy in its response to any enquiry. He described the 'indenturing of Aborigines as altogether wrong' and stated that it should be abolished and that Aboriginal people should receive the same wages for the same work as 'any other section of the community'.[86] He alerted members to the fact that some Aboriginal people had been working plots of land for years and then had them revoked because white people now wanted the

---

82 NSW, *Parliamentary Debates*, Legislative Assembly, 9 November 1937, 1496 (Mark Davidson).
83 Fahrenheit: about 43 to 44 degrees Celsius.
84 NSW, *Parliamentary Debates*, Legislative Assembly, 9 November 1937, 1496–97 (Mark Davison).
85 NSW, *Parliamentary Debates*, Legislative Assembly, 9 November 1937, 1498 (Mark Davidson). Davidson did not provide a date or any other details about the Goodooga removals, but several Aboriginal groups were forced to Brewarrina Aboriginal Station. The first group, around 20 Wailwan Murris from Quambone just south-east of Brewarrina, moved in 1935. The next group, over 100 mainly Yuwalaraay from Angledool to the north-east, were removed in 1936. In 1938 the whole Wangkumara population of 130 from Tibooburra were sent to Menindee, but the Menindee white residents complained, and the Board moved them to Brewarrina. These forced removals caused severe hardship for these communities and placed enormous pressure on the Brewarrina Aboriginal Station. See Goodall, *Invasion to Embassy*, 2008, 241–60.
86 NSW, *Parliamentary Debates*, Legislative Assembly, 9 November 1937, 1498 (Mark Davidson).

land. Ahead of his time, he sought special courts for Aboriginal people as, presently, they did not understand the court processes and 'in all probability the magistrate does not understand them'. His concluding remarks were unambiguous:

> I consider that the Board should be reconstituted, if not abolished. We should aim at the abolition of the so called homes and missions, which are exterminating the aboriginal race by segregating the sexes and sending the girls to domestic slavery.[87]

Mr Henry Bate, member for the South Coast and APB member, endeavoured to set the record straight by informing the Assembly that the Board tried very hard to look after Aboriginal people. He stressed that the Board met regularly 'once a month' and that it 'dealt with difficult questions' and contended that the Board should not be reconstituted.[88] He claimed that the Board 'asks that aboriginal children be allowed' into local public schools, but 'the first people to make an outcry are the local parents'.[89] He explained the position with Mr Brain at Brewarrina, insisting he had to be removed for gross negligence, providing details to which Davidson had not been privy.[90] After a question from opposition leader Mr Jack Lang concerning the recent input from Sydney University's anthropological professor E.P. Elkin, Bate became agitated and stated that Elkin wanted to take the Aboriginal people 'back to their totemic ideas'. Bate declared he knew the Aboriginal people far better than Elkin. He offered to 'step outside' with Lang for 10 minutes to fully brief him on the 'intervention of the Chair of Anthropology'.[91] In his closing remarks there is a plea for understanding and a hint of exasperation:

> We have to deal with their health, education, and employment the same as with other people. We hear people say we took their country from them in the first place, and we should give it back. We made mistakes in the beginning and a desperate effort is now being made to help them.[92]

---

87 NSW, *Parliamentary Debates*, Legislative Assembly, 9 November 1937, 1501 (Mark Davidson).
88 NSW, *Parliamentary Debates*, Legislative Assembly, 9 November 1937, 1502 (Henry Bate).
89 NSW, *Parliamentary Debates*, Legislative Assembly, 9 November 1937, 1503 (Henry Bate).
90 NSW, *Parliamentary Debates*, Legislative Assembly, 9 November 1937, 1507 (Henry Bate).
91 NSW, *Parliamentary Debates*, Legislative Assembly, 9 November 1937, 1508 (Henry Bate).
92 NSW, *Parliamentary Debates*, Legislative Assembly, 9 November 1937, 1508 (Henry Bate).

Bate received support from Mr George Edward Ardill (the son of the former Board member George E. Ardill), who was the member for Yass and a Board member. George Ardill (Jr) (Figure 8.4) joined the Board at the end of 1935. He rose to oppose the motion on the basis that there was no good reason for it. Ardill claimed that the £52,000 allocation to the Board to provide education, housing, clothing, food and ordinary amenities was inadequate, and urged the members opposite to argue not for an inquiry, but for more funds. Ardill claimed that the Board was trying to 'lift them economically … and to lift them politically' so they wouldn't 'merely be recipients of charity'. He defended the Board's policy of retaining apprentice wages in trust and providing endowment moneys in coupons and not cash.[93]

Figure 8.4: George Edward Ardill.
Source: Parliamentary Archives, NSW Parliament Collection (ArdillGE-29P-1930).

The motion was put. William Ferguson had travelled from Dubbo to witness the debate from the gallery.[94] He must have been pleased when, to the government's chagrin, it was passed by the slim majority of 29 to 27. The government had not expected it to pass. Government members had anticipated there would be an adjournment at the end of the debate, but, instead, it went straight to the vote and 'many Government members were missing'.[95] Government numbers on the floor were further reduced by three, when it was realised that regulations disallowed members of the APB to vote. Bate, Ardill and member for Raleigh Roy Stanley Vincent (all APB members) were therefore barred from voting.

---

93 NSW, *Parliamentary Debates*, Legislative Assembly, 9 November 1937, 1512–14 (George Ardill).
94 Horner, *Bill Ferguson*, 47.
95 *Northern Star*, 10 November 1937, 6.

Davidson and Ferguson had got their inquiry. The committee comprised: Captain Chaffey United Australia Party (UAP); C.E. Bennett (UAP); Major A.D. Reid (UAP); Mr Wilson (UAP); Mr E.M. Horsington (ALP); Mr J.M. Tully (ALP); Mr Dunn (ALP); Mr Davidson (ALP); and Dr Fleck (ALP). It began deliberations on 17 November 1937 and Aboriginal activists William Ferguson, Pearl Gibbs and Jack Patten were present at the opening session in anticipation that the inquiry would 'change their lives'.[96] Also present was Joan Kingsley-Strack, who had a chat with Ferguson before the committee meeting. Her diary records:

> the truth will be brought forth showing what a farce the Board is and the scandalous dishonesty right through its dealings with these people ... I sat down beside Mr Ferguson the half-caste who is organising his people throughout NSW to defend themselves and demand the abolishment of the APB. I sat and talked with him for some time and some Aboriginal men and women from La Perouse.[97]

Thirteen witnesses were called, and 3,952 questions asked. No counsel for witnesses was allowed as the 'inquiry might be unduly delayed'.[98] All committee members could ask questions of witnesses, but some witnesses could cross-examine as well. Witnesses called included: Aboriginal spokesperson William Ferguson; Mrs Caroline Kelly from the Department of Anthropology at Sydney University; A.C. Pettitt from the Board; Roy Brain, the ex-manager of the Brewarrina Station; Edith Brain, nurse and matron at Brewarrina; three station managers: James Danvers, Gordon Milne and Edwin Dalley; Agnes Park, wife of the manager at Menindee; Isabel Pratt, a nursing sister; William Morley, Congregational minister and longstanding member of the Association for the Protection of Native Races (APNR); and Aboriginal labourers Monty Tickle and Lindsay Grant. Unfortunately, due to the unexpected early termination of the inquiry, many more witnesses were unable to be called, including Aboriginal activists Jack Patten and Pearl Gibbs, Michael Sawtell (APNR) and Mrs Joan Kingsley-Strack, who could have provided much information on the Aboriginal girls in domestic service.[99] Other Aboriginal men expecting to make contributions were Jack Kinchela, Frank Roberts, Arthur Gayton, Jim Barker, Selwyn Briggs and Archie Reid.[100]

---

96 Horner, *Bill Ferguson*, 48.
97 Diaries, 15/16 November 1937, Joan Kingsley-Strack Papers, MS 9551, Series 2, Folder 10, National Library of Australia (hereafter NLA).
98 *SMH*, 23 November 1937, 12.
99 Horner, *Bill Ferguson*, 53.
100 Horner, *Bill Ferguson*, 53.

The first week of sittings was marred by numerous adjournments, repetition and personal agendas. The Sydney newspaper *Truth*, although not an entirely reliable source, was scathing of the initial proceedings. It reported that Ferguson and Patten, although earnest in their efforts, required help to properly cross-examine. It alleged that the real problems confronting the Aboriginal people were not being addressed, and implored: 'Let the natives tell their story'.[101] It also criticised the committee for a number of adjournments due to the absence of a quorum, and noted that while Mark Davidson was taking his role seriously, the same could not be said of others who 'did not listen to all the questions or answers being too busy attending to their private and parliamentary correspondence'. *Truth* pointed out that some answers were too long and the 'activities of the whole week could easily have been packed into one business morning'.[102] On Thursday, 2 December, the sitting had to be cancelled and a 'great deal of inconvenience was caused to the aborigines who were in attendance'.[103] William Ferguson said that he would have to return to Dubbo and 'wait until he was informed of the next sitting'.[104]

The committee stumbled through its 13 witnesses without a coherent strategy. Instead of canvassing a broad cross-section of Board policies as they affected Aboriginal people, the inquiry focused on a more localised, combative, personal and accusative approach. Considering the circumstances in which the committee was formed it was always going to be a very loaded inquiry.

Yet, for all its failings, it revealed much. First, the gross negligence and malpractice of some managers were exposed. The inquiry showed that the ex-manager of Brewarrina, Mr Brain, had not opened the station school for some months, and 'many of the mothers complained at the absence of education for their children'. A visit to the schoolroom, by Board officers, saw the 'floor littered with pupils' exercise books'.[105] His negligence was demonstrated by his failure to reply to no less than 33 communications by the Board.[106] Although not part of the inquiry, Jimmie Barker, an

---

101 *Truth*, 28 November 1937, 21.
102 *Truth*, 28 November 1937, 21.
103 *Truth*, 5 December 1937, 39.
104 *Sun*, 17 December 1937, 3.
105 *Select Committee on Administration of Aborigines Protection Board, Proceedings of the Committee, Minutes of Evidence and Exhibits*, NSW Parliamentary Papers, Session 1938–40, Vol. 7, 34 (hereafter *Select Committee, 1938–40*).
106 Parry, 'Such a Longing', 306.

Aboriginal man who had worked on Brewarrina station for 21 years, recalled that Brain 'was a cruel man; he faked cheques and was merciless with his baton'. Barker recorded that Brain's 'dishonesty was flagrant'. He had regularly banked, for himself, war pension cheques belonging to an old Aboriginal woman whose husband who was killed in 1916; there was 'little doubt that he had been appropriating money from the residents'.[107] Witness E.J. Dalley, the current manager of Brewarrina, had to defend accusations that his son, aged 21, had been sexually interfering with girls in the dormitory at the station.[108]

Second, William Ferguson stated that endowment money for Aboriginal mothers, particularly those on the stations and reserves, was not given in cash but through 'an order on a storekeeper' and that the mothers must buy what was available, from only that person. Ferguson argued that the mothers should receive a cash payment like others in the community.[109] Mr Morley, from the APNR, also raised concerns about the misuse of endowment funds.[110] In a damning admission, Secretary Pettitt stated that some of the endowment money was withheld and used for 'timber and iron to make further additions to houses not owned by the natives but the Board' – a clear misuse of money earmarked for Aboriginal mothers.[111]

Third, testimony exposed the conditions and life under which Aboriginal people lived on the stations and reserves. The evidence from Sister Pratt, who had worked at Walcha, Taree, Brewarrina, Cumeroogunga and Angledool, unmasked the endemic problem of trachoma, which occurred in conditions of overcrowding and poor sanitation.[112] Sister Pratt also reported that trachoma was exacerbated by the lack of vegetables and the 'dust, heat and flies'; and she claimed the fact that the 'board refused to provide hot water for bathing'.[113] Aboriginal man Lindsay Gordon Grant, while a resident at the Cowra Aboriginal station, stated that many residents complained of inadequate rations, substandard housing and overcrowding. On a personal note, he accused the Board of stopping him from working 'relief work' because the Board felt 'that we dark people did not like to work'.[114]

---

107 Matthews (as told to), *The Two Worlds of Jimmie Barker*, 157–58.
108 *Select Committee, 1938–40*, 108.
109 William Ferguson, *Select Committee, 1938–40*, 61, Question 1647.
110 William Morley, *Select Committee, 1938–40*, 71.
111 W.C. Pettitt, *Select Committee, 1938–40*, 48, Question 1438.
112 Sister Pratt, *Select Committee, 1938–40*, 2–4.
113 Quoted in Parry, 'Such a Longing', 307.
114 Lindsay Gordon Grant, *Select Committee, 1938–40*, 69–70.

One incident laid bare the level of corruption that occurred on these Aboriginal stations particularly clearly. Gordon Milne had been assistant manager to James Danvers at Cumeroogunga Aboriginal station when a fire broke out in a station hut killing a young Aboriginal girl. Danvers wrote to Milne instructing him to claim £80 from the Board for the replacement of the hut – an amount vastly inflated from the estimated £10 replacement cost. Danvers suggested the extra money could be spent on renovations to Milne's verandah.[115] 'Milne was horrified, telling the Inquiry that it was "an awful thing" to make money out of an incident that had destroyed a man's home and his only remaining child'.[116] Danvers indicated, in the letter, that the idea to inflate that cost of the rebuild came from the Board's inspector Ernest Smithers.[117] Smithers denied all wrongdoing and was instructed to investigate. Accusations swirled between the three men. Some months later, when Milne complained to the Board about misuse of station timber by the new manager Arthur J. McQuiggan, Smithers was sent to investigate. Milne was subsequently sacked as assistant manager without notice or appeal.[118] Personalities, retribution and power politics seemed very much in play. Jack Horner wrote that the committee was 'very sceptical' about the events of the fire incident.[119]

The committee lurched towards its final meeting held on 17 February 1938, but the only committee member in attendance was Mr Davidson and the sole witness was Mrs Caroline Kelly.[120] However, also present were 38 women from various organisations, and several clergymen keen to demonstrate their commitment to improving the conditions for Aboriginal people. After a brief, rousing speech by Davidson they all adjourned to the Feminist Club to 'continue and extend the good work the committee had done' and to discuss further strategies.[121] At the reconvened meeting, William Morley (APNR) spoke to a motion that deplored the 'farcical nature of the Select Committee proceedings' and posited that Premier Stevens had 'blocked every effort to get something done' on the behalf of Aboriginal people.[122]

---

115 James Danvers, *Select Committee, 1938–40*, 89.
116 Davis, *Australian Settler Colonialism*, 109.
117 James Danvers, *Select Committee, 1938–40*, 89.
118 Ernest Smithers, *Select Committee, 1938–40*, 87.
119 Horner, *Bill Ferguson*, 52.
120 Captain Frank Chaffey – as colonial secretary, the most senior member of the committee – did not attend one meeting. *Select Committee, 1938–40*, analysis of committee members represented at all sessions, 1–124.
121 *Workers' Weekly*, 22 February 1938, 2.
122 *Workers' Weekly*, 22 February 1938, 2.

The Inquiry failed to report.[123] Alan Duncan suggests that it was more of a 'witch-hunt' on the behaviour of individual Board officers than an examination of general policy.[124]

A crumbling veneer

On 26 January 1938, one day after the Board held its 'managers conference' that warned of conspiracies and spies, 100 Aboriginal people gathered at Australia House at 120 Elizabeth Street in Sydney to protest directly against the Board and call for citizenship rights. One may have thought this would have unsettled the Board, but it did not. The upcoming protest was noted in the Board minutes but it came and went without further Board comment.[125]

In terms of Aboriginal activism, it was a watershed moment. Russell McGregor asserts the Day of Mourning protest (Figures 8.5 and 8.6) signalled the call for 'Aboriginal citizenship' and it was 'Aboriginal activists who first made this call loudly' on 26 January.[126] Only Aboriginal people were supposed to attend, but two policemen insisted that they be present and took up a position at the back of the meeting.[127] At the protest meeting Jack Patten and William Ferguson launched their now-famous pamphlet *Aborigines Claim Citizen's Rights!* Their message to the Board and to the country was brutally honest and clear. Aboriginal people wanted equality, inclusion and respect, and they asked the nation to 'be proud of the Australian Aboriginal, and to take his hand in friendship'.[128]

---

123 Horner, *Bill Ferguson*, 51; Goodall, *Invasion to Embassy*, 2008, 275.
124 Duncan, 'A Survey of the Education of Aborigines in New South Wales', 335.
125 *APBM*, 5 January 1938, Item 11: Billhead advertising: 'Day of Morning' to be held on Wednesday 26 January under the auspices of the Aborigines Progressive Association. The minutes recorded: 'Seen'. It was never mentioned again.
126 McGregor, *Indifferent Inclusion*, 34. For a comprehensive coverage of events leading up to the Day of Mourning see Attwood, *Rights of Aborigines*, 54–78; see also Horner, *Bill Ferguson,* 56–67; and Attwood and Markus, *Thinking Black*, 18–24.
127 Egan, *Neither Amity nor Kindness*, 151–52.
128 Patten and Ferguson, *Aborigines Claim Citizen Rights!*, 7.

8. WINDS OF CHANGE

Figure 8.5: The Day of Mourning.

From left to right: William Ferguson, Jack Kinchela, Helen Grosvenor, Selina Patten, Louise Ingram (holding Ollie Ingram), Jack Patten; children in front, Abe Ingram, Esther Ingram, Neno Williams and Phillip Ingram.

Source: Reference code: 423597, IE Number: IE3157975. Mitchell Library, State Library New South Wales.

Figure 8.6: Day of Mourning.

From left to right: Tom Foster, Jack Kinchela (partly obscured), Doug Nicholls, William Cooper and Jack Patten.

Source: Reference code: 423597, IE Number: IE3157975. Mitchell Library, State Library New South Wales.

The strong words in their seven-page pamphlet chronicled a tragic history of dispossession, neglect, exclusion, punitive policies and '150 years of misery and degradation' on the sesquicentennial celebrations in 1938. This should have caught the attention of the APB, but it did not. At the February Board meeting, a report of the 150-year celebrations was tabled but no response recorded. The Board remained resistant to change. At the same Board meeting, William Ferguson's second request to visit the reserves and stations was flatly rejected.[129]

It was not Aboriginal voices that finally shook the Board, but the words of the deputy premier, M.F. Bruxner. The tipping point came six weeks later at Wagga Wagga. On 12 March 1938 Bruxner, leader of the United Country Party of New South Wales, made a significant policy speech. He touched on Aboriginal affairs asserting there should be a 'new deal for aborigines and improved machinery of native administration'.[130] The Board minutes reveal that he said a good deal more. He accused the Board of neglect and advised that it was the government's intention to appoint a 'permanent protector of aborigines': a man of 'breed and sympathetic outlook' who would be assisted by an advisory committee.[131] The Board was indignant. On 6 April 1938, concerned about the allegations of 'neglect', it forwarded the following letter to the premier:

> If the remark has reference to the alleged neglect on the part of the Board then the Board desire to bring under the notice of the Minister the fact that for many years past successive Governments have failed to provide the Board with the funds necessary to carry out the plans of the Board for the education and welfare of the aborigines, and other phases of this most complex and difficult sociological problem, and in its opinion the criticism is therefore unwarranted.[132]

The Board also regarded the Bruxner proposal as 'a direct reflection on the ability, capacity and sympathy of the Board'. Five members – including the chair and vice-chair – offered their resignation if it was the government's intention to follow Bruxner's suggestion.[133]

---

129 *APBM*, 2 February 1938, Items 2 and 9.
130 *Truth*, 13 March 1938, 18.
131 *Truth*, 13 March 1938, 18; more detail of the speech was reported at a Board meeting, *APBM*, 6 April 1938.
132 *APBM*, 6 April 1938 (no item numbers).
133 W.J. Mackay, chair and commissioner (previously inspector-general of police); E.B. Harkness, vice-chair; B.C. Harkness, chief inspector of public schools, Education Department; E. Sydney Morris, Director-General of Public Health; G.A. Mitchell, ex-metropolitan superintendent of police.

The Board was now under siege. On 6 June 1938 it was reported in the press that G.A. Mitchell had offered his resignation because of Bruxner's comments.[134] To calm the waters, Colonial Secretary G.C. Gollan reassured Board members that their work was 'keenly appreciated' and the matter would soon be discussed in Cabinet.[135] However, government action took a very different tack. A letter from Colonial Secretary Gollan was read out to the Board at its 8 June meeting, indicating that there would be a reconstitution of the Board. Members carried the following motion:

> We feel and resent the fact that we are carrying on without the confidence of the Government and it is imperative that the position be clarified at the earliest moment. Either the Government should reconstitute the Board as suggested from various sources or should support the Board whole-heartedly in carrying out its difficult problem on behalf of the Government.[136]

In the meantime, Mr Mitchell agreed not to insist at present upon any decision regarding his tendered resignation.[137] In June 1938, Colonial Secretary Gollan asked the Public Service Board to review the whole question of the Aborigines Protection Board.[138] The Public Service Board began its inquiry with little fuss and completed its findings on 16 August 1938.[139]

Public Service Board recommendations

In its deliberations, the Public Service Board (PSB) members visited 16 stations and reserves, and a further nine were visited by PSB inspectors. The PSB had access to all Board documents and consulted with the police, the Department of Anthropology at Sydney University, missionaries and medical officers. It also 'perused' the evidence of the Select Committee of 1937 and took account of inquiries and legislation in other states.[140]

---

134 *Daily Telegraph*, 6 June 1938, 3.
135 *Daily Telegraph*, 7 June 1938, 5.
136 *APBM*, 8 June 1938, Item 3.
137 *APBM*, 8 June 1938, Item 3.
138 Duncan, 'A Survey of the Education of Aborigines in New South Wales', 336.
139 *Aborigines Protection: Report and Recommendations of the Public Service Board of New South Wales*, 4 April 1940, 6/4501.1 (SRNSW) (hereafter *PSB Report, April 1940*).
140 *PSB Report, April 1940*, 7.

The PSB made one overarching policy recommendation. It adopted a major recommendation from the *Initial Conference of Commonwealth and State Aboriginal Authorities* in April 1937. It determined that the 'ultimate aim of the administration should be the gradual assimilation of aborigines into the economic and social life of the general community'. Interestingly, it made no distinction between 'full-blood' Aboriginal people and those with 'less of an admixture of aboriginal blood'. This omission may have been an oversight, or perhaps members may not have felt competent to comment. Perhaps because 'full-blood' numbers had been declining, they felt it did not need addressing. Or perhaps they simply let this absurd distinction go.[141] To facilitate the 'gradual assimilation', the PSB suggested that 'present policy of aggregating aborigines on stations under the immediate control of qualified persons is the proper one'. The qualified Board persons should be drawn from the Colonial Secretary's Department and the departments of health, education, police, and agriculture, and should include someone specialised in social and anthropological work.[142]

There were numerous other recommendations, all of which reflected badly on the Board. They can be condensed to five.

First, the PSB recommended that the chair of the Board would no longer be the Inspector-General (now Commissioner) of Police. The new chair would now be the under-secretary to the colonial secretary. It recommended that the police force still maintain a role on the reserves and elsewhere, but only as 'agents of the specialised body dealing with aborigines rather than as the persons in control'.[143]

Second, the PSB report picked up an inconsistency in the *Aborigines Protection (Amendment) Act 1918* (NSW). The definition of an 'aborigine' was 'any full-blood or half-caste aboriginal who is a native of Australia, and who is temporarily or permanently resident in New South Wales'. That meant that all 'quadroons' and 'octoroons' were not Aborigines under the Act and yet, as the report correctly pointed out, these people were still subject to various restrictions under the Act, such as that concerning the purchase of liquor. It recommended to extend the definition with the

---

141 By the end of June 1939, Board census figures: 'Full-bloods': 794 and 'Half and Lesser Castes': 10,144. *Protection of Aborigines: Report of the Board* (the APB Report: hereafter *APBR*) 1941–42, 2. Accessed via *Journal of the Legislative Council*, Q328.9106/7, *NSW Parliamentary Papers, Consolidated Index* (hereafter *Journal of LC*), State Library of New South Wales (hereafter SLNSW), Vol. 1, Part 2.
142 *PSB Report, April 1940*, 30 and 17 (a) and (b).
143 *PSB Report, April 1940*, 21 (B) (i).

words 'or person having apparently an admixture of aboriginal blood'.[144] This would effectively widen the Board's reach, returning it to the original definition expressed in the 1909 Act.

Third, the Department of Education would take responsibility for the education of all Aboriginal children. Separate Aboriginal schools on stations and reserves would continue but they would be staffed, over time, by qualified teachers from the Department of Education.[145] A station manager would no longer double as the teacher. Aboriginal children should be able to attend local public school but the report recognised the antipathy toward them from the white community. It proposed to set up local committees of 'public spirited citizens' to deal with the problem.[146]

Fourth, it was recommended that rations, employment opportunities, medical facilities and housing for all the residents on stations and reserves be improved; moreover, the overcrowding 'that exists on most, if not all, of stations … must be eliminated'.[147]

Fifth, the Board was criticised for its scant record keeping. It was 'rather disappointing that after such time, records of individuals, generally, are so meagre'.[148] Records of the apprentices were not complete and the follow-up left much 'to be desired'.[149] Insufficient records relating to the inmates kept at Kinchela and Cootamundra meant that there was no way of determining the success of placements.[150]

These were damning indictments on the Board. Yet, in October 1938, the Board complained to the colonial secretary:

> It is now understood that the Public Service Board by direction has reported to the Honourable Chief Secretary upon all the phases of the Board's administration … the Aborigines Protection Board wish to state quite definitely its regret at not having been afforded an opportunity of perusing the report before it was considered by

---

144 *PSB Report, April 1940*, 36 (d).
145 *PSB Report, April 1940*, 34 (9) (i).
146 *PSB Report, April 1940*, 30 (17) (d).
147 *PSB Report, April 1940*, 31–32 (2) (a); also 14 (b) (i).
148 *PSB Report, April 1940*, 12.
149 *PSB Report, April 1940*, 19.
150 *PSB Report, April 1940*, 25–26.

Cabinet ... the Government could, no doubt, have been furnished with much valuable information as an aid to it when considering such report.[151]

At the December 1938 Board meeting, E.B. Harkness resigned. There was no Board acknowledgement of his service after 23 years. At the same meeting, still trying to influence matters, the Board passed a motion seeking the transcript from the Australian Broadcasting Commission of a speech that was to be broadcast by the Aboriginal activist, Jack Patten, to ensure his statements were 'strictly in accordance with the facts'.[152]

Aboriginal people had the last say. The final incident that exposed the Board's neglect and incompetence was the well-publicised Cumeroogunga 'walk-off'. One hundred residents from the Cumeroogunga Aboriginal station left it on 3 February 1939 and crossed the Murray River into Victoria at Barmah.[153] The appointment of a series of bad managers by the Board had finally come unstuck. Arthur J. McQuiggan had been placed at Cumeroogunga in the early part of 1937 after his removal as superintendent from Kinchela Boys' Home where he had been repeatedly cautioned against 'insobriety, ill-treatment of the inmates and indebtedness to local tradespeople'.[154] The gun-toting McQuiggan unsettled the residents at Cumeroogunga. Residents feared that the station would be quarantined due to health scares and to escape the poor food and general ill-treatment, some residents moved into Victoria.[155] McQuiggan 'denied the charges of malnutrition' and downplayed the seriousness of the situation.[156] Geraldine Briggs, a resident at Cumeroogunga recalled that McQuiggan, of all the managers, was particularly nasty. He was a 'pig and everybody knew it'. He carried a revolver and made sick people sit in the back of his truck when driving to see the doctor.[157] This was a crisis for the Board. At the Board meeting of 8 February 1939, realising that

---

151 *APBM*, 5 October 1938 (no item numbers).
152 *APBM*, 7 December 1938, Item 15. For the Board still trying to cling to power, see Davis, *Australian Settler Colonialism*, 116.
153 Davis, *Australian Settler Colonialism*, 117. See also Goodall, *Invasion to Embassy*, 2008, 294–307; Attwood, *Rights for Aborigines*, 48–53; Horner, *Bill Ferguson*, 76–80.
154 Quoted in Davis, *Australian Settler Colonialism*, 109.
155 An outbreak of polio had occurred at the Station in January 1938 and an Aboriginal girl had died after being released from the hospital at Echuca. There was fear among the residents that the Station could become a closed compound. See Davis, *Australian Settler Colonialism*, 111–13; Horner, *Bill Ferguson*, 76–77.
156 Horner, *Bill Ferguson*, 77.
157 Quoted in Rintoul, *The Wailing*, 64–66.

Aboriginal activist Jack Patten had been talking to residents, the Board immediately revoked his permission to visit stations and reserves.[158] Soon after, he and his brother George were arrested for inciting the walk-off.[159]

The 'striking' residents had a good deal of support from the AAL, the Women's Temperance Union, the Young Communist league, the Australian League for Democracy and the National Australian Railways Union.[160] The APB played down the strike, suggesting an agitator had caused the problems. After six weeks, 80 residents returned on the promise of an inquiry and immediate improvements. When neither eventuated, they left the station once more.[161] The strike was finally broken when the APB convinced the Victorian Government to withhold rations to those camped at Barmah. During the Cumeroogunga crisis, in May 1939, the chair of the Board, William MacKay, resigned.

From 10 May 1939, in a transition phase until the *Aborigines Protection (Amendment) Act 1940* (NSW) formally ushered in the new Aboriginal Welfare Board, Alfred William George Lipscomb replaced MacKay as the Superintendent of Aborigines Welfare, the senior executive officer and Board member. Stanley Llewellyn Anderson (new under-secretary to the colonial secretary) replaced E.B. Harkness as vice-chair of the Board. Lipscomb, a teacher, author and graduate of Hawkesbury Agricultural College with diplomas in agriculture and dairying, immediately applied himself to his role by visiting 'every Aboriginal Station and Home … and submitted many recommendations'.[162]

The new Aborigines Welfare Board comprised: Lipscomb (Superintendent of Aborigines); Anderson (Under-Secretary to the Colonial Secretary); B.C. Harkness (Chief Inspector of Primary Schools); E. Sydney Morris (Director-General of Public Health); T.R. Schumacher (Inspector of Police); H. Bartlett (Senior Experimentalist, Department of Agriculture); Professor A.P. Elkin (Department of Anthropology, Sydney University); G.E. Ardill (MLA); H.J. Bate (MLA); and W.F. Dunn (MLA).[163] Harkness, Morris, Bate and Ardill survived the restructure and provided

---

158 *APBM*, 8 February 1939, Item 4.
159 Davis, *Australian Settler Colonialism*, 117.
160 Egan, *Neither Amity nor Kindness*, 160.
161 Horner, *Bill Ferguson*, 78.
162 *APBR* 1939, 1–2. Accessed via *Journal of LC*, (Ref. Q342.912) 1934–54, Vol. 5.
163 *Aborigines Welfare Board*, Report for year ending 30 June 1940, 1. Accessed via: aiatsis.gov.au/sites/default/files/docs/digitised_collections/remove/23928.pdf.

the institutional memory of the last decade and more of Aboriginal affairs. The addition, however, of another parliamentarian, an inspector of police, Under-Secretary Anderson and of public servant Bartlett did little to change the dynamic of the new Welfare Board. Professor Elkin brought a new element. Heather Goodall notes that Elkin's influence, which began prior to the establishment of the Welfare Board, was a refocus through terminology: 'training', 'education' and 'the development of social cohesion' replaced 'disciplinary supervision' and 'concentration'.[164] But despite the move from 'protectionism' to welfare and 'gradual assimilation', little was to change.

Secretary Arthur Charles Pettitt – perhaps the second most influential Board officer after Robert T. Donaldson – remained until late 1942, serving under the new Aborigines Welfare Board for a brief period. There is no date for his departure.[165] In 1977, Pettitt provided an interview to Jim Fletcher that was very revealing, not for Pettitt's insight, but for his lack of detail and his apparent memory loss. For instance, he failed to recollect any disputes regarding the exclusion of Aboriginal children from local schools. Asked about the exclusions, Pettitt replied, 'I can't recall any instances where objections were raised'.[166] Also, he could not remember the dispute over the choice of inspector that lasted for several months, and nor could he recall George Ardill (senior) seeking full Board control of education. Moreover, he only had a distant recollection of the reconstitution of the Board in 1916 as an idea 'to team up with the Departments'. His most lucid moment was when talking about the end of the Board in 1940:

> I was sick of it, I had a belly full of it you know, the inquiry, and that sort of thing and the target of a lot of criticism and the Board and so forth, I was tired of it ... I was the king pin really and it all rebounded on me ... I enjoyed the work I was really interested in the abos ... got a boomerang from La Perouse.[167]

---

164 Goodall, *Invasion to Embassy*, 2008, 233.
165 There is a reference to Pettitt still as the secretary to the Aborigines Welfare Board in September 1942. He took out a lease on an oyster and fisheries farm on the south coast. *Government Gazette*, 26 September 1942, 2678. There is no mention of him thereafter on the Board. He was transferred (on loan) to the National Emergency Service. See Horner, *Bill Ferguson*, 117.
166 A.C. Pettitt, interview by J.J. Fletcher, 1977, Audio-tape J01-018426, PMS 5380, Australian Institute of Aboriginal and Torres Strait Islander Studies (hereafter AIATSIS).
167 A.C. Pettitt, interview by J.J. Fletcher, 1977, Audio-tape, J01-018427, PMS 5380, AIATSIS.

His 'memory loss', overall vagueness about events and his final words combine to paint a depressing picture. It seems incredible that he would not recall some pivotal moments during the life of the Board. By his own words, he confirmed the importance of his role and his detachment from Aboriginal people. For someone to reflect upon nearly two-and-a-half decades of wielding enormous power over thousands of Aboriginal people with such indifference and 'blurred recollection' is a tragic indictment of what transpired in Aboriginal affairs in New South Wales from 1916 to 1940.

The demise of the Board did not see the lives of Aboriginal people fundamentally change. Despite the groundswell of Aboriginal activism and humanitarian agitation, it was still considered best practice to forcibly move Aboriginal people onto the stations and reserves; Aboriginal children were still excluded from public schools and many remained in segregated station and reserve schools; young Aboriginal girls and boys continued to be removed from their communities and apprenticed in far-flung parts of state.

Irreparable damage

That the Board for the Protection of Aborigines was able to function in an almost totally unaccountable environment for the last two decades of its life was a gross oversight of government. It also reflected the deep indifference and prejudice towards Aboriginal people from the wider New South Wales community. The inadequacies of the Board were many and they were laid bare in its latter years. Its reclusive nature, disjointed structure and personnel limited its ability to respond to new thinking and embrace Aboriginal voices for change. The conference of Board managers in January 1938 reflected a body unable to manage change and one mired in secrecy and suspicion. Importantly, the consequence of such an extended state of neglect was the irreparable damage done to Aboriginal communities, particularly over the last three decades of the Board's tenure.

Aboriginal activists and an array of humanitarian groups seeking equality for Aboriginal people fought the Board all the way to the end. For its part, the Board never once conceded that it may have misjudged, overstepped or acted negligently. Compounding this depressing picture was that the Board's attitude to Aboriginal people themselves, insisting that they could not be part of a solution or be involved in any decision-making forum. Tragically, Aboriginal people would have to wait until 1969, another 29 years, when the Aborigines Welfare Board was disbanded, before they would be finally released from special legislation and control that set them apart from other Australians.

Conclusion

The story of the Board for the Protection of Aborigines is mostly troubling. In its very early stages, it had shown itself to be a cautious and, in some ways, a compassionate entity tasked with assisting and supporting an Aboriginal population that had been devastated by a brutal dispossession. However, by the turn of the century the Board, driven by some forceful individuals, was squarely focused on a legislative agenda that sought policies to control, segregate, expel and remove. Through the last 20 years of its life, the Board allowed its punitive measures to be driven by a small cabal of non-Board officials who were virtually unaccountable. In the 1930s when the Board was finally challenged by Aboriginal and non-Aboriginal groups seeking its abolition, it had become moribund, paranoid and secretive and it railed against all detractors.

This examination of the Board over its 57-year tenure that ended close to the middle of the twentieth century has exposed several Board traits. First was the fact that the Inspector-General of Police, or later, the Police Commissioner (of which there were six), always chaired the Board. This tradition both reflected and reinforced the inextricable involvement of police with the Aboriginal people of New South Wales. Local police carried out Board policy on the ground – it was they who primarily interreacted with Aboriginal people and not the Board. For Aboriginal people, the police 'became the Board'. Even though this 'heavy-handed' approach was recognised in 1940 and discontinued under the new Aborigines Welfare Board, the police continued to be very visible in New South Wales Aboriginal communities.

Second, the Board's loose structure, absence of protocols and lax attendance requirements underpinned another lasting feature of its history – it allowed powerful individuals to control the agenda and others to disengage. As documented earlier in this book, George E. Ardill, who was appointed in controversial circumstances, was a catalyst for the Board to embark on a more 'hard-edged' policy direction. From the moment he appeared on the Board in 1897, he brought his intense and obsessive character to bear on several of the Board's pressing issues and facilitated the removal of Aboriginal children into his established network of Homes, well before the Board acquired legislation to do so. Also, where possible, he tried to influence policy positions from outside Board structures. Equally, Robert T. Donaldson's persistent and public pronouncements, without obvious Board approval, did much to convince the broader community to accept his views and for the parliament to pass Board-initiated legislation. While only attending one third of all Board meetings, he spoke widely in public on Board issues and pressed doggedly on one matter – the removal of the girls from the camps. Then, as an inspector for the Board, freed from any Board commitments and with no obvious protocols, oversight or requirements to maintain records, he traversed the state to identify children for removal. This process went to the heart of a significant Board failing – its lack of accountability. The Board also permitted lamentable attendance practices for its meetings. As a result, many Board members did not effectively engage in Board matters at all. Serial offenders in this were the parliamentarians on the Board who made up almost one third of all members.

Third, major policy positions of the Board such as the creation of segregated reserves and stations, the establishment of separate Aboriginal schools, the removal of Aboriginal children from their families and the regular expulsion of Aboriginal people from the reserves and stations were never fundamentally challenged. Apart from occasional dissent from parliamentary Board member Robert Scobie on the removal of children, or Board member and justice of the peace Henry Trenchard on the removal of the Aboriginal community from La Perouse, these big policy platforms were not disputed by Board members, and only occasionally contested by non-Aboriginal members of the public.

Fourth, the Board reinforced the marginalisation of Aboriginal people from mainstream Australian society. Aboriginal people were accepted in white society, for short periods of time to undertake domestic duties and some forms of employment, but were unable to participate as full members of New South Wales society.[1] This is most clear in the exploration of Aboriginal exclusion from local public schools. Five high-ranking public

---

1   Goodall, *Invasion to Embassy*, 2008, 108.

servants in education served on the Board, one of whom was considered the most progressive and thoughtful educators of his time.[2] Yet, all these men allowed, and indeed facilitated, the removal of Aboriginal children from public schools because white parents objected to their presence in the classroom. Moreover, for 57 years, as the exclusions continued at many locations across the colony and state, the Department of Public Instruction (later Education) contravened its own legislation that required *all* children in New South Wales to receive free and equal education at a public school.[3] When the Aboriginal children were 'locked out' of the classroom, their families had to home educate their children or move to another district where their children may be accepted at the local school.

Lastly, underpinning all the above was the Board's basic premise: its collective belief that Aboriginal communities had no worth. The Board never acknowledged kinship, the importance of family, claims to Country, language, spirituality, clan connections or the need for Aboriginal people to maintain employment and educate their children. This ignorant, arrogant and paternalistic mindset caused the Board to fail to implement some policy positions. In 1900, the attempt to remove the La Perouse community failed, not only because of stringent opposition, but because the Board dismissed Aboriginal attachment to Country and the need for the residents to maintain employment and education for their children. Similarly, in its bid to have Aboriginal families at Bombaderry removed to Roseby Park, the Board failed because it railed against the mobility of Aboriginal people in what were considered to be 'white spaces' and ignored Aboriginal employment that was crucial to white farmers. When its education policy of allowing small numbers of Aboriginal children to attend public schools was challenged by the prejudice of white parents, the Board raised concerns but never demanded their right to stay – in the end, the Board saw no requirement for Aboriginal children to have full and equal access to education. Also, the Board could not stop Aboriginal girls from returning to their communities after their apprenticeships. Put simply, it never accepted that Aboriginal families loved their children just as much as white families. This remains the most ruthless and pitiless policy of the Board, and the fact that it continued into the early 1970s stands as one of the greatest indictments on white Australia and successive governments of New South Wales.

---

2   Peter Board, director of education, see Chapter 7.
3   *The Public Instruction Act 1880* (NSW).

From 1940 under the new Aborigines Welfare Board, many difficulties for Aboriginal people remained. Winding back the policies of the old Board was a slow process. Some gains were made such as Aboriginal representation on the Board in 1943.[4] But the postwar period brought little comfort to Aboriginal communities. Housing shortages and a 'slump in employment opportunities drove many from the cities and towns to camp on reserves and riverbanks as they had done in the 1930s'.[5]

The new policy of 'assimilation' emphasised finding employment for station residents and selecting 'suitable' families for removal into the white community.[6] An instrument of rehousing under assimilationist policies was 'pepper-potting'. In rural towns Aboriginal families were placed in houses next to white families, separate from other Aboriginal people, and encouraged to lose their Aboriginality. Aboriginal families in these situations complained of the stress of keeping the 'dog quiet', their 'relations away' and the 'children from running on the neighbour's lawn'.[7]

Unfortunately, the legacy of lawless managers and rough justice on the stations and reserves took time to abate. Sonny Simms reflected that as a 10-year-old in 1953 on the mission at La Perouse, his Dad had beaten up the local 'mission policemen' called Beecroft who was trying to arrest him for drunkenness. After the incident Beecroft was forever after Sonny and his brothers. The policeman could come onto the mission at any time and do whatever he liked. Sonny recalled:

> we kids were up on the golf course looking for balls and Beecroft come after us but we would run away and hide in the bush – we knew all the tracks through the bush. Then we would see the smoke and flames and Beecroft had set the bush on fire trying to flush us out! But we were up on the hill watchin' him! On Sunday he would come home from church and he would shoot the dogs on the mission from his side car![8]

---

4   The 1943 amendment to the Act allowed for one position to be filled by a 'full-blood' and the other a 'half-caste'; Walter Page and William Ferguson were the first two Aboriginal representatives on the Aborigines Welfare Board. See Miller, *Koori: A Will to Win*, 174. New research by Victoria Haskins and John Maynard will soon reveal that these Aboriginal representatives were restricted by the Aborigines Welfare Board in their access to the stations and reserves. It appears they were still considered 'suspect' like William Ferguson, Jack Paten and Pearl Gibbs during the late 1930s. Victoria Haskins, Workshop presentation, *Protection and Institutions*, 17 May 2018, University of Technology Sydney.
5   Horner, 'Pearl Gibbs: A Biographical Tribute', 16.
6   Read, *A Hundred Years War*, 99–100.
7   Read, *A Hundred Years War*, 109–10.
8   Sonny Simms (a Bidigal man, from La Perouse Aboriginal Reserve, now living in Nowra), interview by the author, 28 June 2016, Nowra.

A lingering legacy?

Controlling Aboriginal lives was a constant theme during the life of the Board. Yet white interference in Aboriginal life has been constant ever since. The intrusion of the 2007 Howard Government's controversial Northern Territory Intervention was a case in point. Mick Dodson lamented at the time:

> Why do you keep doing this? What's the problem with you people that you always feel you have to come in and fix things rather than support us to fix the things?[9]

Sarah Maddison argues that white Australia persists with what she terms 'the Colonial Fantasy'. Just like the Board had wanted the 'problem' of an Aboriginal presence to disappear, Maddison contends that the mainstream view that the idea of 'Australia as a colony', with its attended history of violence and acceptance of *terra nullius*, ended with Federation is false. As a result, the survival and obvious presence of Indigenous communities today does not sit well with white Australia – it is a 'constant reminder that settler society has been imposed on Indigenous lives and territories'.[10] Just like the fundamental policies of the Board were never challenged, Maddison believes that the time has come to jettison the continued interference in the lives Indigenous Australians. Answers to 'entrenched issues' can only be 'located outside of settler control' and in the 'hands of Aboriginal and Torres Strait Islander people themselves'.[11]

The New South Wales Aboriginal people have paid a heavy price for being Aboriginal. The period of the Board explored here is just one episode in their long journey of survival and resistance. Ann Curthoys and John Docker's observation that the 'temptation to declare that the historian can objectively establish the truth about the past is to be resisted' is relevant here.[12] The complete truth about the New South Wales Board for the Protection of Aborigines will never be fully known, but some light has been shed on a body that has remained hidden. Incremental knowledge of this past leads us closer to the resolution of the big issues that still confront us as a nation. The Board never allowed Aboriginal people to be

---

9   Maddison, *The Colonial Fantasy*, 109.
10 Maddison, *The Colonial Fantasy*, xix.
11 Maddison, *The Colonial Fantasy*, 234.
12 Curthoys and Docker, *Is History Fiction?*, 5.

Aboriginal. Archie Roach's seminal song 'Took the Children Away', which has the lyric 'we were acting white but feeling black', is still pertinent. Our country will never be calm until we, as a nation, acknowledge and accept the past, remove the trappings of our colonial past that fails to fully include and recognise Indigenous Australians as equal citizens and their pre-eminent place prior to European contact, and provide the platforms for all of us to have a voice concerning governance, treaties and healing.

Appendix 1: Board members in order of appearance

1. George Thornton: Start date: June 1883; finish date: four weeks later. Occupation: politician.

All major references to Thornton are found in Chapter 1.

Figure A1.1: George Thornton.
Source: Parliamentary Archives, NSW Parliament Collection (ThorntonG-936).

Figure A1.2: Richard Hill.
Source: Parliamentary Archives, NSW Parliament Collection (HillR).

2. Richard Hill: Start date: June 1883; finish date: August 1895. Occupation: politician.

For major references to Richard Hill see Chapters 1 and 2. From the available records, Hill attended 218 meetings from a possible 248 from September 1890 until his last meeting in August 1895, an attendance of rate of 87.9 per cent.[1] An extrapolation of his overall attendance would have been close to 530 meetings over his 12-year period.

3. Philip Gidley King: Start date: June 1883; finish date: 18 November 1897. Occupation: politician.

Figure A1.3: Philip Gidley King.
Source: Parliamentary Archives, NSW Parliament Collection (King Philip Gidley-752).

For major references, see Chapter 2. Philip King was the grandson of the third governor of New South Wales, a pastoralist, landowner of a large property south of Tamworth, mayor, president of the Australia Club, director of the Mercantile Bank of Sydney and a member of parliament for 24 years.[2] His last recorded attendance (contrary to some reports that he was a member up to 1904) was 18 November 1897.[3] From the available minutes he attended 100 meetings out of a possible 311; an attendance rate of 33 per cent.[4]

4. Alexander Gordon: Start date: June 1883; finish date: sometime in 1885. Occupation: barrister.

Reference in the text: Chapter 2. Alexander Gordon was a barrister and Queen's Council with strong connections to religion and philanthropy; he served on many charitable committees and undertook roles within the Anglican Church, mainly of a legal nature.[5] There are no extant records of attendance patterns for Gordon.

---

1   Analysis of all APB Minutes (hereafter *APBM*) for Hill's tenure on the Board. All *APBM* accessed via: Minute Books (Aborigines Welfare Board), NRS 2, NSW Department of Aboriginal Affairs, Sydney.
2   O'Grady, 'King, Philip Gidley (1817–1904)'.
3   *APBM*, 18 November 1987. The website of the NSW Parliament (www.parliament.nsw.gov.au/members) has him leaving the Board in 1904.
4   Analysis of all *APBM* for King's tenure on the Board.
5   Cable, 'Gordon, Alexander (1815–1903)'.

APPENDIX 1

5. William J. Foster: Start date: June 1883; finish date: sometime during 1887. Occupation: Attorney-General/politician.

Figure A1.4: William J. Foster.
Source: Parliamentary Archives, NSW Parliament Collection (FosterWJ-asJudge).

Reference in the text: Chapter 2. William J. Foster, lawyer, politician, militant temperance advocate, devout evangelical and a member of 'every diocesan, provincial and general synod of the Church of England', became attorney-general in the Parkes Government.[6] Foster was present at the inaugural meeting of the Sydney-based Aborigines Protection Association (APA) in February 1880 and was elected as one of two vice-presidents. There are no extant attendance records for Foster.

6. Hugh Robison: Start date: June 1883; finish date: sometime in 1888. Occupation: inspector of the charities.

Reference in text: Chapter 2. Hugh Robison served for a period of five years. There are no attendance patterns for Robison. As inspector of charities he was perhaps an obvious choice for the Board as its main function was, in the beginning, basically a charitable body. It appears his contribution was minimal. The 1888 Board report mentions, in a seemingly discourteous fashion, 'Mr Hugh Robison, who served as a member … for five years, resigned on the 15 October last'.[7]

7. Edmund Fosbery: Start date: June 1883; finish date: 1904. Occupation: Inspector-General of Police.

---

6   Rutledge, 'Foster, William John (1831–1909)'.
7   *Protection of Aborigines: Report of the Board* (the APB Report: hereafter *APBR*), 1888, 1. Accessed via 'NSW', To Remove and Protect, AIATSIS: aiatsis.gov.au/sites/default/files/docs/digitised_collections/remove/22809.pdf.

For all major references to Fosbery see Chapters 2 and 3. Edmund Walcott Fosbery was born at Wotton, Gloucestershire, in 1834 and educated at the Royal Naval School in Surrey but did not continue a career in the services. He joined a solicitor's firm and then migrated to Australia in 1852, joining the Victorian police and rising to the most senior position as inspector-general in 1874.[8] As an able administrator he was member of the Board of Health, chair of the Public Service Tender Board, on the Committee of the Discharged Pensioners Society, chairman of the Charity Organization Society, a director of the Trustee New South Wales Savings Bank and a director of the Bank of New South Wales.[9] He was, it seems, heavily involved in Sydney society. As there are significant gaps in the Board minutes it is impossible to accurately record Fosbery's attendance. But for the extant years, it was quite remarkable. He attended 466 meetings from a possible 490, an attendance rate of 95 per cent.[10] The highest attendance record of any Board member, over two decades, during the 57-year life of the Board.[11]

Figure A1.5: Edmund Walcott Fosbery.
Source: Australian Police (australianpolice.com.au). Courtesy: Greg Collander.

Figure A1.6: Harman John Tarrant.
Source: Parliamentary Archives, NSW Parliament Collection (Tarrant Harman).

8   Rutledge and Dickey, 'Fosbery, Edmund Walcott (1834–1919)'.
9   Rutledge and Dickey, 'Fosbery, Edmund Walcott (1834–1919)'.
10 Analysis of *APBM* for Fosbery's tenure on the Board.
11 Lipscomb and Anderson, new members of the Aborigines Welfare Board (AWB), attended every meeting for a year before the AWB was officially formed.

APPENDIX 1

8. Harman John Tarrant: Start date: 20 July 1886; finish date: after May 1888 and before April 1889.[12] Occupation: medical practitioner and politician.

Harman Tarrant was a London-educated medical practitioner and member for Kiama in the New South Wales Legislative Assembly for nearly seven years. He only spent one and half years on the Board and there are no extant attendance patterns. It appears his medical commitments were heavy.[13]

9. Sydney Burdekin: Start date: 1887; finish date: 9 March 1899. Occupation: businessman and politician.

Sydney Burdekin was a member of parliament from 1880 until 1894. He was an alderman and mayor of the Sydney Municipal Council, director of Sydney Hospital from 1878 to 1899, and in 1885 was appointed as a magistrate and presided over the Royal Commission into city and suburban railways.[14] He remained on the Board for 12 years, but his attendance record was extremely poor. Of a possible 445 Board meetings over eight years of extant records he attended only 12, an attendance rate of 2.4 per cent.[15]

10. Albert Maxwell Hutchinson: Start date: 26 August 1887; finish date: 20 April 1896. Occupation: unknown.

Reference in the text, Chapter 2, suggests he was a well-respected member. Of the available minutes Maxwell attended 149 meetings out of a possible 192 – an attendance rate of 77.6 per cent.[16] I have been unable to find any details regarding his background.

11. George O'Malley Clarke: Start date: 24 April 1889; finish date: 31 October 1899. Occupation: magistrate.

---

12 Because no Board minutes are available, a departure date can be deduced from Board reports.
13 Maxwell, *Australian Men of Mark*, 367.
14 Humphries, 'Burdekin, Sydney (1839–1899)'.
15 Analysis of *APBM* 1888 to March 1899.
16 Analysis of *APBM* 20 September 1890 to 20 April 1896.

George O'Malley Clarke played a significant role in community life involving himself in the arts, schools, hospitals, the church, horse racing and cricket. By 1889 he was presiding magistrate at the Central Police Court in Sydney.[17] Over his ten and a half years on the Board, his attendance of 53 meetings out of possible 233 (a rate of 22.7 per cent) suggests he was not committed to the Board. The Board reports 1894–95 and 1896 do not recognise O'Malley Clarke as even being part of the Board, though he made five Board appearances during those years.

Figure A1.7: William H. Suttor.
Source: Parliamentary Archives, NSW Parliament Collection (SuttorWH-(jr)).

12. William H. Suttor: Start date: 25 July 1890; finish date: 9 March 1899. Occupation: politician.

Reference in the text: Chapter 2. William Suttor was MLA for East Macquarie and was later nominated to the Legislative Council in 1880.[18] From the available records he attended 181 meetings out of a possible 371, an attendance rate of 48.7 per cent.[19]

13. Thomas Colls: Start date: 11 November 1891; finish date: 1 June 1894. Occupation: politician.

Thomas Colls was born in Liverpool in 1822, schooled in the Campbelltown area and apprenticed as a wheelwright in Liverpool. He ran for the seat of Yass Plains in 1886 at the age of 64 and won by a large majority, holding the seat until 1894. Colls was a justice of the peace and highly active in Yass society.[20] He made three contributions to Aboriginal issues in the Legislative Assembly.[21] He attended 58 meetings out of a possible 129, an attendance rate of 44.9 per cent.[22]

---

17 Teale, 'Clarke, George O'Malley (1836–1899)'.
18 Teale, 'Suttor, William Henry (1834–1905)'.
19 Analysis of *APBM*, 25 July 1890 – 9 March 1899.
20 Schulz, 'Colls, Thomas (1822–1898)'.
21 Doukakis, *The Aboriginal People*, 157.
22 Analysis of *APBM*, 11 November 1891 – 1 June 1894.

14. Robert Hoddle Driberg White: Start date: 16 February 1894; finish date: 12 May 1898. Occupation: politician.

Figure A1.8: Robert Hoddle Driberg White.
Source: Parliamentary Archives, NSW Parliament Collection (White Robert).

Reference in the text: Chapter 2. Robert Hoddle Driberg White was born in 1838, educated in Melbourne and started a career in banking in 1857. He was elected member for Gloucester in the New South Wales parliament for four years and became a life member of the Legislative Council.[23] He made one parliamentary contribution to Aboriginal issues in early 1884.[24] From 156 Board meetings he attended 69, an attendance rate of 44.2 per cent. [25]

15. John Moore Chanter: Start date: 6 September 1894; finish date: sometime during 1910. Occupation: politician.

Reference in the text: Chapter 2. John Moore Chanter, educated in Adelaide, became the first secretary of the Victoria Farmers Union in 1878 before moving to Moama in New South Wales, on the Murray River, where he worked as an auctioneer and became mayor in 1881.[26] Chanter held the seats of Murray (later Deniliquin) and Riverina.[27] He was a politician for 37 years and was 'praised as a hard-working local member who was well acquainted with the vast areas he represented and considered every request from his constituents'.[28] However, his Board attendance was poor. From the available records he attended 86 Board meetings out of a possible 292, an attendance rate of 24.4 per cent.

---

23 'Mr Robert Hoddle Driberg White (1838–1900)', Members, Former Members, Parliament of New South Wales. Accessed via: www.parliament.nsw.gov.au/members/formermembers/Pages/former-member-details.aspx?pk=732.
24 Doukakis, *The Aboriginal People,* 176.
25 Analysis of *APBM,* 1894–98.
26 Hawker and Rydon, 'Chanter, John Moore (1845–1931)'.
27 'Mr John Moore Chanter (1845–1931)', Members, Former Members, Parliament of New South Wales. Accessed via: www.parliament.nsw.gov.au/members/Pages/profiles/chanter_john-moore.aspx.
28 Hawker and Rydon, 'Chanter, John Moore (1845–1931)'.

16. James Richard Hill: Start date: 26 September 1895; finish date: 14 July 1898. Occupation: banker and financier.

The third son of Richard Hill, born in Sydney 1836, became a banker and financier. He was active in charity, a director of Tooth's Brewery, deputy-chair of the Australian Mutual Provident Society, director of the Sydney Hospital and of the APA. He was 'hard-working, touchy, cautious and likeable'.[29] His time on the Board was relatively short but was a regular attender: 61 meetings out of a possible 85 – a rate of 71.7 per cent.[30] There is nothing to suggest that his short stay on the Board had any significant impact.

17. John See: Start date: 25 June 1897; finish date: sometime during 1902, See resigns. Occupation: politician (colonial secretary and premier).

Figure A1.9: John See.
Source: Parliamentary Archives, NSW Parliament Collection (SeeJ-4584).

Reference in the text: Chapter 3. John See was born in Huntingdonshire in England, 1845, and migrated to Australia in 1852. He was elected to the seat of Grafton in 1880, which he held for the next 14 years, becoming premier in 1901. His interest in Aboriginal issues was evident. See proposed that the 'blacks in higher lands, the colder portions of the colony' should receive more than the ordinary allowance. He also felt that the amount of money was insufficient, in the Richmond district 'there were upwards of 1000 blacks – men, women, and children, and in the majority of cases, they were insufficiently clad'.[31]

---

29 Walsh, 'Hill, James Richard (1836–1898)'.
30 Analysis of *APBM*, 1895–98.
31 NSW, *Parliamentary Debates*, Legislative Assembly, 29 June 1887, 2403–4 (John See).

However, he was a poor attender of Board meetings. In October 1902, when the member for Barwon, Mr Willis, criticised the Board on several fronts, Mr See interjected: 'I am on the board!' Mr Willis replied: 'But the hon. Member never attends meetings'.[32] This was true: of the available Aboriginal Protection Board (APB) minutes, See only attended 16 meetings out of a possible 197, an attendance rate of 8.12 per cent.[33]

18. Unni William Carpenter: Start date: 27 August 1897; finish date 27 December 1900. Occupation: returning officer.

Unni William Carpenter was born in Gloucestershire, England, in 1822 and died 1901. He came to New South Wales in 1855 living in Darlinghurst, Sydney. He was elected to City Council, and became a returning officer and a justice of the peace. He was closely associated with the Benevolent Asylum, the Randwick Asylum and other charitable institutions.[34] He was also president of the powerful APA and gained his Board appointment as a result. He joined the Board at the age of 75 in 1897 and, despite his health, his attendance over a period of three years was very commendable indeed – he attended 140 meetings out of a possible 163, an attendance rate of 86 per cent.[35]

Figure A1.10: George Edward Ardill.
Source: *The Rescue* 2, no. 10 (August 1882): 2. Mitchell Library, State Library of New South Wales.

19. George Edward Ardill: Start date: 27 August 1897; finish date: April 1916. Occupation: private enterprise (running homes for the destitute).

References in the text: Chapters 3, 4 and 5. From the available records Ardill attended 475 meetings from a possible 555, an attendance rate of 85.6 per cent.[36]

---

32 NSW, *Parliamentary Debates*, Legislative Assembly, 21 October 1903, 3474 (John See).
33 Analysis of *APBM* for the period of See's tenure.
34 *Evening News*, 5 February 1901, 5.
35 Analysis of *APBM*, 1897–1901.
36 Analysis of *APBM*, 1897–1916.

20. William Charles Hill: Start date: 1898; finish date: during 1910. Occupation: pastoralist.

William Hill was a member of the Legislative Council for nearly 19 years. Prior to joining the parliament, he spent most of his life in the country and had been a wool broker, stock and station agent and pastoralist.[37] His interest in Aboriginal issues may have come from his father Richard Hill, original Board member, and his brother Richard James Hill, who was also a Board member. However, he was a non-attender; from available records, Hill attended just 10 meetings from a possible 219 up to the end of 1909, a rate of 4.5 per cent.[38]

21. Frank Norrie: Start date: 14 November 1899; finish date: June 1905. Occupation: solicitor.

Frank Norrie practised as a solicitor for many years at Grafton. He became mayor of Grafton for two years; he was honorary secretary to the Grafton Hospital and his advice was of 'great value to the institution'.[39] After moving to Sydney, he joined the Board and spent over five years in its service. Norrie was quite active in that he sought a meeting with the Minister for Education regarding the establishment of a Aboriginal school at Runnymede and Burnt Bridge on the north coast of NSW.[40] He inspected the Home at Runnymede, the Aboriginal Station at Cumeroogunga in August 1901 and the Home at Grafton in September 1904.[41] He attended 33 meetings out of a possible 84 over the time that records were kept – an attendance rate of 39 per cent.[42]

22. Henry Trenchard: Start date: 22 November 1899; finish date: April 1916. Occupation: unknown.

References in the text: Chapter 3. Henry Trenchard spent just over 16 years on the Board. He attended 280 meetings out of a possible 415 – an attendance rate of 67.5 per cent. Over that length of time, he was a very consistent contributor. Unfortunately, there is little known of Henry

---

37 'Mr William Charles Hill (1838–1919)', Members, Former Members, Parliament of New South Wales. Accessed via: www.parliament.nsw.gov.au/members/formermembers/Pages/former-member-details.aspx?pk=731.
38 Analysis of *APBM*, 1898–1910.
39 *Northern Star*, 3 June 1905, 4
40 *Evening News*, 23 November 1901, 3.
41 *Northern Star*, 17 October 1900, 5; *Evening News*, 3 August 1901, 2; *Evening News*, 7 September 1904, 8.
42 Analysis of *APBM*, 1899–1905.

Trenchard, other than he was a justice of the peace. He must have been a good friend, or at least known to George Ardill, as Ardill felt the need to write to the colonial secretary to request that Trenchard be appointed to the APB.[43] Trenchard was outspoken on the Board and opposed the removal of the Aboriginal people from the La Perouse reserve in September 1900.[44]

23. Edward Dowling: Start date: March 1901; finish date sometime in 1910. Occupation: general philanthropy and secretary of several educational organisations.

Figure A1.11: Edward Dowling.
Source: Government Printing Office 1-16186. New South Wales State Archives & Records.

References in the text: Chapter 4. Edward Dowling was the son of a painter, and after an elementary education in Sydney he worked for a merchant at the age of 10 and then as an office boy at the age of 13. In later life he became an advocate for the education of working men and was the first secretary of the Board of Technical Education in 1883.[45] He was secretary of the New South Wales branch of the Australian Natives' Association and opined that there are 200,000 Aborigines on the Australian continent and that 'sufficient attention has not been paid [to them] by the Colonial Governments'.[46] While on the Board, Dowling attended 62 meetings from a possible 92, an attendance rate of 67.4 per cent.

---

43   Letter from Ardill to Colonial Secretary, Colonial Secretary's In-Letters (hereafter CSIL), 5/6508, Item 99/19477, State Records of New South Wales (hereafter SRNSW).
44   *APBM*, 6 September 1900, Item 4.
45   McMinn, 'Dowling, Edward (1843–1912)'.
46   Dowling, *Australia and America*, 71.

24. Robert Scobie: Start Date: 1901; finish date 26 July 1918. Occupation: politician.

References in the text: Chapters 4 and 5. Scobie's attendance at Board meetings was abysmal and goes to the heart of one of the major failings of the Board – poor attendance did not disqualify ongoing membership. For the first seven years of available records Scobie only attended eight meetings – an average of one per year. Of the last five years on the Board his attendance improved slightly. Overall, he attended only 33 meetings out of a possible 399, an average rate of 8.27 per cent.[47]

Figure A1.12: Robert Scobie.
Source: Parliamentary Archives, NSW Parliament Collection (ScobieRobert-19P-1901).

Figure A1.13: Thomas Garvin.
Source: Inspector General of Police, Government Printing Office, 1-12252, New South Wales State Archives & Records.

25. Thomas Garvin: Start date: 31 December 1903; finish date: 27 January 1916. Occupation: Inspector-General of Police.

Reference in the text: Chapter 4. Garvin's work ethic in the force was matched by his commitment to the meetings of the APB. Between 1905 and 1916, of the available records, he attended 303 meetings out of a possible 365, an attendance rate of 83 per cent.[48] Garvin presided over the most important legislation with the New South Wales *Aborigines Protection Act 1909* and the controversial 1915 amendment to the Act.

---

47 Analysis of *APBM*, 1901–16.
48 Analysis of *APBM*, 1905–16 (records missing between 1906 and 1909).

26. Edward MacFarlane: Start date: 31 March 1904; finish date: 26 May 1910. Occupation: Under-Secretary of the Department of Lands.

Edward MacFarlane was educated at Fort-Street Model School and Sydney Grammar and after a competitive examination he entered the Surveyor-General's Office. He rose through the ranks to become the Under-Secretary of the Department of Lands. Although not a strong attender at Board meetings (25 from 73, an attendance rate of 34 per cent), he did visit several Aboriginal stations such as Warangesda, Macquarie, Cumeroogunga and Brungle.[49]

27. George Henry Varley: Start date: 1 July 1904; finish date: 1 April 1916. Occupation: newspaper proprietor and politician.

George Varley spent most of his working life in the newspaper business, first as a journalist and then as an owner, and was elected life member of the Australian Provisional Press Association. He was elected to the Legislative Council in 1917 and remained until 1934. During his 12 years on the Board his attendance was not very satisfactory, only attending 77 meetings from 374, an attendance rate of 20.5 per cent. While a member he visited two Aboriginal stations, one at Ulgundahi Island and the other at Grafton Home.[50]

Figure A1.14: Robert Thomas Donaldson.
Source: *Third Australasian Catholic Congress*, St Mary's Cathedral Book Depot, Sydney, 1909.MG/1/U11/ (set), 480. Mitchell Library, State Library of New South Wales.

28. Robert Thomas Donaldson: Start date: 14 December 1904; finish date: 1915? Occupation: politician.

References in the text: Chapters 4 and 5. Robert Thomas Donaldson resigned from the Board in latter half of 1915 to take up his position as inspector for the Board in the October of the same year. During his time on the Board, pre-1915, Donaldson's attendance at the weekly meetings did not reflect

---

49 *Evening News*, 10 August 1904, 5; *Wellington Times*, 28 September 1908, 2; *Riverina Herald*, 25 September 1908, 2; and *Gundagai Times and Tumut, Adelong and Murrumbidgee District Advertiser*, 31 August 1909, 4.
50 *Evening News*, 29 April 1908, 8; *Clarence and Richmond Examiner*, 17 November 1906, 4.

his overall influence on policy and impact upon Aboriginal people. Of the available records, he attended 107 meetings from a possible 350, an attendance rate of 30.6 per cent.[51] His attendance from 1910 to the beginning of 1914 was poor indeed, only averaging 10.4 per cent.

29. **Peter Board**: Start date: 1 August 1907; finish date: 30 November 1911. Occupation: Director of Education, New South Wales.

Figure A1.15: Peter Board.
Source: Crane and Walker, *Peter Board: His Contribution to the Development of Education in New South Wales*, iii. Mitchell Library, State Library of New South Wales.

References in the text: Chapter 7. Peter Board was born on 27 March 1858 at Wingham, NSW. He commenced a career in the Department of Public Instruction as a teacher at Glebe School in January 1873. He rose through the teaching ranks to become a headmaster at the Macdonaldtown School (now Erskineville) in 1882, at the age of 24. He graduated at Sydney University with a Bachelor of Arts in 1889 and then with a Master of Arts, with honours, in mathematics in 1891.[52] He quickly rose in the ranks of the administrative arm of the department and was appointed inspector of schools in 1893. Following an education conference in 1904, at which Mr Board was 'an outstanding figure', and the reorganisation of the higher officers of the department, he was appointed by the government as Under-Secretary and Director of Education in February 1905. An office he occupied with 'marked distinction and great benefit to the state' for 18 years.[53] From the extant records, he attended only 18 meetings from a possible 88 – an attendance rate of 20.5 per cent.

---

51   Analysis of *APBM*, 1905 to 1906 and 1910 to 1915.
52   'Peter Board, M.A., C.M.G', by E. Williams, Peter Board Papers, 1872–1944, MLMSS 1095, Part 3, 25, Mitchell Library (hereafter ML).
53   'Peter Board, M.A., C.M.G', by E. Williams, Peter Board Papers, 1872–1944, MLMSS 1095, Part 3, 25 (ML).

30. Robert McDonald: Start date: 16 June 1910; finish date: 1 February 1912. Occupation: Under-Secretary of the Department of Lands.

He attended 25 Board meetings from a possible 79, an attendance rate of 31.6 per cent. There is no mention of McDonald in any press reports during his time on the Board or in the minutes.

31. Robert T. Paton: Start date: 16 June 1910; finish date: 6 March 1912. Second appointment, start date: 30 April 1916; finish date: 17 August 1921. Occupation: Director-General of the Board of Health, New South Wales.

Figure A1.16: Robert T. Paton.
Source: 'Geoffrey and Dr Paton (on the right)'. obj–140625882, PIC10515/1-32 LOC Album 82, created c.1889. National Library of Australia.

After studying medicine in Edinburgh, Paton left for Australia in 1876 and worked as a doctor's assistant in Wallsend and Bathurst. He returned to Edinburgh, completed his medical training, qualified for the Royal College of Surgeons and graduated from the Free University of Brussels in 1885. On his return to New South Wales, he was promoted to 'medical officer and vaccinator in Sydney' and was also a police surgeon.

He was appointed medical inspector of charities in 1908 and while in this position he was appointed to the Board in 1910.[54] Paton, for all his work responsibilities, was a productive member of the Board with a strong attendance record: 63 meetings from 77, a rate of 78.6 per cent.[55] He reported on the Aboriginal Station at Roseby Park and visited Cootamundra Hospital, along with Ardill, with a view to establishing the Aboriginal Girls' Home.[56] Because of his position as director-general on the Board of Health, he was again appointed to the Board on the Board's reconstitution in 1916 and remained until his resignation in 1921. His attendance at Board meetings during his second appointment was just as consistent as the first: 42 meetings from 67, an attendance rate of 62.7 per cent.

32. Mark Fairlies Morton: Start date: 16 June 1910; finish date: 18 November 1915. Occupation: member of parliament.

Reference in the text: Chapter 7. Mark Morton's attendance at Board meetings was poor, attending only 29 meetings from a possible 271, a rate of 10.7 per cent.

33. William Millard: Start date: 16 June 1910; finish date: 21 March 1921. Occupation: politician and dairy farmer.

Millard was born in Wollongong and moved to Ulladulla in 1854. He became a dairy farmer and tanner, and was a noted rifle shot and amateur boxer, referred to as Captain Millard due to his extensive military service in the Ulladulla Voluntary Rifles, the Corps Reserve and as captain of the 2nd Infantry regiment from 1884 until 1893. He joined the Legislative Assembly as member for Moruya in 1895 and remained in the parliament for next 27 years until his death.[57]

His attendance was not all that good but indicative of many members of parliament who served on the Board. He attended 60 meetings out of a possible 326, an attendance rate of only 16.6 per cent. He was on the Board during two major pieces of legislation: the 1915 and 1918 amendments to the Act.[58]

---

54 Cummins, 'Paton, Robert Thomson (1856–1929)'.
55 Analysis of *APBM*, 1910–13.
56 *APBM*, 18 August 1910, Item 7; *APBM*, 20 July 1911, Item 5.
57 'Mr Mark Fairlies Morton (1865–1938)', Members, Former Members, Parliament of New South Wales. Accessed via: www.parliament.nsw.gov.au/members/formermembers/Pages/former-member-details.aspx?pk=1157.
58 Analysis of *APBM*.

APPENDIX 1

34. Ernest Day: Start date: 31 December 1910; finish date: 12 November 1914. Occupation: Inspector-General of Police.

Born in Dorsetshire, England, and son of a surveyor, Day completed his education and after a short time as a manager of a large Southampton brewery he migrated to Australia and joined the New South Wales Mounted Police in 1883. He had several postings out in the west of New South Wales and performed his duties successfully and was a 'crack shot with both revolver and rifle'.[59] He was a skilled tracker and bushman and was responsible for the apprehension of several bushrangers. A notable capture occurred in Bourke when he disguised himself as a woman to arrest 'Jack the Ripper' who had been molesting women in the district.[60] He was promoted to sub-inspector in 1897 and served at Narrabri and Newcastle. He was promoted to inspector in 1904 and, after a move to Sydney as a superintendent, he succeeded Thomas Garvin in the job of inspector-general in 1911. 'His courteous manners, his wide experience' and the fact that he had risen through the ranks, earned him the title of 'The General' by the 2,800-strong police force. He was a regular attender at meetings: he was present for 145 out of a possible 183, a very credible attendance at 79 per cent.[61] He oversaw the lead-up to the 1915 amendment to the *Aborigines Protection Act 1909* and led the deputation to the colonial secretary that sought the necessary changes to the Act.

35. Rowland Smith Hill: Start date: 25 July 1912; finish date: 9 October 1913. Occupation: unknown.

Justice of the peace Rowland Hill attended 22 meetings from a possible 88, an attendance rate of 25.6 per cent.[62] The minutes record his resignation from the Board on 7 May 1914, but his last attended meeting was 9 October 1913; there is no acknowledgement of his work on the Board.[63]

---

59   King, 'Day, Ernest Charles (1857–1915)'.
60   King, 'Day, Ernest Charles (1857–1915)'.
61   Analysis of *APBM*, 1911–14.
62   Analysis of *APBM* for his period of tenure.
63   *APBM*, 28 May 1914, Item 1a.

36. Dr Walter Hull: Start date: 10 April 1913; finish date: 20 November 1913. Occupation: medical doctor.

Reference in the text: Chapter 5. Dr Walter Hull, for his short time on the Board, was a particularly good attendee – 23 meetings from a possible 28, an attendance rate of 82 per cent. He resigned on a matter of principle after the Board had been on strike over the payment on members to visit stations and reserves.

37. Alfred Hill: Start date: 15 January 1914; finish date: 30 April 1916. Occupation: unknown.

Alfred Hill attended 38 meetings from a possible 102, or 37.3 per cent. I have been unable to locate any details of Alfred Hill.

38. T.H. Abbott: Start date: 10 July 1914; finish date: 30 April 1916. Occupation: unknown.

Abbott attended 65 out of 88 meetings, an attendance rate of 73.9 per cent.

39. James Mitchell: Start date: 10 December 1914; finish date: 22 March 1929. Occupation: Inspector-General of Police.

James Mitchell, a Scot from Aberdeenshire, came out to Australia in 1884, and after an apprenticeship as a coach builder signed up with the New South Wales Police Force. A stint as part of a special 'strike-breaking' force propelled him through the ranks to become acting inspector in 1899.[64] He replaced the ailing Charles Ernest Day in late 1914 in the top job of inspector-general. After Edmund Fosbery, Mitchell was the next longest serving chair of the APB, from 1915 until 1929 but his influence appeared minimal. The Board minutes do not attribute any initiatives or undertakings by Mitchell. In 1929, the transition of chair from Mitchell to Walter Henry Childs was seamless and uneventful; there was not even a vote of thanks or even an acknowledgement of Mitchell's 14 years of service on the Board. During his 15-year period on the Board he attended 158 meetings from a possible 198, an attendance rate of 79.8 per cent, which was very creditable.[65] As the chair he oversaw the tumultuous

---

64   'James Mitchell: Law and Order in the Pioneering Days of NSW', Australian Police. Accessed via: www.australianpolice.com.au/nsw-police-history-index/police-commissioners-of-nsw/james-mitchell/.
65   Analysis of *APBM*, 1914–29.

proceedings, with three resignations, in early 1916 when the Board was reconstituted. He also presided over a period of unprecedented removal of Aboriginal children from their communities.

40. G.S. Briner: Start date: 28 October 1915; finish date: 10 February 1916. Occupation: member of parliament and journalist.

Figure A1.17: George Stuart Briner.
Source: Parliamentary Archives, NSW Parliament Collection (BrinerGS-19P-1901).

George Stuart Briner was educated in Melbourne and was employed as a teacher before coming to New South Wales in 1881, resuming teaching duties until 1891. He became a journalist and then editor of the *Raleigh Sun* in Bellingen before entering parliament in 1901, where he remained for the next 20 years.[66] He only attended 4 meetings out of a possible 33, an attendance rate of 12 per cent, which would deem him a virtual non-attender.[67] His only significant contribution in the Legislative Assembly on Aboriginal affairs was in 1906 when he advocated in favour of not forcing the Aboriginal population of Yass to be moved out of town. He was concerned that they would not receive proper medical attention. He stated that he had been opposed to the relocation of the Aborigines at La Perouse some six years ago.[68]

---

66 'Mr George Stuart Briner (1862–1920)', Members, Former Members, Parliament of New South Wales. Accessed via: www.parliament.nsw.gov.au/members/formermembers/Pages/former-member-details.aspx?pk=1102.
67 Analysis of *APBM*, 1915–16.
68 NSW, *Parliamentary Debates*, Legislative Assembly, 6 December 1906, 4530 (George Briner).

41. Edward Burns Harkness: Start date: 6 April 1916; finish date: 7 December 1938. Occupation: public servant.

Reference in the text: see Chapter 5 for more details on Harkness.

As vice-chair of the Board for over 22 years, his attendance was only better than half. Of 210 meetings he attended 128, a rate of 61 per cent. This reflected the period when the cabal was dictating most of the agenda and Board members remained very much at arm's length.

Figure A1.18: Edward Burns Harkness.

Source: 'Returning Officer for the liquor referendum E.B. Harkness at his desk, New South Wales, September 1928', 1 [picture], FXT269071, Fairfax archive of glass plate negatives, Nine Content.

42. James Dawson: Start date: 30 March 1916; finish date: 26 October 1922. Occupation: chief inspector of education.

See Chapter 7 for further information. Glaswegian James Dawson arrived in Sydney in 1880 and took up a teaching position at Sydney Grammar School. At the age of 25 he was appointed a school inspector and in 1905 was elevated to chief inspector.[69] His name does not appear in the Board minutes as undertaking any other extra duties; the minutes record that his resignation in 1923 was 'accepted with regret'.[70] Dawson's attendance rate at Board meetings was adequate, attending 47 from a possible 79, an attendance rate of 59.5 per cent.

43. Hugh Ross: Start date: 30 March 1916; finish date: 1 April 1916. Occupation: Chief Inspector for the Department of Agriculture.

Hugh Ross was appointed as part of the restructure in 1916 but was only on the Board for one day.

---

69 *Goulburn Evening Penny Post*, 12 February 1935, 2.
70 *APBM*, 18 January 1923, Item 1.

44. Alfred William Green: Start date: 21 June 1917; finish date: 11 January 1934. Occupation: president of the State Children's Relief Department.

Career public servant Alfred William Green joined the State Children's Relief Department in 1884 where he remained for his entire career, becoming president of the Board in 1914. His obituary in the *Sydney Morning Herald* in 1935 mentions nothing of his time on the APB but was more concerned with his contributions to New South Wales Cricket as its president and his philanthropic work with many Sydney Homes, such as the Mittagong Farm Home for Boys and homes for the 'feeble-minded' at Mittagong and Parramatta, and his association with several metropolitan hospitals.[71] Green was an active Board member, proposing motions and undertaking Aboriginal Station inspections. Naomi Parry notes that he was a mediator in the troubles at Cumeroogunga in 1919 but also asserts that his views about Aboriginal people were far from complimentary – he considered Aboriginal children to be 'lazy and unreliable' and were not suited to 'white foster families'.[72] Green attended 108 Board meetings from a possible 146, an attendance rate of 74 per cent.[73]

Figure A1.19: Brian James Doe.
Source: Parliamentary Archives, NSW Parliament Collection (DoeBJ-25P-1920).

45. Brian James Doe: Start date: 31 January 1918; finish date: 31 August 1928. Occupation: parliamentarian.

Brian James Doe was born at Portland and educated at Warrnambool in Victoria, and was a blacksmith by trade. After moving to Broken Hill around 1906, he became involved in local council politics.[74] Over his

---

71   *SMH*, 22 August 1935, 2.
72   Parry, 'Such a Longing', 279–83.
73   Analysis of *APBM* for relevant years.
74   'Mr Brian James Doe (1862–1941)', Members, Former Members, Parliament of New South Wales. Accessed via: www.parliament.nsw.gov.au/members/formermembers/Pages/former-member-details.aspx?pk=1097.

10 years on the Board, he attended 58 from a possible 92 meetings, a rate of 63 per cent; a more credible attendance than most parliamentarian members of the Board.[75]

46. William George Armstrong: Start date: 7 August 1921; finish date: 15 August 1924. Occupation: doctor.

Born in Essex, England, and educated at King's School Canterbury, William Armstrong came out to Australia and settled at Hunter Hill, attended Sydney Grammar School, and gained his medical qualifications from Sydney University. Armstrong moved into the Department of Health as a senior medical officer and between 1904 and 1920 he lectured at the university. After acting in the position for one year, he was appointed in July 1922 Director-General of Public Health and president of the Board of Health. It was in this capacity that he joined the APB. He attended 17 from 23 meetings, at a rate of 74 per cent.[76]

47. H.D. McLelland: Start date: 25 May 1923; finish date: 3 December 1926. Occupation: chief inspector of schools.

Over two and half years McLelland attended 6 meetings out of 26, or a rate of 23 per cent. There was no mention in the press of McLellan in his role on the Board. His resignation was only noted in the Board minutes.[77]

48. Theodore Hooke Hill: Start date: 24 August 1923; finish date: 2 September 1927. Occupation: parliamentarian/bank manager.

After a background in banking, Hill moved into politics.[78] Over a period of four years Hill attended 22 Board meetings from 30, an attendance rate of 73 per cent.[79] There was no mention of any connections with Aboriginal people in the press; the Board mentioned his resignation in the minutes but without comment.[80]

49. Robert Dick: Start date: 15 August 1924; finish date: 12 September 1934. Occupation: Director-General of Public Health.

---

75 Analysis of *APBM* for relevant years.
76 Analysis of *APBM* for relevant years.
77 *APBM*, 3 December 1926, Item 1.
78 'Mr Theodore Hooke Hill (1855–1942)', Members, Former Members, Parliament of New South Wales. Accessed via: www.parliament.nsw.gov.au/members/formermembers/Pages/former-member-details.aspx?pk=986.
79 Analysis of *APBM* for relevant years.
80 *APBM*, 27 December 1927, Item 1.

Robert Dick spent most of his working life in the Newcastle-Hunter district as a full-time medical officer, then as the senior medical officer of health prior to his promotion to director-general. His period in high office was characterised by fiscal restraint, epidemics and the Great Depression.[81] There is no mention in the press of Dick's connection with Aboriginal people and after 10 years on the Protection Board, the Board minutes record: 'Convey the Board's best wishes to Dick in retirement'.[82] He attended 55 from a possible 73 meetings, a credible attendance rate of 75.3 per cent.[83]

50. Samuel Lasker: Start date: 27 August 1926; finish date: 17 December 1929. Occupation: chief inspector, education department.

There was no mention in the press of any connections with Aboriginal people while Lasker was on the Board. The board minutes record on his resignation: 'Accepted with regret appreciation placed on the record'.[84] Over three years he attended 13 from 24 meetings, or an attendance rate of 54 per cent.

Figure A1.20: Roy S. Vincent.
Source: Parliamentary Archives, NSW Parliament Collection (VincentRS-348).

51. Roy S. Vincent: Start date: 23 March 1928; finish date: 1936. Occupation: journalist and newspaper proprietor and parliamentarian.

Roy Stanley Vincent was educated in Uralla, New South Wales, and became editor and owner, along with his brother, of the *Don Dorrigo Gazette* on the mid-north coast. He entered parliament as the member for Oxley and later Raleigh, and remained a Legislative Assembly member for over 30 years.[85] During

---
81 Cummings, *A History of Medical Administration in NSW 1788–1973*, 85–86.
82 *APBM*, 16 November 1934, Item 1.
83 Analysis of *APBM* for relevant years.
84 *APBM*, 17 December 1929, Item 1.
85 'Mr Roy Stanley Vincent (1892–1965)', Members, Former Members, Parliament of New South Wales. Accessed via: www.parliament.nsw.gov.au/members/formermembers/Pages/former-member-details.aspx?pk=1525.

his eight years on the Board he only attended 16 from 67 meetings, an attendance rate of 23.8 per cent.[86] Like many MLA Board members his attendance was poor. He did, however, show some concern for the plight of Aboriginal people. In early December 1930 he inquired of the chief minister about the appalling condition of the Aborigines at Urunga, and three months later he asked Premier Jack Lang to provide the Board with more funds to address the 'deplorable conditions' of the Aboriginal people at South West Rocks and Bellbrook.[87]

52. John Henry Bate: Start date: 19 October 1928; finish date: continued after 1940 with the 'new' Aborigines Welfare Board (AWB). Occupation: parliamentarian.

Reference in the text: see Chapter 8. John Henry Bate was MLA for the South Coast for over 15 years. During the 1936 amendment to the *Aborigines Protection Act 1909* (NSW), Bate informed members that he 'had longer experience that any other current Board member' that he was 'born among the aboriginals' and his first school was 'an aboriginal school'. From his 'well-credentialed position' he argued that it was imperative that the Board been given powers to insist on medical examinations of all Aboriginal people. If not, the 'health of our people is very seriously threatened'.[88] He was educated at Newington College and the Sydney Technical and Hawkesbury Agricultural Colleges. He had strong connections with the agricultural communities on the south coast and was vice-president of the primary producers union. His attended 56 meetings from 104, an attendance rate of 53.8 per cent. He remained on the Board from 1928 until its demise in 1940. He was reappointed to the AWB and remained until 1943.

53. Walter Henry Childs: Start date: 22 March 1929; finish date: 13 March 1935. Occupation: commissioner of police.

Born in Bega on the south coast, Childs entered the police force at the age of 20 in 1892. Over the next four decades he worked his way through the ranks to become the top policeman in 1929.[89] He spent six years as chair of the Board, from 1929 until 1935, and was a regular attender of meetings. When Childs retired from the position, unlike his predecessor

---

86 Analysis of *APBM* for relevant years.
87 NSW, *Parliamentary Debates*, Legislative Assembly, 3 December 1930, 131 (Roy Vincent).
88 *Shoalhaven News and South Coast District Advertiser*, 4 July 1936, 3.
89 Lindsay, *True Blue: 150 Years of Service*. 140.

James Mitchell, the secretary was 'instructed to place on the record the Board's high appreciation of the service rendered by Mr Childs not only at the meetings but to the aborigines generally throughout the state'.[90] He attended 38 meetings from a possible 42, a very credible attendance rate of 90 per cent.

54. George R. Thomas: Start date: 20 February 1930; finish date: 13 November 1930. Occupation: chief inspector of schools.

George Ross Thomas replaced Samuel Lasker. Thomas only attended three meetings, but as there were only five held for the whole year, his attendance rate was 40 per cent. There is no mention of any contribution from him in the press or in the Board minutes. His influence on the Board could be considered negligible.

Figure A1.21: George R. Thomas.
Source: Royal Australian Historical Society, Inspectors of Schools, PXA 1538, 2039/67. Mitchell Library, State Library of New South Wales.

Figure A1.22: Bertie Clarence Harkness.
Source: 'NSW Inspector of Schools', 1932. Royal Australian Historical Society, Inspectors of Schools, PXA 1538, 2039/24. Mitchell Library, State Library New South Wales.

---

90 *APBM*, 13 March 1935, Item 14.

55. Bertie Clarence Harkness: Start date: 16 January 1931; finish date: 1940. Occupation: chief inspector of schools.

Reference in the text: Chapter 8. Bertie Clarence Harkness spent nine years on the Board and appeared to be quite an active member. In October 1934 he inspected the Bomaderry Home for Aborigines, and in November, to honour the 19 Aboriginal men who served in the First World War, he visited the Walhallow Aboriginal Station.[91] In April 1937 he visited, along with Inspector Withers from the Board, the station at Ulgundahi Island.[92] He also attended the opening of a new recreational hall at the Burnt Bridge Aboriginal Station near Kempsey in May 1938.[93] Harkness was a consistent attender of meetings, present at 55 from a possible 76, an attendance rate of 72.4 per cent.[94]

56. William James Scully: Start date: 6 February 1931; finish date: sometime in 1937. Occupation: parliamentarian.

William James Scully was the member for Naomi in the Legislative Assembly. Over the course of the six years he spent on the Board, he only attended 4 meetings from a possible 54. An attendance rate of 7.4 per cent would dismiss any influence he had on Board matters.[95] Unusually for the Board, his poor attendance was noted in the minutes.[96]

57. Alfred McClelland: Start date: 6 February 1931; finish date: 4 December 1935. Occupation: parliamentarian.

Alfred McClelland was the member for Northern Tablelands and later Dubbo. Over the four years he spent on the Board he only attended six meetings from a possible 33; an attendance rate of 18 per cent.[97] He was not effectively engaged with the Board.

58. Emmanuel Sydney Morris: Start date: 16 November 1934; finish date: 1940. Occupation: medical practitioner.

---

91 *Shoalhaven News and South Coast District Advertiser*, 6 October 1934, 4; *Daily Telegraph*, 20 November 1934, 10.
92 *Daily Examiner*, 10 April 1937, 4.
93 *Macleay Argus*, 31 May 1938, 4.
94 Analysis of *APBM* for relevant years.
95 Analysis of *APBM* for relevant years.
96 *APBM*, 12 June 1935, Item 12.
97 Analysis of *APBM* for relevant years.

Sydney Morris was a Quaker and a 'kindly man ... with a deep spiritual conviction'.[98] He devoted his life to government service. After graduating at Sydney University in 1911, he moved into health administration, was appointed director of public health in Tasmania and in 1934 took over from Robert Dick as director-general for New South Wales. Sydney Morris remained on the Board to the end and was appointed to continue the new AWB. He attended 41 meetings from a possible 62, an attendance rate of 66 per cent. There is no evidence in the minutes or the press that he engaged in any direct way with Aboriginal people.

59. William John Mackay: Start date: 12 June 1935; finish date: June 1940. Occupation: police commissioner.

For major reference to Mackay, see Chapter 8. William MacKay's attendance was very solid, attending 29 from 37 meetings, at a rate of 78.4 per cent. His deputy, T. Lynch, stood in for MacKay at eight meetings during 1936 but was never officially appointed to the Board.

Figure A1.23: William John MacKay.
Source: Lindsay, *True Blue: 150 Years of Service*, 143.

Figure A1.24: George Edward Ardill.
Source: Parliamentary Archives, NSW Parliament Collection (ArdillGE-29P-1930).

---

98   Cummins, *A History of Medical Administration in NSW 1788–1973*, 86.

60. George Edward Ardill: Start date: 4 December 1935; finish date: 1940. Occupation: parliamentarian/dairy framer, grazier and auctioneer.

George Ardill was the son of George Ardill who served on the Board until 1916. He followed in his father's footsteps and was the executive director of the Sydney Rescue Work Society for providing homes for neglected children from 1945. He was the member for Yass for 10 years and was a Board member for over four years. He was appointed to the new AWB. He attended 33 of 55 meetings, an attendance rate of 60 per cent.

61. George Alexander Mitchell: Start date: 4 December 1935; finish date: 6 June 1938. Occupation: former metropolitan superintendent of police.

Although a regular attender – 31 from 37 meetings, an attendance rate of 84 per cent – there is nothing to indicate that Mitchell influenced policy or directly connected with Aboriginal people. He was, however, the first to resign from the Board in protest at the speech from the deputy leader of the government, Mr Bruxner, who had cast aspersions upon the Board and its members.[99]

62. Hugh Gilmore Wallace: Start date: 29 May 1936; finish date: 6 January 1937. Occupation: medical doctor/health administrator.

Hugh Wallace was appointed to the Board for a brief period to fill in for Sydney Morris. He attended seven from eight meetings (88 per cent) for a period of six months. He was appointed to the AWB.

63. Stanley Llewellyn Anderson: Start date: 7 December 1938; attended 100 per cent of meetings and then continued in the AWB. Occupation: Under-Secretary to the Colonial Secretary.

64. Alfred William George Lipscomb: Start date: 8 March 1939; attended 100 per cent of meetings and then continued as chair of the AWB. Occupation: teacher, author, employee of Dr Barnardo's Homes.

---

99   *Daily Telegraph*, 6 June 1938, 4. See also Chapter 8.

Appendix 2: Member attendance for all Board members from 1883 until 1916

It should be noted that there were nearly 50 meetings each year under the 'old' Board. Therefore, these members were attending many more meetings than their successors after 1916.

Note: attendance details are unavailable for Gordon, Foster, Robison and Tarrant.

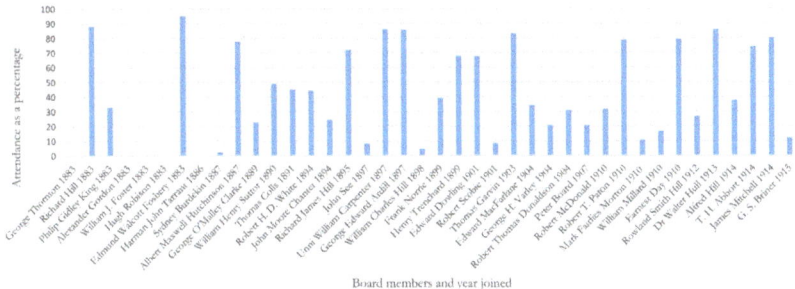

Figure A2.1: Board member attendance from 1883 to 1916.
Source: Author's analysis of *APBM*, 1883–1916.

325

Appendix 3: Member attendance for all Board members from 1916 until 1939

It should be noted that the number of Board meetings during this period was severely reduced. Members were only required to attend, on average, one meeting every six weeks.

Note: no attendance details for Ross are included, as he was replaced immediately after his appointment.

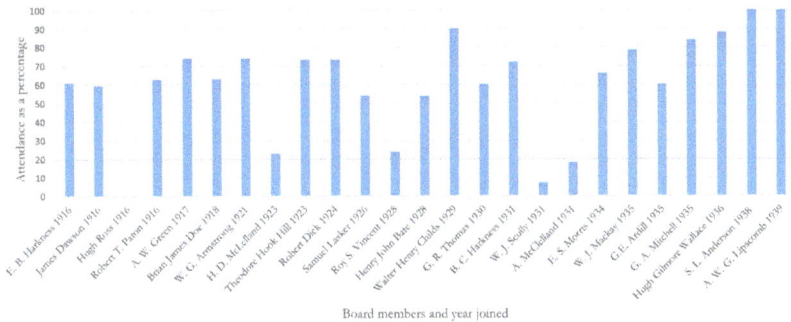

Figure A3.1: Board member attendance from 1916 to 1939.
Source: Author's analysis of *APBM*, 1916–39.

Appendix 4: Statistics of removals (see Chapter 6)

All data from the author's analysis of the Ward Registers, 1916–28.

Aboriginal girls

Data on removal from institutions and within each region shows that some Aboriginal stations and reserves bore a disproportionate burden of removals in raw figures (Figures A4.1–A4.9).

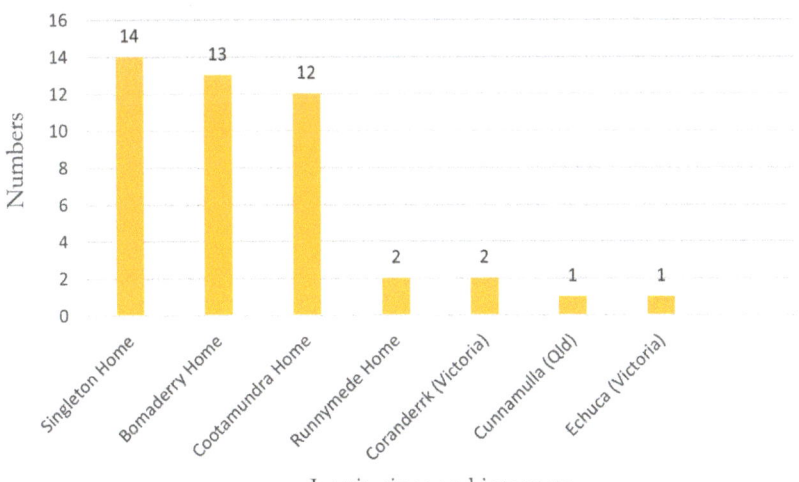

Figure A4.1: Numbers of Aboriginal girls removed from institutions and interstate who were placed in apprenticeships (1916–28). Total: 45.

POWER AND DYSFUNCTION

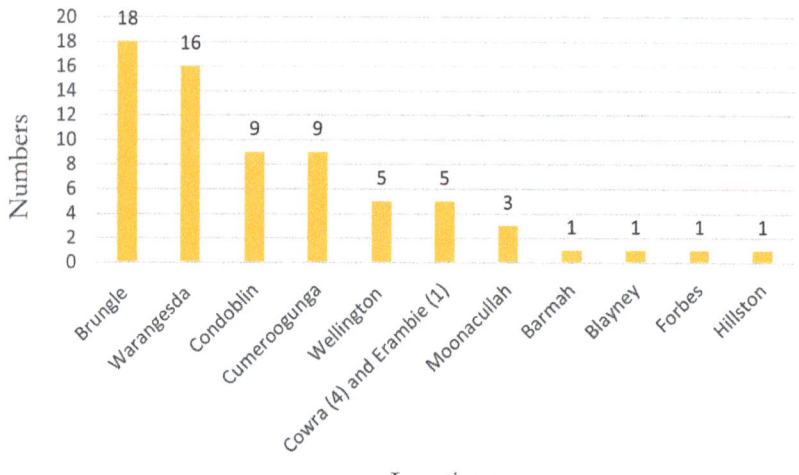

Figure A4.2: Numbers of Aboriginal girls removed from locations within the Wiradjuri region (1916–28). Total: 69.

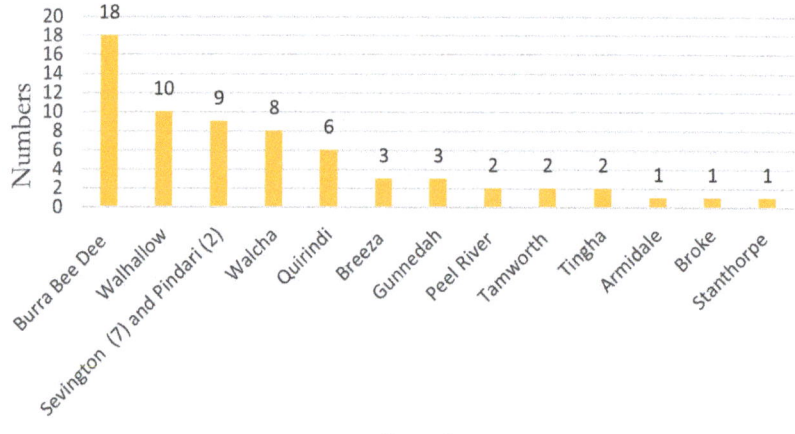

Figure A4.3: Numbers of Aboriginal girls removed from locations within the Northern region (1916–28). Total: 66.

APPENDIX 4

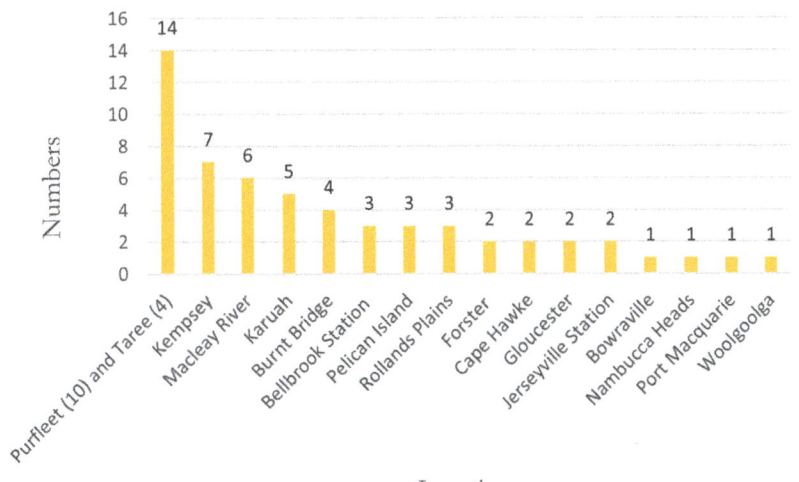

Figure A4.4: Numbers of Aboriginal girls removed from locations within the Mid-North Coast region (1916–28). Total: 57.

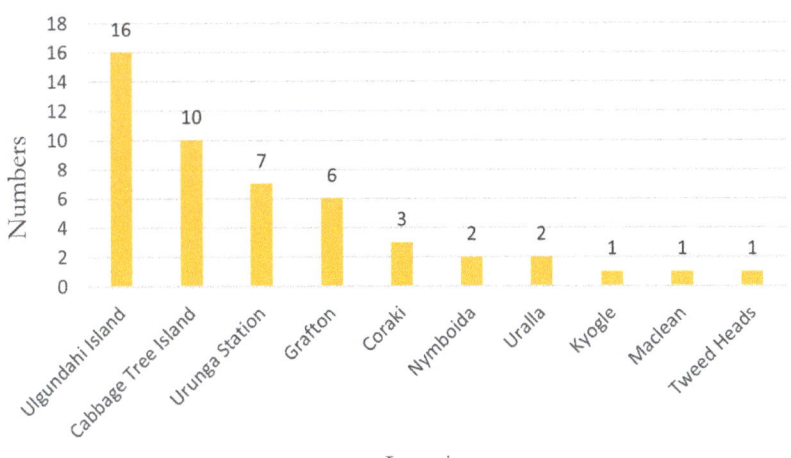

Figure A4.5: Numbers of Aboriginal girls removed from locations within the North Coast region (1916–28). Total: 49.

POWER AND DYSFUNCTION

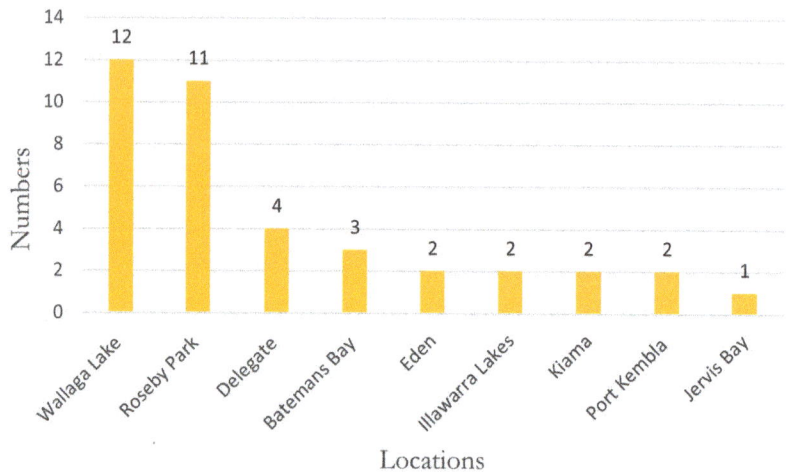

Figure A4.6: Numbers of Aboriginal girls removed from locations within the South Coast region (1916–28). Total: 39.

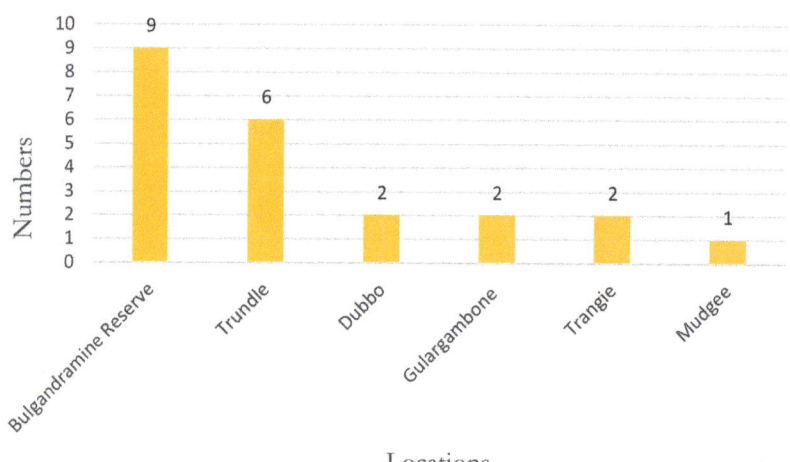

Figure A4.7: Number of Aboriginal girls removed from locations within the Central region (1916–28). Total: 22.

APPENDIX 4

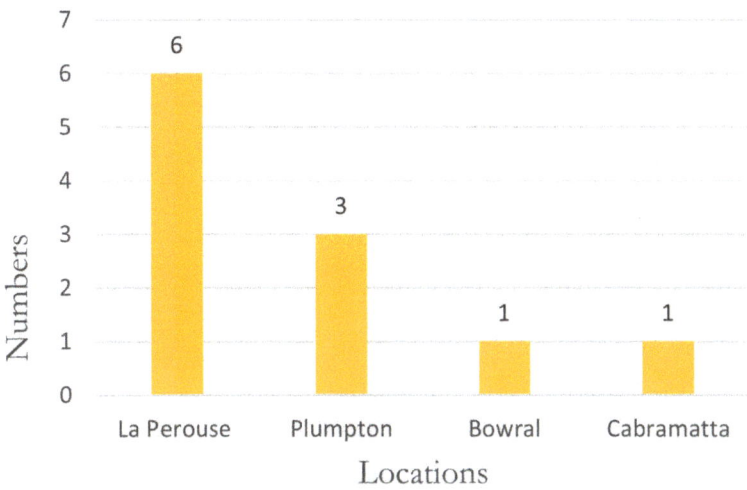

Figure A4.8: Numbers of Aboriginal girls removed from locations within the Sydney/Newcastle region (1916–28). Total: 11.

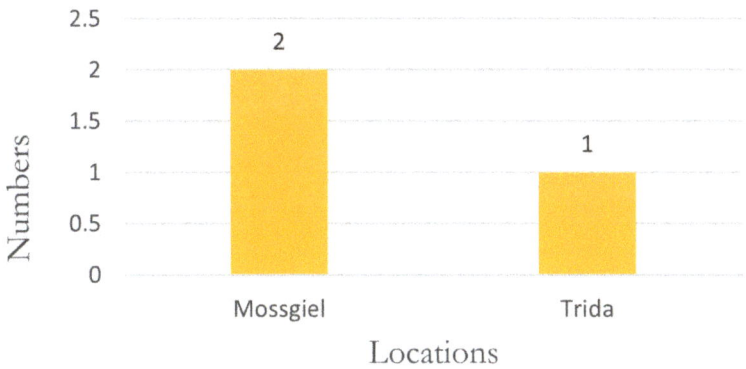

Figure A4.9: Numbers of Aboriginal girls removed from two locations in the Western region (1916–28). Total: 3.

Aboriginal boys

A similar pattern of disproportionate removal from stations and reserves within a region is demonstrated for the boys (Figures A4.10–A4.17).

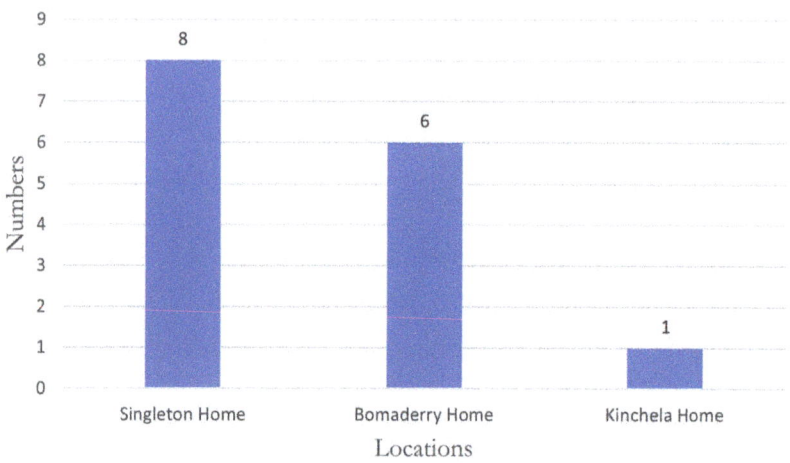

Figure A4.10: Numbers of Aboriginal boys removed from institutions who were placed in apprenticeships (1916–28). Total: 15.

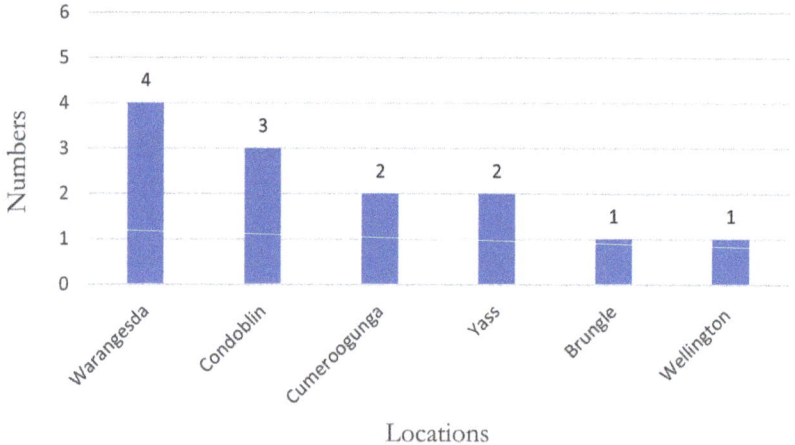

Figure A4.11: Numbers of Aboriginal boys removed from locations within the Wiradjuri region (1916–28). Total: 13.

APPENDIX 4

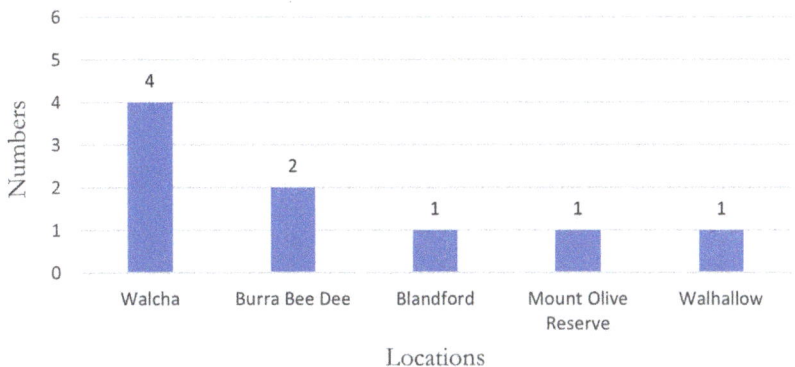

Figure A4.12: Numbers of Aboriginal boys removed from locations within the Northern region (1916–28). Total: 9.

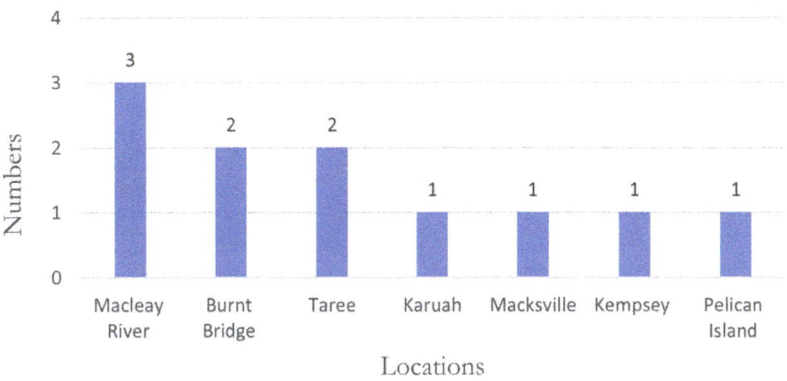

Figure A4.13: Numbers of Aboriginal boys removed from locations within the Mid-North Coast region (1916–28). Total: 11.

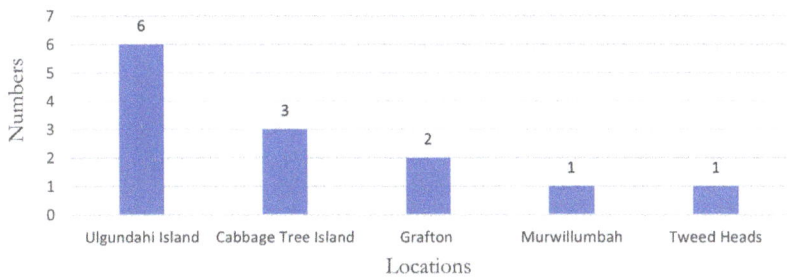

Figure A4.14: Numbers of Aboriginal boys removed from locations within the North Coast region (1916–28). Total: 13.

POWER AND DYSFUNCTION

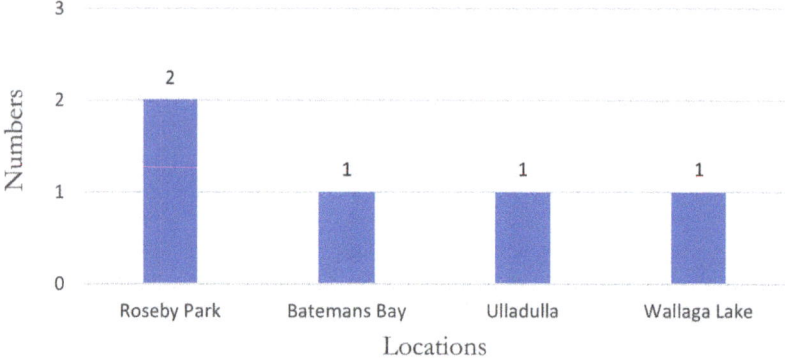

Figure A4.15: Numbers of Aboriginal boys removed from locations within the South Coast region (1916–28). Total: 5.

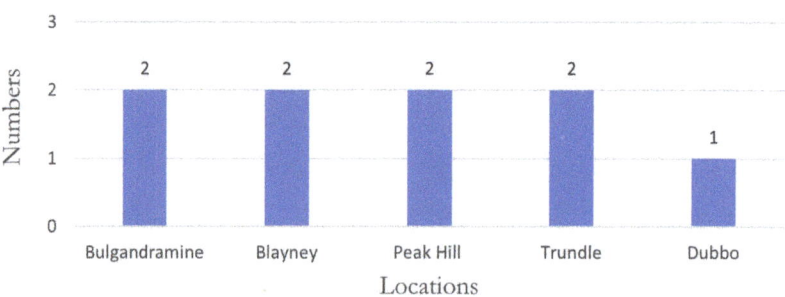

Figure A4.16: Numbers of Aboriginal boys removed from locations within the Central region (1916–28). Total: 9.

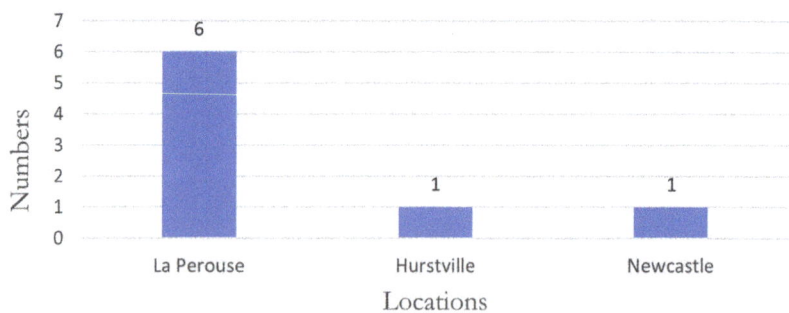

Figure A4.17: Numbers of Aboriginal boys removed from locations within the Sydney/Newcastle region (1916–28). Total: 8.

There were no boys removed from the Western region.

Bibliography

Primary Sources – Archival

Aborigines Protection Board Records

Aborigines Welfare Board – Ward Registers 18 January 1916 – 2 June 1926; 28 May 1924–27 and December 1928, NRS 26, Original location 4/8553 and 4/8554; Reel 2793. Kingswood: State Records of New South Wales (hereafter SRNSW).

Copies of Letters Sent, 1914–27, 4/7128, NRS 5, Reel 1853. Kingswood: SRNSW.

Indexes to Ward Registers, 1916 – circa 1938, NRS 27, Reel 1649, SRNSW (accessed at NSW Department of Aboriginal Affairs in Sydney).

Register of Aboriginal Reserves, 1875–1904, 2/8349, NRS 23, Reel 2847, Aborigines Welfare Board Archives. Kingswood: SRNSW.

Registers of Letters 1910–13, NRS 7 7/3644 (1 September 1910 – 25 September 1911); 7/3645 (10 October 1912 – 4 July 1913). Kingswood: SRNSW.

Colonial Secretary's Papers

Colonial Secretary's Papers, NRS 905. Main Series of Letters Received [Colonial Secretary], 1826–1982, (Colonial Secretary's In-Letters, hereafter CSIL). Kingswood: SRNSW.

CSIL: **1899**, Box 5/7541; **1900**, Boxes 5/7542, 5/5922, 5/6417, 5/6507, 5/6508, 5/6574, 5/6512; **1903**, Box 5/6721; **1904**, Boxes 5/6817, 5/6810, 5/6816F; **1908**, Box 5/6990; **1909**, Box 5/7030; **1910**, Box 5/7073; **1911**, Box 5/7121; **1912**, Box 5/7165; **1913**, Box 5/7204; **1914**, Box 5/7260; **1915**, Box 5/7324; **1916**, Boxes 5/7392, 5/7401–5/7412, 5/7417–5/7423; **1917**, Box 5/7483; **1918**, Box 5/7956; **1919**, Box 5/8018; **1920**, Box 5/8099; **1934**, Boxes 5/9245–5/9268, 5/9283–5/9284; **1935**, Boxes 12/7512–12/7530, 9/2421; **1936**, Boxes 12/7532–12/7546; **1937**, Boxes 12/7545–12/7559, 9/2420; **1938**, Boxes 12/7560–12/7562.

Premiers Department Correspondence

Premiers Department Correspondence Files, Letters Received, NRS 12060, 1927, A903–1342, Box 9/1957. Kingswood: SRNSW.

Premiers Special Bundles, Treatment of Aborigines in NSW 1936–63, NRS 12061, 62/1515 (Part 1) (ref. 12/8749–12/8750). Kingswood: SRNSW.

Department of Public Instruction/Education

Education Files, Department of Education in Letters, 20/12561, Chief Inspectors Reports 1915. Kingswood: SRNSW.

Education, Subject Files, 1875–1948, 20/12730, Government Correspondence 1902. Kingswood: SRNSW.

School Files – SRNSW

Note: All school files from NRS 3829.

Appin School, Pre-1939, File 5/14665.2 (Bundles A and B).

Bomaderry School, Pre-1939, File 5/14993 (Bundles A and B).

Breeza School, File 5/15077.1 (Bundle A).

Dapto School, 1876–1909, File 5/15645.2 (Bundles A and B).

Euroka School, File 5/15854 (Bundle A).

Gerringong School, File 5/15979.29 (Bundle A).

Greenwell Point School, File 5/16146.2 (Bundles A and B).

Huskisson North School, 1876–1919, File 5/16347.2; 1919–1939, File 5/16348.1.

Jervis Bay Aboriginal School, Pre-1939, Files 5/16388.3 and 5/16388.4.

Kangaroo Valley School, 1876–1913, File 5/16418.2 (Bundle A).

Kiama School, 1876–1897, File 5/16465; 1897–1925, File 5/16466 (Bundles A and B); 1925–1939, File 5/16467 (Bundles A and B).

La Perouse Public School, File 5/16561.2.

Larry's Flat School, File 5/16564.1.

Minnamurra School, Pre-1939, File 5/16863.1.

Minto East School, Pre-1939, File 5/16865 (Bundle A).

Minto School, Pre-1939, File 5/16864 (Bundle A).

Nowra School, 1876–1905, File 5/17181 (Bundle A).

Roseby Park Aboriginal School, File 5/17511.2.

Sans Souci School,1926–33, 5/17593 (Bundles A, B and C).

Shellharbour School, 1877–1909, File 5/17617.4; 1909–1939, File 5/17618 (Bundles A and B).

Unanderra School, 1914–39, File 5/17938.1 (Bundle A).

Wallaga Lake School, File 5/17986.2.

Wreck Bay School, 1876–1939, File 5/18213.2.

Archives of Victoria

Correspondence Files, VPRS 1694/P0000/15, Question 2127, South Australian Royal Commission. Melbourne: Public Records Office of Victoria (hereafter PROV).

Victorian Board for the Protection of Aborigines, Correspondence Files, VPRS 1694, P00001/5/15 and VPRS 10768/Units 1–24. Melbourne: PROV.

Archives of South Australia

Correspondence Files – Advisory Council of Aborigines, GRG 52, Series 10, 1/1921 – 5A/1937. Adelaide: State Records of South Australia.

NSW Local Government

Berry Council Minute Book (1928–1936). Nowra, NSW: Shoalhaven City Council.

Berry Council Minute Book (1936–1938). Nowra, NSW: Shoalhaven City Council.

Nowra Council Minute Book (November 1933 – December 1935). Nowra, NSW: Shoalhaven City Council.

Randwick Municipal Council Minute Books: May 1900 – Nov 1909, Yv1532, CY 2933. Bowen Library, Randwick.

Unpublished Manuscripts

Aborigines Inland Mission Records, 1904–1988, MLMSS 7895 1(8); 1905–1923 correspondence primarily from the NSW Office of the Board for the Protection of Aborigines (one of seven folders). Sydney: Mitchell Library (hereafter ML).

Australian Christian Endeavour Union Records, 1892–1998, MLMSS 8088 9(9). Sydney: State Library of New South Wales (hereafter SLNSW).

Daniel Matthews Papers, 1861–1917, Vol. 2, A3384, Parts 1 and 2 (unfortunately, Vol. B 1339 has gone missing since 1993 (only from ML)), ML.

George Thornton Papers, MS 3290. Canberra: National Library of Australia (hereafter NLA).

J.B. Gribble Collected Papers, 1873–1905, 2 Boxes, MS 1514. Sydney: ML and Canberra: Australian Institute of Aboriginal and Torres Strait Islander Studies (hereafter AIATSIS).

Joan Kingsley-Strack Papers, MS 9551: Series 2 – Diaries, Box 3, Folder 10 (1937–1938); Series 7 – Aboriginal Domestic Workers, Folders 1–11 (1924–1973); Series 8 – Committee for Aboriginal Citizenship, Box 11, Folders 1–4 and 9 (1935–1953). Canberra: NLA.

John See Papers, 1885–1905, A 3649–A 3677. Sydney: ML.

Pearl Gibbs Collection, 1915–1983, MLMSS 6922/5 (8). Sydney: ML.

Peter Board Papers, 1872–1944, MLMSS 1095. Sydney: ML.

Primary Sources – Published

Official Printed Sources

Aboriginal Mission Stations at Warangesda and Maloga (Report On Working Of.), Legislative Assembly, New South Wales, 18 January 1883. Available via 'NSW', To Remove and Protect, AIATSIS: aiatsis.gov.au/sites/default/files/docs/digitised_collections/remove/91936.pdf.

Aboriginal Welfare: The Initial Conference of Commonwealth and States Aboriginal Authorities, April 1937, Canberra, 1937, Q353.53499/10. Sydney: ML.

Aborigines: Minutes of Evidence taken before the Select Committee on the Aborigines, Mahroot alias the Boatswain, 8 September 1845, 1–5.

Aborigines Protection: Report and Recommendations of the Public Service Board of New South Wales, 4 April 1940, Government Printer NSW, 6/4501.1. Kingswood: SRNSW.

Central Board Appointed to Watch Over the Interests of the Aborigines in the Colony of Victoria, First Report, 1861. Available via 'Victoria', To Remove and Protect, AIATSIS: aiatsis.gov.au/sites/default/files/docs/digitised_collections/remove/24372.pdf.

NSW Government Gazette, 1910, Vol. 2, from 1 April to 30 June. Regulations for Aborigines Protection Act, 1909, No. 92, 8 June 1910, 3060–64. Sydney: SLNSW.

NSW Government Gazette, 1915, Vol. 2, from 1 April to 30 June. Management of Stations, No. 97, 2 June 1915, 3073. Sydney: SLNSW.

NSW Government Gazette, 26 September, 1942. Sydney: SLNSW.

Protection of the Aborigines (Minute of the Colonial Secretary, Together with Reports), Legislative Assembly, New South Wales, 2 March 1883. Available via 'NSW', To Remove and Protect, AIATSIS: aiatsis.gov.au/sites/default/files/docs/digitised_collections/remove/91930.pdf.

Report from the Select Committee on Aborigines (British Settlements); With the Minutes of Evidence, Appendix and Index, House of Commons, 26 June 1837, VQ 354.9400814/10. Sydney: Main Library, UNSW.

Report of the Select Committee of the Legislative Council, The Aborigines. Victorian Parliamentary Papers, 1858/9, Vol. 1, D.8. Available via 'NSW' To Remove and protect, AISTSIS: aiatsis.gov.au/sites/default/files/docs/digitised_collections/remove/92768.pdf.

Select Committee on Administration of Aborigines Protection Board, Proceedings of the Committee, Minutes of Evidence and Exhibits. NSW Parliamentary Papers, Session 1838–40, Vol. 7, Q328.94401/2, 609–732. Sydney: SLNSW.

Thornton, G. *Aborigines: Report of the Protector, to 31 December 1882,* Legislative Assembly, New South Wales, 1883. Available via 'NSW', To Remove and Protect, AIATSIS: aiatsis.gov.au/sites/default/files/docs/digitised_collections/remove/91912.pdf.

Aboriginal Protection Board Reports

Annual Reports for the Board for the Protection of Aborigines from 1884 to 1942. These reports are not in one location and have been obtained from four sources:

a. 'NSW', To Remove and Protect, AIATSIS: aiatsis.gov.au/collection/featured-collections/remove-and-protect. Accessed between January 2015 and March 2018. Contains the following digitised reports: 1884–1889; 1894; 1903; 1907–1908; 1910–1915; 1917–1918; 1919–1921; 1923–1937; and 1940.

b. CSIL, 1903, 5/6721, Board report for year ending 1901. Sydney: SLNSW.

c. *NSW Legislative Assembly*: *Aborigines Report of Board for the Aborigines 1915–1922*, Q572.991 N. A slim volume that holds reports 1915 through to 1922 and contains, importantly, the report for 1916 – it is a typed carbon copy and was never printed. Sydney: SLNSW.

d. *Journal of the Legislative Council*, Q328.9106/7. Found in *NSW Parliamentary Papers, Consolidated Index* (Ref. Q342.912) Vol. 2, 1874–1893; Vol. 3, 1894–1913; Vol. 4, 1914–1934; and Vol. 5, 1934–1954 for the following Board reports:

1890, Vol. 47, Part 2, 1263; **1891–92**, Vol. 49, Part 2, 1017; **1892–93**, Vol. 50, Part 2, 301; **1892–93**, Vol. 50, Part 2, 327; **1894**, Vol. 52, Part 2, 157; **1896**, Vol. 55, Part 1, 683; **1897**, Vol. 56, Part 1, 607; **1898**, Vol. 57, Part 1, 391; **1899**, Vol. 61, Part 1, 859; **1900**, Vol. 62, Part 2, 255; **1902**, Vol. 64, Part 1, 1101; **1903**, Vol. 65, Part 2, 251; **1906**, Vol. 69, Part 1, 835; **1906** Vol. 69, Part 1, 853; **1907**, Vol. 71, Part 2, 79; **1910**, Vol. 75, Part 1, 395; **1922**, Vol. 94, Part 2, 945; **1941–42**, Vol. 1, 1151 (tabled in Assembly only). Sydney: SLNSW.

Aboriginal Protection Board Minutes

Minute Books (Aborigines Welfare Board), NRS 2, 25 Sep 1890 – 4 Jul 1901 (4/7108–15; microfilm copy SR Reels 2788-2789), 23 May 1905 – 11 Dec 1906 (4/7116, 4/7118, 4/7120; microfilm copy SR Reel 2790), 17 Mar 1910 – 14 Sep 1938 (4/7119, 4/7117, 4/7121–27; microfilm copy SR Reels 2790–2792). Accessed at the NSW Department of Aboriginal Affairs, Sydney.

NSW Parliamentary Debates

Legislative Assembly: 20 November 1879; 10 July 1890; 18 February 1892; 29 June 1887; 20 September 1900; 21 September 1900; 11 October 1900; 3 July 1902; 21 October 1903; 6 December 1906; 13 July 1909; 15 December 1909; 27 January 1915; 28 September 1915; 13 October 1915; 9 October 1917; 5 March 1918; 3 December 1930; 18 June 1936; 9 November 1937. Available via: www.parliament.nsw.gov.au/Pages/home.aspx.

Legislative Council: 20 September 1882; 17 April 1884; 17 December 1909; 24 November 1914; 17 October 1917; 18 October 1917; 5 February 1918. Available via: www.parliament.nsw.gov.au/Pages/home.aspx

Legislation

Aborigines Protection Act 1909 (NSW)
Aborigines Protection Amending Act 1915 (NSW)
Aborigines Protection (Amendment) Act 1918 (NSW)
Aborigines Protection (Amendment) Act 1936 (NSW)
Aborigines Protection (Amendment) Act 1940 (NSW)
Aborigines Protection Act 1869 (Vic.)
Aborigines Protection Act 1886 (Vic.)
Aborigines Act 1910 (Vic.)
Aborigines Protection Act 1886 (WA)
Aborigines Act 1915 (WA)
Aborigines Protection and Restriction of the Sale of Opium Act 1897 (Qld)
Aborigines Act 1911 (SA)
Apprentices Act 1901 (NSW)
Cape Barren Reserve Act 1912 (Tas.)
Children's Protection Act 1892 (NSW)
Deserted Wives and Children's Act 1901 (NSW)
Industrial Schools Act 1866 (NSW)
Neglected and Juvenile Offenders Act 1905 (NSW)
Public Instruction Act 1880 (NSW)
Reformatory and Industrial Schools Act 1901 (NSW)
State Children Relief Act 1881 (NSW)
Vagrancy Act 1935 (NSW)
Victorian Aborigines Act 1890 (Vic.)

Interviews

Bursill, Les, interviewed by the author, 12 July 2017 at Worrigee (near Nowra).

Pettitt, Charles Arthur, interviewed by J.J. Fletcher, 1977, Audio-tape, J01-018426 and J01-018427, PMS 5380. Canberra: AIATSIS.

Simms, Herb, interviewed by Fred Maynard, 7 April 2001, La Perouse, Bib ID: 950973, ORAL TRC 5000/263, NLA.

Simms, Sonny, interviewed by the author, 28 June 2016 and 4 June 2017, Nowra.

Smith, Bryan, interviewed by the author, 12 July 2017, at Worrigee (near Nowra).

Timbery, Laddie, informal discussion with author, June 2016, Huskisson.

Publications

Brennan, Martin. *Reminiscences of the Gold Fields*. Sydney: William Brooks & Co, 1907.

Course of Instruction for Aborigines' Schools. Sydney: Department of Education New South Wales, William Applegate Gullick, Government Printer, 1916.

Course of Instruction for Aborigines' Schools. Sydney: Department of Education, New South Wales, Government Printer, 1940.

Dowling, Edward. *Australia and America in 1892: A Contrast*. Chicago: Published by Authority of the New South Wales Commissioners for the World's Columbian Exposition, 1893 (Rare Books – UNSW Library).

Fraser, John. *The Aborigines of New South Wales*. Chicago: Published by Authority of the New South Wales Commissioners for the World's Columbian Exposition, 1893 (Rare Books – UNSW Library).

The Golden Link, Vol. 3, No. 29, 1 December 1894.

Gribble, J.B. 'Black But Comely: Annual Report of the New South Wales Aborigines Protection Association for 1892', Sydney: (Daniel Mathews Papers, SLNSW) 1893.

Hill, Richard and G. Thornton. *Notes on the Aborigines of New South Wales – With Personal Reminiscences of the Tribes Formerly Living in the Neighbourhood of Sydney and the Surrounding Districts*. Phillip Street, Sydney: Charles Potter, Government Printer, 1892.

Matthews, Daniel. *The Story of the Maloga Aboriginal Mission*. Melbourne: Rae Bros., Polygraphic Printers, 1892.

The New South Wales Aborigines' Advocate. Issued under the auspices of the NSW Aborigines' Mission. A Monthly Record of Missionary Work Amongst the Aborigines, REF.1/MAV/FM4, 23 July 1901 – 31 Dec 1914. Sydney: SLNSW.

Patten, J.T. and W. Ferguson. *Aborigines Claim Citizen Rights! A Statement of the Case for the Aborigines Progressive Association*. Sydney: The Publicist, 1938.

Suttor, W.H. *Early Christian Missions among our Aborigines*. 1889. DSM/572. 9901/S. Sydney: ML.

Sydney Rescue Work Society, *The Rescue*, 30 May 1896; Vol. 6 No. 2, Sept 1896; Vol. 2, No. 10, Aug 1889; (new series) Vol. 3, No. 5, Oct 1890; Vol. 3 No. 6, Dec 1890; June 1894; May 1900 – Dec 1915. Sydney: ML.

Telfer, E.J. *Amongst Australian Aborigines Forty Years of Missionary Work: The Story of the United Aborigines Mission.* Melbourne: Fraser & Morphet Pty Ltd, 1939.

Third Australasian Catholic Congress, held at St. Mary's Cathedral Sydney 26th September – 3rd October 1909. Sydney: St Mary's Cathedral Book Depot, 1909, MG/1/U11. Sydney: ML.

Third Report of the Royal Commission on Public Charities; Subsidised Benevolent Institutions, Legislative Assembly, NSW, 1899. Sydney: ML.

Australian Dictionary of Biography

Note: All entries below from *Australian Dictionary of Biography*, National Centre of Biography, The Australian National University. Accessed between January 2015 and March 2018 at adb.anu.edu.au.

Cable, K. J. 'Gordon, Alexander (1815–1903)'. Accessed at: adb.anu.edu.au/biography/gordon-alexander-3636.

Cain, Frank. 'MacKay, William John (1885–1948)'. Accessed at: adb.anu.edu.au/biography/mackay-william-john-7381.

Cummins, C. J. 'Paton, Robert Thompson (1856–1929)'. Accessed at: adb.anu.edu.au/biography/paton-robert-thomson-7979.

Felton, Philip. 'Donaldson, Robert Thomas (1851–1936)'. Accessed at: adb.anu.edu.au/biography/donaldson-robert-thomas-5994.

Goodall, Heather, and John Maynard. 'Maynard, Charles Frederick (Fred) (1879–1946)'. Accessed at: adb.anu.edu.au/biography/maynard-charles-frederick-fred-11095.

Hawker, G.N., and Joan Rydon. 'Chanter, John Moore (1845–1931)'. Accessed at: adb.anu.edu.au/biography/chanter-john-moore-5553.

Horner, Jack. 'Ferguson, William (Bill) (1882–1950)'. Accessed at: adb.anu.edu.au/biography/ferguson-william-bill-6160.

Humphries, Shirley. 'Burdekin, Sydney (1839–1899)'. Accessed at: adb.anu.edu.au/biography/burdekin-sydney-3331.

King, Hazel. 'Day, Ernest Charles (1857–1915)'. Accessed at: adb.anu.edu.au/biography/day-ernest-charles-5923.

McMinn, W.G. 'Dowling, Edward (1843–1912)'. Accessed at: adb.anu.edu.au/biography/dowling-edward-6006.

O'Grady, Frank. 'King, Philip Gidley (1817–1904)'. Accessed at: adb.anu.edu.au/biography/king-philip-gidley-3957.

Radi, Heather. 'Ardill, George Edward (1857–1945)'. Accessed at: adb.anu.edu.au/biography/ardill-george-edward-5048.

Radi, Heather. 'Long, Margaret Jane (Retta) (1878–1956)'. Accessed at: adb.anu.edu.au/biography/long-margaret-jane-retta-10857.

Rutledge, Martha. 'Foster, William John (1831–1909)'. Accessed at: adb.anu.edu.au/biography/foster-william-john-3560.

Rutledge, Martha. 'Hill, Richard (1810–1895)'. Accessed at: adb.anu.edu.au/biography/hill-richard-1141.

Rutledge, Martha, and Brian Dickey. 'Fosbery, Edmund Walcott (1834–1919)'. Accessed at: adb.anu.edu.au/biography/fosbery-edmund-walcott-3558.

Schulz, C. P. 'Colls, Thomas (1822–1898)'. Accessed at: adb.anu.edu.au/biography/colls-thomas-3246.

Teale, Ruth. 'Clarke, George O'Malley (1836–1899)'. Accessed at: adb.anu.edu.au/biography/clarke-george-omalley-3221.

Teale, Ruth. 'Suttor, William Henry (1834–1905)'. Accessed at: adb.anu.edu.au/biography/suttor-william-henry-4936.

Newspapers

The Age (Melbourne)
Albury Banner and Wodonga Express (Albury–Wodonga)
The Australian (Sydney)
Australian Star (Sydney)
Australian Town and Country Journal (Sydney)
Australian Workman (Sydney)
Bathurst Free Press (Bathurst)
Bega Budget (Bega)
Bird O' Freedom (Sydney)
The Burrowa News (Burrowa)
The Camden News (Camden)
Clarence and Richmond Examiner (Clarence)

Daily Examiner (Sydney)
Daily Herald (Adelaide)
Daily Telegraph (Sydney)
Echuca and Moama Advertiser and Farmers Gazette (Echuca)
Evening News (Sydney)
Goulburn Evening Penny Post (Goulburn)
Gundagai Times and Tumut, Adelong and Murrumbidgee District Advertiser (Gundagai)
Illawarra Mercury (Wollongong)
Inverell Times (Inverell)
Jerilderie Herald and Urana Advertiser (Jerilderie)
Labor Daily (Sydney)
Macleay Argus (Macleay)
Maitland Daily Mercury (Maitland)
Manning River Times and Advocate for the Northern Coast Districts of New South Wales (Taree)
Narrandera Argus (Narrandera)
News (Adelaide)
Northern Champion (Newcastle)
Northern Star (Newcastle)
Nowra Leader (Nowra)
The Richmond River Express and Casino Kyogle Advertiser (Casino)
Riverina Herald (Griffith)
Riverina Recorder (Griffith)
Shoalhaven News and South Coast District Advertiser (Nowra)
Shoalhaven Telegraph (Nowra)
Sun (Sydney)
Sydney Morning Herald (Sydney)
Truth (Sydney)
Tumut and Adelong Times (Tumut)
Wellington Times (Wellington)
Workers Weekly (Sydney)
Yass Tribune-Courier (Yass)

Other

Bate, H.J. 'Conference on the plight of the Aborigines 1938', 24–6 January 1938, JaHQ 2014/1905. Sydney: ML.

Camden Boys Home, Camden, New South Wales: Camden Historical Society Archives.

Courts of Petty Sessions, Kiama, Copies of letters sent, 9 March 1862 – 31 March 1892, City 4/5578. Kingswood: SRNSW.

'In Living Memory' Exhibition, Number 8470. Kingswood: SRNSW.

Secondary Sources

Theses

Barwick, Diane. 'A Little More than Kin: Regional Affiliation and Group Identity Among Aboriginal Migrants in Melbourne'. PhD thesis, The Australian National University, 1963.

Bell, Tracey. 'A Benevolent Tyranny: The Role of Managers on Aboriginal Stations in New South Wales 1880–1969'. PhD thesis, The Australian National University, 1970.

Bennett, Michael. 'For a Labourer Worthy of His Hire: Aboriginal Responses to the Colonisation of the Illawarra and Shoalhaven 1770–1900'. PhD thesis, University of Canberra, 2003.

Cole, Anna. 'The Glorified Flower: Race, Gender and Assimilation in Australia, 1937–1977'. PhD thesis, University of Technology Sydney, 2000.

Curthoys, Ann. 'Race and Ethnicity: A Study of the Response of British Colonists to Aborigines, Chinese and non-British Europeans in New South Wales, 1856–1881'. PhD thesis, Macquarie University, 1973.

Djenidi, Valerie. 'State and Church Involvement in Aboriginal Reserves, Missions and Stations in New South Wales, 1900–1975 and a Translation into French of John Ramsland, *Custodians of the Soil: A History of Aboriginal-European Relationships in the Manning Valley of New South Wales,* Taree: Greater Taree City Council, 2001'. PhD thesis, University of Newcastle, April 2008.

Duncan, Alan T. 'A Survey of the Education of Aborigines in New South Wales, Vols. 1 & 2'. Master of Education thesis, University of Sydney, 1969.

Egan, Richard. 'An Analysis of White Organisations in Victoria and New South Wales Concerned with Aboriginal Welfare 1929–1958'. Bachelor of Letters thesis, The Australian National University, 1991.

Goodall, Heather. 'A History of Aboriginal Communities in New South Wales 1909–1939'. PhD thesis, University of Sydney, 1982.

Greer, Susan. 'Governing Indigenous Peoples: A History of Accounting Interventions in the New South Wales Aborigines Protection and Welfare Board 1883–1969'. PhD thesis, Macquarie University, 2006.

Hankins, Carla. 'The Missing Links: Cultural Genocide through the Abduction of Female Aboriginal Children from their Families and their Training for Domestic Service'. BA (Honours) thesis, University of New South Wales, 1982.

Holland, Robin. 'The Impact of "Doomed Race" Assumptions in the Administration of Queensland's Indigenous Population by the Chief Protectors of Aboriginals from 1897 to 1942'. MA thesis, Queensland University of Technology, 2013.

Irish, Paul. 'Hidden in Plain View: Nineteenth-Century Aboriginal People and Places in Coastal Sydney'. PhD thesis, University of New South Wales, 2014.

Johnston, Susan Lindsay. 'The New South Wales Government Policy Towards Aborigines 1880–1909'. Master of Arts thesis, University of Sydney, 1970.

Maynard, John. 'Fred Maynard and the Awakening of Aboriginal Political Consciousness and Activism in Twentieth Century Australia'. PhD thesis, University of Newcastle, 2002.

Nugent, Maria. 'Revisiting La Perouse: A Postcolonial History'. PhD thesis, University of Technology Sydney, 2000.

Parry, Naomi. 'Such a Longing: Black and White Children in Welfare in Tasmania and New South Wales, 1880–1940'. PhD thesis, University of New South Wales, 2007.

Phelps, Elizabeth. 'A Long Time to Learn: The Process of Change Amongst the Aboriginal people of the Shoalhaven 1960–1989'. BA (Honours) thesis, University of Sydney, 1989.

Read, Peter. 'The History of the Wiradjuri people of NSW 1909–1969'. PhD thesis, The Australian National University, 1983.

Smith, L.R. 'The Aboriginal Population of Australia'. PhD thesis, University of New South Wales, 1975.

Publications

Arkley, Lindsey. *The Hated Protector: The Story of Charles Wightman Sievwright, Protector of Aborigines 1939–42*. Mentone: Orbit Press, 2000.

Attwood, Bain. 'The Founding of *Aboriginal History* and the Forming of Aboriginal History Author(s)'. *Aboriginal History* 36 (2012): 119–71. doi.org/10.22459/AH.36.2013.06.

Attwood, Bain. *The Making of the Aborigines*. Sydney: Allen & Unwin, 1989.

Attwood, Bain. *Rights for Aborigines*. Crows Nest: Allen & Unwin, 2003.

Attwood, Bain. 'The Stolen Generations and Genocide: Robert Manne's *In Denial: The Stolen Generations and the Right*'. *Aboriginal History* 25 (2001): 163–72. doi.org/10.22459/AH.25.2011.10.

Attwood, Bain. *Telling the Truth about Aboriginal History*. Crows Nest: Allen & Unwin, 2005.

Attwood Bain and S.G. Foster. *Frontier Conflict: The Australian Experience*. Canberra: National Museum of Australia, 2003.

Attwood, Bain and Andrew Markus. *The Struggle for Aboriginal Rights: A Documentary History*. Crows Nest: Allen & Unwin, 1999.

Attwood, Bain and Andrew Markus. *Thinking Black: William Cooper and the Australian Aborigines' League*. Canberra: Aboriginal Studies Press, 2005.

Austin, Tony. 'Cecil Cook, Scientific Thought and "Half-Castes" in the Northern Territory 1927–1939'. *Aboriginal History* 14, no. 1/2 (1990): 104–22. doi.org/10.22459/ah.14.2011.05.

Ballantyne, Tony. *Orientalism and Race: Aryanism in the British Empire*. Basingstoke: Palgrave, 2002. doi.org/10.1057/9780230508071.

Barwick, Diane. *Rebellion at Coranderrk*. Canberra, Aboriginal History Inc., 1998.

Bayley, William, A. *The History of the Shoalhaven*. Nowra Shire Council, 1975.

Bell, J.H. 'The Aborigines of New South Wales'. In *A Goodly Heritage ANZASS Jubilee Science in NSW*, Sydney (1962): 111–17.

Bell, J.H. 'The Economic Life of Mixed-Blood Aborigines on the South Coast of New South Wales'. *Oceania* 26, no. 3 (1956): 181–99. doi.org/10.1002/j.1834-4461.1956.tb00678.x.

Bell, J.H. 'Some Demographic and Cultural Characteristics of the La Perouse Aborigines'. *Mankind* 5, no. 10 (1961): 425–38. doi.org/10.1111/j.1835-9310.1961.tb00270.x.

Benton, Lauren, Adam Clulow and Bain Attwood. *Protection and Empire*. Cambridge: Cambridge University Press, 2017. doi.org/10.1017/978110 8283595.

Beresford, Quentin, Gary Partington and Graeme Gower. *Reform and Resistance in Aboriginal Education*. Perth: University of Western Australia Press, 2012.

Bickford, Anne. 'Contact History: Aborigines in New South Wales After 1788'. *Australian Aboriginal Studies*, no. 1 (1988): 55–61.

Biskup, Peter. *Not Slaves, Not Citizens: The Aboriginal Problem in Western Australia 1898–1954*. St Lucia: University of Queensland Press, 1973.

Blake, Thom. 'Deported … at the Sweet Will of the Government: The Removal of Aborigines to Reserves in Queensland 1897–1939'. *Aboriginal History* 22 (1998): 51–61. doi.org/10.22459/AH.22.2011.04.

Brantlinger, Patrick. *Dark Vanishings: Discourse on the Extinction of Primitive Races, 1800–1930*. Ithaca: Cornell University Press, 2003.

Brock, Peggy. *Outback Ghettos: Aborigines, Institutionalism and Survival*. Melbourne: Cambridge University Press, 1993.

Brook, J. and J.L. Kohen. *The Parramatta Native Institution and the Black Town: A History*. Sydney: New South Wales University Press, 1991.

Broome, Richard. *Aboriginal Australians*. Sydney: Allen & Unwin, 1989.

Broome, Richard. *Aboriginal Australians*. Sydney: Allen & Unwin, 1994.

Broome, Richard. *Aboriginal Australians*. Sydney: Allen & Unwin, 2010.

Broome, Richard. *Aboriginal Victorians: A History Since 1800*. Sydney: Allen & Unwin, 2005.

Broome, Richard. 'The Great Australian Transformation: An Argument About our Past and its History'. *Agora* 48, no. 4 (December 2013): 16–24.

Broome, Richard. '"There Were Vegetables Every Year Mr Green was Here": Right Behaviour and the Struggle for Autonomy at Coranderrk Aboriginal Reserve'. *History Australia* 3, no. 2 (2006): 1–16. doi.org/10.2104/ha060043.

Broome, Richard. *Treasures in Earthen Vessels: Protestant Christianity in New South Bran linger Wales Society 1900–1914*. St Lucia: University of Queensland Press, 1980.

Broome, Richard. 'Victoria'. In *Contested Ground: Australian Aborigines under the British Crown*, edited by Ann McGrath, 133–34. St Leonards: Allen & Unwin, 1995.

Bursill, Les, Mary Jacobs, Deborah Lennis, Elder Aunty Beryl Timbery-Beller and Merv Ryan. *Dharawal: The Story of the Dharawal-Speaking People of Southern Sydney*. Sydney: Dharawal Publications, 2007.

Caine, Barbara. *Biography and History*. London: Red Globe Press, 2019.

Carey, Jane and Claire McLisky, eds. *Creating White Australia*. Sydney: Sydney University Press, 2009. doi.org/10.30722/sup.9781920899424.

Carruthers, J.H. *A Lifetime in Conservative Politics: Political Memoirs of Sir Joseph Carruthers*. Edited by Michael Hogan. Sydney: University of New South Wales Press, 2005.

Cato, Nancy. *Mister Maloga*. St Lucia: University of Queensland Press, 1993.

Chesterman, John and Brian Galligan. *Citizens Without Rights: Aborigines and Australian Citizenship*. Melbourne: Cambridge University Press, 1997. doi.org/10.1017/CBO9780511518249.

Christie, M.F. *Aborigines in Colonial Victoria, 1835–86*. Sydney: Sydney University Press, 1979.

Clare, Monica. *Karobran: The Story of an Aboriginal Girl*. Chippendale, Sydney: Alternative Publishing Cooperative Limited, 1978.

Clark, Manning. *History of Australia,* Volume 3. Melbourne: Melbourne University Press, 1987.

Clark, Mavis Thorpe. *The Boy from Cumeroogunga*. Sydney: Hodder & Stoughton, 1979.

Clendinnen, Inga. *Dancing with Strangers*. Melbourne: Text Publishing, 2017.

Coastal Custodians 2, Issue 2. National Parks and Wildlife Service, NSW.

Cole, Anna. 'Unwitting Soldiers: The Working Life of Matron Hiscocks at the Cootamundra Girls Home'. *Aboriginal History* 27 (2003): 146–61. doi.org/10.22459/AH.27.2011.11.

Conservation Management Plan – Warangesda Aboriginal Mission & Station. Lithgow: High Ground Consulting, 2014.

Cowman, Krista. 'Collective Biography'. In *Research Methods for History*, edited by Simon Gunn and Lucy Fair. Edinburgh: Edinburgh University Press, 2012.

Crane, A.R. and W.G. Walker. *Peter Board: His Contribution to the Development of Education in New South Wales*. Melbourne: Australian Council of Educational Research, 1957.

Crotty, Martin and David Andrew Roberts. *Great Mistakes in Australian History*. Sydney: University of New South Wales Press, 2006.

Cruickshank, Joanna. 'Race, History, and the Australian Faith Missions', *Itinerario* 34 (2010): 39–52. doi.org/10.1017/S0165115310000677.

Cullunghutti: The Mountain and its People: A Documentary History of Cullunghutti Mountain, Aboriginal People and the Shoalhaven (1770 to 1920). Office of the Environment & Heritage, NSW National Parks and Wildlife Service, 2013.

Cummins, C.J. *A History of Medical Administration in NSW 1788–1973*, 2nd edition. Sydney: NSW Department of Health, 2003.

Curthoys, Ann. *Freedom Ride*. Crows Nest: Allen & Unwin, 2002.

Curthoys, Ann. 'Good Christians and Useful Workers: Aborigines, Church and State in NSW 1870–1883'. In *What Rough Beast? The State and Social Order in Australian History*, edited by the Sydney Labour History Group, 50–51. Sydney: Allen & Unwin, 1982.

Curthoys, Ann and John Docker. *Is History Fiction?* Sydney: University of New South Wales Press, 2006.

Curthoys, Ann and Jessie Mitchell. 'The Advent of Self-Government 1840s–90'. In *The Cambridge History of Australia*, Vol. 1, edited by Alison Bashford and Stuart Macintyre, 149–69. Melbourne: Cambridge University Press, 2013. doi.org/10.1017/CHO9781107445758.009.

Curthoys, Ann and Jessie Mitchell. 'Bring this Paper to the Good Governor: Aboriginal Petitioning in Britain's Australian Colonies'. In *Native Claims: Indigenous Law Against Empire, 1500–1920*, edited by Saliha Belmessous, 182–203. Oxford: Oxford University Press, 2011. doi.org/10.1093/acprof:oso/9780199794850.003.0008.

Curthoys, Ann and Clive Moore. 'Working for the White People: An Historiographic Essay on Aboriginal and Torres Strait Islander Labour'. In 'Aboriginal Workers', special issue, *Labour History* 69 (1995): 1–29. doi.org/10.2307/27516388.

Davis, Fiona. *Australian Settler Colonialism and the Cummeragunja Aboriginal Station: Redrawing Boundaries.* Eastbourne: Sussex Academic Press, 2014.

Day, David. *Claiming a Continent.* Sydney: HarperCollins, 2001.

Dickey, Brian. *No Charity There: A Short History of Social Welfare in Australia.* West Melbourne: Thomas Nelson Australia, 1980.

Docker, E.G. *Simply Human Beings.* Sydney: Angus & Robertson, 1965.

Donaldson, Mike, Les Bursill and Mary Jacobs. *A History of Aboriginal Illawarra*, Vol. 1, *Before Colonisation.* Yowie Bay, Sydney: Dharawal Publications, 2016.

Donaldson, Mike, Les Bursill and Mary Jacobs. *A History of Aboriginal Illawarra*, Vol. 2, *Colonisation.* Yowie Bay, Sydney: Dharawal Publications, 2017.

Doukakis, Anna. *The Aboriginal People, Parliament, & 'Protection' in New South Wales 1856–1916.* Annandale: The Federation Press, 2006.

Dunn, Mark. 'Vernon Nautical Training Ship'. *Dictionary of Sydney*, 2008.

Edmonds, Penelope. 'Unpacking Settler Colonialism's Urban Strategies: Indigenous Peoples in Victoria, British Columbia, and Transition to a Settler-Colonial City'. *Urban History Review* 38, no. 2 (2010): 4–20. doi.org/10.7202/039671ar.

Edwards, Coral and Peter Read. *The Lost Children*, Sydney: DoubleDay, 1989.

Egan, Richard. *Neither Amity nor Kindness: Government Policy Towards Aboriginal People of NSW from 1788 to 1969.* Paddington: Self-published, 2012.

Egloff, Brian J. *Wreck Bay: An Aboriginal Fishing Community.* Canberra: Australian Institute of Aboriginal Studies, 1981.

Elbourne, E. 'The Sin of the Settler: The 1835–36 Select Committee on Aborigines and Debates over Virtue and Conquest in the Early Nineteenth-Century British White Settler Empire.' *Journal of Colonialism and Colonial History* 4, no. 3 (2003). doi.org/10.1353/cch.2004.0003.

Elkin, A.P. 'Education of Native Races in Pacific Countries: Report of a Conference'. *Oceania* 7, no. 2 (December 1936): 145–68. doi.org/10.1002/j.1834-4461.1936.tb00449.x.

Ellinghaus, Katherine. 'Absorbing the "Aboriginal Problem": Controlling Interracial Marriage in Australia in the Late 19th and Early 20th Centuries'. *Aboriginal History* 27 (2003): 183–207. doi.org/10.22459/AH.27.2011.13.

Ellinghaus, Katherine. 'Biological Absorption and Genocide: A Comparison of Indigenous Assimilation Policies in the United States and Australia'. *Genocide Studies and Prevention* 4, no. 1 (Spring 2009): 55–79. doi.org/10.3138/gsp.4.1.59.

Finnane, Mark. *Police and Government: Histories of Policing in Australia*. Melbourne: Oxford University Press, 1994.

Flannery, Tim, ed. *Watkin Tench 1788*. Melbourne: Text Publishing, 1997.

Fletcher, J.J. *Clean, Clad and Courteous: A History of Aboriginal Education in New South Wales*. Carlton: Self-published, 1989.

Fletcher, J.J. *Documents in the History of Aboriginal Education in New South Wales*. Carlton: Self-published, 1989.

Flick, Isabel and Heather Goodall. *Isabel Flick: The Many Lives of an Extraordinary Aboriginal Woman*. Crows Nest: Allen & Unwin, 2004.

Ford, Lisa. 'Indigenous Policy and its Historical Occlusions: The North American Indian and Global Contexts of Australian Settlement'. *Australian Indigenous Law Review* 12, no. 1 (2008): 69–80.

Ford, Lisa. 'Protecting the Peace on the Edges of Empire: Commissioners of Crown Lands in New South Wales'. In *Protection and Empire: A Global History*, edited by Lauren Benton, Adam Clulow and Bain Attwood. Cambridge: Cambridge University Press, 2017. doi.org/10.1017/9781108283595.010.

Ford, Lisa. *Settler Sovereignty Jurisdiction and Indigenous People in America and Australia 1788–1836*. Cambridge, Massachusetts: Harvard University Press, 2011.

Ford, Lisa and Andrew Roberts. 'Expansion, 1820–1850'. In *The Cambridge History of Australia*, Vol. 1, edited by Alison Bashford and Stuart Macintyre, 121–48. Melbourne: Cambridge University Press, 2013. doi.org/10.1017/CHO9781107445758.008.

Francis, Mark. 'Social Darwinism and the Construction of Institutionalised Racism in Australia'. *Journal of Australian Studies* 20, issue 50–51 (1996): 90–105. doi.org/10.1080/14443059609387281.

Furphy, Sam. *Edward M. Curr and the Tide of History*. Canberra: ANU E Press, 2013. doi.org/10.22459/ECTH.03.2013.

Furphy, Sam. '"They Formed a Little Family as it Were": The Board for the Protection of Aborigines (1875–1883)'. In *Settler Colonial Governance*, edited by Leigh Boucher and Lynette Russell. Canberra: ANU Press, 2015. doi.org/10.22459/scgncv.04.2015.04.

Furphy, Sam and Amanda Nettelbeck. *Aboriginal Protection and its Intermediaries in Britain's Antipodean Colonies.* New York: Routledge, 2020. doi.org/10.4324/9780429316364.

Gammage, Bill and Andrew Markus. *All that Dirt: Aborigines 1938: An Australia 1938 monograph.* Canberra: The Australian National University, 1982.

Gapps, Stephen. 'Mr Ardill's Scrapbook: Alternative Sources of Biography'. *Public History Review* 2 (1993): 102–3.

Gapps, Stephen. *The Sydney Wars: Conflict in the Early Colony 1788–1817.* Sydney: NewSouth Publishing, 2018.

Gilbert, Kevin. 'Pearl Gibbs: Aboriginal Patriot'. In 'Three Tributes to Pearl Gibbs', *Aboriginal History* 7, no. 1–2 (1983): 5–9.

Golder, Hilary. *Politics, Patronage and Public Works: The Administration of New South Wales,* Vol. 1, *1842–1900.* Sydney: University of New South Wales Press, 2005.

Goodall, Heather. 'Assimilation Begins in the Home: The State and Aboriginal Women's Work as Mothers in New South Wales'. In 'Aboriginal Workers', special issue, *Labour History* 69 (1995): 75–101. doi.org/10.2307/27516392.

Goodall, Heather. *Invasion to Embassy,* St Leonards: Allen & Unwin, 1996.

Goodall, Heather. *Invasion to Embassy.* Sydney: Sydney University Press, 2008.

Goodall, Heather. 'Land in Own Country: The Aboriginal Land Rights Movement in South-Eastern Australia, 1868 to 1914'. *Aboriginal History* 14 (1990): 1–24.

Grant, Stan. *The Tears of Strangers.* Sydney: HarperCollins, 2016.

Gray, Geoffrey. '"Mr Neville Did All in [his] Power to Assist Me": A.P. Elkin, A.O. Neville and Anthropological Research in Northwest Western Australia, 1927–1928'. *Oceania* 68, no. 1(1997): 27–46. doi.org/10.1002/j.1834-4461.1997.tb02640.x.

Griffith, John, and Peter Price, eds. *Kangaroo Valley, Historical Photographs.* Kangaroo Valley: Kangaroo Historical Society, 1989.

Griffiths, Tom. *Hunters and Collectors*. Melbourne: Cambridge University Press, 1996.

Grimshaw, Patricia. 'Interracial Marriages and Colonial Regimes in Victoria and Aotearoa/New Zealand'. *A Journal of Women Studies* 23, no. 3 (2002): 12–28. doi.org/10.1353/fro.2003.0008.

Gulambali, Beverley and Don Elphick. *The Camp of Mercy: An Historical and Biographical Record of the Warangesda Aboriginal Mission/Station, Darlington Point, New South Wales*. Canberra: Gulambali Aboriginal Research, 2004.

Haderer, Stefan. 'Biopower, Whiteness and the Stolen Generations: The Arbitrary Power of Racial Classification'. *Critical Race and Whiteness Studies* 9, no. 2 (2013): 1–17.

Haebich, Anna. 'Between Knowing and Not Knowing: Public Knowledge of the Stolen Generations'. *Aboriginal History* 25 (2001): 70–90. doi.org/10.22459/AH.25.2011.05.

Haebich, Anna. *Broken Circles: Fragmenting Indigenous Families 1800–2000*. Fremantle: Fremantle Arts Centre Press, 2000.

Haebich, Anna. *For Their Own Good: Aborigines and Government in the Southwest of Western Australia, 1900–1940*. Perth: University of Western Australia Press, 1988.

Harris, John. *One Blood*. Sutherland: Albatross Books, 1990.

Haskins, Victoria. '"A Better Chance"? Sexual Abuse and Apprenticing of Aboriginal Girls under the NSW Aborigines Protection Board'. *Aboriginal History* 28 (2004): 35–58. doi.org/10.22459/AH.28.2011.02.

Haskins, Victoria. '"Could You See the Return of my Daughter": Fathers and Daughters Under the New South Wales Aborigines Protection Board Child Removal Policy'. *Australian Historical Studies* 34, Issue 121 (2003): 106–21. doi.org/10.1080/10314610308596239.

Haskins, Victoria. 'On the Doorstep: Aboriginal Domestic Service as a "Contact Zone"'. *Australian Feminist Studies* 16, Issue 34 (2001): 13–25. doi.org/10.1080/08164640120038881.

Haskins, Victoria. *One Bright Spot*. Basingstoke: Palgrave Macmillan, 2005. doi.org/10.1057/9780230510593.

Haskins, Victoria. '"& So We are 'Slave Owners'!" Employers and the NSW Aborigines Protection Board Trust Funds'. *Labour History*, no. 88 (May 2005): 147–64. doi.org/10.2307/27516042.

Hedley, Kevin. *People and Progress: Tumut Shire 1887–1987*. Tumut: Tumut Shire Council, 1987.

Henrich, Eureka. 'Ragged Schools in Sydney'. *The Sydney Journal* 4, no. 1 (2013): 49–65. doi.org/10.5130/sj.v4i1.2803.

Horner, Jack. *Bill Ferguson: Fighter for Aboriginal Freedom*. Dickson, ACT: Self-published, 1994.

Horner, Jack. 'A Letter from Jack Horner'. *Aboriginal History* 20 (1996): 195–200. doi.org/10.22459/AH.20.2011.09.

Horner, Jack. 'Pearl Gibbs: A Biographical Tribute'. In 'Three Tributes to Pearl Gibbs', *Aboriginal History* 7, no. 1–2 (1983): 10–20.

Horsburgh, Michael. 'Subsidy and Control: Social Welfare Activities of the New South Wales Government, 1858–1910'. *Journal of Australian Studies* 1, Issue 2 (1977): 64–92. doi.org/10.1080/14443057709386772.

Horton, Jessica. 'Rewriting Political History. Letters from Aboriginal People in Victoria, 1886–1919. *History Australia* 9, Issue 2 (2012): 157–81. doi.org/10.1080/14490854.2012.11668422.

Huggonson, David. 'Aborigines and the Aftermath of the Great War'. *Australian Aboriginal Studies*, no. 1 (1993): 2–9.

Human Rights and Equal Opportunity Commission. *Bringing Them Home: National Inquiry into the Separation of Aboriginal and Torres Strait Islander Children from Their Families*. Canberra: Stirling Press, Commonwealth of Australia, 1997.

Irish, Paul. *Hidden in Plain View: The Aboriginal People of Coastal Sydney*. Sydney: NewSouth Publishing, 2017.

Jackson-Nakano, Anne. *The Kamberri: A History of Aboriginal Families in the ACT and Surrounds*. Aboriginal History Monograph 8. Canberra: Aboriginal History, 2001.

Kabaila, Peter Rimas. *Home Girls: Cootamundra Aboriginal Home Girls Tell Their Stories*. Aboriginal Affairs, Office of Communities, NSW Department of Education and Communities. Jamison, Canberra: Black Mountain Projects Pty Ltd, 2012.

Karskens, Grace. *The Colony: A History of Early Sydney*. Sydney: Allen & Unwin, 2010.

Kidd, Rosalind. *Black Lives: Government Lies*. Sydney: University of New South Wales Press, 2000.

Kociumbas, Jan. 'Genocide and Modernity in Colonial Australia'. In *Genocide and Settler Society*, edited by A. Dirk Moses, 77–102. New York: Berghahn Books, 2004.

Kohen, Jim. *The Darug and their Neighbours: The Traditional Aboriginal Owners of the Sydney region*. Blacktown, NSW: Darug Link in association with the Blacktown District and Historical Society, 1993.

Kohen, Jim. 'Mapping Aboriginal Linguistic and Clan Boundaries in the Sydney Region'. *The Globe*, no. 41 (1995): 32–39.

La Perouse, the Place, the People and the Sea: A Collection of Writing by Members of the Aboriginal Community. Canberra: Aboriginal Studies Press, 1988.

Laidlaw, Zoe. '"Aunt Anna's Report": The Buxton Women and the Aborigines Select Committee, 1835–37'. *The Journal of Imperial and Commonwealth History* 32, no. 2 (May 2004): 1–28. doi.org/10.1080/0308653041000170 0381.

Laidlaw, Zoe. 'Heathens, Slaves and Aborigines: Thomas Hodgkin's Critique of Missions and Anti-Slavery'. *History Workshop Journal* 64, Issue 1 (Autumn 2007): 133–61. doi.org/10.1093/hwj/dbm034.

Laidlaw, Zoe. 'Integrating Metropolitan, Colonial and Imperial Histories – The Aborigines Select Committee of 1835–37'. In *Writing Colonial Histories: Comparative Perspectives*, edited by Tracey Banivanua Mar and Julie Evans, 75–91. Carlton, Vic.: University of Melbourne Department of History, 2002.

Lambert, David and Alan Lester. *Colonial Lives Across the British Empire: Imperial Careering in the Long Nineteenth Century.* Cambridge: Cambridge University Press, 2006.

Lambert-Pennington, Katherine. 'What Remains? Reconciling Repatriation, Aboriginal Culture, Representation and the Past'. *Oceania* 77, Issue 3 (November 2007): 313–36. doi.org/10.1002/j.1834-4461.2007.tb00019.x.

Lancaster Jones, F. *The Structure and Growth of Australia's Aboriginal Population.* Canberra: Australian National University Press, 1970.

Landon, Carolyn and Daryl Tonkin. *Jackson's Track: Memoir of a Dreamtime Place*. Ringwood: Viking, 1999.

Latukefu, Ruth A. Fink. 'Recollections of Brewarrina Aboriginal Mission'. *Australian Aboriginal Studies* no. 1 (2014): 72–87.

Lester, Alan. 'Personifying Colonial Governance: George Arthur and the Transition from Humanitarianism to Development Discourse'. *Annals of the Association of American Geographers* 102, Issue 6 (November 2012): 1468–88. doi.org/10.1080/00045608.2011.627060.

Lester, Alan and Fae Dussart. *Colonization and the Origins of Humanitarian Governance: Protecting Aborigines Across the Nineteenth-Century British Empire*. Cambridge: Cambridge University Press, 2014. doi.org/10.1017/CBO9781139022026.

Lindsay, Patrick. *True Blue: 150 Years of Service and Sacrifice of the NSW Police Force*. Sydney: HarperCollins Publishers, 2012.

Liston, Carol. 'The Dharawal and Gandangara in Colonial Campbelltown, New South Wales, 1788–1830', *Aboriginal History* 12, no. 1–2 (1988): 49–62. doi.org/10.22459/AH.12.2011.04.

Lydon, Jane. 'Bullets, Teeth and Photographs: Recognising Indigenous Australians Between the Wars'. *History of Photography* 36, Issue 3 (2012): 275–87. doi.org/10.1080/03087298.2012.673315.

Lydon, Jane. 'Christian Heroes? John Gribble, Exeter Hall and Antislavery on Western Australia's Frontier'. *Studies in Western Australian History*, no. 30 (2016): 59–72.

Lydon, Jane. 'H.G. Wells and a Shared Humanity: Photography, Humanitarianism, Empire'. *History Australia* 12, Issue 1 (January 2015): 75–94. doi.org/10.1080/14490854.2015.11668554.

Maddison, Sarah. *The Colonial Fantasy: Why White Australia Can't Solve Black Problems*. Crows Nest: Allen & Unwin, 2019.

Manne, Robert, ed. *Whitewash: On Keith Windschuttle's Fabrication of Aboriginal History*. Melbourne: Black Inc., 2003.

Manning, Corinne. 'The McLean Report: Legitimising Victoria's New Assimilation'. *Aboriginal History* 26 (2002): 159–76. doi.org/10.22459/AH.26.2011.07.

Markus, Andrew. *Blood from a Stone: William Cooper and the Australian Aborigines' League*, Sydney: Allen & Unwin, 1988.

Markus, Andrew. *Governing Savages*. Sydney: Allen & Unwin, 1990.

Matthews, Janet. *The Two Worlds of Jimmy Barker: The Life of an Australian Aboriginal 1900–1972 as Told to Janet Matthews*. Canberra: Australian Institute of Aboriginal Studies, 1977.

Maxwell, Charles, F. *Australian Men of Mark, 1788–1888, Illustrated with Authentic Portraits*, Vol. 1, Sydney (no date or publisher).

Maynard, John. 'Fred Maynard and the Australian Aboriginal Progressive Association (AAPA): One God, One Aim, One Destiny'. *Aboriginal History* 21 (1997): 1–13. doi.org/10.22459/AH.21.2011.01.

Maynard, John. 'Land, Children and Politics: Native Americans and Australian Aborigines 1900–1930'. *Journal of Australian Studies* 38, no. 4 (2014): 415–29. doi.org/10.1080/14443058.2014.953010.

Maynard, John. 'Light in the Darkness: Elizabeth McKenzie Hatton'. In *Uncommon Ground: White Women in Aboriginal History*, edited by Anna Cole, Victoria Haskins and Fiona Paisley, 3–27. Canberra: Aboriginal Studies Press, 2005.

Maynard, John. 'Vision, Voice and Influence: The Rise of the Australian Aboriginal Progressive Association'. *Australian Historical Studies* 34 (2003): 91–105. doi.org/10.1080/10314610308596238.

McGrath, Ann. *'Born in the Cattle': Aborigines in Cattle Country*. Sydney: Allen & Unwin, 1987.

McGrath, Ann. 'Born or Reborn in the Cattle?' *Meanjin* 47, no. 2 (Winter 1988): 171–77.

McGrath, Ann, ed. *Contested Ground: Australian Aborigines under the British Crown*. St Leonards: Allen & Unwin, 1995.

McGregor, Russell. '"Breed out the Colour" or the Importance of Being White'. *Australian Historical Studies* 129 (2002): 286–302. doi.org/10.1080/10314610208596220.

McGregor, Russell. 'The Concept of Primitivity in the Early Anthropological Writings of A. P. Elkin'. *Aboriginal History* 17, no. 1–2 (1993): 95–104.

McGregor, Russell. 'The Doomed Race: A Scientific Axiom of the late Nineteenth Century', *Journal of Politics and History* 39, Issue 1 (April 1993): 14–22. doi.org/10.1111/j.1467-8497.1993.tb00047.x.

McGregor, Russell. *Imagined Destinies: Aboriginal Australians and the Doomed Race Theory, 1880–1939*. Carlton South: Melbourne University Press, 1997.

McGregor, Russell. *Indifferent Inclusion: Aboriginal People and the Australian Nation*. Canberra: Aboriginal Studies Press, 2011.

McGregor, Russell. 'Wards, Words and Citizens: A. P. Elkin and Paul Hasluck on Assimilation'. *Oceania* 69, no. 4 (June 1999): 243–59. doi.org/10.1002/j.1834-4461.1999.tb00372.x.

McKenna, Mark. 'Different Perspectives on Black Armband History'. Research Paper 5, 1997–98. Canberra: Australian Parliamentary Library, Politics and Public Administration Group.

McLisky, Claire. 'Colouring (in) Virtue? Evangelicalism, Work and Whiteness on Maloga Mission'. In *Creating White Australia,* edited by Jane Carey and Claire McLisky, 67–84. Fisher Library, Sydney University: Sydney University Press, 2009.

McLisky, Claire. 'From Missionary Wife to Superintendent: Janet Matthews on Three Independent Murray River Missions'. *Journal of Australian Studies* 39, Issue 1 (2015): 32–43. doi.org/10.1080/14443058.2014.987680.

Mellor, Doreen and Anna Haebich, eds. *Many Voices: Reflections on Experiences of Indigenous Child Separation.* Canberra: National Library of Australia, 2002.

Miller, James. *Koori: A Will to Win, The Heroic Resistance, Survival & Triumph of Black Australia.* Sydney: Angus and Robertson, 1985.

Mitchell, Jessie. '"Are We in Danger of a Hostile Visit from the Aborigines?" Dispossession and the Rise of Self-Government in New South Wales'. *Australian Historical Studies* 40 (2009): 294–307. doi.org/10.1080/10314610903105191.

Mitchell, Jessie. 'A City on a Hill: Aboriginal Missions and British Civilisation, 1830–1850'. In *Exploring the British World: Identity, Cultural Production, Institutions*, edited by Kate Darian-Smith, Patricia Grimshaw, Kiera Lindsey and Stuart Macintyre, 223–36. Melbourne: RMIT Publishing, 2004.

Mitchell, Jessie. '"The Galling Yoke of Slavery": Race and Separation in Colonial Port Phillip'. *Journal of Australian Studies* 33, Issue 2 (2009): 125–37. doi.org/10.1080/14443050902883355.

Mitchell, Jessie. '"Great Difficulty in Knowing where the Frontier Ceases": Violence, Governance, and the Spectre of India in Early Queensland'. *Journal of Colonial History* 15 (2013): 43–62.

Molony, John. *History of Australia.* Ringwood: Penguin Books, 1988.

Moran, Anthony. 'The Psychodynamics of Australian Settler Nationalism: Assimilating or Reconciling with the Aborigines?' *Political Psychology* 23, no. 4 (December 2002): 667–701. doi.org/10.1111/0162-895X.00303.

Moses, A. Dirk. 'Genocide and Holocaust Consciousness in Australia'. *History Compass* 1 (2003): AU 028, 001–013. doi.org/10.1111/1478-0542.028.

Moses, A. Dirk, ed. *Genocide and Settler Society: Frontier Violence and Stolen Indigenous Children in Australian History*. New York: Berghahn Books, 2004.

Mulvaney, D.J. *Encounters in Place: Outsiders and Aboriginal Australians 1606–1985*. Brisbane: University of Queensland Press, 1987.

Musgrove, Nell. *The Scars Remain: A Long History of Forgotten Australians and Children's Institutions*. North Melbourne: Australian Scholarly, 2013.

Nettelbeck, Amanda. 'Creating the Aboriginal Vagrant: Protective Governance and Indigenous Mobility in Colonial Australia'. *Pacific Historical Review* 87, no. 1 (2018): 79–100. doi.org/10.1525/phr.2018.87.1.79.

Nettelbeck, Amanda. 'Equals of the White Man: Prosecution of Settlers for Violence Against Aboriginal Subjects of the Crown, Colonial Western Australia'. *Law and History Review* 31, no. 2 (May 2013): 355–90. doi.org/10.1017/S0738248013000060.

Nettelbeck, Amanda. 'South Australian Settler Memoirs', *Journal of Australian Studies* 25, Issue 68 (2001): 97–104. doi.org/10.1080/14443050109387666.

Nettelbeck, Amanda and Robert Foster. *In the Name of the Law: William Willshire and the Policing of the Australian Frontier,* Adelaide: Wakefield Press, 2007.

Nettelbeck, Amanda and Robert Foster. 'Reading the Elusive Letter of the Law: Policing the South Australian Frontier'. *Australian Historical Studies* 130 (2007): 296–311. doi.org/10.1080/10314610708601248.

Nettelbeck, Amanda and Russell Smandych. 'Policing Indigenous Peoples on Two Colonial Frontiers: Australia's Mounted Police and Canada's North-West Mounted Police'. *The Australian and New Zealand Journal of Criminology* 43, No. 2 (2010): 356–75. doi.org/10.1375/acri.43.2.356.

Nugent, Maria. 'Botany Bay: Voyages, Aborigines and History'. *Journal of Australian Studies* 27, Issue 76 (2003): 27–33. doi.org/10.1080/14443050309387821.

O'Brien, Anne. 'Charity and Philanthropy'. *Sydney Journal* 1, no. 3 (December 2008): 18–28. doi.org/10.5130/sj.v1i3.887.

O'Brien, Anne. 'Hunger and the Humanitarian Frontier'. *Aboriginal History* 39 (2015): 109–34. doi.org/10.22459/AH.39.2015.05.

O'Brien, Anne. 'Kitchen Fragments and Garden Stuff'. *Australian Historical Studies* 39, Issue 2 (2008): 150–66. doi.org/10.1080/10314610802033148.

O'Brien, Anne. *Philanthropy and Settler Colonialism*. Basingstoke: Palgrave, Macmillan, 2015. doi.org/10.1057/9781137440501.

O'Brien, Anne. *Poverty's Prison: The Poor in New South Wales 1880–1918*. Carlton: Melbourne University Press, 1988.

Organ, Michael and Carol Speechley. 'Illawarra Aborigines. An Introductory History'. Wollongong: University of Wollongong, 1997. ro.uow.edu.au/asdpapers/25.

Paisley, Fiona. *Loving Protection? Australian Feminism and Aboriginal Women's Rights 1919–1939*. Carlton South: Melbourne University Press, 2000.

Parry, Naomi. '"Many Deeds of Terror": Windschuttle and Musquito'. *Labour History*, no. 85 (November 2003): 207–12. doi.org/10.2307/27515938.

Parry, Suzanne. 'Identifying the Process: The Removal of "Half-Caste" Children from Aboriginal Mothers' *Aboriginal History* 19, no. 1–2 (1995): 141–53. doi.org/10.22459/AH.19.2011.08.

Perkins, Charles. *A Bastard Like Me*. Sydney: Ure Smith, 1975.

Perry, T.M. 'The Spread of Rural Settlement in New South Wales, 1788–1826'. *Australian Historical Studies* 6, Issue 24 (1955): 377–95. doi.org/10.1080/10314615508595010.

Rae-Ellis, Vivienne. *Black Robinson: Protector of Aborigines*. Carlton: Melbourne University Press, 1996.

Ramsland, John. 'The Aboriginal Boys Training Home, Kinchela, 1924–1970, and the Development of a Culture of Physical Fitness and Sport'. *Journal of Educational Administration and History* 38, Issue 3 (2006): 237–48. doi.org/10.1080/00220620600984156.

Ramsland, John. 'The Aboriginal School at Purfleet, 1903–1965: A Case Study of the Segregation of Aboriginal Children in New South Wales, Australia'. *History of Education Review* 35, no. 1 (2006): 47–57. doi.org/10.1108/08198691200600005.

Ramsland, John. 'George Ardill'. *Dictionary of Sydney*, 2011.

Raynes, Cameron. *The Last Protector: The Illegal Removal of Aboriginal Children from their Parents in South Australia*. Kent Town: Wakefield Press, 2009.

Read, Peter. '"Breaking up These Camps Entirely": The Dispersal Policy in Wiradjuri Country 1909–1929'. *Aboriginal History* 8, no. 1–2 (1984): 45–55. doi.org/10.22459/AH.08.2011.04.

Read, Peter. 'Clio or Janus? Historians and the Stolen Generations'. *Australian Historical Studies* 33, Issue 118 (January 2002): 54–60. doi.org/10.1080/10314610208596179.

Read, Peter. 'A Double-Headed Coin: Protection and Assimilation in Yass 1900–1960'. In *All That Dirt 1938*, edited by Bill Gammage and Andrew Markus, 9–28. Canberra: History Project Incorporated, 1982.

Read, Peter. 'Fathers and Sons: A Study of Five Men of 1900'. *Aboriginal History* 4, no. 1–2 (1980): 96–116. doi.org/10.22459/AH.04.2011.06.

Read, Peter. *A Hundred Years War: The Wiradjuri People and the State*. Canberra and Sydney: Australian National University Press and Pergamon, 1988.

Read, Peter. 'Racial Thought in Early Colonial Australia'. *Australian Journal of Politics and History* 20, Issue 1 (April 1974): 45–53. doi.org/10.1111/j.1467-8497.1974.tb01100.x.

Read, Peter. *A Rape of the Soul so Profound: The Return of the Stolen Generations*. St Leonards: Allen & Unwin, 1999.

Read, Peter. 'A Rape of the Soul so Profound: Some Reflections on the Dispersal Policy in New South Wales'. *Aboriginal History* 7, no. 1–2 (1983): 23–33.

Read, Peter. 'Shelley's Mistake: The Parramatta Native Institution and the Stolen Generations'. In *The Great Mistakes in Australian History*, edited by Martin Crotty and David Andrew Roberts, 32–47. Sydney: University of New South Wales Press, 2006.

Read, Peter. *The Stolen Generations: The Removal of Aboriginal children in NSW 1883 to 1969*. Sydney: Human Services Aboriginal Affairs, 2010.

Reece, R.H.W. *Aborigines and Colonists*. Sydney: Sydney University Press, 1974.

Reece, R.H.W. 'Feasts and Blankets: The History of Some Early Attempts to Establish Relations with the Aborigines of New South Wales, 1814–1846'. *Archaeology and Physical Anthropology in Oceania* 2, no. 3 (October 1967): 190–206.

Reed, Liz. 'Rethinking William Thomas: "Friend" of the Aborigines.' *Aboriginal History* 28, (2004): 87–99. doi.org/10.22459/ah.28.2011.04.

Reynolds, Henry. *Fate of a Free People*. Camberwell: Penguin, 2004.

Reynolds, Henry. *The Forgotten War*. Sydney: NewSouth Publishing, 2013.

Reynolds, Henry. *Nowhere People*. Camberwell: Viking, 2005.

Reynolds, Henry. *The Other Side of the Frontier*. North Queensland: James Cook University, 1981.

Reynolds, Henry. 'Racial Thought in Early Colonial Australia'. *Australian Journal of Politics and History* 20, Issue 1 (April 1974): 45–53. doi.org/10.1111/j.1467-8497.1974.tb01100.x.

Rintoul, Stuart. *The Wailing*. Port Melbourne: William Heinemann Australia, 1993.

Roe, Michael. 'A Model Aboriginal State'. *Aboriginal History* 10, no. 1–2 (1986): 40–44.

Rowse, Tim. *After Mabo*. Carlton: Melbourne University Press, 1993.

Rowse, Tim, ed. *Contesting Assimilation*. Perth: API Network, Curtin University of Technology, 2005.

Rowse, Tim. *Indigenous and Other Australians since 1901*. University of New South Wales: University of New South Wales Press, 2017.

Rowse, Tim. 'The Statistical Table as Colonial Knowledge'. *Itinerario* 4, no. 1 (April 2017): 51–73.

Rowse, Tim. 'Tolerance, Fortitude and Patience: Frontier Pasts to Live With?' *Meanjin* 47, no. 1 (Autumn 1988): 21–29.

Rowse, Tim. *White Flour, White Power*. Melbourne: Cambridge University Press, 1998. doi.org/10.1017/CBO9780511518287.

Rowse, Tim, Mark Hannah and Len Smith. 'Queensland's Exceptional Approach to Cross-Race Marriage? A Reply to Katherine Ellinghaus', *Aboriginal History* 28 (2004): 239–43.

Russell, Lynette, ed. *Colonial Frontiers: Indigenous–European Encounters in Settler Societies*. Manchester: Manchester University Press, 2001.

Ryan, J.S. 'Thomas Garvin (CISO), 1843/1922: A 19th Century Champion of Law & Order'. *Journal and Proceedings (Armidale and District Historical Society)*, no. 52 (2009): 89.

Ryan, Lyndall. *Tasmanian Aborigines*. Crows Nest: Allen & Unwin, 2012.

Silverstein, Ben. *Conflict, Adaption, Transformation: Richard Broome and the practice of history*. Canberra: Aboriginal Studies Press, 2018.

Simon, Ella. *Through My Eyes*. Sydney: Rigby Limited, 1978.

Smith, Jim. 'Aboriginal Voters in the Burragorang Valley, NSW, 1869–1953'. *Journal of the Royal Australian Historical Society* 98, Part 2 (December 2012): 170–92.

Smith, L.R. *The Aboriginal Population of Australia*. Canberra: Australian National University Press, 1980.

Smithson, M.A. 'A Misunderstood Gift: The Annual Issue of Blankets to Aborigines in New South Wales, 1826–48'. *Push*, no. 30 (1992): 73–108.

Stanner, W.E.H. *After the Dreaming: The 1968 Boyer Lectures*. Crows Nest: Australian Broadcasting Corporation, 1991.

Stanner, W.E.H. *The Dreaming and Other Essays*. Collingwood: Black Inc. Agenda, 2010.

Stanner, W.E.H. 'The History of Indifference Thus Begins'. *Aboriginal History* 1 (1977): 3–26. doi.org/10.22459/AH.01.2011.01.

Stone, Sharman. *Aborigines in White Australia: A Documentary History of the Attitudes Affecting Official Policy and the Australian Aborigines,1697–1973*. South Yarra, Victoria: Heinemann Educational Books, 1974.

Sutton, Peter. *Country: Aboriginal Boundaries and Land Ownership in Australia*. Aboriginal History Monograph 3. Canberra: Aboriginal History Inc., 1995.

Swain, Shurlee, 'Enshrined in Law: Legislative Justifications for the Removal of Indigenous and Non-Indigenous Children in Colonial and Post-Colonial Australia'. *Australian Historical Studies* 47, Issue 2 (2016): 191–208. doi.org/10.1080/1031461X.2016.1153119.

Swain, Shurlee. *History of Australian Inquiries Reviewing Institutions Providing Care for Children*. Canberra: Australian Catholic University, 2014.

Tatz, Colin. *Obstacle Race: Aborigines in Sport*. Sydney: University of New South Wales Press, 1995.

Tatz, Colin. *With Intent to Destroy*. New York: Verso, 2003.

Tholfsen, David. 'The Intellectual Origins of Mid-Victorian Stability'. *Political Science Quarterly* 86, no. 1 (March 1971): 57–91.

Thomas, Cora. 'From "Australian Aborigines" to "White Australians"'. *Australian Aboriginal Studies* no. 1 (2001): 21–35.

Thornton, Bruce. *Haste to the Rescue: George Edward Ardill and the Sydney Rescue Work Society (Now Communicare Sydney): The First Twenty-Five Years*. Sydney: Baptist Historical Society NSW, 2008.

Tucker, Margaret. *If Everyone Cared*. Sydney: Ure Smith, 1977.

Twomey, Christina and Katherine Ellinghaus, eds. 'Protection: Global Genealogies, Local Practices'. *Pacific Historical Review* 87, no. 1 (2018): 2–9.

Walden, Inara. '"That was Slavery Days": Aboriginal Domestic Servants in New South Wales in the Twentieth Century'. *Labour History,* Issue 69 (1 November 1995): 196–209. doi.org/10.2307/27516399.

Walden, Inara. 'To Send Her to Service: Aboriginal Domestic Servants'. *Aboriginal Law Bulletin* 3, no. 76 (October 1995): 12–14.

Whitaker, Anne-Marie. *Appin: The Story of Macquarie Town*. Alexandria, NSW: Kingsclear Books, 2005.

Wilkie, Meredith. *The Survival of the Aboriginal Family in New South Wales 1788–1981: A Review of Government Policies and Administration*. Discussion Paper No. 4. Sydney: Aboriginal Children's Project, 1982.

Willey, Keith. *When the Sky Fell Down*. Sydney: Collins, 1979.

Windschuttle, Keith. *The Fabrication of Aboriginal History*, Vol. 3, *The Stolen Generations 1881–2008*. Sydney: Macleay Press, 2009.

Wise, Tigger. *The Self-Made Anthropologist: A Life of A. P. Elkin*. Sydney: Allen & Unwin, 1985.

Wolfe, Patrick. 'Settler Colonialism and the Elimination of the Native'. *Journal of Genocide Research* 8, Issue 4 (December 2006): 387–409. doi.org/10.1080/14623520601056240.

Wolfe, Patrick. *Traces of History: Elementary Structures of Race*. London: Verso, 2016.

Woodrow, Marjorie. *One of the Lost Generation*. Eight Mile Plains, Qld: Self-published, 1998.

Zogbaum, Heidi. 'Herbert Basedow and the Removal of Aboriginal Children of Mixed Descent from their Families'. *Australian Historical Studies* 34, Issue 121 (2003): 122–38. doi.org/10.1080/10314610308596240.

Conference Papers

Edmonds, Penelope and Samuel Furphy, eds. *Rethinking Colonial Histories: New and Alternative Approaches* [online]. Melbourne University Conference and Seminar Series 14. Melbourne, Vic.: RMIT Publishing, 2006. Available via: search.informit.org/doi/book/10.3316/informit.0975839268.

Ellinghaus, Katherine. 'Whiteness as Bureaucracy: Assimilation Policies and People of White/Indigenous Descent in Australia and the United States' [online]. In *Historicising Whiteness: Transnational Perspectives on the Construction of an Identity*, edited by Leigh Boucher, Jane Katherine Ellinghaus, 375–83. Melbourne University Conference and Seminar Series 16. Melbourne: RMIT Publishing in association with the School of Historical Studies, University of Melbourne, 2007. Available via: search.informit.com.au/documentSummary;dn=863507193766266;res=IELHSS.

Evans, Raymond and Orsted-Jensen, Robert. '"I Cannot Say the Numbers that were Killed": Assessing Violent Mortality on the Queensland Frontier'. Paper presented at 'Conflict in History: The Australian Historical Association 33rd Annual Conference', University of Queensland, 7–11 July 2014.

McLisky, Claire. '"All of One Blood"? Race and Redemption on Maloga Mission, 1874–88'. Paper presented at the 'Historicising Whiteness Conference', University of Melbourne, 22–24 November 2006.

Websites

NSW Aboriginal Land Council: alc.org.au/.

Australian Dictionary of Biography: adb.anu.edu.au/biography/.

Dictionary of Sydney: home.dictionaryofsydney.org/.

Former Members, Parliament of New South Wales: www.parliament.nsw.gov.au/members/formermembers/pages/former-members-index.aspx.

Trove (National Library of Australia): trove.nla.gov.au.

www.ingramcontent.com/pod-product-compliance
Lightning Source LLC
Chambersburg PA
CBHW041230020526
44117CB00044B/2980